KING *of the* 40TH PARALLEL

KING

of the

40TH PARALLEL

DISCOVERY IN THE AMERICAN WEST

James Gregory Moore

STANFORD GENERAL BOOKS
An Imprint of Stanford University Press
Stanford, California
2006

Stanford University Press
Stanford, California

This book has been published with the assistance of the United States
Geological Survey.

Printed in the United States of America on acid-free, archival-quality paper

Library of Congress Cataloging-in-Publication Data

Moore, James Gregory, 1930–
King of the 40th parallel : discovery in the American West / James Gregory
Moore.
    p. cm.
  Includes bibliographical references and index.
  ISBN 0-8047-5222-2 (cloth : alk. paper)
  ISBN 0-8047-5223-0 (pbk. : alk. paper)
  1. King, Clarence, 1842–1901. 2. Geologists—United States—Biography.
3. Geological Survey (U.S.)—Biography. 4. Explorers—United States—
Biography. 5. West (U.S.)—Discovery and exploration. I. Title: King of
the fortieth parallel. II. Title.
QE22.D5M66   2006
551.092—DC22

                              2005025806

Original Printing 2006

Last figure below indicates year of this printing:
15   14   13   12   11   10   09   08   07   06

Designed by James P. Brommer.
Typeset in 11/16 Minion.

Special discounts for bulk quantities of Stanford General Books are available
to corporations, professional associations, and other organizations. For details
and discount information, contact the special sales department of Stanford
University Press. Tel: (650) 736-1783, Fax: (650) 736-1784

For Dugan, Nikki, Nathan, Scott, and James

CONTENTS

FOREWORD

The U.S. Geological Survey (USGS) owes much to its first director, Clarence King, whose innovative ideas, scientific and artistic genius, and organizational foresight were widely recognized by his peers.

King's experience, at the age of 25, in organizing and leading a precursor to the USGS called the *United States Geological Exploration of the Fortieth Parallel*—the central subject of this book—testifies to the confidence that he inspired in those who appointed him. King's demonstrated excellence in leading his survey for 12 years, and writing and editing the resulting series of landmark volumes and atlases, made him a logical choice to assume the directorship of the USGS at the age of 37, in 1879. King set the infant USGS on a course of excellence and objectivity that endures to this day.

The pivotal role that Clarence King played in USGS history was celebrated on September 9, 2004, as part of the events marking the USGS 125th anniversary, when the USGS Library in Reston, Virginia, the largest Earth science library in the world, was rededicated as The Clarence King Library. I am confident that many readers will enjoy and be enriched by the insights of this book about King's Fortieth Parallel Survey.

CHARLES G. GROAT

Director, U.S. Geological Survey

PREFACE

William Glen

Jim Moore is singularly equipped from personal experience to tell the story of the pioneering scientists who populate this epochal history. Many of his own field studies, conducted across several decades, retrace and elaborate those of the giants of whom he writes here. By both temperament and accomplishment, he would have found himself particularly welcome around their campfires.

Jim's reserved manner veils a piercing intellect, insatiable curiosity, and great wellsprings of energy. Throughout a diverse career, his knack for discerning details and processes overlooked by others has triggered important new hypotheses. If a maverick nature is indeed—as psychologists hold—the best predictor of achievement in science, then Jim's future was early foretold. As an undergraduate recently trained in rock climbing, he and two colleagues, in the middle of the night, rappelled hundreds of feet down the front face of Stanford University's dominating Hoover Tower and taped five descending 4-foot-long, black footprints to mark a monster's gait: a classic caper now writ large in Stanford lore.

Jim's long and diverse research career has centered on the geology of the southern High Sierra; his work there was begun as a graduate student and then pursued intermittently over three decades. He is recognized as the principal geologic mapmaker of the region, and his reports still shape our understanding of the processes that formed that greatest plutonic rock mass in the United States. A nomination for a scientific medal extolled "Moore's legacy of exquisite published mapping of more than eight fifteen-minute quadrangles [covering about 2,000 square miles] of rugged mountain terrain that stands as the authoritative framework for all related studies of the Sierra Nevada's . . . geochemistry, geochronology, and structure."

But the subject of this book, however broad, concerns only one of the several lives in science that Jim has led—rising to international prominence in each. He knew from childhood camping that he would enjoy a career in field studies. Degrees in geology from Stanford (B.S.), the University of Washington (M.S.), and Johns Hopkins (Ph.D.) prepared him for a lifelong career at the U.S. Geological Survey (USGS), begun in 1956 and interrupted only by stints as a visiting professor at Dartmouth College and later at Stanford.

The architect of several pathbreaking ideas concerning geologic problems of the seafloor, Jim was the first to organize and execute a program of SCUBA ocean dives to document, with sound motion picture equipment, the formation of pillow lava at the front of an advancing lava flow offshore of Hawaii. Their now classic documentary revealed for the first time how water reacts with molten lava to form the most abundant rock on the planet: pillow basalt. That process had been one of the great enigmas of Earth science.

The advent, in 1964, of Jim's radical theory about the nature and history of giant seafloor landslides ignited a quarter-century of heated conflict before the theory was vindicated. That debate and the ascendance of his theory were recently highlighted in an hour-long, globally televised documentary film titled "The Runaway Mountain" which—much like his submarine lava film—now widely pervades geology curricula.

Jim and his brother George were the first to map sedimentary deposits on the flanks of various oceanic islands and to reinterpret them as the products of giant waves (tsunamis). They thus opened the possibility in 1984—now seen to be very real—that such deposits could be laid down by tsunamis driven by massive submarine landslides. Concomitantly, the landslide-tsunami theory—because it appeared at a critical period in which the "volcanists" and the "meteorite impactors" were arguing the cause of mass extinctions—invited thinking about the role of bolide-impact-engendered tsunami deposits at mass-extinction boundaries, triggering a global search for such evidence.

Jim has also shown how the volcanic islands in Hawaii and Iceland have grown and evolved, and early recognized that the Hawaiian Islands are sinking as a result of the downflexing of the oceanic crust under the load of the great volcanic pile produced by the geologically rapid, relatively recent growth of the islands. That revelation facilitated the reinterpretation of coral-reef structures found far below current sea level. And from studies extending over more than a decade in Iceland and Canada, he documented the dynamic processes of volcanoes that had erupted under glaciers (now long since melted).

In seeking to explain the nature of the volcanic seafloor crust, Jim has made dozens of dives far down into the ocean depths in mobile submersibles. While he was aboard *Alvin* during the FAMOUS (French-American Mid-Ocean Undersea Study) program in July 1974, the vessel alarmingly wedged itself in a crack on the seafloor. Those working frantically on the surface marveled at Jim's nonchalance while trapped at 8,000-foot depth for several hours before *Alvin* broke free.

Jim was drawn to the ongoing activity in 1965 at Taal Volcano, in the Philippines, and documented the spectacular eruptions that led to the recognition of the volcanic phenomenon defined as "base surge." Among the most devastating of volcanic hazards, base surge entails high-velocity, ground-hugging clouds of hot gases and incandescent ash traveling at upwards of 90 miles per hour that incinerate everything in their path. Understanding their lethal character has figured prominently in the preparation of volcanic-hazard assessments.

He was among the first USGS geologists to arrive at Mt. St. Helens in March 1980 to measure and document the precursory activity culminating in its cataclysmic eruption on 18 May. As a principal investigator on the pre-blast monitoring team, he documented the awesome deformation of the volcanic edifice. Had large areas not been closed to the public by early warnings based on the work of these USGS scientists, more than 5,000 lives would likely have been lost. After the collapse and explosion, Jim continued his study of the dramatic changes the volcano had undergone.

Possessed of three hundred scientific publications, numerous honors, appointments to positions of institutional leadership, and a cadre of acolytes who have since distinguished themselves, Jim retired from the USGS in 1995 at the highest attainable rank for a federal research scientist. But retirement—which he has accepted only in a formal sense—provided him the opportunity to write *Exploring the Highest Sierra*, a sumptuous volume from Stanford University Press in 2000 that quickly became what one reviewer called "a bible" for the region. As a USGS Scientist Emeritus still engaged in a number of projects, he continues to ride submersibles to the deep-sea floor, deliver invited lectures around the world, and collaborate with an international cast of colleagues. Studies that Jim and a co-author excitedly described to me about two years ago have since been published: the discovery and definition of an entirely new class of disk-like volcanoes, 2–3 miles wide, with remarkably flat tops that lie on the flanks of the Hawaiian ridge. Formed, they postulate, by the impoundment of a submarine lava lake within a circular wall of volcanic rock, the perfectly horizontal lava surface established at inception becomes a guide to later tilting of the seafloor.

Jim's fifty-year pattern of cornucopian productivity extends to this book, which treats the endeavors and triumphs of men he has long regarded as among the most significant contributors to modern Earth science. Foremost among them is Clarence King, the first director of the U.S. Geological Survey. Many of King's accomplishments were familiar to Jim early in his USGS career, but later, after he had looked into King's life story in some depth, he came to realize how much of his own experience and work had touched upon that of King. Like King, Jim reconnoitered Yosemite, climbed Lassen Peak and Mount Shasta, hiked the highest Sierra, and ascended the crest of Mount Whitney (at seventeen, with older brother George). Near the summit of Mount Shasta, Jim warmed his hands over the same hot spring that had comforted

King in 1870, and each—almost a century apart—camped high on the same crest. On a winter trip with two companions, Jim traversed the knife-edged south ridge of Mount Clark, near Yosemite, and—with the vision burned in memory—jumped across the treacherous chasm that King and James Gardner had dared on their pioneering ascent of the mountain, in 1866.

During his first summer job, in 1950, as a USGS field assistant, Jim participated in the geologic mapping of the Virginia City area in Nevada, and traversed Gold Hill, where King and Gardner—after having ridden for three hard months across the plains—were burned out of their lodging, in 1863. Enthralled by the giant stone foundations of the Cornish pumps that remain today at Virginia City, Jim consumed the first published volume of King's Fortieth Parallel Survey, *Mineral Industry*. That remarkable treatise graphically details the mining methods at the Comstock Lode, and the awesome steam-driven pumps—each burning 22 cords of firewood a day—that drew water at the mines from depths of greater than 2,000 feet.

Studying the southern High Sierra for his Ph.D. thesis and later for the USGS, he mapped much of the terrain covered by King in 1864 and avidly perused King's *Mountaineering in the Sierra Nevada*, a volume that some held as the cornerstone of a new school of California literature. During work in the Sierra, Jim attained the summits of Mounts Silliman, Brewer, Tyndall, Williamson, Goddard, and Whitney, all of them first discovered, mapped, and named in 1864 by William Brewer's party, of which King and James Gardner were members. Jim also climbed Mount Clarence King and Mount Gardiner, both named by Brewer and Gardner when King made his second attempt to climb Mount Whitney. The conquest of a major peak bonds one, in ways that defy expression, to those who have gone before.

Studying the geology and ore deposits of Lyon, Douglas, and Ormsby counties in western Nevada from 1958 to 1961—a region that partly overlaps the area of King's Fortieth Parallel Survey—Jim traced the intricate shoreline of ancient Lake Lahontan, a feature that King had discovered and named. The daunting aridity of the Basin and Range country sensitized Jim to the struggles of King and Gardner during their first, fever-stricken season of the Fortieth Parallel Survey in the desolate wilderness of the Carson and Humboldt sinks.

Ascending the peak of Shastina, the parasitic cone on the west side of Mount Shasta that overlooks the jagged ice and giant crevasses of the Whitney Glacier on the north side of the main peak, Jim sensed why King so exulted when he first viewed this world of mobile ice in 1870. It was a scene that refuted the geologists who had previously climbed the mountain, missed the glaciers, and proclaimed the absence of glaciers in the United States. And upon reaching the wind-blasted spot on Shastina's crater rim where King and his party, with primitive equipment, had spent a freezing night above 12,000 feet, Jim poignantly realized the rigors of their trial.

Fifty years with the U.S. Geological Survey have afforded Jim a firm grasp of the workings and history of the organization that seems still to lie in the shadow of its founder. King's polymathic genius and extraordinary accomplishments—particularly the founding and shaping of the most productive Earth science institution in history—moved Jim to write this informative and moving account from an apposite vantage point atop his own distinguished career.

ACKNOWLEDGMENTS

Clarence King was the first director of the U.S. Geological Survey, and many of his accomplishments were familiar to me early in my own career as a geologist with the USGS. Two of the principal regions of my own fieldwork—western Nevada and the region of Sequoia and Kings Canyon National Parks in the Sierra Nevada of California—happened to be among King's primary areas of investigation a century earlier. Having had this opportunity to work in terrain investigated by King so long ago was certainly a factor in inspiring and shaping this book.

For 17 years King had maintained a close relationship with his boyhood friend James Gardner. They were together in high school and at Yale, toured Canada by boat, rode horseback across the country, were captured together—and narrowly escaped torture—by Indians in Arizona, spent a summer of discovery in the Sierra Nevada, and mapped Yosemite Valley. They were very different people, yet mutually complementary in both personality and skills. Gardner worked with King in establishing the Geological Survey of the Fortieth Parallel and served as second in command during the survey's six years of active fieldwork, extending from Nevada to Wyoming. His leadership in preparing the precise basemaps that would be the foundation for all subsequent scientific studies was critical to the success of the enterprise. This practice of coupling topographic and geologic mapping would soon be emulated by the other government surveys in the West.

Gardner left the Fortieth Parallel Survey in 1872, when the mapping of the survey area was completed, and joined Ferdinand Hayden's survey in mapping Colorado. He left active fieldwork in the West in 1875, and King went on to his appointment as first director of the USGS in 1879. Though their paths diverged, the two remained lifelong friends (James Terry *Gardner* changed his surname to *Gardiner* in 1880, but during the period chronicled in this book, the name was Gardner, and I use that spelling here).

One motivation for writing this book was the discovery that Gardner's grandson, now in his eighties, lives nearby. The historic photographs and maps that festoon the walls of his house were alluring enough, but when he permitted me to borrow a packet of letters that had been sent by Gardner to his mother during his travels in the West, I was enthralled.

The letters offer an intimate insight through one man's eyes, and I soon found that additional collections of letters, including some written by King to Gardner, were housed in various libraries. Letter writing was then the chief method of long-distance communication, and was commonly undertaken with a concerted effort. In this book extensive use has been made of both personal and official letters, which provide a remarkable window into the life of that time, as well as into the thoughts and mindsets of those who wrote them.

King relished storytelling, and those who wrote about him were unanimous in praising his ability to spin a yarn that would spellbind his listeners. He was prone, however, to theatrics, and I leave it to the reader to evaluate how much King embellished the stories related here.

Fifty years with the U.S. Geological Survey have given me insight into the history and inner workings of the organization that Clarence King founded. During the research phase for this book, I have benefited from my affiliation with the Survey, and from the counsel of many colleagues connected to that organization, including Robert Christiansen, Mike Diggles, William Glen, Christina Gutmacher, Keith Howard, King Huber, Bryan Knowles, Peter Lipman, Edwin McKee, George Moore, Warren Nokleberg, Dallas Peck, Thomas Sisson, John Stewart, and Robert Tilling. I thank these friends for their help. Further, I wish to acknowledge the generous support of the U.S. Geological Survey, and its director, Charles G. Groat, in the production of this work.

Several libraries have loaned material and provided copies of letters and photographs. Archival material was obtained from the following sources: Bancroft Library of the University of California, California Geological Survey Library, California Pioneers Library, Huntington Library, Library of Congress, National Archives, New York State Library, Smithsonian Institution, Stanford University Library, Yale University Library, Yosemite National Park Library, and the U.S. Geological Survey Library. The collection of William Pier, grandson of J. T. Gardner, includes letters chiefly from Gardner to his mother, as well as family photographs.

Clifford Nelson, historian of the U.S. Geological Survey, has helped with reference material and photographs. Michael Schroeder has shared information on Gilbert Munger, an artist with the Fortieth Parallel Survey, and also provided a copy of a letter of Samuel Emmons to his brother acquired from the Library of Congress. Jim Snyder of the Yosemite Library and William Pier, custodian of the Gardner collection, have been extremely helpful. Joseph McGregor has aided whenever possible in locating photographs from the Denver, Colorado, U.S. Geological Survey Library, and I value his ready hand. The staff at the U.S. Geological Survey Library in Menlo Park has aided whenever possible, and I especially wish to thank research librarians Anna Tellez and Page Mosier. Dugan Moore and James S. Moore have transcribed letters from copies of original handwritten script, and Aida and Lee Larson have prepared the index.

I owe much to William Glen, historian of science, for his encouragement and consultation throughout the years of manuscript preparation and editing. The manuscript has been improved in both readability and accuracy by the labors of four technical critics: George Moore, Kurt Servos, William Glen, and King Huber. I am grateful for their careful readings. Finally, I cannot close this statement without expressing my gratitude for the superlative editing of William Carver, in retirement from Stanford University Press, which has greatly improved the clarity, uniformity, and content of the manuscript.

JAMES GREGORY MOORE

ABBREVIATIONS

BL	Bancroft Library of the University of California
CGSL	California Geological Survey Library
CPL	California Pioneers Library
HL	Huntington Library
LC	Library of Congress
NA	National Archives
NYSL	New York State Library
SI	Smithsonian Institution
SUL	Stanford University Library
USGL	U.S. Geological Survey Library
WPC	The Collection of William Pier
YUL	Yale University Library
YNPL	Yosemite National Park Library

A BIRD OF PARADISE

*His buoyant personality dominated his whole career. Gay, versatile,
debonair, irresistible, gentle, honorable, "tender and true,"
he was greater and dearer than his work.*
—Rossiter W. Raymond

The mid-nineteenth century was probably the most dynamic and promising era in
U.S. history. It was a time that witnessed phenomenal overland migration, driven by
the breathtaking expansion of the nation's boundaries, which provided land for the
taking, and by the lust for gold and other precious metals, which promised wealth beyond imagining. And as steamships replaced sailing ships, and railways replaced ox-
or horse-drawn wagons and coaches, the migration became a stampede. All the while,
powerful concepts and tools—Darwin's theory of evolution, the climactic discovery
of many of the chemical elements, the formulation of crucial laws of physics, the introduction of photography and the telegraph, and much else—were catapulting natural science and technology to the forefront of popular imagination.

Clarence King, a man for all seasons, was ideally suited to the challenging work of
a scientist in exploring and mapping the vast unknown reaches of the American West,
and in assaying the region's natural resources. He had been an exceptional student at
Yale College, the first and most prestigious scientific school in the country. He was
gifted with an athletic build and great physical stamina, a photographic memory, diverse intellectual competencies, an instinctive sense of leadership, and a diplomatic
and gracious manner. Enamored of the wilderness, he struck out for the open country immediately after graduation, just as the Civil War was drawing to a close and
much of America was turning west. King, born and bred in the East, made his career

and fame in the West, and then reentered eastern society and politics, moving seamlessly through the disparate worlds of academia, the frontier, Indian encampments, the parlors and smoking rooms of high society, and the seats of power.

In his younger days, King had become an accomplished athlete, excelling at running, horseback riding, ice skating, rowing, and about anything else he put his hand to. In the West he fearlessly—some might say recklessly—hunted dangerous game when provisions were running low, on one occasion riding into a buffalo herd and killing a prime bull with a single revolver shot, while pinned under his own horse. Another time, he shot a grizzly bear after tracking it to its den and crawling in after it.

After apprenticing as a geologist for three years with the nascent California Geological Survey, initially without pay, King went to Washington to seek support for his own ambitious survey. Enthusiastic and persuasive by nature, he was able to secure the necessary approvals and funding, not only by dint of his rich experience in the high country of California, but also because of his personal charm and his close friendships among influential people. In 1867, at the age of 25, he was appointed Geologist-in-Charge of the Geological Exploration of the Fortieth Parallel, a survey of his own devising charged with mapping and studying an 800-mile long, 100-mile-wide strip across Nevada, Utah, Idaho, Colorado, and Wyoming. This expanse, which included the route of the not yet completed transcontinental railroad, stretched from the California boundary to the east flank of the Rocky Mountains. King had superior assistance in organizing and executing this work, always choosing well-qualified, well-rounded young men as his companions. Salient among his eager associates was his boyhood friend and Yale classmate, James Gardner, a skilled engineer who took charge of the critical topographic mapping for the survey, with great ultimate success.

In 1867, the exploration of this vast and remote rocky region was not without its trials and dangers. King had several near fatal encounters with hostile Indians, bandits, and army deserters, made scores of perilous mountain ascents, was struck by lightning while making measurements on a high peak, endured feverish weeks on alkaline water in the desert, and suffered the icy storms of the high mountains.

This far-flung endeavor, deemed near impossible by many, lasted 12 years and produced superb maps and a cornucopia of scientific monographs that subsumed geology, geography, paleontology, botany, zoology, and mining technology. The scientific community was stunned by the breadth and productivity of the enterprise. The field methods, published scientific reports, and maps resulting from the Fortieth Parallel Survey set new standards for such work, both domestically and abroad, and were quickly emulated in detail by other surveys that followed.

King demonstrated his creative and innovative bent in all aspects of this work, which was the first of the great mapping surveys—both topographic and geologic—undertaken in western America. He accomplished the task by dividing the subject area into a series of rectangles and then surveying them one at a time, all the while examining, sampling, and identifying the geological features of the land and positing their underlying origins. In crafting precise maps of such enormous areas, King and Gardner pioneered the use of elevation contours to portray the details of topography. This was possible only because they realized the critical importance of elevation control, and developed methods to measure land elevation quickly and in many places. On matching maps they depicted the diverse geologic units by the use of bright colors, and set out geologic cross-sections showing the third dimension, to aid the reader in visualizing the mapped units and their structure at depth. King also pioneered the use of photography in field studies, and set up laboratories to analyze rocks, ores, and waters. By bringing a distinguished German microscopist to this country, he fostered the microscopic study of minerals and rocks in America.

King was the first to describe the former course of glacial ice in the Yosemite region, and was the first to discover active glaciers within our nation's boundaries, thus opening the study of glaciology in the West. He unearthed evidence to support the notion—an idea theretofore considered heretical by scientists—that great natural catastrophes had helped shape the American geologic landscape, and had punctuated the course of biologic evolution. His popular book on mountaineering was considered the cornerstone of a new school of western literature and continues to captivate readers today. King's globally heralded exposure of the great Diamond Hoax in Colorado, triggered by the suspicions of his men in the field, saved investors millions of dollars, and made his reputation as an honest and resourceful public servant.

King was a gifted conversationalist and storyteller, his voice deep and natural, his repertoire rich, incisive, and singular. His sense of humor, thriving on double meanings and puns, was infectious. His companions in the field always anticipated his return to camp after an absence, because the good humor he bestowed on all hands seemed to dissipate their petty grievances and complaints. Aware of the privations of fieldwork in the remote western reaches, he ran comfortable camps with good food wherever possible, and even made an attempt at some formality while dining. Men rallied about him, and his natural ability as a leader—and his discerning selections of staff members—engendered a strong morale in all the surveys he led.

King belonged to a class of his own. Henry Adams—professor of history at Harvard, editor of the *North American Review*, and son and grandson of presidents—commented that Clarence King continually captivated and delighted him. Adams wrote glowingly that King knew more than he did about "Art and poetry; he knew America, especially west of the hundredth meridian, better than any one; he knew the professor by heart, and he knew the Congressman better than he did the professor. . . . His wit and humor; his bubbling energy which swept every one into the current of his interest; his personal charm of youth and manners; his faculty of giving and taking profusely, lavishly, whether in thought or in money as though he were Nature herself, marked him almost alone among Americans." He was like "A bird of paradise rising in the sage-brush."[1] John Hay, then Secretary of State, remarked that "the dazzling attraction of his personality won him fame that spanned the Atlantic."[2]

Both these men, like so many of the scientists he worked with in the field, became King's lifelong friends. He enjoyed people. His freedom, following a failed engagement to a young schoolteacher he had met in Virginia City, unleashed considerable female attention in the social circles of Washington and New York City. But although he reveled in the popularity, he was not attracted to what he considered the tradition-bound, seemingly affected and artificial, Victorian women of his own class. Instead, he was drawn to, and felt comfort with, natural, unaffected, dark-skinned women. He was interested in the arts and cultures of other peoples, and enjoyed making modest conversation with older Mexican or Indian women in their villages or camps, and was clearly attracted to younger women from simpler cultures. His liaisons with Indian maidens, and with young working women in Cuba, Hawaii, Central America, and Mexico, were legion.

So it was that at the age of 44, he met and was smitten with a young black woman who cared for the children of his host at a New York dinner party. The relationship became intense, and he secretly married the young woman shortly thereafter, to begin an amazing 15-year duplicity in which she bore him five children. Living a double life for the rest of his days, he led his friends to believe that he was a bachelor, and his wife, ensconced in a home in Brooklyn, believed he was a railroad porter by the name of James Todd, whose work required long periods of absence.

When the four federally funded surveys in the West were consolidated into a single bureau, the obvious candidate for its leadership, and the one selected by President Rutherford Hayes—with the advice of the scientific luminaries he consulted—was Clarence King. In 1879, at the age of 37, he was appointed the first Director of the U.S. Geological Survey. King's genius and farsightedness, his collegial and inspiring leadership style, good humor, and lofty standards of excellence are reflected in the scientific organization that he conceived, organized, and led to global preeminence. He was acutely aware of the virtue of hiring the brightest and most qualified young men for his agency, and was innovative in advocating and employing the newest scientific and cartographic tools and techniques. The U.S. Geological Survey has since served as an exemplar for the establishment not only of federal and state scientific agencies, but also for similar institutions in other countries.

Clarence King is embodied in the aphorism that great institutions are often no more than the shadow of a single individual. Few have known such accomplishment. Fewer still have led lives so rich and beguiling.

CHAPTER ONE

A YOUTHFUL ALLIANCE

There is no influence so powerful as that of the Mother,
but next in rank in efficacy is that of schoolmaster.
—*Sarah Josepha Hale*

In the ranking of personal catastrophes, those at the highest level of emotional trauma are the death of a child and the death of a spouse. Florence King suffered both at nearly the same time when just 22. She was living in Newport, Rhode Island, the wife of James King, a merchant working in the China trade. It was a business that frequently took him and his three brothers abroad, so that one or more of them would always be on hand in the Orient to manage the family's affairs. James had proposed to Florence (born Caroline Florence Little) when she was 14 years old and he 21, and they were married September 5, 1840, when she was 15. Not a year later he felt compelled to return to the company offices in Canton, China, and a few months later, on January 6, 1842, she gave birth to their son Clarence Rivers, soon nicknamed Clare.

In the fall of 1845 James returned home, and remained there for a year and a half. During this brief interval he enjoyed the company of his family, and was present at the birth of their second child, whom they named Florence. She was a fragile child, however, and soon died. It was only during this short interlude that young Clare and his father would spend time together.

King urged Florence to accompany him on his next trip to China, which would mean 3 to 4 months aboard a sailing vessel. She seriously considered going with him, but because of concern for her new third child, Grace, decided against it. James sailed in the spring of 1847, leaving his wife with their two remaining children. Near her

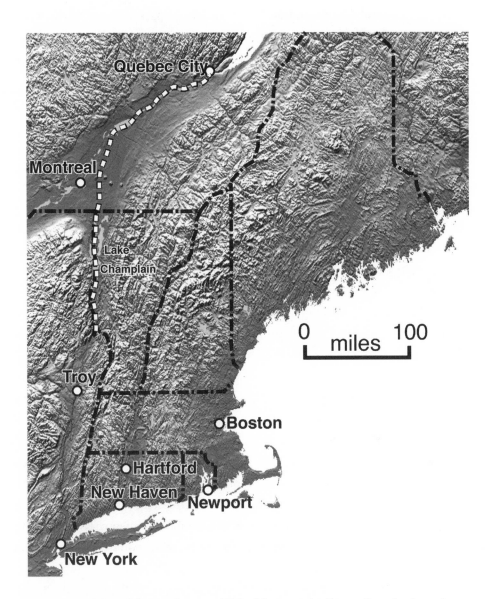

FIGURE 1.1.   Map of the northeastern United States and adjacent Canada, the early
world of King and Gardner. King grew up in Newport, Rhode Island, Gardner in Troy,
New York, and they met halfway between at high school in Hartford, Connecticut. In 1862,
upon completion of studies at Yale College in New Haven, they rowed 300 miles in the
racing gig *Undine* (dotted white line), north along the length of Lake Champlain, into
Canada, and down the St. Lawrence River to Quebec City.

22nd birthday, in the summer of 1847, Florence King's newest child, Grace, fell ill and died, and word of her husband's death from fever in China soon followed.

Crushing grief and depression lasted long after the impact of these two calamities had struck home, but the support of her own close family saw her through this time of trial. Emerging from the depths of despair over the next year, she focused increasingly on five-year-old Clarence, her only remaining child, devoting all her energies to nurturing and educating him. To succeed with this, she felt she had to complete her own education, and she began forthwith a course of classic instruction concentrating on Latin, French, and Greek.

In 1848 young Clarence began school. His mother had moved 30 miles from Newport to Pomfret, in eastern Connecticut, to enroll him in Christ Church Hall, a boarding school with a good reputation. The headmaster of the school, the Reverend Dr. Roswell Park, was a West Point graduate who had become interested in natural history. He left the military to become a professor of natural philosophy and chemistry at the University of Pennsylvania, and in 1841 he published a book on panology, an ambitious systematic survey of human knowledge. He then moved on to Pomfret to become pastor and headmaster of Christ Church Hall. Park preached on Sundays and taught the rest of the week, but still found time to combine his sermons and lectures into several volumes of collected works.

Dr. Park was a strict disciplinarian, and gave his students solid instruction and a good notion of the value of education. The section on geology in his collected works lays out the five primary stratigraphic layers of the Earth, showing that the lowest and oldest is devoid of all evidence of life. The next layers above carry simple fossils, and overlying these the younger layers show traces of progressively more complex life forms. Dr. Park held that "Further investigations are yet required, to complete the theory of Geology, and to reconcile all the facts hitherto collected. We can only add, that the book of nature and the book of revelation will, doubtless, when fully understood, be found to agree entirely. . . . "[1] His work preceded by nearly two decades the debate

FIGURE 1.2. *(opposite)* King's introduction to geology began at Christ Church Hall, a boarding elementary school in Pomfret, Connecticut. This illustration from a book written by his teacher shows some common fossils: 1. Ammonite; 2. Belemnite; 3. Orthoceratite; 4. Trilobite; 5. Orodus, of the shark family; 6. Cephalaspis (a vertebrated fish); 7. Palaeoniscus; 8. Plesiosaurus; 9. Ichthyosaurus; 10. Pterodactylus; 11. Iguanodon; 12. Anoplotherium; 13. Palaeotherium; 14. Dinotherum; 16. Mastodon, or Mammoth. Fossils 1–5 are from the oldest rocks with fossils (Transition); fossils 6–11 are from the intermediate geologic layers (Secondary); and fossils 12–16 are from the youngest layers (Tertiary). (Park, 1841)

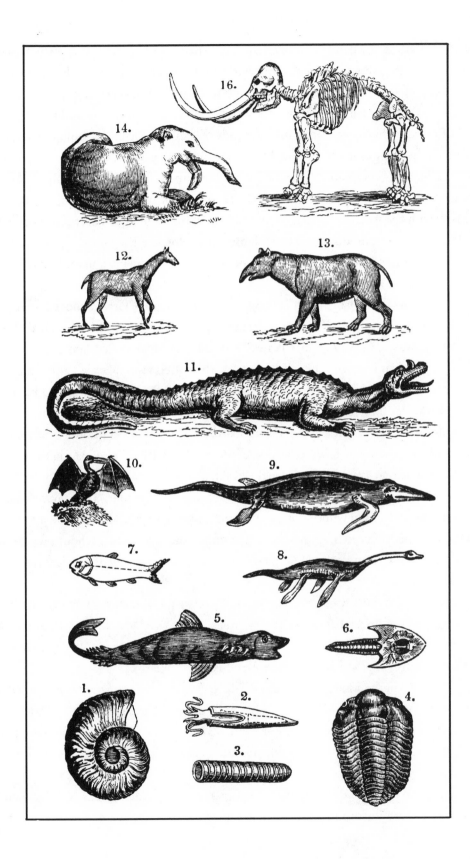

that began in 1859 when Charles Darwin published his *Origin of Species*, which proposed that the diversity of the organic world came about by evolution through natural selection—survival of the fittest—rather than through special creation.

King flourished at this school, captivated by the lessons in science and nature, and encouraged by his mother to collect all kinds of natural objects, including rocks and plants. When he was seven she bought him a magnifying glass. Before long their rooms looked like a museum and laboratory. When he came to her one day, telling of fossil ferns in a rock within a stone wall, she hiked a mile to the place. They examined the curiosity with the magnifying glass, and she helped him look up a description of such things in a book, and discussed their significance. Florence King took a great interest in the things that interested her son and nurtured his lifelong passion for learning.

After six years at Christ Church Hall School, Florence and Clarence moved to Hartford, Connecticut. In October 1855, when thirteen, King enrolled in Hartford High School. It was there that he met James Terry Gardner, nicknamed Jamie. Gardner's parents were familiar with the school because they often visited Jamie's grandparents in Hartford, Judge Seth Terry and Anne Drew Terry. Jamie, born May 6, 1842 in Troy, New York, was four months younger than Clare and would become his schoolmate and lifelong friend. Jamie's father, Daniel Gardner, a lawyer and author of books dealing with international law, became Recorder of the City of Troy. Jamie's mother, Anne, who was active in the Episcopal Church and deeply religious, brought him up with an unshakable faith. In later years Gardner told his daughter, "I have never made an important decision without asking for, and finding God's guidance."[2] Prior to high school, Jamie had grown up in Troy and attended the Troy public schools, where he received a good foundation in language and enjoyed the excellent musical training the school offered.

At Hartford the boys enrolled in the classics division and studied first Latin, then Greek, and later translated from Latin to Greek. In the third year they took courses in ancient history, geography, mythology, and antiquities.[3] Along the way there were lessons in English, mathematics, and modern history.

Clare, Jamie, and fellow student Daniel Dewey became an inseparable band who made the most of available free time. Hiking through the hills surrounding Hartford, the young naturalists noted keenly the birds, animals, and rocks they encountered. Gardner described King's remarkable memory, evident on these trips, "On Saturday, we usually spent the whole day walking in the country. If any question arose as to any object seen during the day, whether we had particularly noticed it or not, King could always describe it from memory with great minuteness. He seemed to photograph unconsciously everything that passed before his eyes, and to be able to recall the picture at will."[4] Fishing trips often included cooking fish over an open fire. In the winter they sledded and skated together.

But King had been suffering from an undefined malady, perhaps the depression that plagued him in later life, and was compelled to quit high school in April 1859. Gardner, for his part, finished out the year and enrolled in the fall at Rensselaer Polytechnic Institute in Troy. There he eventually completed the three-year course in two years.

In January 1860, King sought out a business position, and quickly found a job in New York as a clerk with William Brown and Company, flour merchants. His mother came to New York to live with him. King spent long hours with the ledgers, but he soon found this work burdensome and unappealing. Exhausted after the six-day workweek, he spent Sundays resting. He missed his friends, especially Jamie and Dan, and the carefree times they had spent on the playing field, roaming the fields and woods, and gliding across the ice.

One day, an angry King confronted a junior partner who, he felt, was telling untruths about him to the owner, Mr. Brown. King took the dispute to the owner, who was favorably disposed toward him, but in so doing King alienated Brown's partner. The resulting hostile atmosphere drove King to lose interest in his work and to channel his energies elsewhere. He became attracted to the political arena and to the question, supported by the Republicans, of whether slavery should be prohibited in the territories. Although King was strongly opposed to slavery, he felt that the issue ought not be federally mandated, but that the settlers themselves should decide. He believed that slavery would no doubt be put down in the territories because most of the settlers there had northern sentiments.

In Manhattan, King also discovered the world of art and bought a season ticket for the New York Art Academy. He especially admired Bierstadt's paintings of the Rocky Mountains and Harat's autumn pieces. He invited Gardner to join him in New York to visit the academy.

The business world had become increasingly trying for King, and seeking other diversions in New York, he became aware of women and the social scene. He wrote Jamie: "How many more seductive, wicked, beautiful, fascinating, jolly, voluptuous, apparently modest, artful women there are to one poor chicken here; they show you their necks and bosoms without intending to. . . . "[5] He envied Jamie's spiritual connection and tried to turn to religion, to divert his attention and to restore the purity of his soul, but he felt that the church was failing him. King was unhappy.

In April that year, his mother announced her engagement to George Howland, a widower considerably older than she, who had one child, George, Jr., from a previous marriage. Mr. Howland, the owner of a factory that produced white lead for paint, was financially secure, and saw in Florence King, at 32, a good prospect to care for his young child and to cement the relationship with more children. King wrote to Gardner about this news, but when the letter went unanswered, he sent another letter expressing his disappointment at not receiving a prompt congratulatory letter. By the same letter he asked Gardner to stop using the middle initial R (for Rivers) in his name, and from that time on he was known simply as Clarence King. Gardner had hesitated answering the first letter because he was uncertain whether what it offered was good news or not. On the one hand, Florence was much younger than Mr. Howland, and Clarence would no longer be the sole focus of her energy and affection. On the other hand, the liaison would alleviate the financial straits that had begun to beset mother and son with the dwindling of the family fortune.

In November 1860, Abraham Lincoln was elected president, and on April 12, 1861, Confederate cannon opened fire on the Union-held Fort Sumter in Charleston Harbor, South Carolina. After 36 hours of intense bombardment, which reduced the fort to a smoldering ruin, the Union major in charge surrendered, thus ushering in the Civil War.

Gardner was caught up in the patriotic fever then running high at Rensselaer Polytechnic Institute, where he was a student. Flags were hoisted, drums rolled, cannon fired salutes, and quickly organized drill squads marched in the streets; professors, merchants, lawyers, and church elders enrolled in drill companies; and a mob threatened to pull down the house of a known Confederate sympathizer. A Rensselaer Institute Corps was organized, and Gardner drilled in the streets two hours a day with five of his fellow students, a routine that at the least afforded exercise. Many of the students and citizens enlisted and joined the troops. In addition, hundreds of women, some carrying sewing machines, began meeting in an institute hall to sew for the soldiers, and a group of young ladies made the colors for the regiment. Jamie's mother urged him not to enlist, but he countered by noting that several cousins had already joined up, and that since his great-great-grandfather Ephraim Terry was a major in the militia during the Revolutionary War, the Terry blood that coursed through his body made it hard to ignore the call to arms. He did agree that he would continue his studies for now, because professionals trained in science and engineering might better serve their country as officers.

In addition to his studies at the institute and the demands for military preparedness, Jamie was active in the Episcopal Church. He led the young people's Sunday meeting and continued his independent Bible study. He also became interested in art, read Ruskin's *Modern Painters*, and corresponded with King about artistic matters.

Gardner occasionally joined King in New York, where they went to see displays of modern paintings.

The two young men exchanged letters frequently closing with "your loving brother" or "your affectionate friend and brother." In one long letter to Gardner, King wrote "Do you remember our old Hartford walks how we used to talk whole evenings and tell each other all our feelings and sympathize as to life's trials and hope and wonder for the future and how we declared our love and resolved never to lose our confidence in each other and never get the world's bashfulness of saying 'love'. Yes my brother those were happy days and when life seems to us as a desert land we can look back on them as a bright oasis of shining hours."[6]

Florence King's marriage to Mr. Howland, in July, made it possible for King to leave the clerical position he held at Brown and Company and begin college, with Howland's support. After a fishing trip with his old friend Dan Dewey in Vermont, he enrolled in a chemistry program at the scientific school at Yale College, in September 1860.

The Yale of those days was primarily a conservative Protestant school with an emphasis on the classics. But in response to the changing outlook brought about by the Industrial Revolution and innovative scientific ideas, a new department had been established a few years earlier. This was the Yale Scientific School (soon to be renamed the Sheffield Scientific School), which offered arguably the best scientific education in the country. King, despite his prior training in literature and languages, enrolled in the Scientific School, thereby becoming a "scientific." The "scientifics" were disdained by the "academics," students enrolled in the classics program. He signed up for a three-year course in the analytical chemistry program for a fee of about $200.

The program at the Scientific School consisted of two divisions, one for analytical chemistry and the other for metallurgy. King was in the chemistry division, which included instruction in experimental and analytical chemistry, physics, mineralogy, and crystallography. In the chemistry laboratory, he studied analysis of inorganic, organic, and agricultural materials under the direction of Professor George Jarvis Brush, a young man fresh from study in Germany who became a special mentor to King. Small groups of students would vie with one another in analyzing unknown samples, and in testing chemical theorems by experimental methods. The school also had perhaps the largest collection of rocks and minerals in the country, much of it collected by Professor Brush himself. King became deeply absorbed with these collections and spent hours at the cabinets examining the specimens and studying their significance.

King's natural athletic ability made him popular on the playing field. Short and compact in physique, he had sharp hand-eye coordination, and he was strong. He soon excelled in baseball, cricket, and long-distance walking, and became an excellent ice skater. He joined the rowing team, and before long was elected captain of the four-oared gig *Undine*.

At Rensselaer, Gardner concentrated on mathematics and completed courses in algebra, geometry, plane and spherical trigonometry, analytical geometry, and differential calculus. He excelled in courses in other departments as well, and according to one professor "both in regard to thorough scholarship and to general habits and conduct, he has maintained a position among the best of the students of the institution."[7] Gardner was graduated in the spring of 1861.

After graduation, Gardner continued studies at Troy in a variety of subjects, including mechanics, astronomy, metaphysics, Greek, and Latin. He became more involved in art study, and urged his mother to read Ruskin's book so that she could improve her appreciation of art. Because of a severe eye injury he sustained in October 1861, probably incurred on the playing field, Gardner was forced to give up his studies in Greek and Latin, and to curtail other study in evenings when the light was poor. He did maintain his interest in art, and was especially attracted to the moody paintings of Turner. He admired a large engraving his cousin Mary had bought, titled "Monarch of the Glen," taken from a painting by Landsun. He glowingly described this work as showing "a noble stag just risen from his couch of heather and harebell, his flanks glittering with dew, sparkling in the glorious morning rays that break through the mists which already are rising and wreathing themselves around the rocks, with here and there a rent letting you out into the surrounding mountains, and through one to the clear horizon."[8] At this time King was envious of his friend's growing competence in the art world. He wrote to Gardner "I wish I could pursue art studies with you. I don't know anything about it."[9]

At the beginning of his second year at Yale (in the fall of 1861), King began urging Gardner to leave his studies in Troy and to come to Yale. King sent him a college catalog, and pointed out all the excellent lectures that were offered by Professors Silliman, Loomis, and Dana. Professor Knight offered a course in anatomy, and each student had a body to dissect. King promised that Gardner could board as cheaply in New Haven as at Troy, and added that the opportunity of chumming with his dear friend Jamie again would greatly lift his own spirits. Moreover, Gardner could join the athletic club, ice skate, and participate in gymnastics. Although King still entertained the idea of joining the Army, he was becoming more involved in the college fellowship. He wrote Gardner: "Constantly you force it on me that I don't want to lead men, that mine is not that kind of nature. Now Jim deference to you and your judgement, but I do want to lead men. It will be my life's object. Why can I not? Don't think that because I show you my tender side my weak one if you will, that I have no fire, no firmness, no mental power. Don't think that I never *lead men* for in my own humble way I do. I can see my influence in college plainly enough. I am happy here. I am loved by some people and that is happiness. However, it all seems incomplete to me [because] I lack you. I find no home in my heart but yours."[10]

While Gardner's mother was living in Buffalo, his father was in Brooklyn conducting his law business. Gardner preferred that the two live apart. When his mother pondered moving back to New York, her son asked her: "Why do you wish to leave Buffalo when you have a comfortable home? If you go to Brooklyn you will be alone from morning to night in a small room with no pleasant facilities for going out, in a boarding house which I know from experience to be miserable and untidy. Besides having all the care of father's business which he loves to heap upon you. It needs some very good reason to counterbalance these objections; something beside the longing to be in the neighborhood of your husband and children."[11]

Gardner had been able to eke out his expense money for several months by doing clerical work on ordnance contracts for the Springfield Army Depot, but when these contracts were terminated by the government, his supervisor, Mr. Balch, notified Gardner that there was no further need for his employment.[12]

King sat in on a series of geology lectures by Professor James Dwight Dana, who recounted his work with the U.S. Exploring Expedition commanded by Captain Charles Wilkes in 1838–1842. This expedition discovered and charted a long stretch of the coast of Antarctica, mapped islands in the South Pacific, observed volcanic activity in Hawaii, and mapped several coastal regions in northwestern North America. Dana had joined a land party of the expedition that traveled overland from Fort Vancouver on the Columbia River to San Francisco in 1841, several years before the California gold rush erupted. He described vividly their observations of October 3, 1841, when they rode by the west side of Mount Shasta, the giant volcano in northern California. Some had previously reported the mountain to be 17,000 feet high, thus the highest mountain on the continent. King was spellbound by Dana's eloquent lectures, and longed to visit the untamed West, unaware that he would soon have such an opportunity.

King wrote Gardner about the accomplishments of a fellow student, Othniel Marsh, "Old Marsh (lucky dog) has discovered one of the most important fossils ever found. Lyell has written him offering to publish any communication on the subject in the Royal Geological Society Report. Bully for Othniel." He finished the letter with more personal comments: "You would like the two Stones Hal & Will. They are gen-

FIGURE 1.3.   An etching of Shasty Peak (as Mount Shasta was formerly called) in northern California based on an 1841 field sketch made by James Dwight Dana. He passed the great mountain while traveling overland from the Columbia River to San Francisco with the United States Exploring Expedition (Dana, 1849). A fascination with this mountain was a powerful magnet that lured King west.

tlemen and have a good deal of refinement. Bill loves me very much but it seems to me a sort of farce to have a friendship with anyone but yourself. My heart is taken up with you. Although I don't write much and even when I do write—I don't say much but my love for you grows always and is a most absorbing passion. The deeper I feel the more it becomes an effort to express myself, and at times I almost reason myself into resolving to be silent henceforth. To wait until we reach heaven then we shall see each other face to face."[13]

But King now had a new enticement to draw Gardner to Yale. He offered Jamie a slot on the rowing team, where he could "pull in the bulliest race crew of the jolliest fellows in the fastest boat."[14] Requirements for the team were threefold: entrance fee of $15, swim 100 yards, and approval by the boat captain. All of these could be easily met. Even before Gardner agreed to join the team, King asked him to look into the procedures for transporting a boat through the Albany–Lake Champlain Canal, and from the canal into the lake, and whether any carting would be necessary for such a trip.

The race boat, a four-oared, 35-foot lapstrake racing gig with outrigged oarlocks, was built by one of the best boat builders in America. The white outer hull bore a thin ultramarine stripe below the gunwale, and the inside was salmon-colored. (The seats were simple wooden benches; the sliding seats of modern racing shells would not appear until 1873.) On the transom was the name *Undine* in gold, outlined in blue. King

FIGURE 1.4.   Professor James Dwight Dana (1813–1895), a popular professor at Yale Scientific School, published his *System of Mineralogy* at the age of 24 before he served as geologist on the United States Exploring Expedition of 1838–1842. His stirring and inform-ative lectures excited an interest in geology shared by King and Gardner. (Beach, 1873)

FIGURE 1.5. A sketch of the uniform worn by the rowing crew of the Yale racing boat *Undine*. King's sketch, enclosed in a letter to Gardner of October 10, 1861, was part of his strategy to entice Gardner to come to Yale and join in the activities of the college, including a major boat race. Gardner did come, and although they lost the race, the crew was authorized to take the boat on a 300-mile rowing excursion to Quebec City in Canada. (Courtesy of the New York State Library, Manuscripts and Special Collections)

wrote that "When we race crew are in her she fairly flies and you can feel her shiver all through her kelson from stem to stern."[15] Most exciting to King was that after the July race the crew could make use of the boat for an extended excursion to Canada via Lake Champlain. On this trip they could wear the crew uniform consisting of blue shirt, white trousers, and straw hat. The shirt had anchors on the collar and a gold U on the chest. The boat's flag was of blue satin with the letter U in heavy gold. King loved to think how these trappings would impress the Canadians.

In due course, Gardner decided to attend Yale and moved to New Haven in May 1862, to begin the rigorous training for the upcoming boat race. He also found time to attend Dana's lectures and to explore the opportunities for religious activities at Yale. He was taken by both the science and the spiritualism of Professor Dana's course: "We had a splendid lecture yesterday on volcanoes, which is to be continued today. Dana has wonderful power of description—setting before one the most vivid pictures of scenes from his extended travels." Gardner wrote his mother, "I wish you could have heard the closing lecture of the geological course last night. It was the most sublime lecture in any subject that I have ever listened to. The Six Days of Creation in Genesis was the text: and so deep and high did the magnificent Christian mind of this great Philosopher soar that I felt stunned and overwhelmed. He is one of the few scientists who have not lost sight of the great end of material study. Instead of being lost in the discovery of new phenomena, in classification, or in general laws, he goes through the great storehouse of nature gathering together the letters, and classifying into words, and by laws generalizing into sentences, but all this only that he may read the glorious truths of God revealed to those who for love of their father, labor to understand his languages."[16]

King was captain and stroke oar of the four-man rowing team that now included Gardner, Sam Parsons, Dan Dewey, and a fifth student, the coxswain, who yelled the cadence and steered from the stern, facing the oarsmen. King was careful to enforce the training diet, which included a large portion of honey at breakfast, a sizable midday dinner, and only a single cracker for supper. After exercise, the skin was vigorously sponged, and a half-hour rest period was mandated. The tempo of the training increased as the race approached, and for the last week the crew was taken through paces similar to those they would encounter in the actual race.

The competition the team faced was challenging, because the leading boat was of six oars, and its crew members were older, bigger, and heavier than the men of the *Undine*. Gardner knew, however, that they were less well trained and disciplined. Moreover, the men of the opposing team drank, swore, chewed, and smoked, and

FIGURE 1.6.   A four-oar lapstrake racing boat with outrigger oarlocks in New Haven
Harbor. The forward bending of the rowers indicates that this boat, like King's Yale boat,
had fixed seats. (It was more than a decade later that the present sliding seats first appeared.)
A boat of this kind was raced by Clarence King, James Gardner, and two crew members, and
later taken on a camping trip to Canada in the summer of 1862.

they were fat. Surely the splendid training, exercise, diet, and adequate sleep of the
Undine crew would lead them to victory. Most of the betting men thought so too.

The race was held in the New Haven harbor on June 24, 1862, and the *Undine* got
off to a fast start. The stroke was well coordinated from catch, pull-through, finish,
release-feather, and recovery—and on to the next stroke. *Undine* led for the first part
of the course, but the greater power of the six-oared gig eventually prevailed, and it
barely inched out the *Undine* by 1 second at the finish line. Though King's crew was
cheered loudly for their superior oarsmanship, these hearty congratulations could
not lessen the bitter taste of defeat. They thought the *Undine* might have won the race
if their excited helmsman had steered a less crooked course.

After the race came a festive final weekend at the college, with parades and ceremonies. The promenade concert filled the first evening, and the following day
brought the Wood Spoon Exhibition. At this humorous performance, the most popular senior was presented with a beautifully carved wooden spoon by his friends amid
all manner of speeches and japes. On Presentation Day the seniors were introduced
to the president of the college, and many then took leave of each other. Gardner noted
that, "In the afternoon Clare gave a reception, or a spread as it is called, to the whole
boat club, twenty fellows, ice cream, strawberries, cake and lemonade were served."[17]

King was graduated with honors from the Yale Scientific School July 31, 1862, having completed the three-year course in two. Gardner busied himself with preparing equipment for the Canadian expedition. He sewed several cloth bags by hand to store the pilot bread (hardtack) and meal, and laboriously pieced together a tent, since they would be camping on the trip.

The next day was set for the departure on the excursion to Canada. Gardner had a long discussion with the team, concerning how they could most profit morally from the expedition. His strong Episcopalian convictions led him to regard this trip as an exercise in religious training. He told the group that "By carelessness and thoughtless conversation we may make it a boyish frolic, pleasing at first from its want of restraint, but resulting eventually in disappointment, dissatisfaction, and regret for wasted opportunities. Therefore, if we are diligent in spiritual things and constant and regular in our communion with God, then all the fields and forests and hills, and the changing water and rich clouds shall by day continually tell of our Father, while by night the countless hosts of the starry heavens will declare His glory."[18] The fellows generally agreed with his plan of maintaining a moral and righteous foundation for the expedition, and set about making preparations.

Gardner offered to assemble most of the provisions and equipment needed. He purchased 20 pounds of pilot bread, 10 pounds each of oatmeal and sugar, 12 of baker's flour, plus salt, pepper, soap, and candles. Mrs. Howland, King's mother, contributed an elegant container of Chinese tea. Utensils included three tin kettles, three tin pails for sugar, coffee, and tea, frying pans, sheet iron, teapot, coffeepot, cups, plates, wire grill, and cooking spoon. These supplies and the bedding were to be stowed under the fore and aft decks of the boat.

All were to meet at 5 P.M. at the train station in Troy, so that they could travel together to Whitehall, New York, there to connect with the *Undine*, which was freighted separately on the canal. The equipment was packed in a box to be shipped on the same train to Whitehall. Dan Dewey arrived in Troy by the morning boat, and he and Gardner went to the train station to await King and Sam Parsons from New Haven, and the brothers Will and Hal Stone from Boston. Surprisingly, however, only Will got off the Boston train; Hal had heeded an urgent plea for soldiers at home and had enlisted in the Army. The three then waited patiently for the New Haven contingent, but when the last train arrived, Clare and Sam were nowhere to be seen. At the last minute, the three reluctantly boarded the train for Whitehall without their companions. But while the train was stopped at a junction, another train rushed into the terminal. There was a jolly shout and two men, Clare and Sam, jumped from the train, Clare in his full boating uniform with blue shirt and white trousers. The two had traveled from New York by boat, had missed their train connection, and had only now made it to this junction by a longer route on a different train.

The next day the *Undine* arrived at Whitehall by canal, and the provisions and equipment were loaded. Gardner had developed a bothersome boil on his "sitting down place" and attempted to treat it secretly with poultices. But when they began rowing north on Lake Champlain the next day, friction on the hard rowing bench brought forth tenderness and then intolerable pain. Finally, Gardner was compelled to relinquish his oar and take over a position in the stern where he could relax and sit more comfortably on the baggage pile. That day they rowed 25 miles in 5 hours and stopped at Ticonderoga to camp. It was not a pleasant campsite—nobody slept because hoards of hungry mosquitoes attacked all night. Long-time neighbors in the area said that such an infestation was a rare event, almost unknown previously. Despite the mosquitoes (or perhaps because of them) several excellent fish were caught, milk was obtained from nearby houses, and the crew feasted on a hearty camp meal. A special treat was Mrs. Howland's fine China tea.

By the time they reached Plattsburgh, 70 miles up Lake Champlain from Whitehall, Gardner's boil had become even more painful. Fortunately, he found a doctor in town and had it lanced. Thereafter, he had no further trouble and took regular shifts at the oars. But he did miss his relaxed place in the stern, where he could appreciate the changing natural scenery and contemplate God's creations.

Near the international boundary with Canada, U.S. marshals detained the crew, thinking that they, like many other young men, were attempting to avoid serving in the Army by fleeing to Canada. The crew of the *Undine* was obliged to register at the nearest U.S. office. Signed affidavits were necessary to establish that they were students and therefore exempt from military service.

From the outlet of Lake Champlain they rowed 12 miles down the Richelieu River, past St. John, partly in a canal that skirted a series of rapids, including those at Fort Chambly, near where they camped for the night. The next day's 30-mile trip brought them to a camp on the Lonelle River just 20 miles short of the St. Lawrence River. The camp, dubbed "Camp Stew," would not soon be forgotten. Gardner cooked a mutton stew that was ravenously devoured by a famished crew. After dinner they gathered around a roaring campfire, and as the full moon rose above the forest, King broke into song. Soon the whole crew joined in college songs and hymns. River vessels of various kinds passed silently by in the dark, and sailors could be seen leaning forward and gazing upon this joyous group of young campers.[19]

They next camped at Lake St. Pierre and then rowed on to Quebec City. After fishing for salmon on the Saguenay River, they completed the rowing part of their

FIGURE 1.7. Fort Chambly, on the Richelieu River, as it appeared in 1862 when the Yale rowing crew camped nearby on their excursion from Lake Champlain to Quebec City. The fort was built at the foot of a series of rapids in the river, providing an ideal spot to control river travel by blocking the portage around the rapids. Fort St. Louis had been built at this site in 1665, and Fort Chambly shown here was completed in 1711. (*Scribners Monthly*, v. 17, Nov., 1878, p. 131)

trip, took a steamer to Montreal, shipped the *Undine* back to New Haven, and went on foot to New York City.[20] When they returned, shortly after the Battle of Antietam, Dan Dewey enlisted in the Twenty-fifth Connecticut Regiment.

After the northern cruise, Gardner moved to New York City, and by October 1862 was enrolled in law school. His daily routine was to study the Bible for an hour before breakfast, study law until eleven o'clock, and attend the law school lectures until one o'clock. After lunch he would read and write in his journal until four and exercise until six. The evenings were devoted to study, including French, and to social activities when the occasion arose. The study schedule was necessarily modified when friends and relatives visited. Clarence King, for one, would come to New York, often accompanied by their mutual friend William Hyde.

In October 1862, King happened to visit the office of his professor, George Jarvis Brush. Brush had just received a letter from a friend and former Yale classmate, William Brewer, a letter that would figure significantly in King's subsequent career. Brewer had grown up on a small farm in New York, and attended Yale for two years, concentrating on agricultural science. Two years after graduation, and after he had served for a time as a secondary school teacher, he returned to New Haven, where he

received the degree of Bachelor of Philosophy, in the first Yale class that was graduated from the Scientific School. Brewer next taught several years at the Ovid Academy
in New York and went to Germany for two years to study botany at Heidelberg and
Munich. While there, he took a 600-mile botanical trek through the mountains of
Switzerland, and on the trip became familiar with the geologic features so beautifully
displayed in the Alps. Upon returning to the United States he took a professorship at
Washington College, Pennsylvania, and was married shortly thereafter. But soon after
the birth of a son, his wife died, followed shortly by the child. While deep in mourn-
ing in the summer of 1860, Brewer received a letter from Josiah Whitney, who had just
been appointed the first director of the Geological Survey of California, offering him
a position. It was through their mutual friend, George Brush, that Brewer had been
recommended for the position. Brewer accepted, was appointed first assistant in geology, and departed for California.

In the letter to Professor Brush, Brewer described an expedition in September
1862 to Mount Shasta in northern California, at that time considered to be the highest peak in California. This giant volcano had fascinated King ever since Professor
Dana described it in his lecture. Brewer painted a vivid picture of the mountain as
seen from the Castle Crags on the southwest side. The upper 6,000 feet of the volcanic
cone was mantled with ribs of snow, and the steep skyline on the east side sloped an
impressive 27 degrees. Little was known about the geology of the peak. Its elevation
had been estimated by both Fremont and Williamson at about 17,000 feet, but a recent climber carrying an uncalibrated barometer reported it as somewhat less than
14,000 feet.[21] Many believed it to be the highest mountain in the nation; some said
that its summit was inaccessible, though others claimed to have climbed it.

Josiah Dwight Whitney had graduated in 1839 from Yale, where he studied chemistry, mineralogy, and astronomy under Professor Benjamin Silliman, Sr. He then
studied mineral science in Europe for five years, and returned to the United States to
work at the state geological surveys of New Hampshire, Iowa, and Wisconsin before
being appointed director of the California Geological Survey.

The Shasta party included three local men as packers and helpers in addition to
the scientists. Whitney was the leader, Brewer the botanist, and Charles Hoffmann the
topographer, who carried three 30-inch-long mercury barometers, especially made
with scales that would read to 18,000 feet for elevation measurement. The party
reached timberline on the south side of the mountain at 7,400 feet, using mules to
carry their supplies and instruments, and camped near a small stream. The camp was
overshadowed by the great barren mountain, still towering 7,000 feet above.

Whitney awakened the group at 2 A.M., and after a hasty breakfast they began toiling on foot up a broad ravine in the moonlight. Hoffman stayed in camp, partly because his body was still weak from sickness, but also because his duty was to read one barometer every 15 minutes, for comparison with readings from the two carried to the summit. Much of the slope was littered with sliding debris, making the climbing easier on the snow in sheltered chutes than on the unstable rubble. A 5,000-foot climb up a slope approaching 40° brought them at 8 A.M. to a series of red bluffs at 13,000-foot elevation.

From there to the summit was generally less steep but still difficult, because of uncertain footing where hard snow had melted into jagged points and ridges. The wind was icy and Whitney's fingers suffered from frostbite. They reached the summit at noon after passing a boiling hot spring emitting steam and sulfur-rich gas. Brewer described the inspiring and majestic scenery laid out before them. To the west was range after range extending to the Pacific, to the north were the Siskiyou Mountains, to the east dark storm clouds were building, and to the south appeared the northern extremity of the Great Valley of California. Lassen Peak was clearly visible 75 miles distant. They stayed on the summit more than an hour, taking repeated barometric measurements with the two instruments. Freezing mist encrusted their beards, and three of the party suffered grimly from mountain sickness, with lethargy, headache, and vomiting.

Later comparison with Hoffmann's barometric measurements in camp indicated that the mountain's height was 14,440 feet. Brewer noted, "We were naturally proud of the achievement . . . it was the first time that the altitude of a mountain in the United States, more than 14,000 feet high, had been accurately measured."[22] He noted that despite this great elevation, there were no glaciers on the mountain, which was probably due to the long, hot California summers with little precipitation.

King was fascinated by this account and could not get it out of his mind. The letter convinced him to go west, a decision that was probably the single most important in his life. Brewer in later years wrote, "Both during our earliest conferences and on several later occasions, King told me that Mount Shasta was the magnet that had drawn him irresistibly to the Pacific coast."[23] Brewer's letter intensified King's interest in geology, and he went to Harvard to attend lectures on glaciation by Professor Louis Agassiz.

Late in 1862, King joined Gardner in New York, where the two of them and Gardner's brother Eugene took rooms together. Gardner felt "Clare's jolly nature is as good as sunshine," and was especially pleased when Clare visited his mother on Sunday and returned with "good things in the form of cold roast fowl, etc." to add a special touch to supper.[24] Their cozy room was decorated with the old *Undine* flag they had taken to Canada, prized rock specimens, and a growing art collection, including two water-colors belonging to King. Eugene Gardner enjoyed these new surroundings, which were so much freer than life in the boarding house where he had been living under the shadow of his father.[25]

James Gardner continued his law studies, but now focused much of his energy on art appreciation with King, and he and King became devotees of the Ruskin philosophy. They became so passionate about what they considered a new trend in art, that they formed a group called the Society for the Advancement of Truth in Art. Their credo was "truth in nature" and they championed simplicity and plainness in art and architecture.

Gardner's father, Daniel Gardner, who had maintained his law practice in New York, died rather suddenly early in March at the age of 63. He had apparently been a man hard to live with. Gardner wrote to his mother in Buffalo that "Eugene is changing completely. Father's death lifted a terrible incubus off his life, as he himself expressed it, and now physical, mental, and religion springs up with new life in the sunshine of hope."[26]

In early March 1863, King moved out of the rooms in New York City and relocated at his mother and stepfather's house in Irvington, New York, about an hour north of Manhattan on the Hudson River. The young daughter of King's mother and Mr. Howland, Marian, was a delight to Gardner, who noted that "The baby is a splendid specimen physically and as lovely in temperament as in face. Such a child is an excellent thing to have in the house."[27]

Gardner's intensive law study eventually drove him to nervous exhaustion, and when King broached the subject of a major trip crossing the plains to California he was receptive. The restorative effects of such a total change in schedule and scenery appealed to him, even though he would have to delay his bar examination. Both entertained the possibility of obtaining some form of employment in the West that would match their interest in science and the out-of-doors. Another factor to consider was the ever-present possibility of conscription into the Army, now that both were no longer students. Another friend, William Hyde, became interested in the trip, and proved to be a most helpful companion, in part because his father owned a foundry at the Comstock Lode in western Nevada, near the route they would follow to California.

Plans were rapidly made for a departure in April. The impulse to journey to the West was a momentous one. It would prove to be critical in shaping their careers. Shortly before they left, they learned that their dear friend Dan Dewey, who had enlisted in the Army, had been fatally shot in a canefield during a battle in Louisiana.

CHAPTER TWO

ABLEBODIED MEN

*He couldn't believe that flat could be so flat or that distance ran so far or
that the sky lifted so dizzy-deep or that the world stood so empty . . .
He never had known distance until now.*
—A. B. Guthrie, "The Way West"

The three travelers, King, Gardner, and Hyde, met at Niagara, New York, in April 1863
and took the train bound for St. Joseph, Missouri, then the western terminus of the
railroad and the beginning of the California Trail. At Hannibal, Missouri, a family
group had boarded the train: T. M. Speers, with his wife, two children, and brother
John. Speers, a horse trader, was also heading to St. Joseph, where he planned to take
a wagon train across the continent to California. Speers had originally loaded his entire outfit, including horses, mules, four wagons, and food, onto a riverboat at St.
Louis. At Hannibal everything was transferred from boat to train. Also with Speers on
the train were several wagon drivers and some drovers to handle the stock.

Speers planned to take his draft stock to California, to take advantage of high
market prices. Horses and mules were in great demand by freighters to haul equipment and supplies over the Sierra Nevada to the Nevada mining camps, particularly
the Comstock Lode at Virginia City.

King, in his friendly, jovial style, entertained the children during the long train trip
to St. Joseph and won the gratitude of Mrs. Speers. The Speers invited the three men
to join their wagon party, provided they supplied their own horses. An agreement was
quickly struck for the young men to combine forces with the wagon train, and to help
the drovers care for the livestock in return for food. Ablebodied men were needed in
Indian country to guard the livestock and discourage Indians from stealing everything

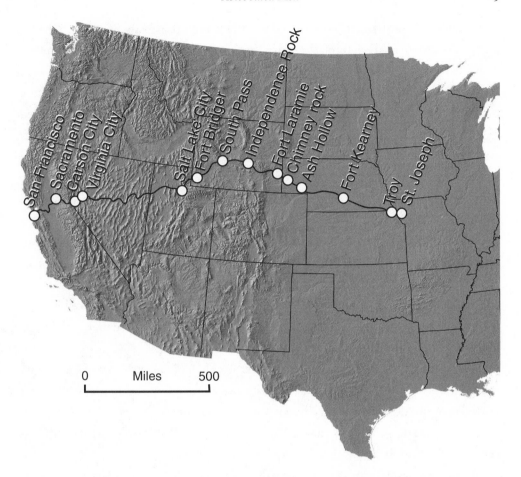

FIGURE 2.1. The California trail traveled by Clarence King and James Gardner in the summer of 1863. They had gone by railroad from the East Coast to St. Joseph, Missouri, where they joined a wagon train accompanied by a herd of horses and mules bound for California. One of the drovers overseeing this herd was Dick Cotter, who became a close friend. Leaving St. Joseph May 1, the three rode horseback with the wagons, eventually travelling nearly 2,000 miles to San Francisco, arriving September 1.

in sight. J. C. Redman, a wagon driver, fortunately kept a journal of the trip that later proved to be a valuable resource, because those kept by King and Gardner were destroyed in a fire near Virginia City.[1] Dick Cotter, one of the drovers entrusted with tending the horses and cattle, became a close friend of King and Gardner.

At St. Joseph the three companions bought riding horses, and on May 1 the trip across the plains began as they crossed the Mississippi River on a newly built bridge. Redman wrote that on the "evening of the 4th while we were preparing to camp for the night we met the first Indians. They came into our camp and stood gazing at us.

They were some of the Pottawotamie Tribe and my enthusiasm about going to the far away golden state nearly left me for a time, but as we traveled on west we were among Indians from one tribe to another all the way through to California."[2]

For several days heavy rain bedeviled the wagon train, turning the trail into a quagmire that slowed travel to a snail's pace. At Troy, Kansas, the wagons were halted by a sheriff's posse that promptly arrested King, Hyde, and Gardner. They were accused of kidnapping some black slaves and taking them into Missouri. The three were hauled into court, but Speers testified that he knew they were innocent, and the charges were dropped. The judge released the men, and the wagons were allowed to continue west.

Food on the trail was simple and plain, mainly cornbread, oatmeal, and fat meat. Special treats were bacon, hardtack, and dried fruit. On May 6, three of the men succeeded in shooting two buffalo. The red meat, especially from young fat buffalo, was tasty, and steak was eaten for a time at breakfast as well as dinner. The jerked buffalo meat that Mr. Speers later bought from hunters became a staple food, but it had to be boiled for a long time before it was tender.

The wagon train reached the Platte River near Fort Kearny, Nebraska, and then followed a swath of green grass and cottonwood trees along the south bank of the river. The water of the Platte was brown and muddy, "too thick to drink and too thin to plow." It was dipped out by the bucketful, and was drinkable only after the silt had settled to the bottom.

King was dazzled by the great herds of buffalo they encountered near Fort Kearny, some 200 miles out on the trail from St. Joseph. He had read and dreamed of these vast herds, and now he wanted to try his luck at hunting. He wished to supplement the wagon train's steady diet of fat pork and cornbread with buffalo hump and tongue. A local stockman advised King that buffalo hunting was easier with a horse trained to run with the buffalo. King borrowed such a horse and, with a hunter, headed out early in the morning, so as to come upon a herd of grazing buffalo that numbered in the thousands. Picking out a magnificent bull, King chased it for two miles, revolver in hand, waiting for a good shot. Finally, the bison stopped and made a stand in a shallow depression on the prairie, whereupon King fired. Immediately, the entire herd broke into a stampede, and many animals raced madly through the depression and past the scene of action. The wounded buffalo turned and charged horse and rider, who were unable, because of the onrushing herd, to move clear. The horse was hurled down, its body pinning King to the ground. King was forced to shoot the injured horse, and finally, when the hunter arrived, was pulled from under the animal, freeing his injured leg. He was taken to Fort Kearny for medical attention and remained there after the wagons resumed their travel west. King later boarded the Overland Stage to overtake the Speers' train. Fortunately, the leg was not broken, but he walked with a limp for weeks.

When they could do so, the three companions rode away from the train to hunt and explore the countryside. On a clear day they spied some high bluffs about five miles from the river, and King and Gardner rode across the prairie to investigate. Gardner rode alone to the base of some cliffs where pines rose from the broken rock. While looking for game, he climbed up among the trees and "suddenly above . . . heard what seemed a human moan, stranger and more sad than any bough rubbing bough in the forest. Above me, stretched at full length on a branch that flung itself out from the face of the bluff lay an Indian chief, wrapped in his crimson serape. His bow and arrows and his lance were lashed to his side on the narrow platform where he rested, and, the thongs straining against their burden, moaned the dirge of some warrior Sioux."[3] Gardner shuddered at the sight, and the image of that funeral platform recurred long after, whenever he was challenged by a mysterious sound.

The wagon train rolled on up the Platte River Valley, past its forks, and then up the South Platte to near the present Colorado state line, where the river was still about as broad as the Mississippi. They crossed the river at a tricky ford; although the water rose barely above the wagon wheels, the bottom was soft and prone to quicksand. The crossing thus had to be made quickly to prevent the wagons from sinking and becoming hopelessly mired. But all went well, and after this crossing, spirits were revived by a dinner of pronghorn antelope meat.

The route then lay across a tableland between the two forks of the Platte and on to Ash Hollow, where a steep descent down the river bluffs brought them to the banks of the North Platte. It was here, just eight years earlier, that General Harney had fought a battle with the Sioux Indians, in retaliation for the "Grattan Massacre" the year before. Small bands of Sioux were frequently encountered moving camp, the horses dragging the travois on which their tepees and other trappings were lashed. The old women led these horses, and the men and young women rode horseback. J. C. Redman wrote, "The bucks are the bosses of the household and never work, but go out and kill the game and leave it wherever they kill it for the squaws to go and bring in, dress it and prepare it to cook for his lordship, while he lays around and grunts and eats, and if there are any skins to tan the squaws have it all to do. And when the Tribe moves to another hunting ground if there are any decrepit and old Indians that are not able to travel, the others usually make a little fire and sit the old ones down by it with a little food and leave them to perish or be eaten by wolves or other wild animals."[4] The wagon train forded the North Platte River and moved westward upstream.

FIGURE 2.2.   Chimney Rock, Nebraska, passed by the wagon train about one month out of St. Joseph. The spire, which rises some 325 feet above the plain between Fort Kearny and Fort Laramie, is one of the most distinctive landmarks on the California Trail. Its lower bluffs of soft sandstone were a favorite place for travelers to carve their initials. (Nebraska State Historical Society Photograph Collections, 1902 photograph)

On May 29, nearly a month after their departure from St. Joseph, the train passed Chimney Rock in northwest Nebraska, one of the most distinctive landmarks on the California Trail. Redman and Dick Cotter resolved to ride over to explore the 325–foot rocky spire, a curious erosional remnant of flat-bedded sandstone. But distance was always underestimated on the broad prairie. The rock was much farther away than they expected; they rode seven tedious miles before reaching its base, and by then the wagon train was barely discernible in the distance. They could afford to spend only a few moments carving their initials in the soft sandstone, to add to those already there.

A few days later they arrived at Fort Laramie on the Laramie River, near its junction with the North Platte, in what is now Wyoming. Up till then they were ahead of schedule, and all hands were pleased to arrive early in the fort's 45-day immigrant season (May 20 to July 4). Wagon trains aimed to reach the fort during that window, so as to give them time to cross the deserts and the Sierra Nevada not later than mid-September, in order to avoid the deadly October snows. (The lesson of the Donner

Party had not been forgotten.) A two-day layover at the fort gave them time to rest, repair equipment, and wash clothes, and it was then time to move on.

On June 9 the wagon train crossed the North Platte, on a bridge that had replaced previous bridges carried away by flood waters. (The first bridge across the river, built in 1851, replaced the ferries that were formerly the only means by which one could cross.) The next day they camped on the Sweetwater River, near Independence Rock in central Wyoming, about three weeks ahead of the main throng of immigrants. (It was common for many wagon trains to celebrate Independence Day, July 4, near this huge, turtle-shaped granite mass, hence the name.) Two days later they passed Devil's Gate, where the Sweetwater River poured through a narrow gap in the mountains. Here they followed the Overland Stage route, which was crowded with wagon trains. Some of the ox teams were headed by a yoke of cows who did double duty; they helped pull the wagons and gave milk morning and evening.

The wagons and stock then funneled over South Pass in western Wyoming, the principal route over the Rocky Mountains and the Continental Divide. This pass, the best over the entire mountain chain, hardly deserved the term, which generally refers to a distinct saddle over a high range. It was, in fact, a broad, low zone some 20 miles

FIGURE 2.3. Fort Laramie in eastern Wyoming, near the junction of the Laramie River and the North Platte River, was reached by the wagon train in early June 1863. The travelers rested at the fort two days, repairing equipment and washing clothes. Gardner was smitten by a young lady traveling with her family, but the romance had little time to mature before the family's party diverged from the route of the main wagon train. (Stansbury, 1852.)

FIGURE 2.4.　Independence Rock in central Wyoming, a landmark granite monolith that is one of the first hard-rock outliers of the Rocky Mountains. The wagon trains commonly arrived at this point on July 4 and here celebrated Independence Day. (William Jackson photograph)

wide between the Wind River Mountains to the north and scattered ranges to the south, including the Green Mountains.

West over South Pass, the Big Sandy River runs in a broad, barren valley where animal feed was hard to find. Indians commonly appeared there when a train stopped for the night and camp was made. One evening Mr. Speers offered a young Indian bread and meat, and asked him where good grass could be found. After he and his friend had eaten their fill, the Indian pointed off toward the hills and offered to lead them to a good place. Redman and Cotter, whose turn it was to look after the stock that night, led the bell mare after the Indians. The horses and mules followed this mare, as they customarily did, and stayed with her. The trail led four miles from camp over rocky ridges and ravines and finally ended in a small basin with good grassy slopes. The bell mare was picketed for the night in the bottom of the basin, and the Indians moved to the opposite side and made preparations to spend the night.

At dusk, the two drovers sensed the danger of their position. They were only two, and a long way from their companions at the wagon train. They knew that they could be surrounded by hostile Indians, who could easily run off their stock. As night fell, coyotes moved in close and began to howl. The herd became restless, yet did not stampede, but remained in the hollow during the night. Now and again, low whistles by the Indians seemed to calm the livestock. The two drovers got no sleep, but remained nervously vigilant all night, expecting an attack at any time. They felt they were in mortal danger, and the night seemed to stretch on forever. When dawn finally came, Redman and Cotter breathed easier, feeling fortunate to have survived till morning without having the horses driven off, or a worse calamity occur. They lost no time in herding the stock back to camp.

Because of rumors of recent raids by hostile Indians, a family of four with their lone wagon joined the party for some days. The Fancher family included two daughters, and Gardner was smitten by the younger one. Redman notes that "Jim Gardner was a little fellow rather susceptible, especially when there was any pretty girls

FIGURE 2.5. On June 12 the party arrived at Devil's Gate, where the Sweetwater River pours through a narrow gorge in the mountains. Here the wagon trail detoured from the river around this water gap. Some of the wagons were hitched to a yoke of cows that worked double duty, helping to pull as well as providing milk morning and evening. (Rendered from a colored painting by William Henry Jackson. Used by permission, Utah State Historical Society, all rights reserved.)

FIGURE 2.6.   South Pass, Wyoming, the principal route over the Rocky Mountains and the Continental Divide. This, the best pass over the entire Rocky Mountain system, hardly deserved the name. Rather than a narrow gap over a mountain range, it is a broad, low saddle some 20 miles wide between the Wind River Mountains to the north and scattered ranges to the south, including the Green Mountains. (Rendered from a colored painting by William Henry Jackson. Used by permission, Utah State Historical Society, all rights reserved.)

around . . . the girls usually rode horseback and both wore bloomers. Miss Amanda being the handsomest, little Gardner seemed quite fascinated with her charms and rode horseback with her as long as they traveled with us, and King was uneasy about him."[5] This element of romance came to an end, however, when the family parted from the wagon train. King then found Gardner interested in riding with him again, when there were opportunities for exploring off the main emigrant trail.

Plodding on day after day, the wagons at length forded the Green River on June 21. It was a dangerous crossing for the stock, thin and wasted as the animals were. Many could scarcely swim through the swift current. They next stopped at Fort Bridger, Wyoming, an important hub on the emigrant trail. It had been abandoned for a period, but the Army reoccupied it in 1862 during renewed Indian raids. At this time, some 900 Shoshone Indians, considered hostile, were being detained at the fort by the Army.

The trail wound up through the Wasatch Mountains (in what is today Utah), and encountered the first deep canyon along the entire route of the trail. The echoes of the rattling wagons reverberated in the canyon, sounding much as if someone were hammering high in the rocks on the steep walls. Reasonably enough, this had been named Echo Canyon.

At Weber Valley they paused at some Mormon settlements and tasted the first fresh fruits and vegetables they had had in two months. Several plain-looking Mormon women offered to wash clothes and furnish wild berries in return for objects from civilization—clothes and cooking utensils. Some of the Mormon men had up to a dozen wives and seemed to be living well.

On June 29 the train crested a ridge and found the whole country beyond the Wasatch laid out before them. The broad reaches of Great Salt Lake lay below like a blue carpet surrounded by the harsh desert of alkali flats and rocky ridges that extended as far as the eye could see. The wagons rolled into Salt Lake City, where stone masons were already at work building the giant Tabernacle, and the party camped in the main city square. Brigham Young, chief of the Mormons, visited them with other church elders in a carriage pulled by two large mules. In a short speech he told of his

FIGURE 2.7.   Fort Bridger in southwestern Wyoming, on Black's Fork of the Green River. The fort was nicely placed in level grassland with fresh streams and plenty of timber. In spite of its rudimentary buildings, the fort was an important stop on the California Trail, because equipment and skins were available for trade there. (Stansbury, 1852)

FIGURE 2.8.   Looking west from a pass in the Wasatch Range at the first view of the Great Salt Lake and the desert country of the Great Basin beyond. When the wagon train arrived at the first settlements in Weber Canyon, the Mormon women offered to wash clothes and trade fresh vegetables and wild berries for objects from civilization, such as clothing and cooking utensils. (Stansbury, 1852)

wish to be left alone, since his people had been driven out of the states and had settled on this site in the desert as a place of refuge. He advised the travelers to "give an Indian a biscuit instead of a bullet."[6]

The real desert travel began west of Salt Lake City. Casks were filled at the sparse water holes, and travel was often only by night, to avoid the heat of the day and conserve water. In places, only bitter alkali water was available for the thirsty beasts. The wagons crossed, or skirted, the ragged mountain ranges and lumbered across the dusty sagebrush plains of the Great Basin, following the Overland Stage route. For more than a month the wagon train traveled the 500 miles from the Wasatch Mountains to the Sierra Nevada, across Nevada Territory. On August 6, the train reached Carson City, in western Nevada, at the east base of the towering Sierra. (It would be about a year—October 31, 1864—before Nevada would be proclaimed the thirty-sixth state.) The forest-covered peaks of the Sierra signaled the end of the desert and the beginning of the well-watered Pacific coastal zone. King, Gardner, and Hyde decided to leave the wagon train at Carson City before the mountain crossing, and to head for the nearby Comstock Lode. As the Speers' wagon train rolled on west, the three companions rode northeast to visit one of the most active mining districts in the country.

Despite new adventures that beckoned, the three riders had grown to love life on the wagon trail and the companionship of the caravan, and would look back fondly on the plains and the desert ranges. Their appetites had never been better, and the simple fare of beans, bacon, bread, and coffee, with two big drinks of water a day, had been sufficient. Gardner wrote home that "Before we left the Plains we had become so fascinated with the life and so interested in the vast loneliness of those deserts, so at home in the little caravan that I would gladly have turned around and traveled right back over the same road. . . . Though I came especially for health and gained new vigor every day yet the bodily improvement and the few discomforts are almost overlooked as I strain the mind to comprehend the total value of this journey to my higher nature. You ask whether I would advise anyone else to take the trip. Most emigrants draw a sigh of relief when they see the dark peaks of the Sierra Nevada cutting

FIGURE 2.9. The Mormon Tabernacle was under construction at the time the wagon train passed through Salt Lake City. Granite slabs were hauled to the site from quarries in Cottonwood Canyon, 17 miles south in the Wasatch Mountains. (Used by permission, Utah State Historical Society, all rights reserved.)

FIGURE 2.10.   The main street in Carson City, Nevada. A stage drawn by a six-horse team is about ready to depart the Ormsby House Hotel. (Lawrence and Houseworth collection, The Society of California Pioneers)

the evening sky; but to us it was like parting with old friends for new ones. To the trials of the desert we were used and had long since ceased to count them as anything compared with the rare pleasures of such a life; before us all was uncertainty. Though there is this feeling among most emigrants yet few of them hesitate to cross again. . . . And I think that every intelligent man whether he at the time realizes it or not gets improvement enough to far outweigh the hardships."[7]

The Speers' party crossed the Sierra into California and arrived in Sacramento on August 14, 1863, 106 days after leaving St. Joseph. King, Gardner, and Hyde rode on to the booming Comstock, which was supplying much of the silver used to finance the Union forces in the Civil War.

The Comstock District had made a slow start. In 1850, a wagon train from Salt Lake City stopped along the Carson River, near where a small stream, one that drained a high range of hills some seven miles west, entered the river. A test panning of the river sand revealed a small amount of gold. This placer deposit was worked in a limited fashion for several years until a resourceful prospector known as "Old Virginny" began panning up the small stream. In 1859, he and three friends found somewhat richer material at the head of the stream, which later became known as the "Old Red Ledge." Other placer miners staked claims in the region, and by the summer of 1859 individual miners were washing out $50 a day in gold from a black sand that was commonly covered by barren slopewash. This sand was associated with a bluish material that clogged the rockers. Some of this was sent to Grass Valley for assay, and on June 27 it was declared to be rich in silver. A short while later, one sample of vein material assayed "$3,876 to the ton, three fourths silver and one fourth gold."[8] The rush was on, and the population of Virginia City rose from about 2,300 in 1860 to 4,000 in 1862 and 15,000 in 1863. This discovery caused the surrounding countryside to be heavily prospected, and several other mining districts were organized in the vicinity.

William Hyde's father owned a ranch in Carson Valley and a foundry at Gold

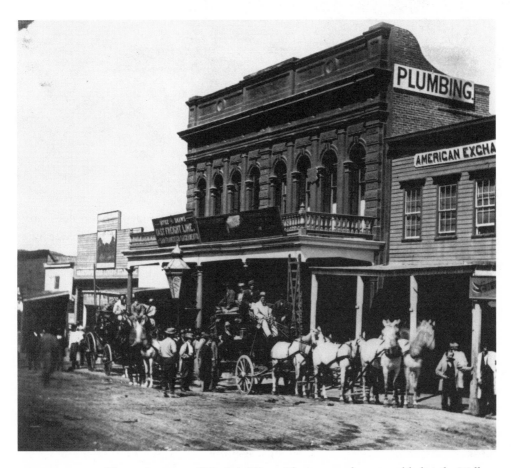

FIGURE 2.11. The main street of Virginia City, with stagecoaches assembled at the Wells Fargo Express office for departure to Sacramento in the early 1860s. (Lawrence and Houseworth collection, The Society of California Pioneers)

FIGURE 2.12.   Freighters stopping to rest and to feed the teams along the crowded road
crossing the Sierra Nevada east of Placerville in the early 1860s. Eastbound wagons are fully
loaded with supplies and equipment for Virginia City and the Comstock mines, and with
hay and feed for the journey. When these wagons returned west into California they were
nearly empty, and it was easy for King and Gardner to get a ride on one to Placerville.
(Lawrence and Houseworth collection, The Society of California Pioneers)

Hill, a town neighboring Virginia City on the southern extension of the Comstock
vein system. The three partners arrived at Gold Hill during a windstorm and stayed
with Hyde's father at the Pioneer Foundry. Late that night, however, a fire started in
the foundry. Despite heroic efforts to save the building, the raging fire burned most
of the night, and at daylight all was ashes, including their possessions. Mr. Hyde lost
everything and was severely burned on the legs. Will, Jamie, and Clare also lost everything: money, clothes, firearms, watches, and the journals that had recorded their trek
across the plains. Even King's letter of introduction to William Brewer of the Califor-

nia Geological Survey was destroyed. They remained in the Virginia City–Gold Hill region for about two weeks, finding employment in the mills that refined the ore from the mines. With many of the locals, they helped Mr. Hyde rebuild his foundry,[9] and enough money was earned for a meager resupply for the trip over the Sierra Nevada to California. King and Gardner left their horses with William Hyde, who stayed in Gold Hill with his father.

The two friends left Gold Hill August 20th, planning to walk the 100 miles over the mountains to the settled parts of California. The Sierra pass was crowded with heavy wagons carrying supplies to the voracious mines and miners of the Comstock. It has been said that "Five thousand teams are steadily employed in the Washoe trade and other commerce east of the Sierra—not little teams of two horses, but generally of six horses or mules, often as many as eight or ten, carrying loads of three to eight

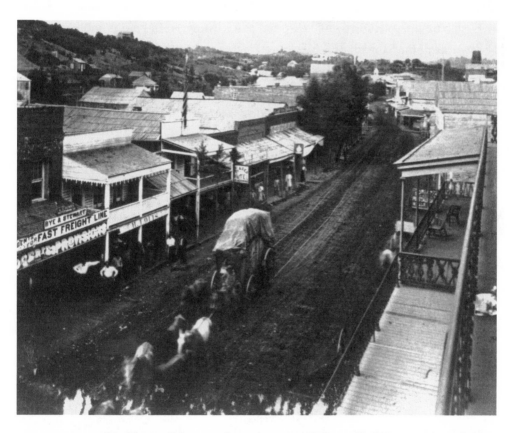

FIGURE 2.13. Muddy conditions on the main street of Placerville (Hangtown), a mining town on the Mother Lode, as it appeared in the early 1860s. It was a major stop on the wagon road from Sacramento over the Sierra Nevada to Virginia City. (Lawrence and Houseworth collection, The Society of California Pioneers)

tons, on huge cumbrous wagons."[10] By day, this traffic of wagons and teams raised clouds of dust when the road was dry or plowed through deep mud when it was wet. At night, the teamsters would crawl under their wagons, roll out their blankets, and sleep on the grimy or muddy ground.

It wasn't long before the partners met a teamster named Lewis, with a wagon lightly loaded for his return trip west. After only a few minutes of friendly talk with King, the teamster offered them a ride in his wagon. He was bound for Stockton, California, and told them that employment could be found there. Several days later they reached the mining settlement of Placerville (Hangtown) in the Mother Lode belt of the western Sierra Nevada foothills.

The next morning, a Sunday, Lewis prepared the horses in the barnyard for the trip to Stockton. As the thoughtful Gardner notes: "Clare and I sat on a bale of hay and deliberated whether we should go on with him or rest as is commanded for and trust our Father to make a way for us. At first we inclined to go on, but the Spirit worked in us and with sorrowful hearts but still trusting, we bid our friend farewell."[10] The two spent the Sabbath on a hill above Placerville in a little grove, joyfully reading the Testaments, and found a pool ideally suited for bathing. After these needs of soul and body were met, they spent the night at an inn. Sensing a spiritual call, they decided to head for San Francisco, not Stockton. The next morning they took the early stage for the river dock in Sacramento.

On September 1, King and Gardner boarded a steamboat in Sacramento and headed downriver for San Francisco. The sidewheel riverboat was crowded with men from the creeks and mines, most wearing rough clothes, flannel shirts, and high boots. They were in California at last, and the long journey from St. Joseph, Missouri, was nearly over. They had been on the trail—mainly on horseback—for four months, and had traveled about 2,000 miles.

One man among the passengers somehow attracted Gardner's attention. "An old felt hat, a quick eye, a sunburned face with different lines from the other mountaineers, a long weather-beaten neck protruding from a coarse grey flannel shirt and a rough coat, a heavy revolver belt and long legs made up the man; and yet he is an intellectual man, I know it." He pointed the man out to King, who studied him and said, "That man must be Prof. Brewer, the leader of Prof. Whitney's geological field party."[11]

King had never met Brewer, had only a sketchy description of him, and knew only that he was a Yale graduate and a biologist with the California Geological Survey. Yet his man had the look of a field scientist. King remembered vividly the letter from Brewer to Professor Brush describing the Mount Shasta climb. Some deep instinct within King sensed that this man was capable of such adventures. King, in his confi-

FIGURE 2.14. The sidewheel steamer *Yosemite* landing at the river docks in Sacramento, adjacent to the Pacific Railroad depot, in the early 1860s. It was on such a vessel that King and Gardner met William Brewer as they were steaming downriver to San Francisco. (Lawrence and Houseworth collection, The Society of California Pioneers)

dent style, approached the man and brashly asked if he were Professor Brewer. Brewer acknowledged that he was, and King then explained that he and Gardner were students from the Yale Scientific School, and that they had carried a letter of introduction from Professor Brush, but that it had burned in a Gold Hill fire a few days before.

Brewer was happy to meet them, and the close acquaintance that began on the riverboat led to a long friendship. They spent the evening together on the boat relating stories of recent travels and future plans. Brewer and his small party had spent the past several months making a reconnaissance of the southern and central Sierra Nevada, because the range was host to much of California's mineral wealth. They had traveled on horseback, carrying only the simplest outfit. Their equipment consisted of notebooks, paper, some instruments, spare clothing (a shirt and socks) packed in the saddlebags, and a rolled blanket and oilcloth tied behind the saddle. In one two-month period, Brewer had ridden his horse 1,100 miles. This latest trip had begun in San Francisco on April 1, meaning that he had been on the trail longer than King and Gardner in their trek across the continent. Brewer's party first traveled south in California's San Joaquin Valley, past Fresno and Visalia to Fort Tejon. They crossed the southern Sierra at Walker Pass to Indian Wells, and upon completing their examination of the mines in that region returned back over the crest to the San Joaquin Valley and Knight's Ferry. Going east, they passed through Yosemite and spent some time in the crestal region, making the first ascents of Mt. Dana and Mt. Lyell (naming the first in honor of what they considered the most eminent American geologist, the second, of the most eminent English geologist). They then crossed the Sierra east at Mono Pass to Mono Lake and the mines at Aurora. Again they recrossed the Sierra west at Carson Pass to Hope Valley and rode up the east side of Lake Tahoe, the deepest lake in California. They then crossed a low ridge north of the lake into the canyon of the Truckee River draining east to Nevada. After examining a new mining district near the river, they made a final crossing west over Donner Pass that took them to the central Mother Lode at Eldorado Canyon, Michigan Bluffs, and Forest Hill.

After having crossed the Sierra Nevada six times, Brewer's party now consisted of just two, he and the packer John Hoesch. Other members of the party had dropped out because of sickness or other business. At Forest Hill, in the Mother Lode mining district, Brewer received a letter from Professor Whitney, who complained that the state still owed him $25,000 for California Geological Survey funding. Whitney was forced to pay for essential expenses from personal funds, and had borrowed up to the limit from his creditors. The survival of the survey was at stake, if funding was not forthcoming in a month. This was not good news for Brewer, who was owed $2,800 in back salary for 14 months, and had also borrowed heavily for personal expenses. Whitney requested that Brewer return to San Francisco. Originally, the survey had planned to work as far north as Mount Lassen, but Indians were reported to be on the rampage from Lassen all the way to the Shasta Valley. Brewer had, therefore, taken a stage south through Auburn and six miles west to the terminus of the railroad, which he rode to Sacramento, and had then made his way to the riverboat and his chance meeting with the partners.

King got on well with Brewer, and expressed his willingness to work for the survey without pay, knowing how invaluable the experience would be. (During these discussions, the cry "Man overboard!" was heard and repeated from deck to deck. Passengers rushed to the rail, but the steamboat did not slacken speed. The captain knew the swimmer. He was a miner who lived on the river bank and was simply swimming home.)

Brewer had not been east for three years, and he was eager to hear the news from Yale, about the activities of his friends and colleagues, and about the changes brought on by the war. They spent the evening together speaking mostly of events in the East, and when the boat arrived in San Francisco, Brewer took the young men to his hotel, where they spent the night. The next morning they used their remaining money to purchase clothes more suited to the city. Brewer then brought King and Gardner directly to the offices of the California Geological Survey in the Montgomery Block Building, a large four-story stone building. It was to be a propitious portal to their professional careers.

CHAPTER THREE

GOLD AND GUNS

The white-topt mountains show in the distance,
I fling out my fancies toward them.
—Walt Whitman, "Song of Myself"

At the offices of the California Geological Survey in the Montgomery Building, King and Gardner met Josiah Whitney, the director of the survey and one of the most respected geologists in the country.

Whitney was a strong and forceful manager with a clear sense of his mission, but was sometimes stubborn and abrasive. He expected the highest standards from his staff, but was generous and just in return. He had worked tirelessly with the state legislature to secure the funding that would keep the survey in the field, doing the work of an agency charged with mapping, sampling, and investigating the geology of this huge and diverse state, with a particular mandate to support the mineral industry. Whitney interpreted his charge in the broadest terms, realizing that detailed maps and an understanding of the geologic structure and age of the rocks must come first, and thereby furnish a proper context for understanding the ore deposits.

Whitney had been appointed State Geologist by act of the state legislature in April 1860 and soon sailed to California, arriving in November. He was to receive a salary of $6,000, part of the total of $20,000 per year that had been set aside for the survey. With Prof. H. W. Brewer, botanist, and William Ashburner, mining geologist, Whitney had begun work in the southern part of the state, principally in the Coast Ranges, and had remained in the field for a year, returning to San Francisco in November 1861. The Survey's appropriation was reduced to $15,000 in 1862, and power-

48

FIGURE 3.1.   The Montgomery Building that housed the offices of the California Geological Survey. When King and Gardner arrived in San Francisco in 1863 they were taken to
this building by William Brewer, where they met the director, Josiah Whitney. When built in
1853, the four-story building was the highest west of the Mississippi. It survived the 1906
earthquake and fire, and was finally razed in 1959 to provide the site now partly occupied by
the Transamerica Building. (1880 photograph, San Francisco Public Library)

ful opponents strove thereafter to further reduce or eliminate its funding. During 1862
the Survey explored the Diablo Range, east of San Francisco Bay, mapping its coal deposits, and then proceeded up the Sacramento Valley and investigated the Mount
Shasta region, climbing the mountain itself. Afterward they worked in the sedimentary sequences of the east side of the Sacramento Valley and then returned to the San
Francisco Bay region, conducting various surveys in the Bay Area. It was the 1863 season that would take Brewer and various other members of the Survey nearly the
whole length of the Sierra Nevada, making a number of crossings of the range.

The staff of the Survey was friendly and open with the visitors. Clarence King had
previously met William Ashburner when Ashburner visited Yale for the purpose of

analyzing California ores at the Sheffield Scientific School laboratories. Brewer, whose letter to Professor Brush at Yale had so intrigued King, helped James Gardner make contact with several civil engineers. And until other arrangements could be made, one of the survey rooms was offered to the two young men as a temporary office.

Brewer needed an assistant to work with him on his continued exploration of the northern part of the Sierra Nevada, which had not yet been investigated by the Sur-

FIGURE 3.2.   Josiah Dwight Whitney at about the age of 30. Whitney became the first Director of the California Geological Survey in 1860, and led it for over a decade despite continual funding problems. He left California in 1874 to become professor of geology at Harvard University. (Brewster, 1909)

FIGURE 3.3.   The principal crest of the Sierra Nevada, looking east from the region of Soda Springs and Tuolumne Meadows near Yosemite Valley. Mount Dana, on the left (13,050 feet), was first climbed by William Brewer and Charles Hoffmann on June 28, 1863, and named for one of America's most eminent geologists. (Whitney, 1865)

vey. Whitney and Charles Hoffmann, the chief topographer, were preparing for an upcoming trip to the Yosemite region, and William Gabb, a paleontologist, was fossil collecting in Oregon. With Whitney's concurrence, Brewer asked King to accompany him on the trip north, as an unpaid volunteer. Although King, then 22, had no real geologic field experience, he was eager to learn and to see some of California, and was excited by the possibility of Indian encounters. Gardner would stay in San Francisco for a time.

On September 5, 1863, Brewer and King left by paddlewheel steamer to Sacramento. King carried with him a Bible, a table of logarithms, and a volume of Robertson's sermons.[1] In Sacramento, where they stayed over Sunday, King attended a church service, the first he had seen west of the Mississippi. There the two travelers parted: King went directly to Grass Valley to reserve himself a horse. Brewer went to Forest Hill, the mining town where the packer was waiting, and the two arrived at Grass Valley later with the pack train.

At Grass Valley, King was outfitted with a horse and later met the packer, John Hoesch, who taught King the fine art of packing a string of mules. Brewer left one of

FIGURE 3.4.   The main planked street of Grass Valley in the 1860s. This town at the northern end of the Mother Lode system is at the center of several underground gold-quartz mines. William Brewer and Clarence King joined forces here at the beginning of their 1863 excursion through the northern Mother Lode and the Klamath district. (Lawrence and Houseman collection, Society of California Pioneers)

his two barometers with a friend in Grass Valley who would use it to monitor regional changes in barometric pressure. It would thus serve as a fixed instrument against which to correct the readings of the roving barometer the expedition would carry to measure altitudes. In this way the fluctuations caused by weather changes could be monitored so elevation measurements made in the field could subsequently be refined.

The gold-bearing quartz veins, so abundant at Grass Valley, were now being mined deep underground, the ore then raised to the surface to be crushed in stamp mills. The pulverized quartz ore was mixed with water and transported through flumes and sluice boxes equipped with riffles to trap the heavy gold. The gold, owing to its great density, would descend through the slurry, where it would be trapped by the riffles. Especially fine-grained gold ore was commonly trapped in blankets fixed across the bottom of the sluicebox. Every 10 or 15 minutes the blankets were washed in a tub where the gold settled to the bottom and was later concentrated by washing in a pan.

At some mines the crushed gold ore was sluiced through flumes which held quicksilver (mercury) in compartments on the bottom. The gold flakes have a strong affinity with the quicksilver and amalgamated with it. The amalgam was collected and baked in a retort or furnace to drive off the quicksilver, leaving a spongy gold residue.

At the mines, many men lost nearly all they possessed despite fruitless labor, but the example of the few who struck it rich encouraged the others to greater effort. King heard the story of two brothers who discovered the Rocky Bar Ledge Mine and in a period of 18 months accumulated $750,000, an immense fortune in the mid-nineteenth century. At the time of Brewer's visit, the brothers were spending their money

FIGURE 3.5. "Piping the bank," hydraulic placer mining in the Tertiary gravels at French Corral, 10 miles north of Grass Valley in California's Mother Lode region in the 1860s. Powerful streams of water were used to disaggregate the ancient uplifted river gravels, so as to pass the water-rich debris through sluices where gold particles were trapped and collected. (Lawrence and Houseman collection, The Society of California Pioneers)

FIGURE 3.6.   Wooden troughs or sluices of the sort used for washing sand and gravel to
obtain placer gold. Commonly the troughs are joined together, and water is introduced at
the uphill end. When dirt is shoveled into the rushing water it rattles down the trough
carried by the force of the water. Various types of riffles or slats are fixed to the bottom
of the sluice to capture the heavy gold particles, while the lighter gravel is carried away.
Commonly, the sluicing is carried on for days, so that a large volume of dirt is washed. The
trough is then drained, and during a careful cleanup, the gold and other heavy minerals are
collected. The residue is gathered up by taking out the riffles, brushing down the length of
the sluice into a pan, and panning up the concentrate to recover the gold. (Hutchings'
California Magazine, Sept., 1860)

as fast as they could on racehorses, women, and the other things that appeal to men
who work hard and think little about the future.

The party of three continued to travel to mineral deposits in the northern
Mother Lode gold district, through Nevada City and Galena Hill, and then as Brewer
wrote "sank into a very deep canyon, perhaps two thousand feet deep, to Poker Flat, a
miserable hole—but what we lacked in accommodations was made up in prices. Ten
white men and two Chinamen slept in the little garret of the 'hotel.'"[2]

Placer mining was active along the streams and rivers that had eroded the bedrock deposits of gold-bearing quartz veins. The eroded material had been carried down streams where the heavier particles of gold accumulated on the margins or bottoms of channels in the stream courses. The gold was associated with heavy black magnetite-rich sand, and this sand was washed by the miners in pans to recover the gold.

Widespread hydraulic mining operations were also underway in this region to recover gold from the ancient stream sediments. In places where ancient rivers had carved broad valleys in the range before it had been uplifted, extensive deposits of ancient sand and gravel blanketed the countryside. These extinct rivers had eroded some of the high-grade vein deposits, and the old sediments contained some placer gold. The gold was recovered by blasting away the ancient river deposits with high-pressure streams of water directed against the banks of barely consolidated sand and gravel. In many places entire hillsides were washed away, leaving ragged scars on the slopes and filling local streams with muddy water. The sediment-laden water was conducted through wooden sluices to collect the heavy gold that settled out.

In most places the richer gravel had already been mined out and only poor material remained. The decline in productivity of these diggings was reflected in the decrepit buildings, half-empty towns, and squalid demeanor of the inhabitants. King described one of these nearly uninhabited mining camps: "Pigs prowl the streets. Every deserted cabin knows a story of brave manly effort ended in bitter failure, and the lingering stranded men have a melancholy look, as of faint fish the ebb has left to die."[3]

The trio moved beyond the Sierra gold fields to the pleasant town of Quincy, county seat of Plumas County, and stayed in a comfortable hotel for a change. The county boasted some 1,500 voters, although it claimed neither church nor schoolhouse. At Genesee Creek, where copper had recently been discovered, Brewer searched for, and found, fossils within the slatey bedrock. The men collected more such fossils at Mormon Station. These fossils indicated that the metamorphic rocks containing them were Jurassic or Triassic in age. This finding would help constrain the age of the mineralization farther south in the Mother Lode gold belt.

Brewer's expeditions rarely carried a tent, for he relied on the uncertain axiom that it rarely rains at night in California in the summer. But at their Mormon Station camp, where they retired early, wrapped only in their blankets, the rains did come in the middle of the night. Brewer remarked, "How cheerless and uncomfortable it is to lie out in the rain—how one looks up at the black sky, and lets the rain patter on his face, saturate his hair and beard, as he thinks of home and its cheerful fireside and luxurious comforts."[4] Luckily, the rains that night did not totally saturate their blankets, but this was the middle of September and summer was in its final days. The next day, a Sunday, they spent in camp, drying out.

James Gardner was not as eager as his friend to begin traveling immediately. He wanted to stay in the same place for a while, get to know the city, and make some money. He took rooms in San Francisco and discovered that the climate in the city ranges from cool to cold, with rain in the winter and fog and wind from the ocean most of the rest of the time. He was able to renew acquaintances with several family friends from the east who had moved to San Francisco, including H. H. Bancroft, a bookseller and later a historian. The Bancrofts entertained him at dinner and insisted that he stay often at their home for the night. Gardner's efforts to find employment were not immediately successful, but he began to attend the Episcopal Church, and wrote his mother about the latest sermons. These letters reaffirmed his strong religious faith. Sunday school, where he derived great pleasure from teaching the youngsters, became a regular activity.

With the Civil War raging in the eastern part of the country, authorities became concerned about the threat of Confederate sympathizers or actual naval forces attacking shipping and shore facilities at San Francisco. On September 3, 1863, General George Wright, the Army commander in the city, received a telegram from the War Department instructing him to take possession of Point San Jose (Black Point) on the north coast of the city, and to construct batteries for defense against raiding warships. The Golden Gate, the entrance to San Francisco Bay, was already defended by gun emplacements on both its north and south sides, and on Alcatraz Island. (Fort Point, on the south side, actually sits below the Golden Gate Bridge today.) The War Department feared that a Confederate warship similar to the privateer *Shenandoah* could slip through the Gate into the bay under cover of the fog banks so prevalent there. Colonel Rene DeRussy, of the Army Corps of Engineers, in charge of coastal defenses, had noted that cannon at Black Point would produce lines of fire that would intersect those from Alcatraz, increasing the effectiveness of both, and forcing an intruding warship to fire in two directions at once. (The Army had first to clear the point of squatters and others who had built houses legally. One of the demolished houses belonged to John C. Fremont, who had rented it to a friend when he went east in 1861 to serve in the Union Army as a general. Litigation over this matter, which continued for decades, was finally settled in favor of the government.)

Professor Whitney, aware of this program of upgrading coastal defenses around the bay, met with Colonel DeRussy, and subsequently Gardner was offered employment mapping and laying out batteries at Black Point (renamed Fort Mason in 1882).

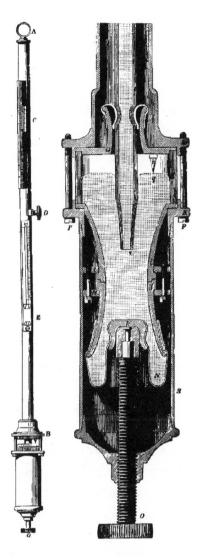

FIGURE 3.7. A mercury (or cistern) barometer, the standard instrument used for
the measurement of air pressure, which in turn furnishes a good estimate of altitude.
Mercury (q), in the lower part of the barometer, is contained in a cistern with a leather
bottom (N) inside the brass cylinder (S). The cistern is fabricated with boxwood sides
and top (G, E, i, j, k). Boxwood is pervious to air but impervious to mercury, and therefore
ensures equilibrium with air pressure without leaking mercury. To calibrate the instrument,
a twist of the thumb screw (O) squeezes the bottom of the bag and raises the surface of the
mercury to the tip of the ivory point (h) visible on the right side of the mercury surface.
When adjusted, the height of the mercury column (which is supported by the local air
pressure) above the mercury level in the cistern can be measured to 2/1,000 inch. The
reading of atmospheric pressure, in inches of mercury, is then converted to altitude with
appropriate corrections. Total length of the instrument is about three feet. (Smithsonian
Institution, Middleton, 1969)

He began surveying the site in mid-September 1863, and by early the next year a garrison of 100 men was stationed at Black Point to man the twelve-gun emplacement on the western brow of the point. Gardner was next directed to work on a battery of ten cannon at Point Knox on the southwest side of Angel Island, which lies in the bay three miles north of San Francisco. Colonel DeRussy directed him to plan the position of the battery, map the site, lay out the work on the ground, and supervise the construction. His salary, the princely sum of $135 a month, was the highest he had ever made. With board and lodging of only $35 a month, he was able to save nearly a hundred a month, and even to return the money his grandfather had advanced him for living expenses.

Meanwhile, Brewer and King rode on toward Lassen Peak in northern California. Arriving at its base, they met a group from the Sacramento Valley on an excursion. They camped with these tourists, were given a quarter of venison, and found good fishing in nearby Willow Lake. They then explored the thermal features of the region, including the many hot springs and the four-acre Boiling Lake, above which rose a great pall of steam over areas of bubbling and boiling water. At Steamboat Springs dozens of jets of hot water and steam roared into the air.

On September 26, setting out early in the morning, they started up Lassen Peak (10,466 feet) and reached the summit by 10 A.M., remaining for five hours. The barometer fell precipitously as a storm approached, bringing with it a fierce wind on the summit. Clouds blanketed most of the lower country below about 8,000 feet. Seventy-five miles to the northwest, rising above the clouds and framed against a background of intense blue sky, appeared the giant snow-capped cone of Mount Shasta, in all its splendor. The spellbound King exclaimed: "What would Ruskin have said if he had seen *this!*"[5] The storm-related pressure changes having degraded their readings, Lassen Peak would have to be climbed again for more meaningful barometric (altitude) measurements. But that night they had a great feast in camp, the fare including the usual coffee, pork, and beans, but also fresh venison and trout. The next day being cloudy, King went down the valley and sketched the mountain.

Three days later, after suffering tentless through intermittent snow, rain, and sleet, the party once again ascended Lassen Peak. They began climbing at night with the thermometer at 18° F, and reached the summit before sunrise. The evidence of volcanic action was everywhere, and as the sun rose, the great shadow of the mountain lay before them, projected on the western sky. Glaciers had once mantled Lassen's slopes, and the polished, grooved rocks showed evidence of their passage. The air was intensely clear, again revealing the massive bulk of Mount Shasta to the northwest.

FIGURE 3.8.   A woodcut of Lassen Peak made from a sketch by Clarence King. Brewer and King made two ascents of the volcano in late September 1863. The peak, which they measured at 10,577 feet above the sea, afforded remarkable views both north and south, encompassing a total straight-line distance of 340 miles. (Whitney, 1865)

Snow had fallen on the awesome peak during the recent storms, leaving its upper slopes mantled with a sharply defined cap of fresh snow. King, aware of Tyndall's work on the glaciers of the Alps, was surprised that no active glaciers had been seen on the much higher Mount Shasta during Brewer and Whitney's climb the previous year.

Brewer wrote that in the country surrounding Lassen "many volcanic cones rise, sharp and steep, some with craters in their tops, into which we can see—circular hollows, like great nests of fabulous birds."[6] Surprisingly, they could discern Mount Hamilton in the crystal-clear air, 240 miles to the south, a peak of modest size in the Coast Range 50 miles southeast of San Francisco. Brewer said, "This is the longest distance at which, as far as I know, I have ever seen a terrestrial object."[7]

As they prepared to continue the journey north, Brewer became concerned about

FIGURE 3.9.   Looking northwest at the giant volcanic cone of Mount Shasta. King had
admired this mountain from the time he had first heard it described in Professor Dana's Yale
lectures, and it became a magnet drawing him to the west. He wrote "The one great point in
the landscape is the cone of Shasta; its crest of solid white, its vast altitude, the pale-gray or
rosy tints of its lavas, and the dark girdle of forest which swells out over canyon-carved foothills give it a grandeur equalled by hardly any American mountain" (King, 1872). He would
have to wait until 1870 to climb it. (From a photograph by Carleton Watkins, Dana, 1895)

Indian trouble, especially since the party consisted of only three men, King, Hoesch,
and himself. Some travelers they had encountered had reported the Native Americans
to be hostile, but to avoid the supposedly dangerous area would require a detour of
200 miles. The party had no rifles and only two working revolvers, but proceeded on
nonetheless (another non-functioning handgun was strapped on for show). Brewer
made sure that the most valuable things they carried—their field notebooks—were
kept in coat pockets, to remain with them if they had to abandon their equipment. As
it turned out, the Indians posed no threat. Along the way, they met two of them, near-
naked, collecting and eating grasshoppers.

On October 3 they reached Fort Crook (now Fall River Mills) on the Fall River.

There, they were able to get hay for their horses, and to replace a lost shoe on one that was becoming lame. Only about a dozen troopers remained at the post, because most were off fighting Indians. Brewer always enjoyed campfire discussions with King, whom he found eager to learn and interested in the features they had observed or examined during the day. Around the campfire they discussed geologic problems such as the age of the gold veins, the action of glaciers on Mount Shasta and elsewhere, and the nature of eruptive materials that built the young Cascade volcanoes. King attempted to apply the philosophy of Ruskin—truth in nature—to all things encountered during the field work. Brewer laid out Professor Whitney's plan to propose a geologic study across the continent from California through the Great Basin and the Rocky Mountains. Whitney thought that the railroad companies would profit from funding such surveys along their routes, once the geologic framework of California became better known. King noted the chance of real funding possibilities for such mapping programs.

Riding north across lava plateaus, the views to the west toward Mount Shasta were dramatic. The peak dominated the landscape as a single, sharp, snow-capped cone— an image that would surely captivate an artist. From this side, the parasitic western cone of Shastina was hidden, and did not divert the eye from the near-perfect symmetry the peak presented. Here they stopped at Pilgrim Camp, where a hunter had just returned with five freshly killed deer. They purchased half of a large buck, an ever-welcome addition to their meager larder, and devoured roasted venison in large quantities.

This hunter, a middle-aged man named More, who supplied traveling parties with meat, was an excellent shot who almost never wounded his quarry, and was unafraid of the marauding Indians who had indeed attacked him on several occasions. The Indians soon learned of his constant vigilance and unerring aim, and knew that he would as soon use his rifle on them as on a wild animal. He profited from selling game and hides and reportedly accumulated a considerable amount of gold, which he buried near his camp. More was a loner who had been born in Kentucky and had moved on to the frontiers of Texas and Missouri, always fighting Indians and making a living as a hunter. As they sat around the fire, King was enthralled by his wild and amusing stories.

King was a good listener, but he also loved to tell stories, and he took his turn entertaining the others. He had a remarkable memory for detail, and a pleasing voice, and was not averse to embellishing his facts for the sake of excitement. He also had a knack for improvisation and the ability to mimic regional accents. His most endearing quality was the good humor he exuded. It was always a pleasure to be in his company and to listen to his tales.

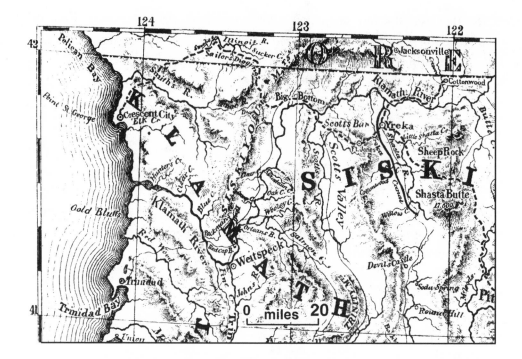

FIGURE 3.10.   Map of northwestern California showing the 1863 route (dashed line) of Brewer and King after they had investigated the gold mines in the northern Mother Lode and traveled north. They skirted the east and north sides of Mount Shasta (Shasta Butte) to Yreka, past Fort Jones and Scotts Bar, across the Klamath River to Sailor's Diggings in Oregon, and then over the Siskiyou Mountains to Crescent City, California, on the Pacific. There they parted; Brewer took a steamer to San Francisco, and King looped back through Oregon to Jacksonville on a wagon road, where he caught a stage to San Francisco. (Modified from part of the 1856 map of George Baker)

The party of three rode into Shasta Valley on the east side of Mount Shasta, and explored Pluto's Cave, a well-known local feature. This large cave—actually a lava tube—formed when an ancient lava flow drained out from beneath its upper crust of cooled and hardened lava. The magnificently arched roof is 50 feet high in places, and the walls are decorated with the fluid forms of once-molten lava. The cave, more than a mile long, was filled with bats end to end. When the candle was extinguished deep in the cave, all were stunned by the unforgettable experience of total blackness. Near the entrance, where the roof had broken down, wild bighorn sheep had fallen in, and their skulls and bones littered the rocky floor.

They went next to the small town of Yreka, where letters for Brewer and King were waiting. A large group of Indians was camped nearby. They were more handsome than the Digger Indians of the central part of the state, and King found some of the women quite attractive; most wore paint on their body and face, in simple patterns of red and black. The party spent three days in the town and then headed out northeast to Cottonwood, on the Klamath River, only a few miles from the Oregon border.

Here they camped near a sadly rundown farm and were given hay for their animals. The farmer was ailing, in pain and barely able to stand, and his young wife—who had five children, the oldest about nine—was distraught and overworked. She asked if Brewer was a doctor or could help her husband; the nearest doctor was 22 miles away and wanted $50–75 per visit, a sum far greater than they could afford. Brewer therefore set about doctoring the sick man, went into town in the evening to purchase some remedies, and was able to see his patient greatly improved late in the evening and the next morning. The poor fellow did suffer a relapse later that day, but remained hopeful, and was certain he would have died if Brewer had not ministered to him. When the time came to move on, the family insisted on providing the travelers with milk and butter, a welcome addition to their supplies.

This was to be their last working camp, and they spent five days exploring the country in all directions. The nights were bitter cold, ranging from 15° to 25° F. The cold and often rainy weather made living outside comfortless, but increased their appetites. The three of them ate 36 pounds of beef in six days in Genesee Valley and 44 pounds of venison in seven days on the Shasta trail, all of this in addition to their normal rations.[8]

Back in Yreka on October 21, Brewer decided to split the party. John Hoesch headed south to San Francisco with his horse and two pack mules loaded with the specimens they had collected and unneeded extra clothes. He faced a long and arduous ride of 400 miles, alone. Brewer and King headed west for the Pacific through Deadwood, Fort Jones, and Scott's Bar. They investigated mining camps along nearly every watercourse in this region. The first gold discoveries here dated to 1851, but by now the mines were nearly exhausted, much of the population had dispersed, and the half-empty towns were in a state of decay. In a few places a lone Chinese miner would be seen panning the river gravels or working his rocker, barely eking out subsistence.

The town of Hamburg, a bustling mining community just two years before, presented now only remnants of its former cabins, most of them long since carried away by the often flooding river. Except for a group of Klamath Indians, the town was now nearly deserted. The wooden grave markers in the local cemetery were rotting and fallen, and soon there would be no trace of the men who had worked so hard at this place. Brewer wrote, "Alas, how many a sad history is hidden in the neglected and forgotten graves that are scattered among the wild mountains that face the Pacific."[9]

The Indian graves nearby were better kept than those of the white folk. Each of their graves was mounded, and surrounded by a small palisade of sticks. Suspended

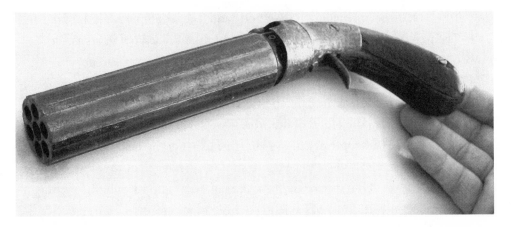

FIGURE 3.11.   Pepperbox pistol found in the ruins of Fort Jones, west of Yreka, California. A garrison was maintained at the fort from 1852 to 1857 to protect settlers from marauding Indians, but the fort had been abandoned when the Brewer party passed by. This type of pistol, perhaps belonging to the officer in command of the fort, employs a cluster of six barrels and was the forerunner of the six-shooter revolver. (Photograph by Michael Diggles)

from poles stuck in the ground were the worldly possessions of the dead, including baskets, weapons, clothing, strings of beads, implements, moccasins, and ornaments.

The way got rougher, and became nothing but a rocky trail, only suitable for riding or packing. In this part of the state no wagon roads had been built because of the great cost of construction and maintenance. On October 27, Brewer and King crossed the Siskiyou Mountains and descended down into the mining camp of Sailor Diggings, just over the border in Oregon Territory. Near the town was an underground mine where a gold-bearing quartz vein was being mined. A Spanish arrastra crushed the ore. The device centered on a shallow basin 12 feet in diameter floored by flat stones. A vertical shaft fitted with horizontal cross arms turned in a hole in the center of the basin. Attached to these arms by chains were several large boulders, each weighing about 200 pounds. A layer of broken quartz ore was placed in the basin with water, and the ore was crushed to a powder as the shaft turned, rotated by water power (or in some cases by mules), and dragged the boulders around and around over the ore. The resulting slurry ran through a sluice box lined with a blanket, and the gold accumulated in the fibers of the cloth. Periodically, the smaller gold flakes would be washed from the blanket. Quicksilver was poured over the crushed ore in the basin, and between charges of ore, the quicksilver was carefully collected, and the gold that had amalgamated with it was recovered by retorting. At this mine, about $25 in gold was concentrated from each ton of ore crushed by this primitive method.

From Sailor Diggings, Brewer and King climbed some 3,000 feet to the crest of a
range that commanded a good view of the Pacific Ocean. A long ride took them down
into the canyon of the north fork of the Smith River and on to Lewis Ranch, back in
California. Here, for $50, they sold their two tired and worn horses, including saddles
and bridles, and continued on foot, walking 18 miles to the mining town of Low Divide. There, Brewer examined the copper deposits in the vicinity, which occur over a
broad mineralized belt. King walked 20 miles on to Crescent City, on the Pacific coast,
where he received letters that called him back to San Francisco. Accordingly, he jour-
neyed 120 miles by wagon road northeast to Jacksonville, Oregon, a transportation
hub for the region. From there he took the stage to San Francisco.

While on the coach, King had plenty of time to review his field notebooks and re-
cap the remarkable two-month journey they had just taken. It was an unforgettable

FIGURE 3.12. A Chinese gold miner washing gravel in a rocker, a device midway between
a sluice and a pan. The original placer-mining operations often did not recover all the gold,
and small amounts of "pay dirt" could be recovered in this way by rewashing the tailings.
(California Geological Survey)

FIGURE 3.13.   An arrastra, a primitive machine used for crushing gold-bearing quartz-vein material drawn from an underground mine. The gold ore was first broken into apple-sized chunks and placed with water in the shallow basin. Attached to the revolving vertical post are four crossbars to which are chained large blocks of stone, each weighing up to 200 pounds. As the post is turned, whether by water power or mules, the large stones are dragged across the ore and crush it to a fine slurry. This material is then washed in a sluice; alternately, the gold is caught by amalgamation with quicksilver in the bottom of the basin. (California Geological Survey)

learning experience, and he realized that the demanding work of a field geologist is both challenging and rewarding. It was one thing to be able to identify and name the hundreds of mineral specimens in the Brush Collection at Yale College, but another to pick up a rock in the field, classify it, and deduce something of its origin and character. He learned the value of collecting and tagging specimens so that unknown material and special features could be more carefully analyzed in the laboratory. Three tasks were always required at collection: break the specimen from its outcrop and shape it to a convenient size with the hammer, and label and number it; write the rock's description, location, and significance in the notebook, with its sample number; and spot the rock's sample number on the map. With this system, if one of the three—sample, notebook, or map—were lost, at least some information would be brought from the field. The collection of fossils and water was treated similarly.

The study of ore deposits also began to take shape in his mind. The existence of ore at a given locality was a special phenomenon—some process had caused an extraordinary concentration of a particular element at this place. He realized that he now knew about as much as anyone did about the nature of the gold deposits of the northern Mother Lode and Klamath Districts. Brewer's strategy—visiting and making detailed studies of as many of these mines and prospects as possible—was the best way to understand them. By comparing and contrasting their features, one could discern the overarching threads common to all. Brewer made a point to examine not only the geologic mode of occurrence of the metalliferous deposits, but also the methods of milling the ores, so as to ensure the best payoff for prospective mining operations. Most of the mines processed low-quality ore and used inefficient milling methods. Some turned a profit because of sensible management, and richer ore, of course, was always a bonus. The elements of chance and luck often drove the equation, and a rich vein or even a single large nugget could make it all worthwhile. Most miners were sustained through the hard times and backbreaking labor by the dream of the lucky strike that would put them on easy street.

Brewer stayed a week at Low Divide (also called Waldo) examining nearby mines and prospects. He stayed in a disreputable hotel, remarking that "a filthier, dirtier, nastier, noisier place I have not struck in the state."[10] The weather was rainy, and as many as 30 wet, noisy, and smelly men tried to get warm at the stove—an impossibility. The sleeping room upstairs had no beds, and 25 men slept on the floor. Not only did some lodgers stumble up and down the stairs all night, but loud card games in the lower room continued till morning.

At dawn on the eighth day he walked four more miles and stopped at a tavern operated by a Dutch couple, where he enjoyed a clean table and room. There he spent two days examining the local copper mines and prospects and then went on to Crescent City, 16 miles west. This walk brought him from the dry scrubby terrain inland to the lush forests of the Pacific Coast, with their moss, ferns and giant redwoods. The largest tree he measured, a Sequoia redwood, was 58 feet in circumference and more than 300 feet tall.

The town of Crescent City, built about 10 years previously, is on a small cove lacking an actual harbor. Brewer stayed there 12 days and spent several evenings enjoying dinners with Mr. Pomeroy and his wife, friends originally from Massachusetts. On a broad coastal flat, lakes and swamps attract a large number of waterfowl, including

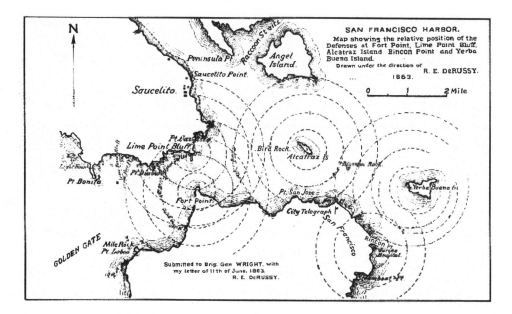

FIGURE 3.14.   Map showing the location of the coastal-defense batteries protecting San Francisco in early 1863. James Gardner supervised the mapping, planning, and construction of additional batteries at Point San Jose (later called Fort Mason) and Angel Island. (Map modified from that commissioned by Colonel R. E. DeRussy, in command of the San Francisco coastal defenses for the Civil War; Scott, 1880)

ducks, geese, swans, and pelicans. An Indian hunter came into town with a horse loaded with perhaps 100 ducks, which he sold for $1.50 per dozen. Brewer took advantage of this bounty, and indulged in duck dinners for most of his stay. All the while, despite frequent rain, he made investigative excursions to neighboring regions, visiting coal and copper mines.

Indian wars were almost continual in this corner of California, because of the ill treatment visited on the native people by the settlers. It was common for white settlers to kidnap Indian children and take them south to San Francisco and elsewhere, to be sold as servants. In retaliation, the Indians killed settlers and stole cattle. A particularly unsavory incident occurred on an island near Eureka when a band of misguided settlers attacked a group of Indian women and children who had been left on the island while the men were out hunting and fishing. During the night, the settlers murdered the whole lot, in cold blood. The avenging Indian raids made the entire region unsafe, and many innocent people lost their lives.

A violent storm struck the entire California coast November 14. In Crescent City it unroofed several houses and cast piles of enormous logs up on the beach, practically to the main street. But about a week after the storm hit, the steamship *Oregon* arrived unexpectedly and anchored 3 miles offshore. Brewer booked passage, took a small boat out to the ship the next morning, and the *Oregon* was soon underway heading south. The ship rolled heavily, and on the second night it passed so close to Point Reyes that one could hear the barking of the sea lions on the rocks (during the foregoing storm a Russian man-of-war had been wrecked on this headland). On November 23 the *Oregon* entered the Golden Gate, and when Brewer landed at dockside and went to the survey headquarters in the Montgomery Block, he found that most of his scientist colleagues were back in the office.

By early November, Gardner had been appointed Resident Engineer in charge of the mapping and design of six batteries at four locations on Angel Island. He was assigned a government barge and rowers who were to transport him daily from the San Francisco dockside to the island, and was aided by an assistant engineer and two surveyors who lived on the island. The exact position and line of fire of every gun had to

FIGURE 3.15. A 10-inch Rodman iron cannon at Point San Jose (Black Point) at the present site of Fort Mason. The mapping, layout, and construction of this gun emplacement were supervised by James Gardner in the fall of 1863, after which twleve such 10-ton cannons were emplaced here for harbor defense. From this battery there is a clear view of any vessel that succeeds in entering the Golden Gate into San Francisco Bay. (Photo by the author)

be determined before the groundworks could be planned. He had to oversee the site survey as well as the battery construction. Among his other responsibilities was the supervision and remuneration of the contractors who transported supplies to the island and did the construction work. The placement of a battery at Point Stewart, on the west side of the island, was a particularly difficult assignment. After Gardner prepared a detailed topographic map and laid out all the plans for the fortification, Colonel DeRussy rejected the plan as being too expensive. It was a challenge to design and build, inexpensively, a gun emplacement on a hillside so steep that a man could barely stand on it. When Gardner spent great effort on several more design options for the battery, the colonel finally gave his approval, and the work went forward.

When King returned from his expedition to northern California, the two friends spent several days in San Francisco, enjoying an extended reunion. The city was growing rapidly at that time, and new buildings were under construction everywhere. Its population had reached about 100,000, but like much of California there was a marked imbalance between men and women. Men outnumbered the women in the city by about 20,000.

King immediately began preparing to leave for another survey expedition. He departed the same day that Brewer returned by ship from Crescent City, and headed for the Mariposa Estate at the southern end of the Mother Lode gold belt in the Sierra foothills. There he joined two other members of the California Geological Survey, William Ashburner, mining engineer, and Charles Hoffmann, topographer, to make a general survey of the estate, including the preparation of topographic and geologic maps and a study of the mineral resources. The property had been purchased by John C. Fremont after his third expedition west in 1846, was now controlled by the Mariposa Mining Company, and was considered one of the most important gold-vein regions in the Mother Lode. The superintendent of the Mariposa Mines was Frederick Olmsted, an old friend of King's from Hartford. A remarkably capable man, Olmsted was the engineer and landscape architect who designed Central Park in New York beginning in 1857, and who also had been general secretary of the United States Sanitary Commission, the forerunner of the American Red Cross.

King delighted in climbing Mount Bullion, five miles northwest of Mariposa, to enjoy the wide views of the range crest that it afforded. "This serrated snow and granite outline of the Sierra Nevada, projected against the cold clear blue, is the blade of white teeth which suggested its Spanish name."[11] Features of the Yosemite region, a scant 25 miles to the east, were visible from this vantage point. One could see the upper part of El Capitan, the giant vertical cliff flanking the north side of Yosemite Val-

FIGURE 3.16. The town of Mariposa at the southern end of the Mother Lode gold belt on the west slope of the Sierra Nevada, in 1859. Clarence King was employed here during the winter of 1863–64 after his trip to northwest California. He contributed to a topographic and geologic study of Fremont's Mariposa Estate, with its productive gold mines. (Hutchings' California Magazine, May 1859)

ley, and the high peaks of the crestal region beyond, including the sharp obelisk of Mt. Clark. At that time, Mounts Dana and Lyell nearby on the main crest were considered to be the highest in the Sierra Nevada, but King's observations, made in the clear winter air of January 1864, revealed to the southeast a snow-covered mass of high mountains, west of Owens Lake, that seemed to be higher. King would become obsessed by this tantalizing, unknown alpine region.

Gardner continued his work on the Angel Island batteries, but found time before Christmas, 1863, to spend $60 for gifts, a handsome sum at that time. He got turkeys for his four boatmen and gifts for their wives and children. He bought Japanese toys for eight little girls in his Sunday School class, and books for four boys in the mission school. He also got gifts for the servant at the boarding house and for Mrs. Bancroft and her daughter.

King arrived from the south for a Christmas break, and the two friends spent two more joyous weeks together. Gardner remarked on how he relished these meetings after separations of a month or so, and noted that their relationship had entered an entirely new phase. Writing of King he noted, "Both of us had scaled heights since our paths parted in November and on his brow shines now a light more beautiful than ever covered it before. Out in the wilderness away from all outside Christian influences, God is bringing him into the closest communion with the things that are unseen and eternal. He is being cleansed for some great work."[12]

But the work for the Corps of Engineers began to wear on Gardner. Colonel DeRussy heaped additional work on him, and when Gardner asked for a raise it was refused. He was tempted by an offer (no doubt brokered by King) from Frederick Olmsted for a permanent position as engineer at the Mariposa Estate.[13] He declined the post because he was enjoying the pleasures of civilization too much in San Francisco and was not yet ready to adopt a more primitive lifestyle. He marveled at how his friend King could remain in an almost constant travel mode for so long. It would soon be a year since they had left New York, and King had been sleeping under the stars virtually ever since.

It was only on Sundays and holidays that Gardner did not work, so on Washington's Birthday he set out early in a small boat to enjoy San Francisco Bay. It was a beautiful morning, the fog and clouds slowly dissipating to reveal the intensely blue water, the green hills of Marin, and the white buildings in the city. Many ships rode at anchor. Suddenly, a white puff of smoke rose from the fort at the Golden Gate, followed by the boom of a cannon, which echoed back and forth from hill to hill and died out in the distance. Then, suddenly, from all the forts and batteries, as well as from the city and from the ships at anchor, came the deep-throated crash and boom of a hundred great guns in answer to the fort's cannon. The thunder reverberated long and loud as it rolled back and forth across the Bay, and finally stilled to a silence deeper than that which preceded it. Although far from home, Gardner would not soon forget this homage to our first president in this new land.[14]

Spring came early to California, and Gardner marveled that in early March on the table were new potatoes, green peas, asparagus and lamb. But the work went on, and DeRussy increased his demands on Gardner's time. On a Saturday in the middle of March the Colonel asked him to accompany him on Sunday for an inspection of some of the works. When Gardner refused to work on the Sabbath, the colonel told him that it would not take long, that he could go to church in the afternoon, and furthermore that he was paid by the month. Gardner remained firm and was told that if he did not obey this order he must resign. After an hour of thought and prayer about the matter, Gardner wrote a note submitting his resignation. The following Tuesday, he received an answer from the colonel declaring that his resignation was accepted.[15]

Gardner was not unaware of the benefits that this work had brought him. He had been able to enhance his engineering skills in surveying the terrain, planning the placement of cannon, and laying out and drafting the blueprints for the fortifications. He had also learned considerable management skills in ordering materials, supervising the construction of the sites, and handling the payroll of the contractors. But his life, once again, was about to change.

King, for his part, had suffered a personal setback during his work at the Mariposa Estate. In the winter, he had continued to climb Mt. Bullion because the crystal-clear views afforded by the cold transparent air fueled his speculations about the high unknown mountains to the southeast. The paleontologist William Gabb observed that King's hours on Mt. Bullion admiring the view could be better spent hunting fossils in the gold-bearing slates; Ashburner complained that many of King's countless yarns around the campfire were exaggerated and tiresome; and Brewer even suggested that King was averse to hard work.

King responded by focusing on his assigned work and repledging himself to science. He spent many hours hammering and splitting the slate and argillaceous rock outcrops in search of some trace of former life. One day, while working in a deep gulch called Hell's Hollow, he happened to stoop over when arising from lunch and spotted a cigarlike shape protruding from the rock. Closer inspection revealed it to be an extinct squidlike mollusk, *Belemnites*. Given its character and location in the rock that carried gold veins, it established the fact that the Mother Lode gold had been deposited in strata of Jurassic age. In attempting to break the fossil free, he broke it in half, but was undismayed, knowing it would be as good as new when glued back together. This find was more significant than the fossils collected with Brewer at Genesee Creek, because they were in rock similar to that which contained gold, whereas this specimen was in the rock that did contain gold veins nearby. King daydreamed on his way back to camp about having his name recorded in the annals of science as the one who had dated the age of gold mineralization in the world-famous Mother Lode.

King got a chance to visit Yosemite for the first time in March 1864. Like all first visitors to this magical valley King gazed in awe at the massive granite cliffs rising thousands of feet above the valley floor. The waterfalls, swollen by spring runoff, poured over the cliffs, contrasting with the tranquil Merced River, which meanders

FIGURE 3.17.   Yosemite Falls, descending 2,500 feet down the north wall of Yosemite Valley. King made his first trip to Yosemite in the spring of 1864 while working on a geological survey of the Mariposa Estate. In the fall of the year he mapped the Yosemite Grant with James Gardner. (Beach, 1873)

through groves and meadowland far below. On the north wall he traced the stupendous face of the El Capitan cliff, the 2,500-foot Yosemite Falls, and the smooth white shape of North Dome, towering above the valley. On the south wall was the delicate but stirring Bridal Veil Falls, the pinnacled Cathedral Spires, and the blocky mass of Sentinel Rock. All were dominated by Half Dome to the east, towering 4,400 feet above the valley floor, "nobly proportioned and lifelike, the most impressive of all the rocks, holding the eye in devout admiration."[16] King did not know that in seven months he would be commissioned to prepare the first detailed map of this extraordinary valley.

Josiah Whitney had long wanted to probe the geology of the Nevada desert ranges east of the Sierra, so as to compare the age and character of their strata with those in California that he and his group had studied. In April he invited King to accompany him on an excursion to western Nevada. King, long intrigued by the lonesome ranges of the Great Basin that he had encountered on the trip west, was quick to accept. He met Whitney in Sacramento, and the two headed over the mountains by stage. From Placerville on, they were slowed by mud and finally, in the summit region, by deep snow. The trip over the crest was made by sleigh.

King talked with Whitney about the snowy mountain mass he had glimpsed toward the southeast from Mount Bullion, thinking that it might well be the highest in the country. The peaks were in the unmapped crestal region of the Sierra Nevada between Mono Pass (southeast of Yosemite) and Walker Pass (near the southern part of the range). Brewer had bypassed this nearly inaccessible high country in his Sierra explorations of the previous summer. King and Whitney discussed the possibility of exploring and mapping this region during the coming summer. King suggested that his engineer friend, Jim Gardner, would be a good man to assist with the topographic mapping.

While Whitney went on to Virginia City and the Comstock mines, King remained at Lake Tahoe to make barometric observations south of the lake, for the purpose of determining the altitude of critical points. This magnificent lake, 30 miles long and 1,600 feet deep, sits at 6,200 feet amidst the encircling mountains. It had been called Lake Bonpland on Fremont's 1850 map, Bigler Lake on Goddard's 1857 map, and Lake Tahoe on a new map of the Pacific States compiled in 1863.[17] When King joined Whitney at Virginia City, he was assigned to head east with a small party to make geologic observations in the West Humboldt Range of central Nevada. This is the eighth of the twenty or so north-trending desert ranges that span the Great Basin from the Sierra Nevada to the Wasatch Mountains, east of Salt Lake City. It lies beyond the Humboldt Sink, the broad alkali desert where the west-flowing Humboldt River eventually disappears. King made a reconnaissance of the range and climbed Star Peak, its highest point, which commands vistas over a broad area. He also explored the next range to the east, where a granite massif intrudes a thick sequence of sedimentary rock.

After resigning his engineering position with the Corps of Engineers, Gardner was able to spend time with his friends exploring San Francisco, continuing his church work, working with young people, and counseling those in bereavement. He was mindful that he had seen little of California during his six-month stay. Travel in the state was expensive, and he had had little free time for excursions.

When Whitney returned from the Comstock mines to San Francisco, he made plans "to send a scientific expedition into the southern Sierra of which very little is known, an immense tract there being as yet entirely unexplored."[18] In introducing the subject of this expedition in his report, Whitney credited King with identifying the significance of this high region: "The glimpses of the high peaks of this portion of the Sierra, obtained during the clear winter weather, from Mount Bullion, on the Mariposa Estate, by Mr. King, had led him to the belief that here were the most elevated summits of the range; and this fact, coupled with the circumstance that, unless explored during this season by the Geological Survey, this region might long remain a blank on the map of California, led to the organization of a small party whose object should be to make as complete a reconnaissance of this portion of the Sierra as their limited time and means would permit."[19] Following King's suggestion, Whitney asked Gardner to join the expedition as volunteer assistant topographer. All provisions, such transportation as would be needed, and other expenses would be provided, but each member had to supply his own horse. Gardner accepted. The expedition was to get under way in May and be in the field for about four months.[20]

While preparing for the survey, Gardner also sought treatment for some medical problems. He had been suffering from a painful throat irritation, which was most severe when he first arose in the morning. After other treatments failed, he went to a doctor who specialized in the latest remedies. First an electric current from a galvanic battery was passed through his throat by means of a silver spoon rammed down to the soft palate. Next the doctor administered African capsicum, a powerful red pepper, mixed with molasses so that it would stick to the throat. This was followed by a gargle of white oak bark, borax, and alum. After ten days of this treatment, the throat irritation was markedly improved. The same doctor also helped him treat his eyes, which had been inflamed. The doctor had accidentally discovered the therapeutic effect of castor oil: Gardner oiled his eyelids and the region around the eyes before retiring at night, and this too proved to be marvelously beneficial.[21]

The exploring party planned to leave San Francisco during the second week of

May and would be led by William Brewer, the botanist-naturalist whom King had accompanied to the northern Sierra and points west during the previous fall. Also in the party would be Charles Hoffmann as topographical engineer, James Gardner as assistant topographer, Clarence King as unpaid assistant geologist, and a camphand-packer. Gardner assured his mother that while in the mountains they would get fresh provisions every two or three weeks, and that he could send letters out at those times. Actually, it would be several months before Gardner's mother would hear from him.

CHAPTER FOUR

ALMOST INACCESSIBLE TO MAN

There's a land where the mountains are nameless
And the rivers all run God knows where.
—Robert W. Service

The party of five—William Brewer, Charles Hoffmann, James Gardner, Clarence King, and Dick Cotter, the drover of the plains—assembled in Oakland, where the horses were stabled. They organized their equipment, made up the packs, and rode south on the east side of San Francisco Bay to San Jose. Except for Cotter on a mule, all were on horseback. Two pack mules, Nell and Jim, carried the loads. King, it seems, disliked John Hoesch, the regular Survey packer, and had convinced Brewer that his friend Dick Cotter should be signed on as camp helper-packer in his stead. Cotter was familiar with handling stock, and he had quickly learned the art of loading a mule in such a way that the pack would stay secure.

Beyond San Jose, at Gilroy, they turned east and crossed from the Santa Clara Valley over the Coast Range, by way of Pacheco Pass, into the vast San Joaquin Valley. Only then, on May 30, 1864, did they become fully aware of the severity of the drought that then gripped California. The Central Valley was hot, dry, and brown, with barely a blade of grass seemingly still alive. They made camp near a ranch house, and the hot northern wind continued to blow dust in their eyes and through their clothes. Visibility was no more than 50 yards. When at last they settled down for supper, dust covered the food, and a gritty layer of sand coated the bottom of their tea mugs. Worse, 300 stinking dead cattle were piled behind the house. Thankfully, the rancher had been able to sell another thousand head that were starving for lack of feed—for just $1.50 apiece.

FIGURE 4.1.   The 1864 field party of the California Geological Survey (Charles Hoffmann absent). From left to right: James T. Gardner, Richard D. Cotter, William H. Brewer, and Clarence King. Gardner is holding a sextant, used for mapping and astronomical location; Cotter is armed with musket, dagger, and pistol; both Brewer and King have mercury barometers, used to measure altitudes, slung on their shoulders; and King holds a geologist's hammer. (U.S. Geological Survey Library)

Within two days, still hot and dusty and still lacking hay for the stock, they crossed to the east side of the Central Valley and reached Fresno. It was near there that Jim, the faithful mule who had been with Brewer for four years, became sick and died, probably from bad water. Such a good mule was worth $150 to $200. Fortunately, Jim's saddle and pack could be loaded aboard a wagon bound for Visalia, where the party would be heading next.

King, a muscular five foot six,[1] had been assigned an incorrigibly bad horse named Buckskin. Slow and halting on the trail, Buckskin could be depended on to

FIGURE 4.2.   View east, toward the snow-covered Sierra Nevada, from the Four Creeks region in the Central Valley. The 1864 Brewer party entered this terra incognita from near this site, traveling through Visalia and into and across the mountains. (Rendered from field sketch drawn during the Pacific Railroad Survey; Blake, 1858)

shy and jump unpredictably at the slightest irregularity in the path, or at any passing animal. And when spurred, the horse seemed unaffected for about twelve seconds, but then went dashing off at a stumbling trot, usually in the wrong direction.

King was delighted, therefore, when they reached Visalia, to meet a Spaniard who was down on his luck and eager to sell his horse, a fine-looking young bay. This one, full of energy and fire, was exactly the kind of horse that suited King. Professor Brewer disposed of Buckskin and bought the new horse for King, who promptly named it Kaweah, for the nearby river. The animal was a wise choice, for in a few months, along the road to Fort Miller, it would help save King's life.

Brewer looked in at Camp Babbitt, near Visalia, to learn when a cavalry escort might be available, if needed, for protection against hostile Indians. While there, he left a mercury barometer in the care of the camp, to be read every day, as a basis for weather-related corrections to be made later on the instrument readings taken in the mountains. The party also left some equipment and extra provisions in Visalia, to be brought up later by the ox teams that pulled wagons to the mountain sawmills.

From Visalia they climbed into the foothills and eventually camped at 5,000 feet at

FIGURE 4.3.   Part of Goddard's California map used as a primary source for the Brewer
party in their exploration of the highest Sierra in 1864. They discovered that the Kern
River did not have its headwaters near Walkers Pass as shown here, but turned north
for some 70 miles, heading north of the latitude of Owens Lake. The party entered the
mountains at Visalia (Visaija on the map) and worked east up the divide between the
Kings and Kaweah Rivers. After his second attempt on Mt. Whitney, King evaded
highwaymen on the road from Visalia to Millerton on the San Joaquin River. (Map
compiled by George H. Goddard in 1857)

FIGURE 4.4. Mount Silliman, seen from the northwest. The peak was named to honor Benjamin Silliman Jr., professor of chemistry at Yale. When the 1864 Brewer party climbed this peak, they saw a high mountain ridge 10 miles to the east that they took to be the main Sierra Crest. But later, after climbing Mount Brewer on this crest, they realized that it lay on a separate ridge, the Great Western Divide, and that the main crest was still 8 miles farther east. Photograph by the author.

Thomas's Sawmill (at the present site of Sequoia Lake), where the cool, clean mountain air and clear water offered profound relief from the scorching alkaline plains below. From this camp, they spent a week studying the forests of Sequoia trees and exploring the uplands between the Kings and Kaweah rivers, the route they planned to take for their approach to the high, snow-clad mountains of the Sierra Crest.

With all of their pack and riding animals carrying their supplies, the men trudged along on foot over the rough trail. They led the horses and mules through forests, up steep slopes, and over rocky ridges to arrive at Big Meadows, a grassland several miles long, where they camped for four days while investigating the surrounding country. Always on the lookout for fresh meat, Brewer managed to purchase two fine deer at a hunter's camp. King wrote that at night the temperature sank to "18°, 16°, 17°, and 20° —surely not comfortable nights for sleeping without shelter."[2] In the morning, two soldiers from Visalia visited the camp, and Brewer, having heard that a band of hos-

tile Indians was in the mountains, asked them to send an escort in two weeks to accompany the survey party.

The men cached much of the baggage at Big Meadows and traveled on with
lighter loads, but at the next camp a sumptuous venison feast was enjoyed by all. The
party then tramped up the Kings–Kaweah Divide and climbed a high peak that they
named for Professor Benjamin Silliman, who had founded the Yale Scientific School.
From Mount Silliman they had a magnificent view of the country above timberline
to the east, toward an impressive alpine ridge that they took to be the principal crest
of the range. (The fact that the real crest of the Sierra was obscured by the intervening Great Western Divide was unknown to them at the time.) They now directed their
efforts toward the highest peak on this ridge crest, believing it to afford a good site for
charting the whole range and the desert country to the east, including Owens Lake, a
major landmark lying below the Sierra on the east.

The expedition's mapping strategy was to occupy a high peak of known position
and from it to measure the angular relations to other major peaks of unknown position. The transit, sextant, and compass were the instruments used for taking horizontal angular measurements on landmarks such as peaks, distinctive parts of ridges,
and valleys and lakes. When the process was repeated from another known point to
the same landmarks, then the intersection of the two lines of sight from the known
points would fix the position of the unknown points. This method of triangulation
was the first step in preparing the base for a planimetric map of the still unmapped
southern Sierra crestal region.

The method for measuring the altitude of occupied points was by readings from a
mercury barometer (or *cistern barometer*, the name reflecting its mercury reservoir).
This instrument measures atmospheric pressure by indicating the height of a column
of mercury that exactly balances the weight of the atmosphere. Inasmuch as about 30
inches of mercury is equal to atmospheric pressure at sea level (the height of the mercury falling proportionately at higher altitudes), and because such instruments thus
have to be at least that long, they are lengthy, cumbersome, and fragile. The glass
barometer was housed in a brass tube which, in turn, was protected in an outer leather
or wooden case. Despite this protection, barometers commonly broke in the field. A
vernier scale measured the height of the mercury column to a precision of two one-
thousandths of an inch. Because the height of the mercury column is affected by temperature as well as by pressure, temperature readings were required so that appropriate
corrections could be made. One could detect a change in the mercury height by raising
the barometer only a few feet, but even a moderate change in the weather could alter
the mercury height equivalent to several hundred feet of elevation change.

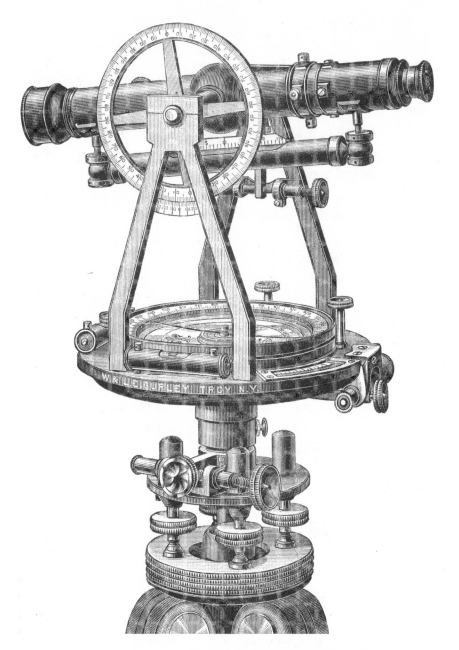

FIGURE 4.5. Surveyor's transit used for measuring horizontal angles (scribed on the horizontal circle outside of the compass), and elevation, or vertical angles (scribed on the vertical circle near the telescope). The instrument is leveled by adjusting four thumb screws at the base until the two spirit levels on the horizontal circle outside the compass are centered. Vertical and horizontal angles can be measured to one-half minute by means of engraved vernier scales. The instrument can double as a level, by using the large spirit level attached beneath the telescope. (Wentworth, 1903)

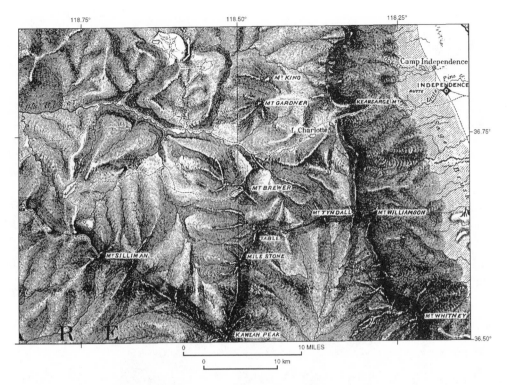

FIGURE 4.6. Part of the Hoffmann map of 1873, showing the route of the Brewer party across the Sierra in 1864 (dashed line). It was from the summit of Mount Brewer (center) that Brewer and Hoffmann sighted the highest peak in the range and named it Mount Whitney (lower right). Clarence King begged to backpack to it and climb it. He and Richard Cotter returned five days later; they had got only as far as Mount Tyndall on the main Sierra Crest (Hoffmann, 1873)

The much more compact aneroid barometer, a device based on the change in volume of a sealed, flexible metal box, had been used by the surveyor George Goddard in 1855, but it did not come into general use until later, because internal stresses in the early versions caused a systematic drift. In order to account for natural changes in barometric pressure caused by shifting weather conditions, both types of barometer were typically corrected with concurrent readings from a stationary instrument at a base station. For the survey's 1864 field campaign, the Army personnel at Camp Babbitt, near Visalia, recorded daily barometric and temperature readings.

From the newly christened Mount Silliman the party descended along Silliman Crest, near Kettle Peak, and followed a mountain stream to a camp near an isolated, rounded pinnacle they called Sugarloaf Rock. The next day they saw a system of ter-

FIGURE 4.7.   Looking east across Roaring River Canyon to the Great Western Divide, with Mount Brewer in the complex of peaks near the center. The long, evenly graded pair of ridges in the center are glacial moraines about 3 miles long. They were deposited on the far (east) side of a glacier moving from right to left down the canyon, and represent two separate advances of the glacier. The Brewer party rode horses up the crest of this moraine system to reach their camp at the base of Mount Brewer. (U.S. Geological Survey oblique aerial photograph taken November 7, 1956)

races of debris on the canyon sides deposited when glacial ice, in the past, nearly filled the canyon. These moraines flank the canyon of Roaring River. "Reaching the brink of this gorge," King wrote, "we observed, about half-way down the slope, and standing at equal levels on both flanks, singular embankments—shelves a thousand feet in width—built at a height of fifteen hundred feet above the valley bottom, their smooth, evenly graded summits rising higher and higher to the eastward on the canyon-wall until they joined the snow. They were evidently the lateral moraines of a vast extinct glacier, and that [one] opposite us seemed to offer an easy ride into the heart of the mountains. . . . By a series of long zigzags we succeeded in leading our animals up the flank to the top of the north moraine, and here we found ourselves upon a forest-covered causeway, almost as smooth as a railroad embankment. Its fluted crest enclosed three separate pathways, each a hundred feet wide, divided from each other by roughly laid trains of rocks, showing it evidently to be a compound moraine. As we ascended toward the mountains, the causeway was more and more isolated from the cliff, until the depression between them widened to half a mile, and to at least five hundred feet deep. Throughout nearly a whole day we rode comfortably along at a gentle grade."[3] At the head of the moraine, the trail became rougher, and finally, when they could take the animals no farther, they made camp at a moun-

FIGURE 4.8. The summit of Mount Brewer (13,570 feet), as viewed from about three miles west. The peak was climbed twice (July 2 and 4) by Brewer and Hoffman, and from its summit the principal Sierra Crest was visible eight miles to the east. (From a sketch by William Brewer; Whitney, 1865)

tain lake at the base of the pyramidal peak atop the ridge crest they had seen from Mount Silliman.

Arising before dawn the next morning, Hoffmann and Brewer spent the day climbing the peak, with great difficulty, and from the summit they commanded a view of a desolate and wild landscape rising toward a vast array of high peaks. Brewer was awed by the sight and wrote, "Such a landscape! A hundred peaks in sight over thirteen thousand feet—many very sharp—deep canyons, cliffs in every direction . . . sharp ridges almost inaccessible to man, on which human foot has never trod."[4] Much to their dismay they discovered that this peak, soon to be named Mount Brewer (13,570 feet) for their party chief, was not on the main Sierra Nevada Crest after all, but on a lesser ridge, the Great Western Divide. The main Sierra Crest lay a formidable eight miles farther east across a wild and rocky region at the headwaters of the Kings and Kern rivers. (The Kern River, which the then existing maps indicated had its headwaters 50 miles to the south, actually extends up to this latitude, making it the longest river in the Sierra Nevada.) The two climbers named several lofty peaks, including Mount Tyndall on the main crest to the east (for an eminent British geologist), Mount Goddard 30 miles north-northwest (for the engineer who had compiled the best California map to date), and Mount Whitney off to the southeast (of course for the director of the California Geological Survey). On setting the level in place, they found that Mount Whitney was clearly the highest mountain in sight and probably the highest in the entire range and indeed in the United States.

Brewer and Hoffmann returned to camp that night exhilarated and exhausted. Hoffmann showed the others, particularly Gardner, his field sketches of the main range crest, and Brewer explained the rugged nature of the terrain that lay between them and the true crest. King felt proud that his guess that this region included such heights had been proved correct. He noted that "For a couple of months my friends had made me the target of plenty of pleasant banter about my *highest land,* which they lost faith in as we climbed from Thomas's Mill—I too becoming a trifle anxious about it; but now that the truth had burst upon Brewer and Hoffmann they could not find words to describe the terribleness and grandeur of the deep canyon, nor for picturing those huge crags towering in line at the east. Their peak, as indicated by the barometer, was in the region of thirteen thousand four hundred feet, and a level across to the farther range showed its crest to be at least fifteen hundred feet higher. They had spent hours upon the summit scanning the eastern horizon, and ranging downward into the labyrinth of gulfs below, and had come at last with reluctance to the belief that to cross this gorge and ascend the eastern wall of peaks was utterly impossible."[5]

Clarence King, however, did not accept this judgment. He was excited about fur-

FIGURE 4.9. William Brewer and Charles Hoffmann were awed by this view when they made the first ascent of Mount Brewer and gazed east. They had assumed that the mountain was on the Sierra Crest, and were dismayed to discover that the main crest in fact lay an additional eight miles farther east. They named pyramidal Mount Tyndall (far left) and helmet-shaped Mount Whitney (right skyline), which they reckoned as the highest peak in the range and probably in the United States. King felt challenged by this unknown terrain, and with Richard Cotter set out on a backpacking trek to climb Mount Whitney. Five days later they returned after climbing Mount Tyndall, realizing that Mount Whitney was too far. (Photograph by the author)

ther exploration among the high peaks, Mount Whitney being his chief objective. He begged Brewer for permission to undertake a backpacking trip with Dick Cotter to explore the crest. King described his feelings in confronting Brewer: "It was a trying moment for Brewer when we found him and volunteered to attempt a campaign for the top of California, because he felt a certain fatherly responsibility over our youth, a natural desire that we should not deposit our triturated remains in some undiscoverable hole among the feldspathic granites; but, like a true disciple of science, this was at last over-balanced by his intense desire to know more of the unexplored region. He freely confessed that he believed the plan madness, and Hoffmann, too, told us we might as well attempt to get on a cloud as to try the peak."[6]

Brewer finally agreed, and the next day King and Cotter shouldered 35- to 40-

pound packs, the supplies and equipment rolled in one blanket each. They carried six days' provisions, including bread, cooked beans, and venison, and equipment that included compass, pocket level, barometer, wet and dry thermometers, rope, notebooks, cooking pot, canteen, and Bowie knife, which would later serve as an impromptu ice axe. Brewer, Gardner, and Hoffmann, helping with the packs, climbed with them to the saddle south of Mount Brewer. King described the view from the pass as, "Rising on the other side, cliff above cliff, precipice piled upon precipice, rock over rock, up against sky, towered the most gigantic mountain-wall in America, culminating in a noble pile of Gothic-finished granite and enamel-like snow . . . I did not wonder that Brewer and Hoffmann pronounced our undertaking impossible . . . our friends helped us on with our packs in silence, and as we shook hands there was not a dry eye in the party. Before he let go of my hand Professor Brewer asked me for my plan, and I had to own that I had but one, which was to reach the highest peak in the range."[7]

From the pass, Brewer, Gardner, and Hoffmann turned north to climb again to the summit of Mount Brewer to complete their observations. King and Cotter traversed south along the crest of the Great Western Divide, looking for a way into the Kern River drainage. But after climbing over the next eminence south of Mount Brewer, a high peak now called South Guard (13,224 feet), they found that progress along the ridge crest was blocked by a series of jagged pinnacles. Thwarted in that direction, they descended by rope near Longley Pass to a small lake draining into East Lake on the Kings River side of the Kings–Kern Divide. From there they turned south and climbed into a cirque at the north base of the divide, where they camped far above timberline. King tells of shaving slivers off the wooden barometer case to build a tiny fire to " . . . warm water for a cup of miserably tepid tea." It was a cold night, the temperature standing at 20°F at 9 P.M. and at 2°F when they arose the next morning.[8]

Beginning before first light, they climbed the precipitous Kings–Kern Divide by a route that may have been near and west of what is now called Mount Jordan (13,344 feet). At one ledge where their advance was blocked by a 30-foot vertical cliff, King lassoed a spike of rock protruding from the next ledge and climbed the rope hand over hand. After King had hauled up the packs, Cotter climbed the rope, and before long they were at the summit of the divide. The descent down the headwall into the upper Kern River Drainage was a hair-raising adventure. They roped down a series of almost vertical faces, until finally they reached the snow slopes at the base of the cliffs.

A long traverse eastward, high in the headwaters of the Kern River, brought them at dark to a campsite probably on Tyndall Creek at about 11,600 feet. Arising at 3:30 A.M. the next morning, they began climbing the north side of Mount Tyndall, in the end realizing that the higher peaks to the south were too distant to attempt. Climbing up steep rock slopes, they were often compelled to divert around cliffs and cut steps in steep snow and ice with Cotter's knife. The culminating challenge was a giant column of ice that stood out from the final cliff below the summit. King recalled that "We climbed to the base of this spire of ice, and, with the utmost care, began to cut our stairway. The material was an exceedingly compacted snow, passing into clear ice as it neared the rock. We climbed the first half of it with comparative ease; after that it was almost vertical, and so thin that we did not dare to cut the footsteps deep enough to make them absolutely safe. There was a constant dread lest our ladder should break off, and we be thrown either down the snow-slope or into the bottom of the crevasse. At last, in order to prevent myself from falling over backwards, I was obliged to thrust my hand into the crack between the ice and the wall, and the spire became so narrow that I could do this on both sides; so that the climb was made as upon a tree, cutting mere toe-holes and embracing the whole column of ice in my arms. At last I reached the top, and with the greatest caution, wormed my body over the brink."[9]

King's account of the difficulty of the climb up Mount Tyndall has been criticized by some as an exaggeration of what is considered today to be only a moderate climb. We must remember, however, that he and Cotter were in a totally unknown wilderness never before penetrated by explorers, an alien place that was two long days distant from their base camp, which was itself in a remote place. It is understandable that they would perceive this forbidding country differently than we do today.

At the summit of Mount Tyndall, now finally on the main Sierra Crest, the mercury level in their barometer stood at only 17.99 inches, water boiled at 192°F, and they made the altitude to be 14,386 feet (the modern U.S. Geological Survey map shows it at 14,018 feet). King noted that "Upon sweeping the horizon with my level, there appeared two peaks equal in height with us, and two rising even higher. That which looked highest of all was a cleanly cut helmet of granite upon the same ridge with Mount Tyndall, lying about six miles south, and fronting the desert with a bold square bluff which rises to the crest of the peak, where a white fold of snow trims it gracefully. Mount Whitney, as we afterwards called it in honor of our chief, is probably the highest land within the United States."[10]

From Mount Tyndall they became aware how the summit region of the Sierra Nevada, as seen at this latitude, is divided into two giant parallel ridges, with the Kern River flowing in the immense south-directed gorge between them. They also saw that a prominent jagged ridge to the southwest was surmounted by the Kaweah Peaks, a well-known landmark visible eastward from Visalia in the Central Valley.

King described the view east of the main crest: " . . . the whole range fell in sharp, hurrying, abruptness to the desert, where, ten thousand feet below, lay a vast expanse of arid plain intersected by low parallel ranges, traced from north to south . . . reaching out to horizons faint and remote, lay plains clouded with the ashen hues of death; stark, wind-swept floors of white, and hill-ranges, rigidly formal, monotonously low, all lying under an unfeeling brilliance of light, which for all its strange, unclouded clearness, has yet a vague half-darkness, a suggestion of black and shade more truly pathetic than fading twilight. No greenness soothes, no shadow cools the glare. Owens Lake, an oval of acrid water, lies dense blue upon the brown sage-plain, looking like a plate of hot metal. . . . The serene sky is grave with nocturnal darkness. The earth blinds you with its light. That fair contrast we love in lower lands between bright heavens and dark and cool earth here reverses itself with terrible energy. You look up into an infinite vault, unveiled by clouds, empty and dark, from which no brightness seems to ray, an expanse with no graded perspective, no tremble, no vapory mobility, only the vast yawning of hollow space."[11]

Overwhelmed by the western view of the Great Western Divide, the elements of Ruskin's philosophy of "Truth in Art" triggered an eloquent description from King: " . . . the whole region, from plain to plain, is built of this dense solid rock [granite], and is sculptured under chisel of cold in shapes of great variety, yet all having a common spirit, which is purely Gothic. . . . Yet, as I sat on Mount Tyndall, the whole mountains shaped themselves like the ruins of cathedrals—sharp roof-ridges, pinnacled and statued; buttresses more spired and ornamented than Milan's; receding doorways with pointed arches carved into blank façades of granite, doors never to be opened, innumerable jutting points with here and there a single cruciform peak, its frozen roof and granite spires so strikingly Gothic I cannot doubt that the Alps furnished the models for early cathedrals of that order."[12]

The granite landscape is overwhelming in this region, and King had become obsessed by it. The expanse before him, including Mounts Brewer, Tyndall, and Whitney, is all underlain by a single related mass of giant granitic intrusions, or plutons. Fifty miles long and more than ten miles wide, it includes the largest individual intrusive mass in the Sierra Nevada. For miles and miles, the perpetual silver-gray landscape is nowhere moderated by darker rocks.

Two miles east of Mount Tyndall, and considerably higher, was a more massive mountain mass, actually situated east of the Sierra Crest, and surmounting its own giant ridge. This imposing eminence, standing above Owens Valley, they named Mount Williamson to honor Colonel R. S. Williamson of the U.S. Army Corps of Engineers, who had headed a survey of railroad routes in California ten years before. (The choice proved to be a wise one, for some years later Williamson helped King gain the financial support he needed for his Fortieth Parallel Survey.)

The rocks of these granitic masses, particularly coarse-grained, contain large well-formed crystals (phenocrysts) of potassium feldspar set in a finer-grained groundmass. The conspicuous phenocrysts reach several inches in length, and commonly protrude from the surface, owing to differential weathering of the rock. This arresting textural detail was not lost on King, who found that the protruding crystals are hard to sleep on, but offered good handholds for climbing. He wrote that "A single thickness of blanket is a better mattress than none, but the larger crystals of orthoclase, protruding plentifully, punched my back and caused me to revolve on a horizontal axis with precision and frequency." In describing the descent of the Brewer wall, he wrote, "When within about eight feet of the next shelf, I twisted myself round upon the face, hanging by two rough blocks of protruding feldspar, and looked vainly for some further hand-hold; but the rock, besides being perfectly smooth, overhung slightly, and my legs dangled in the air." Speaking of the ascent of Mount Tyndall, he wrote, "We climbed alternately up smooth faces of granite, clinging simply by the cracks and protruding crystals of feldspar, and then hewed steps up fearfully steep slopes of ice, zig-zagging to the right and left to avoid the flying boulders."[13]

With their observations from the Tyndall summit complete, King and Cotter descended the mountain on the west side and circled back to their previous campsite near Tyndall Creek. Their provisions running low, they had no choice but to prepare to return to the base camp and to abandon the climb of Mount Whitney at this time. The next day they selected a new return route, because of the grave difficulty they would have faced in ascending the wall they had roped down before. Instead, they crossed the Kings–Kern Divide to the east of their previous crossing and worked down over steep snow and treacherous rocky cliffs to a lake basin below.

The course was blocked by a long lake, and the only route left to them was to climb a steep slope of blue ice rising from the lakeshore that was surmounted by a forbidding assemblage of crags and cliffs. King and Cotter set about climbing the ice, cutting footsteps where needed, and roped their way to the base of a 40-foot-high rock wall. King led the way until about halfway up the wall, but was unable to reach a crack two feet above his head, and carefully descended to Cotter's side. Cotter thought he could make the reach because of his greater height and length of arm. While King held the rope, preparing to fix himself between ice and rock if Cotter fell, his companion inched up, leapt for the crack, and was able to pull himself up, over the lip, and out of sight. The rope was then used to hoist up the two packs and the barometer, and King, tying the rope around himself, began the ascent, belayed from above by Cotter, who yelled down that it was OK to bear weight on the rope.

King wrote that "I got up without difficulty to my former point, rested there a moment, hanging solely by my hands, gathered every pound of strength and atom of will for the reach, then jerked myself upward with a swing, just getting the tips of my fingers into the crack. In an instant I had grasped it with my right hand also. I felt the sinews of my fingers relax a little, but the picture of the slope of ice and the blue lake affected me so strongly that I redoubled my grip, and climbed slowly along the crack until I reached the angle and got one arm over the edge as Cotter had done. As I rested my body upon the edge and looked up at Cotter, I saw that, instead of a level top, he was sitting upon a smooth roof-like slope, where the least pull would have dragged him over the brink. . . . In all my experience of mountaineering I have never known an act of such real, profound courage as this of Cotter's. It is one thing, in a moment of excitement, to make a gallant leap, or hold one's nerves in the iron grasp of will, but to coolly seat one's self in the door of death, and silently listen for the fatal summons, and this all for a friend,—for he might easily have cast loose the lasso and saved himself,—requires as sublime a type of courage as I know."[14]

Shortly above this difficult place, they made their fourth and final backpack camp in a thicket of gnarled white-barked pine. The next day a long climb out of the basin took them across the shoulder of Mount Brewer via Longley Pass and down to the site of Brewer's camp. The camp was empty, but a note told them that camp had been moved 2,000 feet down to a meadow with good forage. King remarked that upon reaching this meadow camp, "Our shouts were instantly answered by the three voices of our friends, who welcomed us to their camp-fire with tremendous hugs."[15] After King and Cotter recounted their travels, Brewer remarked, "King, you have relieved me of a dreadful task. For the last three days I have been composing a letter to your family, but somehow I did not get beyond 'It becomes my painful duty to inform you.'"[16]

The full party then returned to Big Meadows, but Brewer had been suffering from a brutal toothache for two days. King tried to pull the tooth with a bullet mold, which could double as pliers, but without success, and the tooth became worse. One side of Brewer's face was grossly swollen, and eating was difficult. A trip to Visalia was imperative, and King accompanied him on the long ride. There the tooth was successfully pulled, affording great relief. Seizing the moment, King took advantage of Brewer's good feelings to propose that another attempt on Mount Whitney be made from the southwest. Brewer agreed, gave King $100 for expenses, and directed him to rendezvous in two weeks (August 1) with the main party at Clark's Station, on the road to Yosemite.

With an escort of two cavalrymen out of Visalia, King headed into the mountains on the Hockett Trail. He crossed the Kaweah–Kern Divide between the South Fork of the

Kaweah and the Little Kern River (which was called the North Fork of the Kern in the Whitney Report), then rode across Coyote Pass to the main Kern River. Because the Hockett Trail had not yet been finished beyond this point, King and his escort headed up the river for several miles before climbing cross-country to the east, out of the south-trending canyon. Josiah Whitney writes that in the uplands east of the Kern "in the midst of every difficulty, Mr. King worked for three days before he could reach the base of the mountain. The highest point reached . . . was, according to the most reliable calculations, 14,740 feet above the sea-level. At the place where this observation was taken, he was, as near as he was able to estimate, between 300 and 400 feet lower than the culminating point of the mountain, which must therefore somewhat exceed 15,000 feet in height. So far as known it is the highest point in the United States, and the elevation attained by Mr. King was greater than any other person has reached, within our territories, or anywhere on the continent north of Popocatepetl" (in Mexico).[17] (Mount Whitney remained the highest peak in the country until Alaska was acquired in 1867.)

King was disappointed when this attempt at the mountain fell short, and was no doubt all the more resolved to make another attempt when the time was right. (Mount Whitney was finally first climbed nine years later, in 1873, by three men from the town of Lone Pine, situated below Whitney on the east.) Astride his cherished horse Kaweah, he retraced the Hockett Trail back to Visalia and remained in a hotel there two days thawing his bones, enjoying the food, and delightedly observing the young ladies of the town. While he was withdrawing some gold coins from the Wells Fargo office he noticed two tough Mexican mountaineers, dressed in buckskins and jangling big spurs when they walked. The older, thin and wiry, presented a sparse black beard and a hawk nose. His companion, about 18 and partly of Indian stock, had a "beardless face showing deep brutal lines, and a mouth which was a mere crease between hideously heavy lips. Blood stained the rowels of his spur."[18] King observed that in speaking to the hotel keeper they learned that King planned to ride to Fort Miller on his way to the appointed meeting at Clark's Station.

As he set out on the trail, he could see that Kaweah felt frisky, eager for a quick gallop. He had learned, however, that the horse was a bundle of nervous energy, and that if he were given his head for a breakneck dash, calming him down subsequently would be an arduous task. Accordingly, he urged Kaweah into a more practical trot, and they moved steadily along the road at a leisurely six miles an hour. They reached the Kings River ferry about dusk, and King ate an unsatisfactory dinner at the ferryman's table before tending to Kaweah and preparing to camp for the night. At that time he noticed two riders, about a quarter mile downstream, spur their horses into the river, forcing them to swim across and then struggle onto the farther bank. Were they intent on saving the ferry fee, or had they some other plan?

King wrapped himself in his greatcoat and lay down on the ground with his saddle as pillow, in a position where he could keep an eye on Kaweah. Up before sunrise, he took a quick bath in the river, and at dawn the ferryman took him and his horse across for the half-dollar ferriage. For two miles the trail closely followed the river, but then it led up the bank to reveal the great monotonous plain of the Central Valley, and off in the distance the Sierra, its ragged black crest backlit by the dawn.

Kaweah, fresh and alert, resumed his steady trot, but suddenly his ears pricked up, and he looked off to a clump of willows 150 yards ahead, where a campfire glowed. Two men quickly arose and began saddling their horses, the taller one also grabbing a shotgun. King then knew that they were the Mexicans from Visalia, and that they intended to waylay him on the trail. He decided to give them a run, and after checking the saddle girth and the pistol at his belt, he urged Kaweah ahead and around the campsite, to strike into a gallop across the plain.

In a minute the brigands were mounted, yelling to their horses, and galloping after King. He looked over his shoulder, and " . . . found that the Spaniards were crowding their horses to the fullest speed; their hoofs rattling on the dry plain were accompanied by inarticulate noises, like the cries of bloodhounds. Kaweah comprehended the situation. I could feel his grand legs gather under me, and the iron muscles contract with excitement; he tugged at the bit, shook his bridle-chains, and flung himself impatiently into the air."[19] The three horses galloped on, kicking up clods of dirt and leaving a cloud of dust. Knowing that it was 15 miles to Fort Miller, King tried to slow Kaweah, just enough to conserve his energy and keep the bandits out of gunshot. When the hot sun rose, the gallop began to tell on Kaweah. Bloody foam was flung from his mouth, and when King tried to restrain his dash still further, the pursuers began to gain ground. King could clearly hear their clashing spurs and gasping horses.

King was used to comparing the beats of two mapping chronometers, and so he listened carefully and compared the breathing of Kaweah with that of the mustangs following. He noted that the lead mustang breathed nine breaths for every seven from Kaweah. But after a time, when this ratio slowly approached ten to seven, King was more confident that Kaweah had won this lap. He gave Kaweah more rein and felt him stretch with a greater burst of speed. Once Kaweah had pulled well ahead of the pursuers, King looked cautiously back and saw that both riders had dismounted, and that one horse had fallen.

King soon reached a way station where a man sat holding a rifle. The man had seen the chase and knew that King had narrowly escaped a sorry fate. These same Mexicans had been seen lurking around the stage station two nights before, and had tried to steal some stage horses, but seeing the station keeper vigilant with his rifle they disappeared. King pulled off Kaweah's saddle, sponged out his mouth, and walked him slowly about for some time to cool him down.

King remained at the station, but at midday caught sight of two horsemen passing by far in the distance, intent on returning to the road toward Fort Miller. King stayed all day at the station, enjoyed a simple meal, and departed at nine o'clock, after dark. He avoided the path and rode cross-country, piloting by the stars. Just as he was approaching Millerton, he heard the jangling of spurs on the road, and quickly guided Kaweah off into a thicket, some distance from the trail. The two Mexicans rode by; one broke into song, a passionate evocation of love. King mused that "These Californian scoundrels are invariably light-hearted; crime cannot overshadow the exhilaration of outdoor life; remorse and gloom are banished like clouds before this perennially sunny climate. They make amusement out of killing you, and regard a successful plundering time as a sort of pleasantry."[20]

After the two had passed, King rode on into the village, stabled Kaweah, and found an excellent hotel, where he asked to be awakened early. After a heavy sleep he arose at four o'clock, had a good breakfast, and took to the trail toward Mariposa. After fording the San Joaquin River he soon noticed that Kaweah's were the first tracks of the day on the trail; no one was in front of them.

Around noon he rode into an Indian rancheria, and as always was attracted by the Native Americans' way of life, particularly the women. He saw " . . . one woman of splendid mold, soundly sleeping upon her back, a blanket covering her from the waist down in ample folds, her bare body and large full breasts kindled into bronze under streaming light; the arms flung out wide and relaxed; the lips closed with grave compression, and about the eyes and full throat an air of deep, eternal sleep. She might have been a casting in metal but for the rich hot color in her lips and cheeks."[21]

Toward evening King and his horse arrived at a group of shacks that might be called a small town. The proprietor of a country store offered to put King up for the night and to keep his horse in the corral. The man, a Southerner and a tippler, apparently had little business, and sold mainly firearms, gambling paraphernalia, and liquor. After supper, prepared by a Chinese cook, King was shown to a bed in a separate cabin, across from the corral.

Awakened in the middle of the night by Kaweah's stamping, King soon heard two horses riding down the trail into town. Spurs jangled as two men dismounted and went into the next building, the home of his host. He could hear enough of the ensuing talk to pay close heed. One of them asked when the lone rider arrived and what he was wearing. The host responded, and mentioned that King had told him he planned to set out for Mariposa at seven in the morning. Importuned not to conduct their business within one mile of the town, the Mexicans mounted and rode off north toward Mariposa.

King waited half an hour and then quietly arose. With boots and clothes in hand, he padded out barefoot to the corral. Kaweah came up to him, nuzzled him, and mercifully was quiet. Knowing that the town streets were rock-strewn, and fearing any noise, King muffled Kaweah's hooves with his clothes. He wrapped and tied his pants and shirt around the front hooves, and his coat and drawers around the back. With his boots hung to the saddle horn, he led the horse quietly out of the corral, through the town, and well out on the trail. Noting that all was still quiet in the sleeping town, he stopped, shook as much dirt as possible out of his clothes, dressed, and mounted, with pistol cocked and ready.

After riding for about a mile, he spotted a smoking fire off the trail, and two sleeping forms nearby. The trail here was thick with dust, and Kaweah walked by the camp silently while King kept his pistol aimed at the nearest figure. Neither awoke, and after a suitable distance, Kaweah shook his body and leapt into a gallop. They rode all night and arrived at Mariposa after sunrise. King took a hotel, relieved that he had seen the last of his followers. Resuming his journey the next day, he was able to reach Clark's Station on the Yosemite Road at the appointed time of August 1. But Brewer's party was not to be seen. They had encountered difficulties in the High Sierra and would arrive three weeks later.

Brewer had left Visalia July 14 and rejoined the main party at Big Meadows, which by then was resupplied with a month's provisions on three pack mules. Strengthened by the addition of seven soldiers, the party followed a series of Indian and animal trails northeast toward the brink of Kings Canyon, the great glacially carved "yosemite" of the South Fork of the Kings River. They descended on a "horrible" trail, apparently west of the present Don Cecil Trail, perhaps down Lightning Creek, to judge from the route indicated on the Hoffmann map of 1873. Brewer wrote, "We sank into the canyon of the main South Fork of Kings River, a *tremendous* canyon. We wound down the steep side of the hill, for *over three thousand feet*, often just as steep as animals could get down."[22]

The Whitney Report recounted that "The canyon here is very much like the Yosemite. It is a valley from half a mile to a mile wide at the bottom, about eleven miles long and closed at the lower end by a deep and inaccessible ravine like that be-

FIGURE 4.10. A general view of Kings River Canyon, as viewed from the trail descending into the gorge from the southwest. William Brewer remarked, "Next to Yosemite this is the grandest canyon I have ever seen. . . . On both sides rise tremendous granite precipices, of every shape, often nearly perpendicular, rising from 2,500 feet to above 4,000 feet" (Brewer, 1930). (Drawn by Charles Robinson; Muir, 1891)

low the Yosemite, but deeper and more precipitous. It expands above and branches at its head, and is everywhere surrounded and walled in by grand precipices, broken here and there by side canyons, resembling the Yosemite in its main features. The Kings River canyon rivals and even surpasses the Yosemite in the altitude of its surrounding cliffs, but it has no features so striking as Half Dome, or Tutacanula [El Capitan], nor has it the stupendous waterfalls which make that valley quite unrivaled in beauty."[23]

Members of the Brewer party next attempted to explore side canyons, but in most places the climb out of the canyon was precipitous and difficult. A soldier discovered that a rough route on the north side, up Copper Creek, was passable, and they climbed up this drainage to the crest of the Monarch Divide near Granite Pass (10,673 feet), between the canyons of the South and Middle Forks of the Kings River. From the crest, they took angles on Mount Goddard, 25 miles north-northwest on the San Joaquin–Kings Divide, and on the Palisades, 15 miles northeast on the main Sierra Nevada Crest. Two nearby peaks, about 10 miles east, were named Mount Gardner and Mount King to honor members of the party. Mount King was later changed to Mount

FIGURE 4.11.   The south wall of the Yosemite-like canyon of the South Fork of the Kings River. (Drawing by J. Clement; Muir, 1887)

Clarence King, and the name Mount Cotter was added to a lesser peak between Mounts Gardiner and Clarence King.

After extended reconnaissance, Hoffmann found that the pack animals could not descend into the Yosemite-like Middle Fork Canyon. The party therefore retraced its steps, descended into the South Fork Canyon, and headed east toward the main Sierra Crest up the south branch of the river (now called Bubbs Creek). This venture might have failed had it not been for the good fortune of their meeting a group of prospectors who had just carved a rough trail for their horses from Owens Valley, crossing the main Sierra Crest at Kearsarge Pass.

One of the prospectors was Thomas Keough, of Independence, who in later years said of the trip from Owens Valley, "Our first task was to build a trail up Little Pine Creek [now called Independence Creek] on the east cliff of the mountains. I have

FIGURE 4.12. Roaring River Falls, entering Kings Canyon through a side canyon cut in the south wall. (Muir, 1887)

FIGURE 4.13.   Mount King, now Mount Clarence King (12,905 feet), from the west. The peak was named by the Brewer party during the 1864 exploration of the highest Sierra. (Rendered from a sketch by William Brewer; Whitney, 1865)

sometimes heard it said that the trail over what is now called *Kearsarge Pass* is an old Indian trail. The fact is, however, that our party built this trail in order to get our animals up over the top of the Sierras. It might have been possible for a man to work his way on foot up over this pass, but there was no sign even of a foot-path until we built the trail in the summer of 1864 when we started on this prospecting tour. . . . It was a rough trail we built, but it sufficed for our purposes and we got our animals up over it." After crossing the pass, Keough continues, "We went westerly down the South Fork of the King's River until the cañon became impassable. In the cañon we met a number of scientists headed by Professor Brewer. They named Mt. Brewer after him. Prof. Brewer was trying to find a way across the mountains, and we told him how to get into Owen's Valley over the pass by the trail we had just built."[24]

By following the prospectors' very rough trail, the Brewer party reached Kearsarge Pass (11,823 feet) on the main Sierra Crest and descended the steep escarpment down to Owens Valley, near the present town of Independence.

Brewer wrote that: "Camp Independence was located in the valley, and for a year fighting went on, but at last the Indians were conquered—more were starved out than killed. They came in, made treaties, and became peaceful. One chief, however, Joaquin Jim, never gave up. He retreated into the Sierra with a small band, but he has attempted no hostilities since last fall."[25]

After a long trip north up Owens Valley, with daytime temperatures at 102°–106° F, the party reentered the mountains at Rock Creek, crossed Mono Pass, entered the drainage of the South Fork of the San Joaquin River, and camped on Mono Creek in Vermilion Valley (now flooded by Lake Edison). They then probably passed through Helms Meadow and east across Dusy Creek.

Brewer and Hoffmann were determined to climb Mount Goddard, the high, dark peak they had seen before and named from Mount Brewer, and had identified again from the crest of Monarch Divide. This point, they knew, would command vistas of a huge region of unmapped territory, and would thus be important for their topographic surveys. They traveled as far as horses could go and camped for the night at about 10,000 feet, perhaps in upper Red Mountain Basin. The next morning a party of four—Brewer, Hoffmann, Cotter, and Spratt (a soldier)—headed toward the peak.

FIGURE. 4.14. View looking west from the Sierra Crest at double-peaked Mount Gardiner (12,907 feet) on the left and the pyramidal Mount Clarence King (12,905 feet) on the right. Long after the 1864 expedition the lower peak between the two was named Mount Cotter to honor Richard Cotter, packer and mountaineer. The conical crag at lower right is Fin Dome. (U.S. National Park Service photograph)

FIGURE 4.15.   Indian camp, or rancheria, in the Sierra Nevada foothills of the type visited by Clarence King on his solitary ride from Visalia to Clark's Station (near Yosemite), where he joined up with the Brewer party. (Lawrence and Houseworth collection, The Society of California Pioneers)

After crossing six granite ridges all over 11,000 feet in altitude, Brewer and Hoffmann gave out from sheer exhaustion when they viewed the great dark mountain from atop a 12,000-foot peak and saw that it still lay some 6 miles distant. (They were probably on the crest of the LeConte Divide near Hell-for-Sure Pass, viewing the mountain across Goddard Canyon.). Too weary to go on, they turned back, walked until long after dark, and camped at 11,000 feet, with little food and no blankets. They fired a pitch-laden stump and huddled around the blazing fire for a long freezing night.

Cotter and Spratt, however, had continued on toward the mountain. They traveled all night, walked continuously for 36 hours, 26 without food, and finally were forced to turn back after getting within 300 feet of the peak's summit. Brewer noted the abundant dark metamorphic rock in this region, primarily mica slate, and Cotter described alternating veins or beds of slate and granite near the Goddard summit. (This mass of dark metamorphic rock underlying Mount Goddard is 25 miles long, the largest separate mass of metamorphic rock in the central Sierra Nevada.)

After this unsuccessful foray to the mountain, the party rejoined and returned to Vermilion Valley, where they met up with a group of soldiers who had just arrived from Fort Miller with fresh provisions of salt pork, flour, coffee, and sugar. They spent two days at this spot, recuperating, washing clothes, and reading about the Civil War in the somewhat dated newspapers that had arrived with the provisions.

They next climbed over a steep ridge and down into the canyon of the Middle Fork of the San Joaquin, and thence north up onto a highland where Hoffmann took more observations on surrounding peaks to extend the triangulation net. For some time he had been complaining about a leg that had caused him much pain and inconvenience. Although no injury was visible, the leg continued to worsen, and when Hoffmann became quite lame, Brewer decided, on August 21, to strike out for a populated area where they could get help. The next day they rode 23 miles, and poor Hoffmann was much worse. At the end of the day he had to be lifted from his horse. To add to his discomfort, it began to rain that night. Without a tent, all were soon soaking in their blankets from the cold rain, and suffered on the hard ground. In addition to severe rheumatism, Hoffmann developed an abscess in the left thigh.[26] After two more days of travel he got much worse, and travel was now very slow. Finally, on August 23, the ragged and weary party reached their rendezvous point at Clark's Ranch (now Wawona).

King, who had arrived at Clark's August 1, was waiting with Frederick Olmsted's party, which included Mr. and Mrs. Ashburner and some of their friends. He took rides with the ladies, related his engaging stories around the campfire, and particularly savored the offerings of a cook who spread a good table and had plenty of trout and venison on hand. Clark's Station was a rustic lodge owned by Galen Clark, a bearded mountaineer. It was a favorite way station for those traveling to Yosemite. Clark had been a New England miner, but had come west for health reasons in 1856 and was homesteading 160 acres of big trees in the Mariposa Grove. He loved Yosemite and the big trees and lobbied extensively for the creation of a park that would preserve them for posterity. The land that would become the park had just been withdrawn from the public domain by an act of Congress, which then ceded it to the State of California. Two years later, in 1866, Clark would be appointed "Guardian of Yosemite" to oversee the new state park.

Brewer's battered party rested. The long hard ride was over and the animals were gaunt, close to starvation. Brewer had lost 30 pounds, and Hoffmann was in desperate shape. He could not stand and was confined to his bed, members of the party always tending him.

After three days at Clark's, Brewer and Olmsted went to Yosemite Valley. The meadows were parched and brown and the waterfalls almost dry, owing to the terribly dry summer. After inspecting the region and discussing methods of managing the area as a "public pleasure park" they traveled on to camp at Mono Pass for a week. From there they attempted to climb Mount Dana, but Olmsted had trouble breathing in the thin mountain air, and instead they turned to the next major peak south of Dana, where they actually rode their horses to the summit. Olmsted named the peak Mount Gibbs in honor of Oliver Walcott Gibbs, Professor of Science at Harvard.

When Brewer arrived back at Clark's Station, Hoffmann was no better despite attentive nursing by King and Gardner. He could neither walk nor ride horseback, and was eager to get to San Francisco, where the best medical attention would be available. A litter was made, and on September 10 four men began to carry him down the long trail to Mariposa. But soon the trail narrowed so tightly that only two could struggle with the litter, navigating between the rocks and trees. Finally, after the group reached the crest of a steep hill, the way got easier, and King and Cotter (the strongest of the group) carried the litter on to Mariposa, while Brewer and Gardner returned to Clark's to get the livestock. They met soon at Mariposa, where a carriage was outfitted with a bed, and King and Cotter rode with Hoffmann the 100 miles to Stockton, where they boarded a steamer bound for San Francisco. Hoffmann's malady was slow to heal; he remained nearly immobile for the whole next year, but was able to work on his maps in the office.

Gardner and Brewer spent a few days at the Mariposa Estate studying the mines and mills. They then rode with Olmsted in his carriage to Stockton, carrying $28,000 in gold bullion from the mines.

Upon reaching San Francisco, William Brewer learned that he had been appointed professor of agriculture at Yale. After conferring with Josiah Whitney, he resigned his position with the California Geological Survey, and made preparations to take passage to the East Coast. Referring to his notebooks, he determined the distance that he had traveled during his geologic surveys in California over the preceding four years. It amounted to 15,105 miles—7,564 on horseback, 3,101 on foot, and 4,440 by public conveyance.

The 1864 expedition of the Brewer party, despite its extraordinary accomplishments, was of short duration and insufficient budget. Of the five members, both King and Gardner were unpaid volunteers. In his synopsis of the fieldwork, Whitney observed that "the Sierra Nevada [is] a chain of mountains nearly as extensive as the Alps . . . and, when we consider that the number of Alpine explorers and of the published volumes of their results may be counted by the hundreds, their researches extending over nearly a century, we feel that we need not apologize for the imperfections of our work, believing, as we do, that we have done the best which our time and means have permitted."[27]

Despite the reconnaissance nature of their work, these men had made the first topographic, geologic, and botanical survey of a vast area. They identified, mapped, and named the highest peak then in the nation, and they crossed what is still the most usable pass over the remotest section of the range crest. They were the first to outline the course of the Kern River, which flows in a major canyon some 75 miles south from the Kings–Kern Divide before turning west to the Central Valley. They mapped out the position of the Great Western Divide, to the west of the Kern Canyon, and that of the main Sierra Crest, to the east of the canyon. They demonstrated that recent glacial action is widespread in the higher parts of the range. And they measured for the first time the altitude of many points on their route, utilizing the mercury barometer, and their data compare favorably with modern determinations.[28]

The expedition demonstrated that granite overwhelmingly predominates in the southern Sierra. In the gold country to the north, a broad metamorphic belt flanks the range along its west side, and is the primary host to the Mother Lode gold belt. In the 26-page section of the Whitney report on "The Region About the Head of Kern and Kings Rivers," the words "granite" or "granitic" are used 49 times. Although William Brewer's background was in botany, and his position on this survey was that of botanist, he had a keen interest in geology and developed a good knowledge of the science. In a letter written to Professor George Brush of Yale during the expedition, he praised the work of Clarence King, who had been a student of Brush. Brewer remarked that King had been converted from the metamorphic theory of the origin of granite to the intrusive theory. This debate, whether granite is formed by the solid recrystallization of preexisting rocks (granitization), or by crystallization from molten material (magmatism), continues today.

CHAPTER FIVE

GRAND COLD FURY OF THE SIERRA

The noble walls—sculptured into endless variety of domes and gables,
spires and battlements and plain mural precipices—all atremble
with the thunder tones of the falling water.
—John Muir, The Yosemite

When Clarence King and Charles Hoffmann returned to San Francisco to seek medical help for Hoffmann, the news, discussed at length at Survey headquarters, was about the withdrawal of Yosemite Valley from the public domain to serve as a state park. The region had been granted to the State of California by an act of Congress, signed by President Lincoln, June 30, 1864. (Yosemite would become a U.S. National Park 26 years later, in 1890, but this action was the beginning of the National Park movement). The bill had been backed and ushered through Congress by California Senator John Conness. A board of eight commissioners was appointed by California's governor to oversee the proper use and preservation of the new park, the world's first natural public park. Included on this commission were Frederick Olmsted (chairman), Josiah Whitney (State Geologist), William Ashburner (mining geologist), and Galen Clark (who was also appointed on-site guardian).

The first order of business for the commission was to establish the park's boundaries, prepare a detailed map of its topography, and study its general geology. And for that Whitney was designated to select a team of experienced men. Hoffmann's disability removed him from consideration for the mapping task; he was bedridden, and the outlook for his recovery was uncertain. James Gardner was chosen to supervise the mapping because of his considerable experience under Hoffmann in mapping by triangulation in the High Sierra, and he brought as well a knowledge of detailed sur-

FIGURE 5.1.   Looking east from the Mariposa Trail up Yosemite Valley, with the great cliff of El Capitan on the left, Bridalveil Falls right of center, and the rounded peak of Half Dome on the right skyline. King and Gardner spent about two months in the fall of 1864 mapping the valley and its walls, investigating its geological features, and fixing the newly mandated state park boundary line. (Hutchings' California Magazine, October, 1859)

veying, gained at the Mariposa Estate, and with the Army Corps of Engineers in laying out the San Francisco fortifications at Black Point and Angel Island. King, a man of many talents, would head up the geological survey.

The commission had wasted no time, and just a week after returning to San Francisco from the arduous 1864 summer campaign in the Kings River Sierra, King, Gardner, and Richard Cotter headed back to Yosemite, arriving October 5. It was crucial that the mapping be completed before the winter snows closed the mountain roads and trails, and important that reports and maps be prepared before December, when the California Legislature would meet. Frederick A. Clark, a surveyor on loan from the Mariposa Company, joined the others in Yosemite. Two locals from the valley were also taken on by the team: Longhurst as cook, and Wilmer to work with Dick Cotter, who would be serving as the survey's chainman. William Hyde—the friend who had traveled with King and Gardner across the plains and mountains—arrived from Nevada and volunteered to help. They also had the use of two pack mules, Pumpkinseed and the nearly blind Bonaparte.

Gazing at the immense face of El Capitan, King felt the more somber aspect that fall had brought to the valley, and pondered once again the forces that could build

FIGURE 5.2.   Portrait of Clarence King at age 22. (Photograph by Galen Clark, Guardian of Yosemite; courtesy of the Bancroft Library, University of California, Berkeley)

such a spectacle. Alluding to Whitney's rift hypothesis for the origin of the valley, he wrote, "In this cold, naked strength, one has crowded on him the geological record of mountain work, of granite plateau suddenly rent asunder, of the slow, imperfect manner in which Nature has vainly striven to smooth her rough work and bury the ruins with thousands of years' accumulation of soil and debris."[1]

The mapping crew took over two cabins on the valley floor, directly facing the north wall and the marvelous spectacle of Yosemite Falls. Early the next morning a group of Indians, including two teenage girls, entered their camp and watched spellbound as Longhurst prepared breakfast. He made flapjacks over an open fire and, as King relates, "scorning such vulgar accomplishments as turning the cake over in midair, he slung it boldly up, turning it three times,—ostentatiously greasing the pan with a fine centrifugal movement, and catching the flapjack as it fluttered down,—and spanked it upon the hot coals with a touch at once graceful and masterly . . . our Indian friends . . . wrestled affectionately for [the] frequent unfortunate cakes which would dodge Longhurst and fall into the ashes."[2]

The surveyors first climbed the north wall and set up camp near the brook that feeds Virgin's Tears Fall (now called Ribbon Fall). At the nearby brink of El Capitan— that massive cliff that drops a sheer 3,200 feet to the valley floor—the entire Yosemite Valley was laid out before them. King gazed down and pondered again Whitney's rift hypothesis, which posited that the valley was bounded by two giant rifts or faults marking the sides of a central block that had descended when support was somehow withdrawn from below.

Back in camp, cook Longhurst rewarded them with a hearty dinner, one that turned out surprisingly well, considering that he was somewhat tipsy. "He had found among our medicines a black bottle of brandy, contrived to induce a mule to break it, and, just to save as much as possible while it was leaking, drank with freedom."[3] Longhurst regained favor, however, by producing a delicious duff for dessert. The duff was made by mixing about two cups each of flour, suet, and broken bread with a draft of molasses and sugar, a handful of dried plums, a few eggs, and a pinch of baking soda. To this mixture he added enough water that a stiff dough could be kneaded into a ball, and the ball was then tied up in a canvas bag. The bag was put in a bowl placed in the bottom of a covered iron pot filled with an inch or two of water. After boiling for 2–3 hours on the campfire (water added as needed) the duff was removed from the canvas and served. Longhurst, attempting to redeem his past transgressions, topped it off with a sauce flavored with the last bit of remaining brandy.

Next day, Gardner set up the transit on a suitable knoll near camp, alongside a great dead pine tree, and began laying out the boundary line. Wilmer and Cotter chained along the line in a northeasterly direction through forests and over smooth

FIGURE 5.3.   Galen Clark, a miner from New England who had come west in 1856 and homesteaded 160 acres south of Yosemite Valley at the site of present-day Wawona. He provided a good bed and meal at his lodge, which came to be called Clark's Station. Clark loved Yosemite, and worked tirelessly toward its creation as the nation's first large state park, in 1864. He was on the first Board of Commissioners governing the Yosemite Grant and was appointed Guardian of Yosemite. (The Society of California Pioneers)

FIGURE 5.4.   Looking east-northeast from near Glacier Point toward Half Dome with Clouds Rest to the left on the skyline. A human figure stands atop the overhanging rock on Glacier Point, at the upper right. Josiah Whitney (1870) commented about Half Dome that "It is a crest of granite, rising to the height of 4,737 feet above the Valley, inaccessible, being probably the only one of all the prominent points about the Yosemite which never has been, and never will be, trodden by human foot. . . . On the side fronting Tenaya Canon, it is *absolutely vertical* for 2,000 feet or more from the summit." (Photograph by F. Matthes, U. S. Geological Survey.)

plateaus of bare granite, keeping their route about one mile from the brink of the valley, as mandated by Congress. When they reached the first ridge to the east—the crest
that extended north from the prow of El Capitan—they found that the abrupt slope
down into the valley of Yosemite Creek was too steep for chaining, and most of the
line thereafter had to be continued by triangulation. But the segments of the boundary that were already measured would suffice as a base line from which to establish
the map scale. Every prominent point, including those on the verge of the chasm, was
fixed by triangulation from at least two other points on the line. From the points on
the rim, they took secondary bearings to features in the valley. The valley floor was
thus laid out like a map three thousand feet below, and they could easily sketch in its
details, as controlled by the bearings taken.

    Gardner and his men mapped topography, watercourses, roads, trails, and build-
ings, and laid out and marked the park boundary on the ground, mainly with rock
cairns. Using the mercury cistern barometer, they established the altitude of occupied
points and determined the heights of cliffs and waterfalls. The map would need to stand
alone, however, since the ground it delineated could not yet be fixed in its exact position
in California. They did not have the astronomical instruments needed to determine latitude and longitude, and the positions of the surrounding peaks had not yet been established. That would have to await a later expedition, one equipped for such work.

    King, as was his wont, found time to explore the surrounding region, and made
forays to the brink of Yosemite Falls—by then a feeble stream compared to its spring
grandeur—where barometric measurements indicated a drop of 2,537 feet. He
climbed to the crest of the Three Brothers, and to the summit of North Dome, where
he studied the well-displayed onionskin fracture, which had produced the giant concentric shells that cap the dome. In several places he noted that the bedrock granite
had been polished to such a brilliant surface that it reflected light almost like a mirror. He recognized these polished surfaces, scored as they were with deep parallel
scratches and gouges, as resulting from the work of glaciers. Massive rivers of ice—
carrying countless embedded rock fragments—had moved across the granite, over
thousands of years, and left the marks of their passage.

    The survey camp was then moved to the North Dome area, where the mappers
made traverses to trace out these glacial markings, as well as the piles of glacial debris
(moraines) that marked the extent of past glaciers. And from established stations, they
took bearings to prominent points across the chasm, preparatory to continuing the survey and boundary line there on the south side. The nights, meanwhile, had turned cold,
and the men awoke in the morning stiff from sleeping on the frozen ground. Longhurst
did his best in the cooking realm, but the rations were lean. At length, the party was reduced to bread, beans, and bacon, not enhanced by the delicacy of a tasty plumduff.

Even the beans were relished, however, when King and Gardner talked around the campfire of their good fortune in being the first to undertake making a map of this magical place—one of the world's most incomparably beautiful valleys.

King climbed nearby Mount Hoffmann, which had been named by Brewer to honor the Survey's topographer the previous year, and then followed down Yosemite Creek, where he reckoned that in places the ice had been 700 feet thick, and found clear evidence that it had advanced into the main Yosemite Valley. He crawled to the very edge of the cliff where the waters of Yosemite Falls gush over a granite lip.[4]

The party then descended to the valley floor, where they reoccupied the two cabins and rested for a day. The Indians had left the valley, and Yosemite Falls was dry; the cold nights had largely frozen the streams that fed the falls. They climbed south out of the valley, onto the Mariposa Trail, and made camp at Meadow Brook, not far from Inspiration Point west of Cathedral Rocks. At that point, Gardner began the southern boundary. They laid out the line for about two miles to the east before turning northeast to the region of Glacier Point—always remaining one mile, or a bit more, from the canyon rim. Bill Hyde took on the task of sketching the details of talus slopes and river displayed thousands of feet below them.

King commonly left the surveying party at their work and continued alone to conduct his geologic observations, now along the south rim of the canyon. From Sentinel Dome and Glacier Point he marveled at the finely sculptured bulk of Half Dome. "You see it now edgewise and in sharp profile, the upper half of the conoid fronting the north with a sharp, sheer fracture-face of about two thousand feet vertical. From the top of this a most graceful helmet curve sweeps over to the south, and descends almost perpendicularly into the valley of the Little Yosemite." He continued, "Observation had taught me that a glacier flowed over the Yosemite brink. As I looked over now I could see its shallow valley, and the ever-rounded rocks over which it crowded itself and tumbled into the icy valley below. Up the Yosemite gorge [Tenaya Canyon], which opened straight before me, I knew that another great glacier had flowed; and also that the valley of the Illilouette and the Little Yosemite had been the bed of rivers of ice; a study, too, of the markings upon the glacier cliff above Hutchings's house, had convinced me that a glacier no less than a thousand feet deep had flowed through the valley, occupying its entire bottom."[5] Despite this overwhelming evidence for glacial action, King did not argue against the Whitney rifting model. He assumed, rather, that the glacier advanced into the valley after the valley had first formed by block subsidence, and that subsequent modification of the valley shape by glaciation was not extensive.

More than a month had been spent by now on the mapping, and the work was nearing completion. Gardner had carried the 30-mile park boundary back on itself

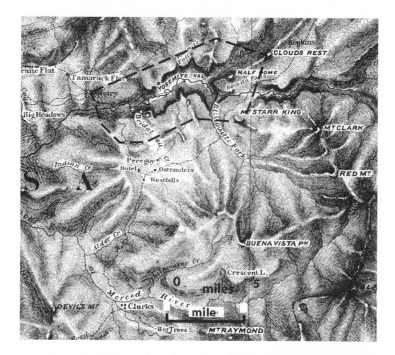

FIGURE 5.5.   Yosemite Valley and the boundary (dashed line) of the state park laid out
by Gardner's team in the late fall of 1864. When the survey of the valley and boundary line
was completed, Clarence King and Dick Cotter attempted to climb the high spire of Mount
Clark, east of the valley, but the climb was aborted by a severe snowstorm which also forced
the mapping team to leave the valley. They retreated in mid-November, south through deep
snow and blizzard conditions, first to the sheep cabin at Westfall's, and then on south to
Clark's Station near the Big Trees. The first ascent of Mount Clark was made two years later
by King and Jim Gardner. (Modified from Charles Hoffmann, 1873)

with a closure that was within permissible error. King, meanwhile, had become increasingly interested in the isolated grandeur of The Obelisk, which dominated the
eastern skyline. He decided to rename it Mount Clark, for the Guardian of Yosemite,[6]
and determined to make an attempt for the summit. On November 10, he and Cotter
loaded Bonaparte and Pumpkinseed with a week's meager supplies and one blanket
each—all tied behind the saddles—and, leaving their friends in the valley, rode back
up the Mariposa Road. This was just three months after the two had made their
memorable backpack trek to Mount Tyndall in the southern Sierra. On this more
northerly Sierra venture, they turned off near Meadow Brook, traveled cross-country
over frozen ground, and camped near an eastern tributary to Bridalveil Creek. They
filled their canteens in the evening and slept with them in their blankets, knowing
that the stream would be frozen in the morning. The next day they crossed the divide
into the drainage of Illilouette Creek and rode all afternoon, up the crest of a wonderfully formed medial moraine, to the base of Mount Clark.

That evening they bivouacked in a grove of fir and noted a dark threatening cloud bank to the west, the first storm clouds they had seen since April. By morning, gray clouds engulfed them, and when the mist parted, exposing the upper reaches of Mount Clark, they found that a dusting of fresh snow had covered the higher slopes. Soon a low, moaning wind rose to stronger blasts, but King—unwilling to give up the prospect of a first ascent—spent the day examining glacial erratics. In early evening he climbed a nearby ridge to evaluate the prospects for an improvement in the weather. But the wind increased, and the clouds became more threatening. That night, after a hearty dinner of double rations, they bundled up together tentless, rolled in their blankets, after arranging all equipment and provisions in neat piles, ready for a quick departure. By 9 o'clock the wind died down, and snow began falling in large flakes. King and Cotter covered their heads in their blankets and slept well most of the night, until breathing became difficult, as the covering of snow became thicker.

By morning a foot and a half of snow had fallen. The surroundings had been transformed into a white landscape, and the air was filled with blowing snow. After digging out and preparing breakfast, they concluded that the attempt on The Obelisk had to be abandoned. They gathered their equipment, saddled the mules, wrapped

FIGURE 5.6. Looking southeast from north of Yosemite Valley, toward the Mount Clark Group. King changed the name of the spire-like peak, formerly called The Obelisk, to Mount Clark, to honor Galen Clark, the Guardian of Yosemite, one of the nation's first park rangers. (Whitney, 1865)

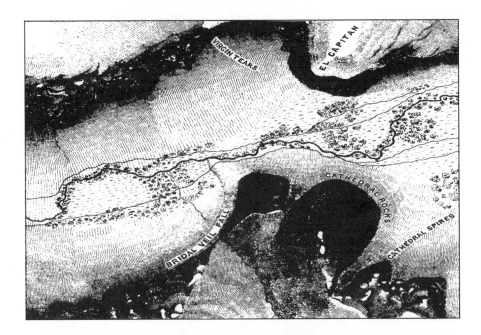

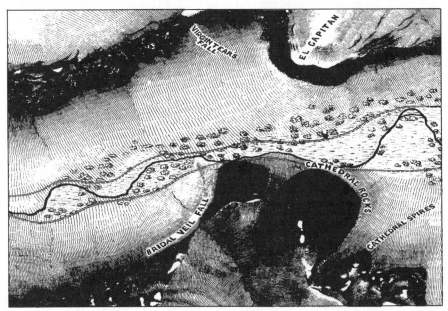

FIGURE 5.7.   Part of the map of Yosemite prepared by James Gardner and Clarence King in the fall of 1864. The map was titled "Map of the Yosemite Valley from Surveys made by order of the Commissioners to manage the Yosemite Valley and Mariposa Big Tree Grove, by C. King and J. T. Gardner, 1865." The first version (top) was published in 1868 in Whitney's *Yosemite Book*. After publication, Whitney noticed, when reviewing the new 1867 mapping of Charles Hoffmann, that the meanders of the Merced River were incorrectly defined, and angrily labeled King's mapping "a complete sham" (Wilkins, 1988). A revised map based on Hoffmann's new versions of road and river placement (bottom, still dated 1865) appeared in the 1869 and 1870 editions of Whitney's *Yosemite Guide-Book*. King attributed the erroneous river mapping to sketches made by William Hyde.

themselves tightly in blankets, and began the long trek back to Yosemite Valley. Fortunately, the regular trend of the long moraine, which they had followed on their way up, guided them back for the first mile or two, until the wind-driven snow reduced visibility to only a few feet. From there on, finding the trail became nearly impossible, and the mules stumbled, blinded by violent blasts of wind-driven snow. King wrote that "It was a cruel necessity, but we spurred them inexorably forward, guiding them to the right and left to avoid rocks and trees which, in their blindness, they were constantly threatening to strike. . . . The snow constantly balled upon our animals' feet, and they slid in every direction."[7]

In due course, they crossed the Illilouette and began the long hard climb to the ridge separating it from the drainage of Bridalveil Creek. It was there that the mules nearly gave out. Only by dismounting, breaking trail, and dragging the animals uphill through the tempest could they reach the summit. From there the terrain was easier, but the wind did not abate and only by compass could they maintain a proper course. Suddenly, without warning, they were struck by a violent blast of horizontally driven snow and hail, which drove them into the closest shelter, a cluster of fir trees. Here man and beast turned their backs to the wind to protect face and eyes, and hunkered down among the trees. They endured the blast for more than an hour, frozen to the bone. Bonaparte and Pumpkinseed were heavily frosted, and they stared pitifully at the men.

When a lull came, the men remounted and headed west. Near Inspiration Point the mules suddenly recognized the trail, and Bonaparte quickened his pace to a trot. Pumpkinseed needed no added encouragement, and the animals could scarcely be controlled as they took the trail down to the valley. Gradually, the wind died down, and the clouds brightened. Now on the Mariposa Trail, they saw great avalanches tumbling off the canyon walls near El Capitan, and heard their thunder. The two travelers attained the valley floor at dark and shortly smelled the smoke from their valley lodge. After giving the mules a full ration of barley, they joined their friends in the cozy cabin and shared a savory pot of beans and mugs of hot coffee.

But it was clear that the storm doors had opened. That night the tempest resumed and brought gale force wind and rain. Sleep became impossible. The Merced River rose, overflowed its banks, and flooded parts of the valley. Yosemite Falls swelled to a thunderous torrent. Fearing that the mountain trails would become hopelessly blocked, the team decided that one group should haul most of the equipment down to Clark's Station immediately. Cotter, Hyde, and Wilmer packed up the animals with instruments and equipment and left at first light.

In the morning there was a break in the storm, the sun shone briefly, but by evening dark clouds once again choked the valley and shut off the light. A chill pervaded the air, and snow resumed its fall. By the following morning, eight inches of snow was on the ground on the valley floor, and it was apparent that a major storm had begun, and might seal up the mountains. King and Gardner decided to pack up all the remaining equipment and escape as soon as possible. King started first, to break trail and make some last barometric measurements, and Gardner and Frederick Clark followed. By noon King had reached Inspiration Point, where on a fine day the view into the Valley would have been stunning, but now nothing was visible through the falling snow, now a foot and a half deep on the ground. King occupied two final barometric reading sites, and finally, at 4 o'clock, after nine hours of hard travel through the snow-covered forest, he arrived at Westfall's sheep cabin, near upper Bridalveil Creek, 3,000 feet above the valley floor.

The snowfall increased, and by evening when Clark and Gardner arrived at the cabin, worn and tired, King decided it was imperative that someone press on to Clark's Station, to bring back help before the storm made travel impossible. But just at this time, the indomitable Cotter stumbled in from the dark exhausted, having walked up from Clark's Station to help bring the remaining equipment down. The four ate a cold supper, and it was decided that King and Cotter would make up the advance team and slog on to Clark's in the stormy night. At first, Cotter's recent trail guided them, but his footprints soon filled in as the wind and snow increased. The long miles they had already traveled that day took their toll, and exhaustion slowed the pace. In places, they lost their way and had to return to previous landmarks for a fresh start. Well-known blazes on trees were covered by snow, and sometimes they had to thrust a hand down into the snow along the tree trunks, feeling for the blazes on the bark. Around midnight, after a long trek, they reached the brink of a steep slope.

King relates that "Here Cotter sank with exhaustion and declared that he must sleep. I rolled him over and implored him to get up and struggle on for a little while longer, when I felt sure that we must get down to the South Fork Canyon. He utterly refused, and lay there in a drowsy condition, fast giving up to the effects of fatigue and cold. I unbound a long scarf which was tied round his neck, put it under his arms like a harness, and, tying it round my body, started on, dragging him through the snow, to see if by that means I might not exasperate him to rise and labor on."[8] Braced by this treatment, Cotter revived, and was able to continue on his own down the long incline to the river, and from there on to Clark's, where they arrived about 2 A.M. Pounding on the cabin door, they awakened their friends, and were soon spread out before a roaring fire partaking of hot food and drink.

By morning the storm abated and a period of calm ensued. Gardner and Frederick Clark arrived from Westfall's about noon, just as a new storm erupted in full vigor. They all spent the night in the cabin as the wind howled and the storm continued. The following morning two feet of snow lay on the ground, and more was falling as the now united party loaded instruments, notebooks, and light gear onto the mules. The heavier equipment and blankets were left at Clark's to be recovered in the spring.

The somewhat revived group struggled out through the deep snow, searching for the trail, at times resorting to the simple tactic of following Bonaparte, who, with his inborn natural compass, knew where the trail lay. After surmounting Chowchilla Summit, the trail led downhill, and the snow gradually turned to rain. Eventually, they were walking on bare ground in a violent rainstorm. King wrote, "A more drowned and bedraggled set of fellows never walked out upon the wagon-road and turned toward Mariposa. Streams of water flowed from every fold of our garments, our soaked hats clung to our cheeks, the baggage was a mass of pulp, and the mules smelled violently of wet hide. Fortunately our note-books, carefully strapped in oil-cloth, so far resisted wetting."[9]

The streams they encountered, which had been quiet brooks when they ascended this trail two months earlier, were now swollen torrents, difficult to cross. At one stream, the mules would not cross until "The one-eyed Napoleon was brought to the brink and induced to plunge in by an application of fence-rails *a tergo*, his cyclopean organ piloting him safely across, when he was quickly followed by the other mules. We watched the load of instruments with some anxiety, and were not reassured when their heavy weight bore the mule quite under; but he climbed successfully out, and we ourselves, half swimming, half floundering, managed to cross."[10]

At another stream the pack mule carrying the instruments was swept downstream, where it became caught in a mass of logs with its head under water. King jumped into the stream, swam to the mule, and was able to free it and get its head above water. With help from the others, pulling on head and tail, they were able to drag the poor beast onto the bank, where it lay more dead than alive. While King was trying to revive it by pokes with a tripod, the bank on which he was standing gave way and he sank back into the flood. Cotter grabbed the collar of his coat and hoisted him like a great fish back onto the bank next to the mule; the two of them, man and mule, sputtered, coughed, and finally came to their senses.

After another difficult stream crossing, the tired, dripping, muddy party came to a ranch house occupied by two bachelors, who were just beginning their supper. Bacon and fried onions with tea and biscuits were on the table. The two men were at first a bit apprehensive, but after some hesitation, and King's gentle assurances, a deal was struck, and the bedraggled party entered the house and began the process of tending to body and belly. A rope was stretched across the sitting room in front of the large fire, and the soaking clothes were stripped off and hung to steam on the line. The wayfarers stood naked before the fire, turning slowly to heat and dry all sides. With the evening came comfort, as clothes dried, blood warmed, and more cooked onions and biscuits arrived to satisfy cravings for food.

The next morning turned out to be fine, and the flooded streams had greatly subsided. After rewarding their hosts handsomely for the bounties of their shelter and table, the group continued on to Mariposa, where they parted from Frederick Clark. And after two more days of muddy travel, maneuvering through the San Joaquin Valley they arrived in San Francisco.

In this fashion, the party having been forced from the field by deteriorating weather, the long field season of 1864 came to an end. When they arrived in San Francisco, they found that both Brewer and Whitney had left for the East Coast, Brewer for his professorship at Yale, and Whitney for his home in Boston, where he would continue his landmark work on the California geologic treatise. Brewer's trip, via Central America, took the customary month of travel. He left San Francisco November 14, anchored at San Juan del Sur, Nicaragua, and endured a 12-mile cart ride over the low divide to Lake Nicaragua. After a 50-mile boat trip across the lake, and a rude railroad trip to San Juan del Norte on the Atlantic side, he boarded the steamer *Golden Rule* and arrived at Sandy Hook on December 10, and home in Ithaca three days later.

Gardner turned over the boundary-survey plots and notebooks of the Yosemite work to Frederick Olmsted, who was also planning to leave California, to resume his work on city parks. Shortly after arriving in San Francisco, King and Gardner left aboard the *S.S. Moses Taylor* bound for Nicaragua, on December 11, 1864.[11] After a carriage trip to Lake Nicaragua, they spent several days enjoying the tropical atmosphere while waiting for a boat to cross the lake. King, happily relaxed, wrote "Gardner and I seated ourselves under the grateful shadow of palm-trees, a bewitching black-and-tan sister thrumming her guitar while the chocolate for our breakfast boiled. The slumberous haze of the tropics hung over Lake Nicaragua, but high above its indistinct pearly veil rose the smooth cone of the volcano of Omatepec, robed in a cover of pale emerald green. Warmth, repose, the verdure of eternal spring, the poetical whisper of palms, the heavy odor of the tropical blooms, banished the grand cold fury of the Sierra, which had left a permanent chill in our bones."[12] Delivered to the San Juan River by the lake steamer, they traveled thence to the Caribbean, and on to New York.

CHAPTER SIX

MIRAGE AND BLIZZARD

Earth so huge and yet so bounded—
pools of salt and plots of land
shallow skin of green and azure—
chains of mountains, grains of sand.
—Alfred Lord Tennyson, "Tiresias"

Arriving in New York early in January 1865, King and Gardner went right to Boston to compile the previous season's work and to consult with Professor Whitney about future plans. Whitney urged the two to remain with the California Geological Survey, and at length they agreed. King had been quietly formulating plans for a survey of his own to explore the Great Basin, that open country east of the Sierra that had beguiled him on their first trip west, but he put those plans temporarily aside.

Working from his notes, King wrote up his geologic observations for the Yosemite region and turned this material over to Whitney. He spelled out his evidence for the presence of former glaciers, particularly in the high country surrounding Yosemite Valley, but also indicated that ice masses had combined to form a giant glacial tongue that had swept down the main valley. Soon, however, King took ill and returned home to be with his mother and her two young children in Irvington, New York. He was suffering from fever, probably malaria contracted in the Nicaraguan swamps, and was bedridden for weeks.

Whitney, with great industry, compiled the results of the 1864 fieldwork, and combined this material with that collected from the earlier years of the California Geological Survey. This compilation was assembled in a well-received volume, on the general geology of California, published in 1865.[1] Whitney spelled out his Yosemite

FIGURE 6.1.   A ship entering the Golden Gate from the Pacific Ocean. Until the advent of the transcontinental railroad in 1869, the most rapid method of traveling to California was by sea from the eastern seaboard to Panama, across the isthmus, and on by sea again to San Francisco. King and Gardner made the three-week trip four times: 1864–65 (east), 1865 (west), 1866–67 (east), and 1867 (west). (From Ringgold, 1852)

rift hypothesis, writing that "The Half Dome seems, beyond a doubt, to have been split asunder in the middle, the lost half having gone down in what may truly be said to have been 'the wreck of matter and the crush of worlds'. . . . If the bottom of the Yosemite did 'drop out,' to use a homely but expressive phrase, it was not all done in one piece, or with one movement; there are evidences in the valley of fractures and cross-fractures at right-angles to them, and the different segments of the mass must have been of quite different sizes, and may have descended to unequal depths." He also mentioned the evidence of glaciation in the valley set forth in King's report: "In the course of the explorations of Messrs. King and Gardner, they obtained ample evidence of the former existence of a glacier in the Yosemite Valley. . . . Mr. King thinks it must have been at least a thousand feet thick."[2]

Three years later in the Yosemite Book of 1868, Whitney hardened his position, and fully rejected the possibility of the valley having been carved by ice: "Much less can it be supposed that the peculiar form of the Yosemite is due to the erosive action of ice. A more absurd theory was never advanced than that by which it was sought to ascribe to glaciers the sawing out of these vertical walls and the rounding of the domes. Nothing more unlike the real work of ice, as exhibited in the Alps, could be found. Besides, there is no reason to suppose, or at least no proof, that glaciers have ever occupied the Valley, or any portion of it, as will be explained in the next chapter, so that this theory, based on entire ignorance of the whole subject, may be dropped without wasting any more time upon it." Whitney goes on to contradict King's evidence: "The plateau, or amphitheater, at the head of the Merced was not high enough to allow a glacier to be formed of sufficient thickness to descend down as far as into the Yosemite Valley; at least we have obtained no positive evidence that such was the case. The statement to that effect in the 'Geology of California,' Vol. I., is an error, although it is certain that the masses of ice approached very near to the edge of the Valley, and were very thick in the canyon to the southeast of Cloud's Rest, and on down into the Little Yosemite."[3]

Despite Whitney's defense of his rift hypothesis, it has not fared well through the years as a reasonable model for the formation of Yosemite Valley. No one has ever found any trace of the giant faults along which the valley floor subsidence was supposed to have occurred. John Muir, François Matthes, and others added to the ample evidence of glaciation in and about Yosemite as well as in the other giant Yosemite-like canyons of the Sierra Nevada. Most observers believe, like King, that the canyon was largely filled with ice during the ice ages, and moreover, owes its origin largely to glacial action during several distinct advances of the ice.

For several months, Gardner worked diligently on the Yosemite map. Following

FIGURE 6.2. View from Yerba Buena Island in San Francisco Bay, looking west toward the cluster of sailing ships near the San Francisco waterfront. The entrance to the bay, the Golden Gate, appears on the extreme right. (Ringgold, 1852)

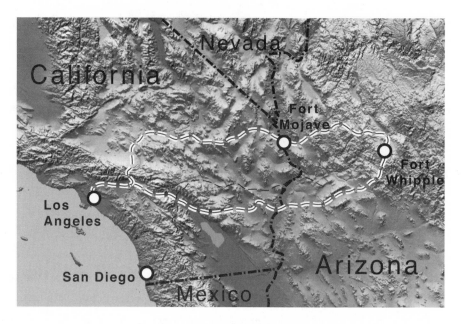

FIGURE 6.3.   Map of southern California and Arizona, showing the 1865 route that King and Gardner made on horseback from Los Angeles to Fort Mojave, Fort Whipple area, and return. The mapping tour in Arizona was cut short when the enlistments of the escorting troopers expired near Fort Whipple, and further work could not be continued because the region was frequented by hostile Indians.

the practice of the time, he depicted topography with fine hachure lines, all directed downhill. To indicate a steeper slope, they were made both heavier and closer together. The result gives a graphic impression of the nature of the terrain. The technique is challenging in a special place like Yosemite Valley, where nearly vertical canyon walls abut flatter ground on the valley floor below and pass into gentle uplands above. On the steepest slopes he used extremely tight hachures, fine lines spaced 30 to 60 to the inch. On the cliffs they all but merge, producing a solid black effect. This exacting pen work strained his eyes, exacerbating previous eyestrain he had suffered in college. The final map, completed in the summer, is designated: "Map of the Yosemite Valley from Surveys made by order of the Commissioners to manage the Yosemite Valley and Mariposa Big Tree Grove, by C. King and J. T. Gardner, 1865, drawn by J.T.G." It would be published three years later in Whitney's *Yosemite Book*.

In assessing his own mapping skills, King realized that he needed training in astronomy if he was to be properly equipped to make the observations and calculations required for the determination of latitude and longitude in remote areas. He therefore went to New Haven and took a course in astronomy from Professor Lyman. At

Yale he also consulted William Brewer, now professor of agriculture, and his old professors Brush, Dana, and William Whitney, brother of Josiah.

In the fall of 1865, King, Gardner, and the Whitney family boarded the side-wheeler steamship *Henry Chauncey* in New York and headed to California via the Isthmus of Panama. When they eventually arrived in San Francisco, it became apparent that funds for geologic fieldwork were limited, and Whitney had to scramble to keep his staff paid. He convinced Army General Irvin McDowell of the importance of surveys in the desert regions of California and Arizona and secured funding for King and Gardner. The two were soon ordered to Fort Whipple, Arizona, to undertake a reconnaissance for military routes.

They went south by ship to San Pedro, a port close to Los Angeles, drew equipment, horses, and an ambulance (to carry equipment) from the Army depot at nearby Fort Drum, and were assigned an escort of soldiers all of whom had volunteered for the duty. They rode through Los Angeles, a town of modest size, crossed Cajon Pass, and followed the Mojave River to its sink. Then, after 150 miles of desert travel, they crossed the Colorado River at Mojave and entered Arizona Territory, in January 1866.

FIGURE 6.4. King and Gardner crossed Cajon Pass between the San Gabriel and San Bernardino Ranges and passed from the humid Coast Ranges into the arid Mojave Desert with its distinctive Joshua trees. (Williamson, 1856)

While still two days away from Fort Whipple (now Prescott), King and Gardner rode early from camp one morning, about an hour ahead of the escort, in order to make observations along the trail. They were armed and carried instruments, including a long mercury barometer for determining altitude. The trail led through dry foothills covered by sagebrush and scattered small junipers. After dropping down a gentle slope, they were traversing a small valley when directly in front of them an Indian rose up from behind a large bush with his bow drawn and his arrow pointed directly at Gardner's face. Jim's first impulse was to grab for his revolver, but King, speaking in a low voice, cautioned him that such a strategy could be fatal. Within moments a second Apache appeared at the side of King's horse, also with bow drawn.

The first Indian motioned to them to dismount. Robbery seemed to be the motive, and because they were evenly matched, the geologists hesitated, realizing that once off their horses they stood little chance of resisting or escaping. Jim, then, signaled that they wished to ride on. At this point the Indian made a loud snake-like hiss, and in response to this signal, about 50 armed warriors appeared from the bushes and surrounded them, silent and ready. The Apaches were nearly naked and wearing no warpaint. When ordered again to dismount, King and Gardner complied, and dropped their revolvers to the ground when commanded to do so.

The leader then ordered King to remove the barometer from his shoulder, thinking that it was a rifle. King unsealed the instrument and began carefully explaining how this great new "gun" worked, using a combination of Spanish words and sign language. King rambled on for many minutes, using his eloquent story-telling abilities to draw in the Indians and to buy time. He showed where the "ammunition" was loaded and how to aim the weapon, and tried to demonstrate how powerful it was. As the Indians grew impatient, Gardner tried to delay matters further by withdrawing his compass from the case on his belt and showing them its remarkable features. The leader, unimpressed, ordered the surveyors to strip off their clothes, and at this point the realization hit home that motives far more serious than simple robbery were afoot.

They pulled off their clothes and boots as slowly as possible, but finally stood naked, surrounded by the host of armed, sullen natives. Some gathered sticks and twigs and built small fires. Others brought forth buckskin thongs. These preparations meant only one thing, death by torture—Apache style. A common technique was to stake the victim spread-eagled on the ground, face up, and nurse a small fire on his belly. Depending on the nature of the fire, the ordeal could be prolonged—a smaller fire burned more slowly down into the vitals. The captives heard the excited voices of the savages, smelled the smoke of the fires, and understood their impending agony.

Just then, the thud of horses' hooves was heard to the west, and before long their escort appeared over the rise. The lead rider signaled to the troops, who fanned out and surrounded the area where the captives were held. Almost immediately, most of the Indians disappeared into the countryside, and after much scrambling only two were captured. The troop was soon joined by General McDowell, who rode up and quickly learned how close the scientists had come to an excruciating end.

The two captive Apaches belonged to a tribe headed by Chief Iritabe, who, as it happened, was a friend of the general. The troop, herding their two captives before them, rode to the main Indian encampment several miles from the site of the ambush. As reported later by Gardner, when the chief was told of the capture and near torture, he said that the headstrong young braves " . . . who captured you were a hunting party that set out this morning, and seeing you, no doubt thought to rob you. But when you were taken, the hate and wildness overtook them and they longed to torture you. I am a friend of the white men, and I am for peace, for if we fight against you, you will sweep us from the earth . . . leave me your prisoners and for two days I will hold them, until you have passed through Willow Canyon. . . . When the two days are past I will call the tribe to council to decide the punishment of these men. If I succeed in the punishing of them—good. If not, the tribe will vote for war, but you will be safe."[4]

The chief was forthright, and his plan was agreed upon. But soon after the Cavalry had reached Fort Whipple, this Apache tribe declared war on the settlers. Two mail carriers were ambushed and horribly killed, close to the spot where King and Gardner had been ambushed. The Army responded, and the tribe was decimated. Chief Iritabe and his family abandoned the area and went north.

This episode left a lasting imprint on the two young men, and reinforced their awareness that they should carry rifles in the field. King later wrote in a book review: "The Apache differs in no wise from the astonishing devil whose lodge is to-day decked with the bloody scalps of last year's pioneers. He is the same whom we have lately seen in the person of Cochise, demurely drawing down the grin of hell into the oily counterfeit of a brotherly smile, and 'swapping' platitudes with a certain childlike general, while his picked warriors only a few miles away danced a veritable *can-can d'enfer* around a writhing soldier whom they grilled for a pastime."[5]

The detachment rode on to Fort Whipple, and from there Gardner and King began working up the topography of the Prescott Road region. While King studied the geology, Gardner carried out the triangulation of high peaks to the north, and im-

FIGURE 6.5. Fort Whipple in northwestern Arizona near the present site of Prescott. It was on the trail two days march west of this fort that King and Gardner were captured by Apaches in January 1866. They narrowly escaped a fiery death by torture. (Photograph by T. O'Sullivan, 1868; U.S. Geological Survey Library)

provised a baseline between Granite Mountain and the highest peak in the San Francisco Mountains. By sighting Polaris, the North Star, he determined latitude at the summit of Granite Mountain (but no longitude, because of the lack of a suitable chronometer). These measurements, coupled with an azimuth to San Francisco Peak, and knowledge of the peak's location from a previous survey by Lieutenant Whipple, provided the two points for the baseline. The ensuing survey showed for the first time that the ranges of northern Arizona follow a linear aspect with a systematic northerly trend. Five distinct ranges were mapped: the Black Mountains, the Cerbat or Hualapais Mountains, the Aquarius Mountains, the Aztec Mountains, and the Sierra Prieta. Previous maps, because of their incompleteness, depicted a maze of irregular mountain masses, their confusion resulting from mistakenly joining parts of one range to parts of another.

Before the surveyors could complete their work, the enlistments of the soldiers expired, whereupon they demanded payment and discharge and prepared to leave. King's only recourse was to ride the long trail to the nearest Army post at Camp Date Creek, 60 miles to the southwest. After a two-day ride to the post, he found no help there, either with replacements or with rations. General Mason, apparently wallowing in his cups, ignored all requests for help, and there seemed no hope of continuing with the exploration. Reluctantly, King and Gardner abandoned their mapping and headed back to California, first to La Paz, on the Colorado River, and then on to San Bernardino.

The two began the long ride back to Los Angeles through some of the most barren country in the Southwest, and even though it was only May, the desert was a furnace. Each rode a mule, but Gardner's was a troublesome animal that had taken an intense dislike to King's mount, John, and refused to follow closer than one-quarter mile. The two therefore had to travel separately on the long journey, too far apart to communicate even with a shout. King wrote of this strange caravan, "Hour after hour, plodding along at a dog-trot, we pursued our solitary way without the spice of companionship, and altogether deprived of the melodramatic satisfaction of loneliness."[6]

They rode day after long day in the blistering sun, across alkali plains and rocky hills almost devoid of vegetation, certainly with no trees that might have afforded shade. Water was scarce, often foul, or bitter with alkali. Staring toward the constant glare of the horizon, they searched for that speck of green that might signal a spring or an oasis. Sometimes the image of the white wasteland would change abruptly into

FIGURE 6.6. Riding across the blistering Mojave Desert, King described the shifting mirages, "the white expanse became suddenly transformed into a placid blue sea, along whose rippling shores were the white blocks of roofs, groups of spire-crowned villages, and cool stretches of green grove. A soft, vapory atmosphere hung over this sea; shadows, purple and blue, floated slowly across it, producing the most enchanting effect of light and color. The dreamy richness of the tropics, the serene sapphire sky of the desert, and the cool, purple distance of mountains were grouped as by miracle" (King, 1871). (From a field sketch by W. P. Blake; Williamson, 1856)

FIGURE 6.7.   Mount San Gorgonio as it appears from the edge of the Mojave Desert looking south. The broad pass, several miles wide, that leads to the Los Angeles Basin is between Mount San Gorgonio and San Bernardino Mountain, out of the picture to the right. (From a field sketch by C. Koppel; Williamson, 1856)

a blue lake with billowing waves and rocky shores, even apparently bordered by the white houses of inviting villages. But the mirage would then shimmer, lift, and vanish, and the thirsty desert would return. As King wrote, "The bewildering effect of this natural magic, and perhaps the feverish thirst, produced the impression of a dream, which might have taken fatal possession of us, but for the importunate braying of Gardner's mule, whose piteous discords (for he made three noises at once) banished all hallucination and brought us gently back from the mysterious spectacle to the practical question of water."[7]

Springs were marked out on the maps they carried, but experience had taught that as often as not they were mislocated or altogether missing. On one torrid afternoon the weary riders headed west toward what appeared to be a bit of green swimming in the mirage. King was sure that the green was a mere hallucination brought on by oppressive heat and the unrelenting glare along the horizon, but John, his mule, nervously tossed his head about and quickened his pace. The mules thereafter were not to be deterred from their chosen path, and after another hour's ride over the flat, dusty desert, two palm trees emerged from the glare. They had indeed come upon a treasure, a spring surrounded by lush green grass. "John lifted up his voice, now many days hushed, and gave out spasmodic gusts of baritone, which were as dry and harsh as if he had drunk mirages only."[8]

The mules were quickly unsaddled, and man and beast drank their fill, after which the travelers built a fire and enjoyed a pot of tea together. While the mules were munching the grass, King and Gardner stripped, plunged into the clear water, and soaked up the moisture that had eluded them along the 150 miles they had come since departing the Colorado River. Thus reinvigorated, they reclined in the shade of the palms, and when water and grass had restored the mules, and canteens were refilled, the trip was resumed. Of course Gardner's mule stubbornly refused to move until King and mount had set out on the trail the required quarter mile.

So it went, through the rocky ranges of the Mojave Desert, but after another interminable ride they spotted San Gorgonio Pass flanked by two snow-covered peaks, San Bernardino on the north and San Jacinto on the south. When at length they reached the pass, the contrast between the arid desert to the east, and the green Pacific slope to the west was absolute. King wrote, "There are but few points in America where such extremes of physical conditions meet. What contrasts, what opposed sentiments, the two views awakened! Spread out below us lay the desert, stark and glaring, its rigid hill-chains lying in disordered grouping, in attitudes of the dead. The bare hills are cut out with sharp gorges, and over their stone skeletons scanty earth clings in folds, like shrunken flesh; they are emaciated corpses of once noble ranges now lifeless, outstretched as in a long sleep. Ghastly colors define them from the ashen plain in which their feet are buried. . . . Sinking to the west from our feet the gentle golden-green *glacis* sloped away, flanked by rolling hills covered with a fresh vernal carpet of grass, and relieved by scattered groves of dark oak-trees. Upon the distant valley were checkered fields of grass and grain just tinged with the first ripening yellow. The bounding Coast Ranges lay in the cool shadow of a bank of mist which drifted in from the Pacific, covering their heights. Flocks of bright clouds floated across the sky, whose blue was palpitating with light, and seemed to rise with infinite perspective. Tranquillity, abundance, the slow, beautiful unfolding of plant life, dark shadowed spots to rest our tired eyes upon, the shade of giant oaks to lie down under, while listening to brooks, contralto larks, and the soft distant lowing of cattle."[9]

Back in San Francisco, King spent the month of May 1866 working up his notes on the Arizona work and Gardner prepared the map. King decided to accept Whitney's offer of a position as assistant geologist in the California Geological Survey. After preparing for a summer campaign in the field, he left for the central Sierra, crossing the Coast Range over Pacheco Pass, and found the Central Valley to be much more lush than it had been during the terrible drought of two years before. When at Mariposa, he climbed Mount Bullion again to enjoy the view of the High Sierra, now much more meaningful after having trod on some of its higher summits. Descending a ridge, he arrived in camp and: "Evening and supper were at hand, Hoover [the cook] having achieved a repast of rabbit-pie, with salad from the Italian garden near at hand. It added no little to my peace that two obese squaws from the neighboring rancheria had come and squatted in silence on either side of our camp-fire, adding their statuesque sobriety and fire-flushed bronze to the dusky druidical scene."[10]

FIGURE 6.8.   An early-morning view of Mount Clark, east of Yosemite Valley. King and Cotter made an attempt on the peak in the fall of 1864, but were turned back by stormy weather. In June 1866 King and Gardner made the first ascent of the mountain up the thin blade-like south ridge, which drops off sheer on both sides. Near the summit the ridge is broken by a chasm that can be crossed only by a frightening leap to a perch with unstable footing. (Photograph by the author)

Gardner and Whitney joined him at Clark's Station, and they spent a week in the Yosemite region reviewing the previous work. But King had not forgotten the aborted attempt on Mt. Clark and yearned to try it again. For triangulation purposes it did occupy a critical position. The peak is of singular shape. When viewed from either north or south, it appears as a sharp, frightfully thin blade, with sheer walls on east and west. Shouldering their backpacks, Gardner and King headed up toward the base of the mountain. Gardner carried a Temple transit with tripod for triangulation, a blanket, and a tin cup. King packed his barometer, blanket, field glasses, compass, level, and food for two. Whitney remained at Clark's Station.

They bivouacked at the base of the south ridge at the same camp which Cotter and King had used in the storm two years earlier. The pair awoke early for a breakfast of bacon and coffee, and began climbing the bare rock of the ridge. As they mounted higher on the blade-like eminence, it fell away to right and left in sheer faces, forcing them to remain on the narrow crest. Before long the exposure was palpably frightening, for one could look down from dizzying heights thousands of feet to a partly frozen lake on the east side and to broken debris and rock on the west. In places, large spires surmounted the crest, and the men were repeatedly forced to climb out on the east face and work up narrow cracks to regain the crest beyond the pinnacles. King recalled, "At last we struggled up to what we had all along believed [to be] the summit, and found ourselves only on a minor turret, the great needle still a hundred feet above. From rock to rock and crevice to crevice we made our way up a fractured edge until within fifty feet of the top, and here its sharp angle rose smooth and vertical, the eastern precipice carved in a flat face upon the one side, the western broken by a smoothly curved recess like the corner of a room. No human being could scale the edge. . . . About seven feet across the open head of a cul-de-sac (a mere recess in the west face) was a vertical crack riven into the granite not more than three feet wide, but as much as eight feet deep; in it were wedged a few loose boulders; below it opened out into space. At the head of this crack a rough crevice led up to the summit. Summoning nerve, I knew I could make the leap, but the life and death question was whether the debris would give way under my weight, and leave me struggling in the smooth recess, sure to fall and be dashed to atoms. There was no discussion, but, planting my foot on the brink, I sprang, my side brushing the rough projecting crag. While in the air I looked down, and a picture stamped itself on my brain never to be forgotten. The debris crumbled and moved. I clutched both sides of the cleft, relieving all possible weight from my feet. The rocks wedged themselves again, and I was safe."[11]

Gardner passed the instruments and knapsack across the chasm, and then made the leap while King watched, "I shall never forget the look in his eye as he caught a glimpse of the abyss in his leap. It gave me such a chill as no amount of danger nor even death coming to myself could ever give."[12]

From the crack they had leapt into, it was only a short scramble to the top, where they marveled at the wild alpine prospect laid out before them, knowing that they were the first ever to have this view. Gardner set up the transit on the summit block, 11,600 feet in elevation, and carefully turned angles to the array of peaks surrounding them. King sat in a notch below, reading the barometer and taking notes. Whitney later wrote that, "Mr. King, who, with Mr. Gardner made the ascent of the peak, says that its summit is so slender that when on top of it they seemed to be suspended in the air."[13] After four hours on the summit they descended the crack to where it fell off into space and faced the leap again. This time, however, it was not so threatening, for they could carefully adjust their footing on the loose stones before the leap, knowing that they would land on solid massive granite. All went well, and a rapid descent down the mountain brought them to camp before dark.

Next, they explored the region of the Clark Range, where King climbed Black Mountain, looked into the upper San Joaquin Basin, and saw the dark-colored Mt. Ritter and the chain of sharp needles of metamorphic rock to its south, which he named the Minarets. In August they entered the Ritter country and attempted to climb Mt. Ritter from the west, just as a thunderstorm threatened. The storm broke when they were a scant 400 feet from the summit, and they were forced to turn back. (It would be ten years before John Muir would make the first ascent of this mountain.) With supplies depleted, they returned to Clark's Station, reprovisioned, and moved on to the country north of the Merced River, into the upper drainage of the Tuolumne River, and on to Soda Springs. Here King went down the river, but a great waterfall brought his exploration to a halt, and he missed the mighty Yosemite-like glaciated canyon of the Tuolumne containing Hetch Hetchy Valley, today the repository of much of the water supplying the San Francisco area.

King and Gardner next turned to the main Sierra Crest east of Tuolumne Meadows and climbed Mt. Dana, 13,050 feet high. They explored along the crest, and seven miles north attempted to make the first ascent of another bold mountain peak, but were forced to take refuge in a crack in the rock during a gale, and spent a cold night in the open. The next day they climbed to the summit and King wrote: " . . . that firm peak with titan strength and brow so square and solid, it seems altogether natural we should have named it for California's statesman, John Conness."[14]

Gardner noted in later years that when he and King were working on the Sierra Crest east of Yosemite Valley they discussed using the latest methods of topographic mapping to underpin a geological survey of the Great Basin to the east, a vast region then largely unknown. He stated, "Sitting on the high peaks of the Sierra, overlooking the deserts and ranges of Nevada to the eastward, we worked out the general outlines of the 40th parallel survey work. It was the natural outgrowth of our journey across the plains, our experience on the California Survey, and our exploration of Arizona, coupled with King's great aggressive energy and consciousness of power to persuade men to do the thing that he thought ought to be done."[15]

They now quit the high country and rode over Mono Pass to magical Mono Lake and recrossed the Sierra at Sonora Pass. Upon returning to San Francisco, King received a telegram from his mother, informing him that her husband, George Howland, had died of brain fever. King, now aware that his mother and her children were solely dependent on him, decided to return to New York as soon as possible.

Both Clarence King and James Gardner resigned their positions with the California Geological Survey and laid out their plan to begin a new mapping program across Nevada and the Rocky Mountains. Whitney tried to entice them to stay with his survey, but when he saw their firm resolve to move on, he endorsed the project, and notified Senator Conness of King's intentions.

Shortly thereafter, late in 1866, King and Gardner sailed from San Francisco, bound for the East Coast via the isthmus. They had just completed an extraordinary three-year postgraduate school in science. Two of their tutors, former professors Whitney and Brewer, were graduates of the most prestigious colleges in the country that offered courses in science, Harvard and Yale, and both had attended European academies as well. The third, Charles Hoffmann, was one of the most accomplished German-trained cartographers in the country. King and Gardner, so steeped in seizing opportunity, were about to seize another.

CHAPTER SEVEN

FEVER ON THE DESERT

Full many a flower is born to blush unseen,
And waste its sweetness on the desert air.
—*Thomas Gray, "Elegy Written in a Country Church-yard"*

When King and Gardner arrived in New York early in January 1867, King found that an examination of his stepfather's business affairs after his death had revealed complete disarray. Little was left of his assets, and King at the age of 24 would now assume the sole support of his mother, her two young children, other family members, and servants. This was a heavy burden that plagued him the rest of his life.

Gardner, meanwhile, worked busily on the Yosemite map and was asked to present an evening address on February 20 before the Connecticut Academy of Science, concerning his work in Arizona. Though it was his first formal public performance, he chose to take a positive view and treat it as an experiment.[1] The talk was well received, and afterward Yale Professor Daniel Gilman asked him to give his class a lecture on the mountains of western America.

King, assessing his new responsibilities, was debating with himself about marshaling support in Washington for the new survey he contemplated along the railroad route from the Sierra Nevada east through the Rocky Mountains. He was certain that he and Gardner were well qualified to head such a program of exploration. They were graduates of Yale and Rensselaer, among the most prestigious scientific and engineering colleges in the nation. They had four years experience in geologic and topographic surveys in the west, much of it in previously uncharted high country, with members of the California Geological Survey, including Whitney, Brewer, Ashburner, and Hoffmann. The results of major parts of their work were included in Whitney's volume *Geology* published in 1865. They had made the first detailed map of Yosemite Valley, and Gardner was in charge of preparing the map for publication. In addition, King had received from Colonel Robert Williamson, who had led the Army-sponsored Railroad Surveys of 1853–54, a letter endorsing his survey program,[2] and Professor Whitney had written California Senator John Conness on his behalf.

King was well aware of another factor in his favor. He had many friends in the academic community, including much of the faculty at Yale, most significantly William Brewer, James Dana, and William Whitney, brother of Josiah and Professor of Language. King also had the foresight to have named a peak honoring Colonel Williamson, and another to honor Senator Conness. It is not surprising that these two supported his enterprise, and who knows how many others did so in anticipation of a like honor.

By that time controversy had begun to boil between the academic and military communities, concerning the role that civilian scientists should take in upcoming surveys of the newly acquired lands, which were being rapidly settled. Traditionally, the military had taken the lead in such surveys, including the celebrated Lewis and Clark Expedition (1803–06) and John C. Fremont's well-known explorations (1841–45). Charles Darwin, it was argued, had sailed on a British naval vessel, the *Beagle*, under the command of Lieutenant Robert Fitzroy (1831–36), and James Dana had sailed on one of several U.S. Navy vessels participating in the United States Exploring Expedition (1838–1842) under the command of Lieutenant Charles Wilkes. Outstanding science was accomplished on these expeditions, usually by the civilian scientists, but in the realms of transport and security they were totally dependent on the military.

The U.S. Army expected to continue to sponsor and manage these territorial surveys. Many areas were deemed dangerous because of hostile Indians, and often an armed force of some size was necessary to ensure safety. Even with these precautions, several civilian scientists had been killed by the Indians. The system of Army forts scattered over the great expanses of essentially uninhabited country provided security, supplies, and communication in time of need, and the military maintained the types of transport necessary to move people and gear from one place to another.

Most agreed, however, that good science required professional scientists—men who were educated at academic institutions, not the military academies. As knowledge advanced, many specialties were required, including topography and geology, but also botany, zoology, paleontology, anthropology, linguistics, and astronomy. These were fields in which the military generally had little expertise. The compilation, digestion, and publication of the voluminous data collected on these expeditions was time-consuming and best done in an academic setting, and with the collaboration of other scientists, including those from foreign institutions. Only in such an environment could independent and innovative thinking thrive. These factors raised the question of who should have managerial control over the surveys, the military officers or the civilian scientists.

King's concerns about funding possibilities for the western survey he had in mind were dispelled when he visited Yale and met with William Brewer, now Professor of Agriculture. Brewer was enthusiastic and firmly supportive of the project, and immediately wrote Edwin Stanton, Secretary of War, with a strong endorsement for the proposed survey. This vast tract of territory, he said, had been largely disregarded during the exploration of the West. Only the most basic reconnaissance mapping existed. It was timely, indeed essential, to prepare a continuous geologic section across the region, in part to explore the extent and quality of the region's mineral deposits, but also to lay out alternative routes of travel and present all manner of modern scientific information on a series of first-class topographic maps.

King lost no time in traveling to Washington to present his proposal to Mr. Stanton. He mentioned Brewer's letter and spelled out his plans for the project. The work would extend from the Sierra Nevada to the eastern Rocky Mountain Front, a distance of 800 miles, and would include a swath a hundred miles wide bracketing the existing wagon road and the proposed route of the continental railroad, both of which roughly followed the 40th parallel of latitude. The survey would not only delineate the geography of the terrain, of primary military importance in the campaigns against hostile Indians, but it would also provide a basis for the settlement and mineral exploration of the region, which would surely burgeon once the railroad was built. Stanton was interested, and referred the matter to General Andrew Humphreys, a skilled surveyor who had managed the Pacific Railroad Surveys, including those conducted by Colonel Williamson, and who now commanded the Army Corps of Engineers. Humphreys responded favorably. Little did the General realize at that time that by the appointment and funding of a civilian to carry out geologic and geographic surveys in the West, he was spelling disaster for his own establishment. The organization of King's survey was the beginning of the end for military control of western mapping.

Whitney was upset that King would propose working east of the Sierra in Nevada in an area where he had some interest and had already done some work. However, he did write a letter of support for King to Spencer Baird of the Smithsonian Institution: "Allow me to introduce Mr. Clarence King, for some time one of my assistants on our Survey and a gentleman whose acquaintance I feel sure that you will be pleased to make. If you can aid him in any way in getting up geological and topographical work in the Far West I am sure that you will be glad to do so. I cordially recommend him to your good offices."[3] Endorsements for the survey were received from Baird and Williamson.

Senator Conness, instrumental in the establishment of Yosemite State Park, became a strong supporter of King's project and convinced several of his colleagues in Congress of its potential, and was able to attach its funding to the pending appropriations bill. Gardner wrote to his mother, "I have been waiting my letter till I could hear from Washington as to the fate of our bill. I have every reason to believe from the newspaper reports that it passed on Sunday night. There are still several slips possible between us and our object yet; but Clare has done nobly to work it through Congress."[4]

Indeed, the bill passed, and the *United States Geological Exploration of the Fortieth Parallel* was created and funded March 2, 1867. It marked the first time that the Congress had funded a survey in which geology would be the principal activity. King was appointed U.S. Geologist in Charge, serving under the Chief of Army Engineers, General Humphreys, and was authorized to hire two assistants in geology, two in topography, and one each in botany, zoology, and photography. In the field he would draw a per diem allowance for all expenses, and his salary was set at $250 a month.[5] His financial worries were now over; sufficient resources would be available for Florence Howland's needs.[6] To the surprise of many, the appointment placed all of the operations of the survey in the hands of a civilian. In the field, a military escort of 15 men would accompany the survey.

King accepted the appointment and wrote General Humphreys that he planned to depart for San Francisco by May 1, 1867. With the financial support of some wealthy friends, he prepared the required $20,000 bond that was necessary for a government official entrusted with public monies.[7] The selection of an able group of scientists was made in consultation with Gardner. For the first assistant in geology he hired James D. Hague, Professor of Mining Geology at the Boston Institute of Technology (later known as the Massachusetts Institute of Technology), who had been recommended by Professor Dana. James Hague, a graduate of Harvard, had studied abroad at the Freiberg Academy of Mines and at Göttingen, Germany. He had previously been superintendent of the Albany and Boston Copper Mine in Michigan. His brother, Arnold Hague, a classmate of King's at the Sheffield Scientific School, was chosen as second assistant in geology. He, like his brother, had studied abroad at Freiberg and Göttingen, and also at Heidelberg. Arnold Hague strongly endorsed the hiring of Samuel F. Emmons, who graduated from Harvard in 1861. Emmons had also

studied in Europe, two years at the Paris Ecole des Mines and two years at the
Freiberg Academy. Although King had no authorization to take on a third assistant in
geology, Emmons was so attracted to the program that he offered to work without
pay, which was acceptable to King (and how King and Gardner had themselves begun
their careers). Gardner, for his part, was designated first assistant in topography and
the second in command of the survey.

On April 28 the faculty of the Yale Scientific School gave a farewell dinner for several of the members of the new Fortieth Parallel Survey on the eve of their departure
from New Haven. The upcoming expedition was regarded as one of the most important scientific projects ever supported by the United States Government. King was
suffering from a severe cold, could not attend, and Gardner became the spokesman
for the group. About 30 people attended, including several professors, six members of
the survey staff, Yale president Woolsey, Governor Hawley of Connecticut, and other
dignitaries. Before dinner the group assembled in the parlor, where a large map of the
western U.S. had been pinned to the wall. Gardner described the history of the project, the area to be studied, the nature of the terrain, and the strategy to be used in investigating such a vast and remote region.

With King still ill, and in the care of his mother, Mrs. Howland, Gardner was saddled with preparations for the survey. As the time for departure approached, King was
still unable to make any of the travel arrangements. Gardner wrote, "I could not get
onto the steamer till fifteen minutes before she sailed; and then I left many things un-
done. I had calculated that I should have just time enough to finish up my affairs in
New York, when Clare's illness at this critical juncture threw all his work on me, increasing mine more than tenfold. I only barely succeeded in getting the party off by
neglecting all my own personal matters."[8]

The first survey group embarked at New York bound for San Francisco on May 1,
1867. They would sail south through the Caribbean, cross the isthmus by rail, and
meet another sailing vessel that would take them on to the Golden Gate. Thereafter,
the plan was to travel east from San Francisco over the Sierra Nevada to Nevada, and
there begin the survey of that broad swath embracing the 40th parallel of latitude.

Gardner sailed with the first group, and once at sea there was time to relax and
enjoy the company of new friends and the mild climate of the Caribbean. He noticed
that the sea voyage to California was always easier than the trip back to the East Coast,
because the confined shipboard life contrasted with the easy sedentary eastern existence so much less than with the strenuous, free life of the western fieldwork.

King, though still weak from fever, left ten days later with a second group on the
steamer *Henry Chauncey*, the same sidewheeler he had taken west in 1865. By leaving

in the second group he knew he would have more time to recover his health and prepare his plan of operations. He shared a cabin on the hurricane deck with Henry Custer, a Swiss who had surveyed with the Northwest Boundary Commission and was the second assistant in topographic mapping for the new expedition. Another cabin was occupied by Timothy O'Sullivan (photographer), Robert Ridgeway (zoologist), and William Bailey (botanist). O'Sullivan had worked with Mathew Brady in photographing some of the major battles of the Civil War. Some found his habit of retelling war stories tedious, but he proved to be an outstanding scientific photographer who would contribute much to the reports of the survey. Ridgeway was a boy of 17 with an interest in hunting and collecting. He had undergone a few months of training in the preparation of specimens with Professor Baird at the Smithsonian Museum. The distinguished Harvard Professor Asa Gray sponsored Bailey, son of a biology professor and a graduate of Brown University.

The seas were calm as the *Henry Chauncey* sailed past the Bahamas, Cuba, Santo Domingo, and Navassar, that last an island where guano was actively mined. On May 11, they arrived at the port of Aspinwall, Panama, which Bailey described as "a most forsaken hole . . . where the houses can hardly stand alone and pigs, carrion fowl and offal surround them."[9] About 10 A.M. they boarded the westbound train but were delayed repeatedly as preparations for departure were made. A young mother with a babe in arms, accompanied by a small child, arrived late and was in the process of boarding when her little boy ran down the station platform. She quickly handed her baby to King to hold while she ran to fetch the boy. At that instant the train started with a clatter, and pulled out of the station, leaving mother and son wailing on the platform.

King had no choice but to care for the infant, and assumed that the mother would take the next possible train, allowing them to meet on the Pacific side. Surprisingly, he was unable to find any fellow passenger who was willing to help with the baby. He became doubly worried when he recalled that the mother had told him she was to meet a southbound steamer for Peru. As Gardner later reported, "It remained therefore for King, while at Panama, to find the ways and means of supplying the crying needs of the baby, who by this time was in want of everything a baby ever does want."[10] When they arrived in Panama, King—with the baby in one hand and an umbrella for shade in the other—began to walk the streets, looking for a residence giving some hint that small children were part of the household. He found a cabin where a young English-speaking woman was nursing an infant, and when his story had been told and a multitude had gathered, he found the help he sought. While waiting for the next train to arrive, he found pleasure in talking to this young woman and her friends, while she provided the help that the infant needed. King rewarded the woman for her services, and found upon the arrival of the next train that the anxious mother indeed was aboard, thus giving to this singular event a happy ending. Little did he know that several years later he would have a second encounter with his emergency wet nurse.

The botanist, William Bailey, was delighted with the abundant and varied plant life while crossing the isthmus. He wrote, "I saw the most gorgeous vegetation which I have ever yet beheld. The trees were hung down with vines and creepers, and huge palms, bamboos and an infinite number of other plants were matted together. The mimosas were very beautiful. It is winter here and there were not as many flowers as at other times—but still there were many and gorgeous. Several strange things were brought me by the passengers, who would dive into the woods at the stations and come back with plants, nuts, and lizards."[11]

Northbound passengers were taken by tugboat out to the steamer *Constitution*, at

FIGURE 7.1.   The wooden, side-wheel steamship *Constitution*, a 342-foot, 3,300-ton ship driven by 40-foot paddle wheels. The walking beam transfers power from a giant steam cylinder 8-3/4 feet in diameter with a 12-foot stroke to the side wheels. Clarence King, with photographer T. O'Sullivan, zoologist R. Ridgway, botanist W. Bailey, and topographer H. Custer, crossed Panama by rail and then voyaged on this ship 3,500 miles north in the Pacific to arrive in San Francisco June 3, 1867. (The Mariner's Museum, Newport News, Va.)

anchor in the Gulf of Panama. Bailey wrote, "The Constitution is an immense vessel with a promenade deck all around it—which is gay on moonlight evenings. . . . Gorgeous butterflies, humming birds, and dragon flies are constantly wafted out to the vessel."[12] On the voyage up the coast they stopped and let off passengers at Acapulco and at Cabo San Lucas on the southern tip of Baha California. Later Bailey remembered that while on the ship "One of our greatest sources of amusement was to gather around Clarence King and listen to his innumerable stories. . . . For him to start a story was but a signal for a crowd to gather. Our own little group became secondary to a large audience embracing all sorts and conditions of men. . . . To know King at his best one had to hear his voice, and above all his musical infectious laugh."[13]

When the ship arrived at San Francisco on June 3, the men who had not been in the city before were instantly impressed, and Bailey was " . . . astonished at the vast size and exceeding elegance of the hotels and the busy hum of this *very* large city. It is the size of Boston—and has horse cars in all the streets—and the general aspect of one of our larger eastern cities."[14]

King soon made contact with Gardner, who was registered at the Occidental Hotel, and the two were privileged to set up a temporary office at the headquarters of Colonel Robert Williamson, who had conducted some of the early railroad surveys in California. Equipment was drawn from the quartermaster, and camp helpers were hired—among them Dick Cotter, who had just returned from a trying expedition to Alaska. He had worked with a party exploring possible telegraph routes from Alaska to Siberia, so as to establish intercontinental communication via an undersea cable across Bering Strait.

King met with Whitney at the offices of the California Geological Survey and found Whitney to be a bit testy over King's delay in completing his reports from the previous summer's work and Gardner's delay in preparing the central Sierra map. Understandably, he felt some resentment over King's success with Congress in pushing through the conception and funding of the Fortieth Parallel Survey. Whitney had dreamed of conducting his own geologic survey across the Great Basin and Rocky Mountains when the California work was completed. He believed that King had usurped his plan, but King defended his action by maintaining that the idea had come to him in 1863 while riding across the continent on his first trip west, a trip that Whitney had never experienced.[15]

Josiah Whitney's brother, William, professor at Yale, tried to defuse a latent discord between the two men by writing his brother and posting the letter on the same steamer that King left on from New York: "His [King's] plans and his party are tho[ugh]t very well indeed of here, and everyone has hope and confidence that he will

FIGURE 7.2. James Gardner (left) and Clarence King (middle) took on Richard Cotter (right), the trusted packer of the Sierra Nevada expedition, to work with them on the Fortieth Parallel Survey. Their first major camp was on the plain near Sacramento, California, where they spent a month organizing supplies and equipment and becoming familiar with their instruments and livestock. (Photograph by Timothy O'Sullivan, summer 1867; courtesy of the Bancroft Library, University of California, Berkeley)

make a great thing of his expedition. It seems to me that considering his youth, he has done not a little already, in the way of exploration and observation, and I should think his talent well suited to the management of such a party as he will have in hand. He has certainly exhibited a very extraordinary capacity as a lobbyist. His allegiance to you is very marked; he always speaks of you with the warmest affection and highest admiration. I must sincerely hope that the two surveyors are going to work fraternally, helping one another."[16]

The main body of the group traveled by the side-wheel river steamer *Yosemite* to Sacramento, where they set up camp a half-mile from the capitol. Here they assembled the equipment, provisions, and animals for the trek over the mountains to begin the Nevada fieldwork. The entire month of June was spent in preparation, with Gardner in charge, and he felt that if it were to be done again, he wouldn't know how to get the organization pulled together any quicker.

Much of the effort was devoted to acquiring the livestock needed for riding and pulling wagons. The animals were branded with two crossed hammers, the seal of the survey. The scientists who had not previously ridden much had nonetheless to select a mount and become accustomed to it. Bailey wrote that "At present my tail is raw and discharging water from the effects of a ride I took yesterday. King says for my comfort that there is no bum on earth but that will get hardened to it. My condition is a source of much amusement to the rest of the fellows who have all in their day been through a similar mill. I have a white mare, a gentle creature, to whom I can always go up even in the pasture, without corralling her."[17]

FIGURE 7.3.   Construction of the Central Pacific Railroad was under way when the Fortieth Parallel party crossed the Sierra in 1867. Chinese immigrants using horse-drawn equipment graded the roadbed and constructed tunnels to complete this monumental enterprise. This giant earth fill on the west slope of the Sierra Nevada was under construction in the mid-1860s 35 miles west of the crest at Donner Pass. (Lawrence and Houseworth Collection, The Society of California Pioneers)

The corps lived in wall tents that were pitched on the Sacramento Plain. Each housed two to four men sleeping on wooden bunks, under which clothing and gear were stored. The tents had a porch-like canvas fly at the entrance to provide shade in the desert heat, and a washstand and saddle rack were part of the equipment at each tent door. Cooking for the camp was done over a fire made in a trench, with iron bars to support the cook pots. Bread was baked in iron Dutch ovens placed on the coals.

During this period of preparation a group of four scientists, including Bailey, Emmons, and O'Sullivan, took the train up to the railroad terminus at 6,000 feet, beyond which active construction was under way. Bailey writes that "I went into the new tunnels beyond Cisco and saw the Chinamen at work. The mule teams for Virginia City were a peculiar feature. Some of them have twelve or more mules and some three or four carts fastened together. One man appeared to guide all the mules. The language of these drivers is vociferous and sweary. Their expressive 'Git' can be heard in every direction. It is wonderful what a talismanic power this expression has in California. The slang here is rich anyway—being a mixture of Yankee and Spanish with a dash from all other nations."[18]

The mountain of equipment, including camp and cooking gear, duffel, and provisions, was sorted and arranged so that it could be packed in two heavy wagons carrying 3,000 pounds of gear apiece. The instruments were carried in a smaller thoroughbrace wagon, a type of wagon suspended by leather strapping, which helped to cushion the ride. Each wagon was pulled by four mules, and a fifth, extra mule was led from the tailgate.

On July 3, 1867, they broke camp and headed up toward Donner Pass on the road across the Sierra Nevada. Gardner led the main group, because King had to return to San Francisco for last-minute business matters. Railroad building was under way on the transcontinental route over the Sierra, and the track had already reached 40 miles east of Sacramento to Cisco, at 6,000 feet above sea level. Much of the baggage went by rail to Cisco, and the main party of ten men on horseback, followed by three wagons, took the road that paralleled the railroad. They traveled 18 miles the first day with little incident, although one scientist was thrown twice from his mule and chased it three miles before it was caught.[19] The cooks, sad to say, had failed to pack the lunch supplies at places easily accessible in the wagons. Since breakfast had been served at 5 A.M., the grumbling for food forced a lunch stop at 4 P.M., just one hour before dinner.

Near the village of Alta, where they stopped, the peculiar nature of their caravan brought out curious townspeople who thought that a circus had come to town. Here a young black man, Jim Marryatt, who supplied the party with waterfowl, joined them and showed great interest in the expedition and in the new country they would be ex-

FIGURE 7.4. Cisco, California, at the eastern railroad terminus in 1867. At this major transfer point, at mid-elevation on the west slope of the Sierra Nevada, eastbound passengers and freight were switched from the train to horse-drawn stages and wagons for the pull over the Sierra, a route used at the time primarily to the Comstock mines in Nevada. For the cross-country travelers a 1,000-mile gap still lay between the advancing ends of the transcontinental railroad. (Lawrence and Houseworth Collection, The Society of California Pioneers)

ploring. Gardner hired him as cook's mate and he stayed with the survey, proving to be a dependable camp helper. He had been born in Jamaica, had sailed over much of the world as a cabin boy, and eventually had ended up in Alta as a cook, having lost track of his family and believing that his mother was probably dead. King took a great interest in Jim, who later became an excellent camp cook and King's valet. (A few years later, King would discover that he had previously met Jim's mother.)

At the Cisco terminus, they loaded the wagons with the baggage that had arrived by train and continued the remaining 14 miles to the summit at Donner Pass. Here the road was jammed with huge freight wagons carrying loads of three to six tons and drawn by teams of eight to ten mules. These supplies, loaded at the Cisco depot, were bound for locations over the mountains, much of them going to the Comstock Lode in Nevada.

Construction work on the Central Pacific Railroad over the summit was also going forward actively, with the hope of finishing within the month. The laborers, many of them Chinese, were blasting deep cuts in the granite bedrock, filling depressions with immense piles of rubble, and constructing trestle bridges over the gorges. Sev-

FIGURE 7.5.   Snowshoeing (skiing) in the high Sierra near Donner Pass. Railroad engineers whom Gardner had met at the summit region had been making use of such Norwegian conveyances during the winter, both uphill and down. Gardner became quite expert with them during the winter of 1867–68 near Virginia City, when exceptional snows blanketed the Virginia Range. (Lawrence and Houseworth collection, The Society of California Pioneers)

eral tunnels had been completed, and blasting of the 1,700–foot-long summit tunnel was under way.

At camp near the summit, Gardner met some of the railroad engineers. They said that snow the previous winter was up to 16 feet deep, and was double that depth in a really heavy snow year. Avalanches were therefore common, and for that reason much of the track on the sidehill near the summit was covered by a unique system of snow sheds. For cross-country travel in the winter the engineers used snowshoes ten or twelve feet long made, as Gardner wrote, "in the Norwegian fashion—a long narrow board turned up at the end."[20]

The party crossed the Sierra at 7,200 feet, and after a steep descent skirted Donner Lake, where only 20 years before a party of pioneers, snowbound for the winter and reduced to starvation, turned to cannibalism. The next 25 miles of road passed down the canyon of the Truckee River, a robust mountain stream draining from Lake Tahoe. This road was soon to be the next stage for the railroad builders. It would be a difficult route and would require several bridges, but nothing could equal the formidable task of pushing the railway over the mountain crest.

Beyond the canyon, the pine-covered hills gave way to sagebrush desert and the road passed into Nevada, established as the 36th state three years earlier, in 1864. Here, in the rain shadow of the great mountain range, the only greenery was along the Truckee River. The men made camp at Hunter's Station, a midway stage stop where six-horse coaches traveling between Virginia City to the east and Cisco to the west stopped to change horses. In the evening, for a short time, three of these coaches came from each direction, all to get a change of fresh horses. Gardner described the

FIGURE 7.6. Map of the area that embraces the five mapped quadrangles of the U.S. Geological Exploration of the Fortieth Parallel that are aligned along the railroad route in Nevada, Utah, Colorado, and Wyoming. The 100- by 165-mile quadrangles are numbered in Roman numerals from east to west, but they were mapped from west to east. The transcontinental railroad was not yet completed when the survey began in 1867. The three eastern quadrangles do not include the 40th parallel (white dashed line), owing to the northeastern route of the railroad. (After King, 1876)

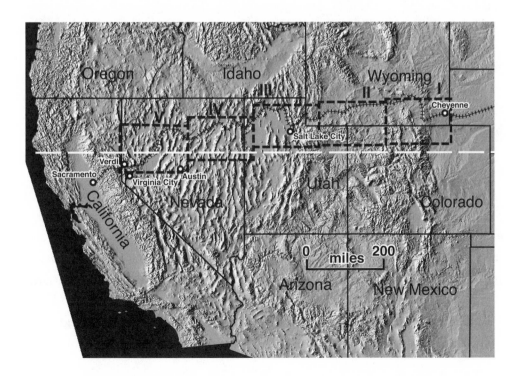

F I G U R E 7.7.   Camp of the party of the Fortieth Parallel Survey on the Truckee River near Wadsworth, Nevada. The river continues 20 miles north of Wadsworth to Pyramid Lake. Bluffs in the background are a sequence of uplifted late Tertiary lake beds. (Photograph by Timothy O'Sullivan, 1867; Hague and Emmons, 1877)

action: "As they changed horses thirty six were taken out and the same number put in, so that there were seventy-two stage horses there at one time. There were about ninety passengers. It was a very lively scene."[21] With the advent of the railroad, this horse-based transportation system would soon wind down.

The first working camp was at Glendale, a village of a dozen houses at a green area where at high water the Truckee River spreads out over a considerable area. (It would not be long before the city of Reno would grow near this place.) The survey party camped there July 15–22, 1867, investigating the surrounding countryside. Operations were hindered because necessary items of equipment were missing and money was short, a draft for which had been lost in the mail. King had to scrape and pinch and dip into his own purse to sustain the party during this difficult time. Gardner supervised the day-to-day operations, and confided that he gets "along pretty well with the party but it is so large and so new that it requires very careful management to reconcile the discordant elements. . . . Fifteen men from all grades of society; from all parts of the Union; of every age and disposition; are not easily made into a homogeneous party at first. But I think we made a decided advance."[22]

It was here that mosquitoes first began to bedevil the party, and there was no escape from them. Even at night the insects bit the men through their blankets. From this camp King, Gardner, and James Hague climbed Peavine Mountain, an isolated peak some five miles north of Glendale that afforded excellent views not only west to the Sierra, but also to several ranges to the east and south. The pale-blue waters of Pyramid and Winnemucca Lakes were visible to the northeast. Here they established their first geodetic station, so as to provide a basis for the topographic mapping to come. For this first season King hoped to map a swath of territory 100 miles wide, from the east base of the Sierra 150 miles to the east toward the middle of Nevada. Despite their late start he knew it was imperative that they make a good showing of results this first summer, thus providing a basis for support in future seasons. A fundamental strategy of the exploration was that high-quality topographic mapping, under the supervision of Gardner, would be made of all the territory explored, so as to serve as a base for the other studies, primarily those focusing on geology. The photographer, Timothy O'Sullivan, also began extensive work with his camera. In later years William Brewer noted that, "King was the first to carry out these ideas [photographic documentation] on a grand scale; and now the camera is an indispensable part of the apparatus of field-work in such surveys."[23]

The survey then moved east down the Truckee River to a point near where the river makes a sharp bend (near the present site of Wadsworth) and flows north toward Pyramid Lake. This lake, like the other saline lakes in the Great Basin, fills a depression with no outlet. Evaporation of the ponded water balances the river inflow, maintaining a relatively constant lake level.

Exploration soon revealed that Pyramid Lake, Carson and Humboldt Sinks, Winnemucca Lake, and Walker Lake are all remnants of a single, much larger and deeper lake (that existed during the Ice Age as recently as 18,000 years ago). Above the surface of these lakes, dramatically exposed in the facing mountains, are well-preserved terraces that proved to be ancient shorelines carved by the restless waters of this former giant lake. The highest lake level was 4,388 feet above sea level, some 500 feet above the level of Pyramid Lake. King named this great western Nevada prehistoric lake *Lake Lahontan*, to honor the noted French explorer of the Great Lakes region.[24] The Baron Louis de La Hontan is remembered for his memoirs, published in France, which provided fascinating descriptions of life in the New World and the "American Wilderness." A similar, even larger prehistoric lake, *Lake Bonneville*, of which Great Salt Lake in Utah is the remnant, covered a huge area in eastern Nevada and western

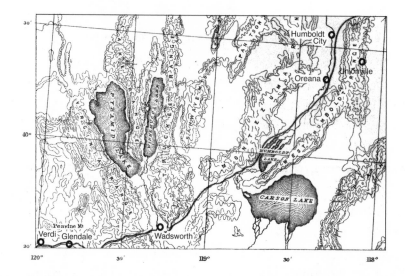

FIGURE 7.8.   Map of west-central Nevada showing the area of the principal camps of
the Fortieth Parallel Survey during the first field season (1867). Carson Lake and
Winnemucca Lake have both since evaporated because of their shallowness, and because of
water diversion and drier weather since the time this map was made. The present city of
Reno is near Glendale. Map includes an area 105 miles wide. (King, 1868)

Utah. It was named by Karl Gilbert—a geologist with the Wheeler Survey—to honor
Captain G. L. E. Bonneville, who saw Great Salt Lake in 1833, 14 years before Brigham
Young led the Mormons to the region.[25]

　　At this time an escort of twenty cavalrymen from Fort Churchill near Virginia
City, under the command of a sergeant, joined the survey. Fifteen pack mules, as well
as a wagon drawn by six mules, carried their supplies and provisions. These soldiers
were a rough bunch who at times seemed more troublesome than useful, considering
their drunkenness, carousing, and disloyalty. King, however, had not forgotten the
near-fatal encounter with the Apaches in Arizona, and bore the inconvenience in order to maintain the security they provided.

　　At the Big Bend of the Truckee River, King and Gardner occupied a tent together.
It contained a large writing table and folding chairs. Personal baggage and boxes of
papers and books were heaped on the ground, and instruments and firearms were
close at hand. Following the custom of the California Geological Survey, they would
usually sleep outside on the ground behind the tent, where they could enjoy the fresh
air and stars. On work trips away from the main camp, some lasting two weeks, tents
were not used, and camp was made where the blankets were unrolled.

　　From the Big Bend Camp, investigators fanned out to examine the nearby terrain. Zoologist Ridgeway was active, shooting and collecting birds and small animals. Botanist Bailey had by then collected more than 500 plant specimens. He also collected samples from the ancient, white lakebeds near camp, which contained diatomaceous earth. Diatoms are single-celled plants that produce a tiny, lacelike skeleton of almost pure silica, their classification requiring microscopic study. He sent several samples of the diatomite to his brother, a professor in Nova Scotia, who was an expert on such fossils and would make a microscopic examination. Bailey also busied himself with boiling down water samples of measured volume, from the lakes and springs. The resultant solid matter was carefully packed away for later

FIGURE 7.9.   The boat *Nettie* drawn up on the shore of Pyramid Lake in the summer of 1867. The boat made the first trip down the Truckee River, from Glendale to the lake. It capsized upstream from the camp at Wadsworth, and clothes, pistols, and other equipment were lost. Later, a party including James Hague, Samuel Emmons, Timothy O'Sullivan, and Robert Ridgeway brought the boat down to the lake. The flag flying by the boat records an early use of crossed hammers as the survey emblem, but earlier survey horses and mules were branded with the symbol at the Sacramento camp. The crossed pick and hammer was later adopted as the official symbol and flag of the U.S. Geological Survey. (Photograph by Timothy O'Sullivan; National Archives and Records Service)

chemical analysis. It was in this camp, however, where Bailey first began suffering from attacks of fever, that alternated with the shakes and aching of the joints. Although he took quinine and other medications, they provided little relief, and the attacks would continue.

It was at the Truckee River that a curiously tall and shy derelict of a man stumbled into camp barefoot, dusty, and travel-worn. King quickly learned that Sereno Watson, who had just walked across the Sierra Nevada, had completed the chemistry course at Yale. He carried a letter of introduction from a friend of King's and earnestly begged for a place with the survey. No funding was available for yet another scientist, but King sensed that the man was capable. Watson was offered a position as unpaid volunteer in topography, and he quickly and gratefully accepted. He would become one of the nation's foremost botanists.

Two men were sent back to Glendale to bring the sailboat *Nettie*, belonging to the local Indian Agent, downriver to camp. The river had not been navigated before, and they soon found—halfway to the Big Bend—that as Bailey wrote, "The river is very

FIGURE 7.10.   Tufa domes and The Pyramid, seen from the east shore of Pyramid Lake. The domes are formed of shell-like layers of calcium carbonate that were deposited from thermal springs. The Pyramid, for which the lake was named, rises some 400 feet above the water surface, with a hot spring halfway up its side. (Photograph by Timothy O'Sullivan; King, 1878)

FIGURE 7.11.   The party of the Fortieth Parallel Survey in camp in Nevada in 1867. Clarence King is in the center, in front of the pole that Dick Cotter has climbed. The men to King's right and left are possibly Jim Marryatt and James Gardner. (Photograph by Timothy O'Sullivan; U.S. Geological Survey Library)

rapid and shallow and they grounded. They lost most of their clothes, pistols and all they had, and were a most forlorn looking set when they got in. By the help of more men, the boat was finally dislodged from the rocks and brought safely to camp."[26] A party including James Hague, Emmons, O'Sullivan, and Ridgeway then went with the boat on down the river to Pyramid Lake, where it was used for surveys around the lake and to land on the islands. Bailey was unable to join this group for botanical studies, due to his continued ill health.

At this camp Bailey noted that "About this time we began to suffer terribly from

FIGURE 7.12.   Looking south down the length of Osobb Valley (now called Dixie Valley), the first basin east of the Pahute Range (now called Stillwater Range). An accumulation of hot-spring deposits has built up a broad low mound 60 feet high and 12 acres in extent around several hot springs. The temperatures of the hot-spring pools range from 185° F down to those comfortable for bathing. In the lower part of the valley is an extensive field of white salt covered by a thin sheet of brine that completely evaporates in the dry autumn months. The salt layer, 5 feet thick, has been mined for use in the refining of silver ores. (Photograph by Timothy O'Sullivan, whose wagon containing photographic equipment is near the center; Hague and Emmons, 1877)

mosquitoes—which cheerful little insects literally swarm here and 'sing as they toil.' To escape their abominable torture, several of us flee nightly for the high grounds at the base of the mountains. They are fewer there, but we do not entirely avoid them. I never saw such persistent devils—or any of the genus with such long bills. A net is no impediment to them—it is only a means of corralling them where they can bite at their leisure. They do not confine their attention to the night—but gobble you at any time when it suits their convenience."[27]

Watson, in addition to his surveying duties, proved to be an energetic and diligent collector of plant specimens. On the one hand, Bailey found Watson to be competent and agreeable; on the other hand, the duplication of expertise began to irritate Bailey. And with his persistent illness curtailing his field activities and draining camp resources, a tension developed between Bailey and his supervisor, Gardner. (Bailey decided that he would much rather be in a party with King than with the second officer, Gardner.)

It was from this camp that a topographic crew scaled a nearby mountain and was blessed by far-ranging visibility. The air was so clear that they could see more than 200 miles. Gardner spent all day on the peak planning the strategy for the upcoming mapping program. A primary triangulation net would be laid down, utilizing the major peaks over the entire 100-mile wide swath of the project area. These peaks would serve as apices of the primary triangles. Then a net of smaller triangles would be fixed on the larger ones to locate the positions of lesser peaks. From the latter, still other visible points, including stream intersections, prominent outcrops, and habitations, would be sighted in to serve as guides for the sketching of the map itself.

The elevations of the primary points within the mapped swath were determined by measurements with the cistern barometer, and barometric base stations were established at intervals of 100 to 150 miles. While establishing the elevation measurements of the triangulation points and other key places, a second barometer, installed at the nearest base station, was read continuously to monitor the ever-changing weather-induced variations in barometric pressure. The ultimate determination of the elevation of the base stations was made by a later comparison with elevations determined by the leveling surveys on the Pacific railroad.

Another party left the Big Bend camp heading east to investigate the alkali deserts near the sink of the Carson River. Included were Custer and Anthony (topographers), Arnold Hague and Emmons (geologists), Watson (botanist), and Marryatt (teamster and cook). They then moved southeast to an area of numerous hot springs in Osobb Valley. Calcium carbonate deposits from the springs there had built a broad mound some 80 feet high. Some of the scalding hot springs discharged gas, but others were at a good temperature for bathing.

On August 20, Gardner, with a party of topographers and geologist James Hague, headed north to begin mapping in the vicinity of Mud Lake, north of Pyramid Lake (today the "lake" has totally dried and is called the Smoke Creek Desert). Some soldiers and a pack train accompanied them.

The next day the main party, with the wagons, struck the Truckee River camp and moved on to the east to a desolate spot called Coffman Station. It was here, where it was terribly hot in the sun, that the men enjoyed the sight of Samuel Emmons—a very slender man—attempting to squeeze himself into the shadow of a telegraph pole.

After another parched campsite with only alkaline water, they traveled east over barren country and made camp at the sink of the Humboldt River. Near this desolate alkaline desert, a mine and quartz mill were operating. Bailey reported that "the mosquitoes were more numerous and venomous than I ever supposed them capable of being. None of us pretended to sleep after the first night—but walked about attempting to beat off these fearful pests. Bars were of no use and the 'pesky devils' could get under our blankets and scorch us until we would 'git up and git.' The miners suffered in the same way, and would build smudge fires of cow dung and sit in this way between Scylla and Charybdis. To make things worse—the fever came upon me here with redoubled force—and several times I was delirious with pain—and wished that my life would end then and there."[28]

Several other men became sick at this camp. King arrived and got feverish, yet drove himself to keep working. With Samuel Emmons he examined the Hot Springs Range, and while there, suffering a severe attack while out in the blazing sun, crawled under a ledge and lost consciousness. When he awoke, he stumbled about and realized he was blind. Emmons helped him on his horse, and together they rode slowly back to camp, with Emmons leading King's horse.

King's sight returned in a few days, and the main camp moved up the Humboldt River Valley. He and Emmons traveled west to review some of the terrain already covered, but the main group left the quartz mill camp on August 28 in a driving rainstorm. By nightfall they camped at a place called Parker Station, where there was only a single cabin. The owner offered to take Bailey, still suffering from a raging fever, into the cabin during the rain. Bailey wrote, "My blankets were stretched for me on the rough pine boards and Charley Stables (one of the teamsters) sat and sponged my head for a long time—and gave me beef tea. I was doomed to have a wretched night though. A lot of soldiers were in the next room—cursing and talking at the tops of their voices—and after the rest had gone, two remained to a late hour to bake bread in the stove, and then the up stage stopped in the middle of the night—bound for Idaho and there was another row."[29]

The next morning Bailey's fever had broken and the weather cleared. They moved on to the small settlement of Oreana on the Humboldt River, where Gardner's group joined them, half of them sick with fever and ague. The topographic work in the north had not gone well because, as Gardner noted, "The worst obstacle to geodetic and topographical work has been a dense smoky haze which prevailed from the middle of August till the breaking up of the warm weather 3 days since. Some days the atmosphere was so thick that one could not see six miles. As none of my triangles requires sights at mountain peaks less than twenty miles off, many of them sixty, it is easily seen how much the geodesy has been delayed."[30]

King became concerned about the rampant sickness that was afflicting so many with malaria-like symptoms. Seeing that this health issue jeopardized the success of the enterprise, he decided that they should get away from the lowlands, to cooler air and purer water. Accordingly, they moved camp to Wright Canyon, on the west side of the Star Peak Range (now called the Humboldt Range). The main camp was set up

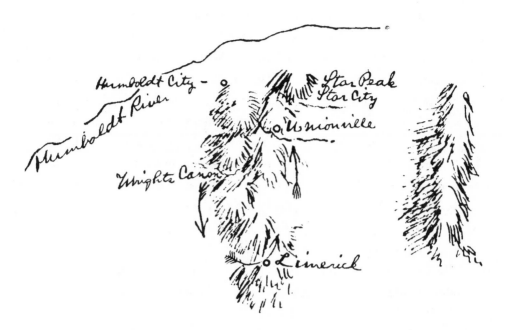

FIGURE 7.13. Sketch map drawn by botanist William Bailey showing the route traveled during the worst phase of his fever, from Humboldt City to Unionville, Nevada. In order to accommodate the sick, camp was first moved up into Wright's Canyon, where the water was good and the air cooler. However, the fever persisted and camp was moved again, over the pass past Limerick to Unionville, where use was made of a headquarters building and a small hotel. After a month many were still on the sick list and the Survey finally moved west, in late October, to winter quarters at Carson City and Virginia City. (From letter by Bailey to his brother, October 16, 1867. This item is reproduced by permission of The Huntington Library, San Marino, California.)

near the mouth of the canyon, and a second, for the sickest men, was up the canyon at higher altitude. Here the terrain was hospitable, with trees, grass, and flowers, and sparkling water flowed in the stream.

At first the ill men seemed to get better, but the fever returned and again ravaged the men in both canyon camps. Some got better but others worse. Gardner was immobilized for several days. The cook, Longhurst, famous to them for his tasty duff at the Yosemite camp, became so ill in the high camp that it seemed he would not pull through. Seeing all this, King abruptly moved the camps to get the men "under shelter, for the barometer had indicated the approach of a great storm, and already the change of wind announced its approach."[31] They struck out for Unionville, a mining town on the other side of the range about 28 miles distant, where there were a hotel and other amenities of civilization. Longhurst was carried down from the upper camp on a stretcher and placed in the bed of the thoroughbrace wagon, which rode a bit easier than the other wagons. Bailey, too sick to ride horseback, rode on the seat with the driver, who himself had just suffered a bout of chills and shakes. Before long, cold rain began to fall, and the men became soaked and thoroughly chilled.

The sick men were put up in a small hotel at Unionville, and the next day King managed to rent a house with two large rooms plus kitchen and cellar. Bailey wrote that, "My diarrhea continued bad and the room was cold and damp. The floor re-echoed to every step of the heavy boots of the party. On the 16th Sept., it began to snow and they tell me the ground was white but I was down with the fever again and knew nothing but the pain of that. Every step on the floor set me in agonies, and the next day I asked King to let me go to the hotel where I could be comparatively comfortable. He consented at once and I moved over. On the 18th I had a violent attack of the chills and then a tremendous fever and suffered beyond all expression. . . . I have lost about 8 pounds since leaving Sacramento and am decidedly weakened. Emmons is sick in bed today with the same disease."[32]

King continued to drive himself between bouts of sickness and conducted several long trips from Unionville. Once, in the range 80 miles east, he was making sights

Looking up the cañon. From Camp 19. Unionville, Nevada.

FIGURE 7.14.   Sketch by botanist William Bailey, showing Buena Vista Canyon, above the mining town of Unionville, where the survey had its last main field headquarters during the first field season, 1867. Because of illness, Bailey remained at Unionville for several weeks, and between bouts of fever worked up this canyon. (From letter by Bailey to his brother, October 16, 1867. This item is reproduced by permission of The Huntington Library, San Marino, California.)

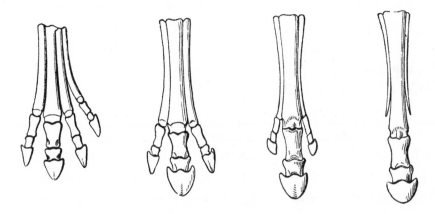

FIGURE 7.15.   Foot bones of three fossil horses and one modern horse (left to right), arranged from oldest (about 50 million years) to youngest (present-day). The systematic loss of lateral toes and the size increase of the third toe apparently resulted as an adaptation to harder ground, where speed was the animal's best defense. Clarence King learned of horse fossils uncovered in Oregon in 1867, and notified his friend Othniel Marsh, a Yale paleontologist who had an interest in such material. Marsh described this succession of horse genera that showed a direct line of descent with important intermediate forms. This sequence was considered a solid confirmation of Darwin's theory of evolution. (Marsh, 1874)

from a high ridge with topographer Frederick Clark when a storm developed and charged the air with electricity, causing their hair to buzz and stand on end. Nearby lightning flashed and thunder boomed. When King sighted the theodolite on a distant target an "electrical flash came through the instrument, striking my right arm and side. I was staggered and my brain and nerves severely shocked. The theodolite was thrown and badly injured. Mr. Clark and I hastened back to our camp in Salt Valley. In the course of a week the effects of the [lightning] stroke wore off. I was able to work all the time, although distressed at times by the stoppage of circulation in the right side."[33] But King took all this in good humor and, as was his habit, constructed from the adventure one of the choice tales he would be telling around the campfire or in the drawing room.

Bailey recovered and felt well enough to botanize in Buena Vista Canyon, a stream course that rose into the mountains above Unionville. Emmons and Custer were still ill, but each insisted on leading groups out on long expeditions into desolate desert country, where the only moisture to be found was in bitter alkali springs. Worse, perhaps, dangerous Indians roamed the region.

King and James Hague took this opportunity to make an extended trek north to

Idaho. Hague had completed work on the Humboldt mines and was eager to examine the booming Silver City mines in southwest Idaho. Though this region was clearly outside of the mandated area of the Fortieth Parallel Survey, King justified the trip by the fact that some of the ores carried $3,000 in gold per ton. Since the mine would be relying on the railroad for transport, he considered that it should be a sanctioned part of his study of economic ore deposits.[34]

After several weeks examining the mines, they traveled on to The Dalles, Oregon, where King had an opportunity to examine some unique fossils that had recently been found in the John Day Beds of eastern Oregon by the geologist Thomas Condon. This collection included a unique three-toed horse. King alerted his Yale paleontologist friend, Othniel Marsh, who had a long-standing interest in fossil horses. Marsh was excited about the find, and soon obtained samples that he compared with other horse fossils he and others had collected, from strata spanning the last 50 million years. Through time the horses became larger with a longer neck, and the feet developed from an original four-toed arrangement to the single hoof of the modern horse. Marsh noted that "The line of descent appears to have been direct, and the remains now known supply every important intermediate form."[35] This fossil sequence provided strong support for Darwin's theory of evolution. Othniel Marsh would not forget King's kindness in drawing his attention to the John Day horse fossils.

Longhurst, the cook, did not recover from the fever until he returned to California. Gardner also traveled to San Francisco for several days of relaxation to recover his health. He quickly improved in the City by the Golden Gate, and even found time for other activities. He wrote that he visited "an acquaintance in San Francisco who was selling out the library of a deceased friend, an Englishman, and there saw *Ruskin's Modern Painters* and *Elements of Drawing & Treatise on Perspective & Seven Lamps of Architecture*. The books had never been read and were as good as new except the binding. He gladly sold me the whole for $21.00 gold. On consulting Bancroft I found that I should have had to pay $90.00 gold for them if bought in the regular way."[36]

Back at Unionville, Jim Marryatt took over the duties of cook and produced excellent meals appreciated by all. William Bailey described the last bill of fare for dinner, "leg of mutton, caper sauce, mutton stew, tomatoes raw and stewed; cabbage, onions, turnips; potatoes mashed—and baked; cornbread and hot biscuits—canned jellies, baked beans, tea and coffee."[37]

Timothy O'Sullivan, the photographer, was left in charge of the camp in the absence of King and Gardner. He found that he could make money on the side by taking portraits, and began filling his free time photographing the townspeople. They had not had such a service previously, and eagerly bought O'Sullivan's prints to send home to their families.

Bailey suffered a new attack of the fever. Fortunately, it occurred while he was seeing the doctor in the hotel, and he was immediately put to bed. This was a great relief for him, after sleeping on the cold floor of the common room wrapped in dusty blankets. Henry Custer, also feverish, was brought in very weak after returning from a topographic expedition. A telegram from Gardner in San Francisco reported that his own recuperation was complete, and that he would return to the field. A message from King in Silver City, Idaho, ordered the group at Unionville to proceed immediately to Glendale, in western Nevada, where arrangements would be made for winter quarters.

The Unionville contingent, which by now consisted of O'Sullivan, Bailey, Watson, Ridgeway, two teamsters, and the cook, started the retreat back to Glendale on the

FIGURE 7.16.   Mill and smelter for silver, lead, and antimony ores from the Montezuma mine at the settlement of Oreana, Nevada. The dark smoke is probably from the fires for the steam boilers, and the light smoke is dust from the stamp mills used for crushing ore. The Unionville contingent of the survey (shown here) spent a bitter cold night here in late October 1867 on their way to winter quarters at Carson City. (Photograph by Timothy O'Sullivan; U.S. Geological Survey)

morning of October 28, 1867. Bailey had recovered sufficiently from the on-and-off sickness to be able to ride his mule, but Custer was bedridden, too sick to travel, and was left with a soldier at the Unionville Hotel. Before departing, they discovered that one of the soldiers had deserted. He had taken his horse and saddle, and had also stolen another saddle and several days' rations from the storehouse.

O'Sullivan's party headed south from Unionville, passed through the deserted town of Limerick, over the rocky pass of the West Humboldt Range, and reached Oreana at dark. It was bitter cold the next morning (13° F), and O'Sullivan spent the day photographing the mill and smelting works that reduced the ore from the Montezuma Mines in the Trinity Range. The ore contained silver, lead, and antimony.

They camped the next night at Palmer's Station, where Bailey had spent a long feverish night in the tiny cabin on the way out. Bailey wrote, "One of the charms of the place is the extreme difficulty of obtaining any kind of fuel. It was only after diligent search and much digging that we succeeded in raising enough greasewood to boil our tea and fry what little fresh meat we had left. The night was so cold—that we all slept in the corral in the hay. O'Sullivan and I slept together for the sake of the additional blankets—and for such animal heat that each might impart to the other. Even then—we were cold."[38]

The following day the small group continued on west toward Glendale. Bailey wrote "we had a heavy pull all day through deep sands—and a most monotonous view of desert plains and still more desert mountains. Watson and I rode ahead of the train—and about three o'clock came in sight of the Truckee with its tall cottonwood *trees*—yes! actually trees! They were tinged yellow or brown by the frosts—but still looked pretty to our eyes long unused to any form of arborescent beauty. And then to know that they grew next to good fresh water—that we wouldn't have to drink any longer the disgusting alkali of the desert."[39]

After two more days of travel they reached Glendale on November 4, and there took a pleasant house that provided the most comfort they had had for months. Gardner, O'Sullivan, and Watson were already there when they arrived, but left the next day with a pack train for the region of Pyramid Lake, where they wished to complete topographic work that had been curtailed earlier by both sickness and hazy air.

Emmons brought his party to Glendale from a dangerous survey in the Black Rock Desert region of northwestern Nevada. A teamster had been ambushed by Bannock Indians near their camp, his body pierced by both arrows and bullets, and the local people had called on Emmons to release part of his military escort to punish the renegade Indians. Four soldiers and a group of citizens had gone on patrol but had encountered no Indians. The Emmons party, by now weary and hungry, eagerly joined O'Sullivan's troop for a Thanksgiving turkey, good Oregon cider, and fun-filled ceremony. Bailey wrote that "In the midst of the fun—and there was lots of it—in came Gardner and his party—but too late for the feast. King made his appearance a few days after and we got ready to move to winter quarters."[40]

Just as the group was leaving Glendale, a band of Paiutes rode up and planted a pole in the ground with a fresh scalp attached. They had come—as emissaries from the friendly chief Winnemuch—to convince King that they had done right in attacking some outlaw Indians who had roamed from Pit River in California to steal stock from the ranches. James Hague took the scalp, wrote a note explaining the situation, and rode off to give the evidence to H. G. Parker, the Indian Agent.

The main group of the survey arrived at Carson (now Carson City) the next day and engaged a large house for winter quarters—a former hotel called the White House. Each had his own bedroom. A large common room was set aside for writing and drafting. They ate in another, smaller house. A second group, including King, the Hague brothers, Emmons, and O'Sullivan, planned to spend the winter in Virginia City at the site of the Comstock Lode. The rents there being double those in Carson, it was decided that only the geologic division would spend the winter in Virginia City. There they could work underground, examining the geology of this rich silver deposit. James Hague would take the lead.

Gardner assembled his group of three assistants for one last trip to take advantage of clear air before winter really set in. This was the group that had failed to complete their mapping of the country between the California line and Pyramid Lake due to deteriorating weather. This time too they encountered a series of storms. Gardner wrote that he came " . . . from a race that are not easily backed down for weather. Sometimes it seemed that I should be frozen to a mummy on the top of some peak, and sometimes it seemed as if we should all be washed to pieces by the torrents of rain; but God gave us opportunities to finish the work before the last great storms came, in which no human being could have traveled the pathless mountains." He praised the work of his assistant and also botanical expert: "Mr. Watson one of my most untiring assistants was the last man into camp about three hours after dark. In spite of cold and wind he had stood his ground on a mountain and closed up the last gap in our topographical work. His courage that day made the success of our trip complete; for that night a tremendous snow storm set in. The hurricane rocked our poor tent till it seemed as if no cords nor canvas could stand the strain. We rose at earliest light and prepared to abandon the position before the snow became too deep. Our poor animals stood shivering with their tails to the storm; their legs drawn up under them and their arched backs supporting a white frozen mass."[41]

Clearly, it was past time to terminate the field season, and the frozen crew labored south through snowdrifts and over swollen streams. Gardner directed the main contingent to continue to Carson, while he and Arnold Hague rode on to Virginia City. Suffering through an icy cold rain on Christmas Day, they arrived after seven hours in the saddle, wet, cold, and miserable. They were directed to the small house where the team was quartered, and found warm greetings from their friends and a bright fire burning. After thawing out before the fire and changing to dry clothes, they sat down to a finely spread table of delicious food. Gardner wrote his mother that "We five young bachelors made merry round our board and rejoiced in our comfortable home; and the storm raged furiously outside and I felt very thankful to be at rest. That night I slept in Clare's arms on luxurious mattresses and between snowy sheets; instead of rolling myself in a blanket on the ground. Next morning I rose without feeling the slightest ill effects from the previous day's ride."[42]

In discussing his late-season work, Gardner notes that "Clare said it did seem too stormy for any party to continue in the field, but I had set my heart on making this winter a complete map of country 100 miles square and I determined to carry this through in spite of any weather. . . . I feel confident that I can make the truest topographical map that has yet been made of any part of the interior of the country. Professionally the year is a success. I wish I felt so sure of my heart work as of that of the brain; but I fear that too much of my effort has been spent on one part of my nature to accomplish the greatest possible good to others of which I am capable. For a number of years I have bent my energies toward professional progress. I fear it has been at the expense of a broad development of heart."[43]

With the first season of fieldwork over, King reviewed the team's accomplishments and felt lucky to have covered as much terrain as they had. The sickness had seriously impeded their efforts, but pluck and perseverance carried the work forward. They had mapped 12,000 square miles of rough and arid country, and had collected some three thousand samples of rocks, ores, salts, fossils, and biologic materials. King wrote that "In spite of the most adverse circumstances, and almost overwhelming pressure of work, the few of us who kept our health have, by great effort, turned a threatened failure into a very complete success. . . . The party are all well and united by a healthy Esprit de Corps." The bouts of fever and chills suffered by the survey members were not an isolated occurrence. King reported that "The U.S. soldiers, the isolated ranchmen, the Indians, and campaigners, like ourselves, have all been disabled this year by the malaria. The great flood of last year left a vast amount of stagnant waters, which doubtless generated the miasma which has been so fatal to all the inhabitants of the desert. Mining and gold-milling operations were suspended at the

Humboldt Sink, and have been only lately renewed."[44] The now well-established association between malaria and mosquitoes was not known until 1882. Nevada's out-
break likely resulted from the juxtaposition of miners—who had come from all over
the world—with the native mosquitoes during an exceptionally wet spring.

The December storms of 1867 were among the heaviest ever recorded in the West.
The wind and rain wreaked havoc in California, deroofing houses and flooding rivers.
The Sacramento River rose to 22 feet above flood stage, inundating parts of Sacramento and Marysville. But Virginia City, a bustling city of about 10,000 inhabitants
in Nevada, largely ignored the stormy weather. Its main laboring activity was deep in
the mines, which had now reached 1,000 feet below the surface. Many saloons and
gambling halls were open all night, and other social activities beckoned.

Regarding the stormy weather in Carson City, Bailey writes: "For the last three
weeks we have had most awful weather here and a series of floods that have threat-

FIGURE 7.17.   Hoisting works of the Yellow Jacket Silver Mining Company at the south
end of the Comstock Lode at Gold Hill, Nevada. The lumber brought in on railroad cars
(stacked in front of the mill) was used for timbering in the mines to prevent collapse.
Unwanted mined material was dumped on the extensive tailing piles from mine cars.
Valuable ore was taken to the mill for crushing and milling to recover silver and gold.
(Thompson and West, 1881)

ened to float us to the Atlantic. First there would be heavy snows on the mountains and then torrents of rain. A great mountain stream from the Sierra has been turned from its course and has completely encircled the White House. We dine in a smaller house nearby and the stream flows between. At times it has been impossible to reach the other house only next door without making a long detour through the town. The winds accompanying these storms are frightful. They take off the roofs of houses without the least trouble. . . . I have had no letters for a long time. Ordinarily the overland mail goes through to New York in 16 days. I send my letters all that way now, as the passes of the Rocky Mountains are lower and apt to be clearer than those of the Sierra Nevada."[45]

The topographic crew computed the triangulation nets and plotted up their field sheets, and Bailey and Ridgeway wrote up reports on their season's work. With his work completed, Bailey occupied his time with reading and drawing. "Still the time hangs on my hands and I would much prefer to be at work. I have told Mr. King to employ me in copying or any other way he thinks best, but as he is in Virginia City, I see him but rarely. I hate to have given the appearance of idling, especially as Gardner, the second in command, hates me and would do anything he could to remove me. He has treated me meanly from the beginning, and acted so towards others that I have been many times incensed into speaking my mind pretty plainly about him and his doings. He 'smiles and smiles' before my face and abuses me behind my back until in indignation of these underhanded attacks, I have informed Dr. Gray (who recommended me) of the whole matter. I know my natural bitter temper and impulsiveness very well and despise them as much as any one else can, but still I think my continued ill health here is a partial excuse. . . . I was appointed with the understanding that I was to be alone in my special department [botany], but another gentleman [Watson] now shares it with me. He is a man, however, that I greatly admire and respect. The mean slights and misunderstanding of my words and actions have almost made me desperate of what I say or do—so that where I believe I would have achieved a good reputation for cheerfulness and kindness at first, I am naturally looked on now as peevish."[46]

Concern had grown over the absence of Ridgeway, the zoologist, and Palmer, the Indian Agent, who had been out all of December through the heavy storms. They had gone to the region of Pyramid Lake for the purpose of collecting bird and animal specimens. Some speculated that heavy gales had capsized their boat on the lake, or that they were delayed by the high water in the Truckee River. They finally did return in the middle of January with a good collection of birds, but with stories of hard times both in camping and in crossing streams and negotiating roads with their wagon and team.

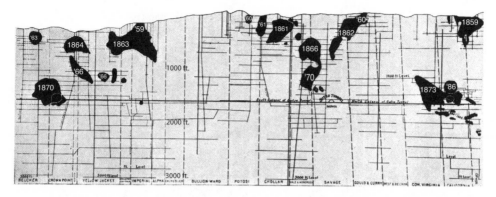

FIGURE 7.18. Vertical section along the Comstock fault-vein system. The diagram traces the system about two miles horizontally and 3,000 feet vertically, with both vertical and horizontal scales the same. The main ore bodies (bonanzas) are shown in black with their years of discovery. Fine lines show mine workings; vertical dashed lines are mine property boundaries; and numbers near the center show depth in feet. The first discoveries in 1859 were at the Gold Hill Mines on the south (left) and Ophir on the north (right). During the winter of 1867–68, when Clarence King and James Hague examined the mines, they were only about 1,000 feet deep. When the Fortieth Parallel Survey fieldwork was completed in 1871 most of the bonanzas had been discovered. (After Smith, 1966)

The Virginia City group spent most of the worktime underground in the active mines, mapping out the extent of the major vein system, which trended north and dipped about 45° down to the east. Giant Cornish pumps were needed to pump the 1,000-foot-deep shafts; otherwise, the mines would soon be flooded. A curious feature of the vein system was that most of the rich ore bodies were not along the main fissure vein, but resided in large isolated pods away from the vein in the hanging wall, that is, in the overhanging eastern wall of the vein. This made exploration difficult, because little evidence of the pods could be found along the vein itself, and blind, exploratory drifts had to be set out into the hanging wall to search for them.

Some of the ore bodies were both large and rich. These bonanzas, when mined out, produced large chambers, or stopes. Such caverns—if allowed to remain open—would rapidly collapse. But a new type of timbering had been invented in 1860 by Philipp Deidesheimer, a young German engineer who had worked previously in the California goldfields. He devised a method of timbering these large stopes, some of which were hundreds of feet in width and height. Heavy six-foot-long timbers were joined together into cubes, and as the ore removal was completed these cubes were affixed to one another to form a stout network that filled the stopes and effectively prevented caving.[47] The system was so successful that an enormous amount of timber

FIGURE 7.19.   Square-set timbering, a system of interconnected 6-foot cubes of heavy timbers used for filling the mined-out caverns, to prevent collapse. The system was invented by Philipp Deidesheimer, a young German engineer who had worked previously in the California goldfields. It permitted almost complete mining of the large rich pockets of silver ore. (Hague, 1870).

came to be used. By 1880, 600 million board feet of lumber had gone into the mines. The slopes of the Sierra were stripped of forest through a span of 100 miles to supply this timber.

O'Sullivan took his burdensome photographic equipment into the mines and made some of the first images ever taken in an active mine.[48] He burned magnesium metal as a light source, and was able to capture miners at work, as well as features of the mine and elements of the mining equipment.

King was lucky in obtaining mine maps from a former mine superintendent of now-closed sections of the mines. By combining old and new mapping he believed that the most complete map ever made of a major silver-lode system would result from their work. On the basis of his mapping, he predicted that more bonanzas

FIGURE 7.20. The margin of a collapsed mine working that had utilized the square-set timbers with mortised ends shown in the previous illustration. In some places, layers of clay occurred within ore zones and expansion of the clay would exert tremendous force on the supports, producing a collapse like this. (Photograph by Timothy O'Sullivan; U.S. Geological Survey Library)

would be discovered as the mines reached greater depth, a view that would prove true eight years later.[49]

At this time it was decided that James Hague would take the lead in working up a volume on mineral deposits, the Comstock Lode to be the featured part. King's strategy was to push this work forward aggressively, ahead of all else, because it made a package that could be finished without reliance on other specialists. Moreover, because of the widespread interest in the Comstock Lode—the most important silver mine in the country—such a work would surely excite popular interest. By so doing, the survey would be delivering one product early, one that could serve as ammunition in requests for further funding for the whole enterprise.

While Hague's group was engaged in the study of the mines, preparations for the

FIGURE 7.21.   Miners waiting to descend in two lifts into the depths of the Savage Mine on the Comstock Lode. These shafts were considered the most dangerous places in the mines. Deaths from falls down the shafts from the various levels were commonplace, and heavy equipment would sometimes fall and strike the men in the cages. Malfunctions of the equipment, such as breakage of the hoist cable, not only would drop the cage at lightning speed but would also drop the heavy cable on top of it. In other cases, the hoist operator would fail to stop the ascending cage, loaded with miners, when it reached the surface, causing it to rise to the top of the headframe, batter against the pulley system, and spill the miners out onto the floor of the hoist house, where they were lucky if they did not fall back down the shaft. (Lithograph from a photograph by Timothy O'Sullivan; U.S. Geological Survey Library)

next summer's field campaign also went forward. King ordered a supply of new instruments, including gradiometers, barometers, and hand levels, all needed for topographic surveying: Gardner had realized that extensive elevation control was necessary for depicting landforms by contour lines, and wanted all the field men to be well equipped to obtain such data. A reply was received February 10, 1868, from the Washington headquarters of the Corps of Engineers: "In compliance with your requisition of the 8th, the following instruments, for which you will find invoices enclosed, will be sent you from New York by Wells Fargo & Co. Express:

FIGURE 7.22.   A Comstock miner picking out fractured vein material that will be loaded into the wheelbarrow. This image, among the first photographs ever made underground in a mine, was illuminated by the flaring of powdered magnesium metal. Normally, the miner labored in the light of a single candle (upper right). (Photograph made in the winter of 1867–68 by Timothy O'Sullivan; U.S. Geological Survey Library)

(2) Two Gradiometers no. 16 & 17, Wurdemann.

(4) Four Square plate pocket Compasses.

(3) Three Double Vernier Barometers.

(4) Minimum Thermometers.

(6) Six pocket Thermometers reading to 212°.

(3) Three pocket Levels.

(2) Two brass Evaporating pans with micrometer screw &c &c.

You will please return the usual duplicate receipts for the above instruments when they shall have reached you. . . . P.S. Your attention is called to the fact that no receipts have been received from you for instruments heretofore sent you, as required by Regulations."[50]

Because of the exceptional winter, the slopes of the Carson Range around Virginia City were covered with three feet of snow, and the young men took up the sport of skiing—called snowshoeing at that time. Gardner wrote that "We are nearly two thousand feet above the valley of the Carson River which runs at the foot of these mountains. We look down there and see the dark ground, showing that they have had rain while the snow has fallen heavily around us. All the slopes about here are very steep and every afternoon we go out to ride down the hill. Not however on old fashioned sleds but on Norwegian snow shoes. These are thin boards about 4 inches wide and twelve feet long, turned up at the end and having a strap on top which holds the foot to the shoes. On these you can travel rapidly over the deepest snow, and down the hills your speed is like lightning. . . . The pole in the man's hand is for balancing and steering. I have known men to slide a mile in fifty seconds on these shoes. It is by the use of them that the mails have been carried over the Sierra Nevada in winter since the earliest settlement of the country. The mail carriers used sometimes to make sixty miles per day. In going up hill you tie a rag around the bottom of the shoes and can travel with about the ease that a person could walk on ordinary ground; but the moment you get to a descending place you pull off the rags and shoot down the slope like an arrow. To balance on such long narrow boards and to guide them was quite difficult at first. One shoe had an irresistible tendency to run over the other, and I got a good many falls; but perseverance soon gave me the knack; and now I enjoy it thoroughly. A little play helps wonderfully in work."[51]

The bad news that Bailey had no doubt expected finally came. He wrote, "At Mr. King's suggestion, very kindly worded, I have resigned my position. He expects the next campaign to be very arduous and unhealthy, and speaks of it as sheer folly for me to undertake what he thinks it quite possible I cannot perform. He moreover speaks of the danger of fixing the malaria in my system. A great part of this is gammon talk intended to deceive and has been talked into King by Gardner, always anxious to get rid of me. It is so understood in the party. Most of the fellows are my warm friends. The Survey's short of funds and gives notice that the salaries for next month cannot be paid. Things look bad."[52] With Bailey's resignation, Sereno Watson assumed all the botanical work for the survey.

Gardner realized that the unremitting work in the field had precluded other activities, but now there was time for some leisure. In his measured analytical manner, he noted that "Heretofore I have avoided parties because I found the position of a non-dancing young man to be very unpleasant unless he has unusual powers of entertaining conversation [here he was no doubt referring to King]. From experience and observation I have deliberately come to the conclusion that the effects of not dancing, considering the way in which society is at present instituted, will probably be worse in the majority of cases than the results of mingling freely but not intemperately in all the dances. . . . Today I commenced taking dancing lessons and pretty nearly mastered the waltz."[53]

King and Gardner were enticed by the social whirl of Virginia City. King outfitted himself with well-cut clothes from a good tailor and became quite a dandy. He wore tight light-colored trousers with a black stripe down the side, a dark coat, sporty hat, and either lemon or violet gloves, and carried a cane. The two eligible bachelors met two young schoolteachers, and were soon leading a busy social life. King's friend was Miss Ellen Dean, and "Kingy" and "Deany" were a common sight at socials and dances and also went swimming together at a nearby hot spring. Gardner met Miss Josephine Rogers, from Oakland, California, and was infatuated. The couples took advantage of the cold weather for skating, and went to the New Year's Ball by sleigh. The two romantic attachments became serious. On one of King's frequent trips to San Francisco to line up field equipment and look into reference material he made a special purchase. He bought a diamond ring, and on Easter Sunday in Virginia City he announced his engagement to Miss Dean. Gardner's romantic liaison with Miss Rogers also blossomed.

The fieldwork began again in May 1868, and King divided the corps into two main groups, so as to cover as much ground as possible. Emmons and James Hague went farthest east—about to the center of Nevada. They worked on mapping the geology of the entire Toiyabe Range and investigated the mines, including those at the boom town of Austin. Custer and Watson studied the area east of Unionville toward the Pahute Range. King went with Ridgeway to Pyramid Lake, where pelicans had returned in large numbers. Ridgeway was able to collect dozens of eggs from several bird species, which he shipped to the Smithsonian Museum; some of the eggs would

FIGURE 7.23.   The mining town of Austin on the west side of the Toiyabe Range. After
King captured a cavalryman who had deserted the Survey camp with stolen equipment, the
fugitive was lodged in the jail here. (Photograph by William H. Jackson)

be used for trading with other institutions for items missing in the Smithsonian collections.

King joined up with the parties at Austin on the west side of the Toiyabe Range in
July and then divided the corps into four groups. Arnold Hague and Clark moved
east to the region of Ruby Valley, with King and Custer paralleling them to the south.
Gardner reoccupied an astronomical station on Job's Peak and then refined the to-
pography in western Nevada. Emmons worked east into the ranges bordering the
Great Salt Lake.

While working in the Reese River region west of the Shoshone Range, a cavalryman sneaked away from camp carrying instruments and equipment. His desertion
was not discovered for 12 hours, at which time King and the sergeant of the detachment gave chase. King was intent on apprehending the man so as to discourage other
desertions, a practice that had become all too common. They trailed the soldier for
over 100 miles, and late on the second day discovered that he was heading for a pass
over the Havilah Mountains. King and his companion rode cross-country most of the

night, circling about the range and rejoining the trail on the far side. They spotted the trooper eating breakfast, and King approached him alone. "I captured him in a hand to hand struggle in which I nearly lost my life, and only saved myself by dodging his shot and cramming my pistol in his ear in the nick of time. I lodged him in Austin jail, and the fact of his capture forever reduced the soldiers and the working men of the survey to obedience."[54]

In August the parties rendezvoused at Fort Ruby near the railroad. James Hague finished his study of the Nevada mining camps and went on to Colorado to study the mining activity there. Emmons investigated the country north of the Humboldt River, and Arnold Hague worked in the southern region, including Humboldt Wells and Pilot Peak. King worked up the length of the East Humboldt Range (now called the Ruby Range). There he noticed that a year-round stream flowed into Franklin Lake at the east foot of the range. To discover the source of the water, he and Jim Mar-

FIGURE 7.24. Fort Ruby, near the Central Pacific Railroad at the southern end of Ruby Lake, and at the east base of the present-day Ruby Mountains in central Nevada, in 1868. The fort was manned from 1862 to 1869, prior to the completion of the railroad, to provide security for the overland road and mail route from marauding Paiute and Goshute Indians. It was a rendezvous point for the several divisions of the Fortieth Parallel Survey. (Photograph by Timothy O'Sullivan; U.S. Geological Survey Library)

ryatt ascended the stream valley and found a cirque occupied by a beautiful mountain lake. While Jim tended the mules, King clambered around the headwall and found ample evidence that several small glaciers had perched in the highest parts of the range, and one of them had carved the bowl for the lake. This lake he named Lake Marian for his young half sister and later wrote a Christmas poem for her describing this remarkable spot, *The Stone Giant's Bowl*.[55]

King chafed under the burden of paperwork he was required to complete in the field. The War Department headquarters was constantly after him to produce reports on the work performed, including the routes of travel and the locations worked by all the various parties. He also was compelled to maintain the accounts on expenditures for food, lodging, equipment, and instruments, forage for the animals when on private property, repair of equipment, etc. In remote areas in the West, where govern-

FIGURE 7.25. A small lake high in the East Humboldt Mountains (now Ruby Range) whose basin had been carved by glaciers during the Ice Ages. King named it Marian Lake for his young half sister and composed a poem about a giant that: "Holds in his rock-arm a basin, cut from the silvery granite, chiseled by ice and by tempest, trimmed with the fir and the pine tree." This poem was presented to his sister in a book he prepared for Christmas, 1870. The lake is now called Overland Lake. (Painting by Gilbert Munger, in King, 1878; poem in King, 1870, see Appendix R for complete poem)

FIGURE 7.26. King Peak, in the northern Ruby Mountains of central Nevada. The peak, named in the 1960s to honor Clarence King, stands just 1.5 miles northwest of Overland Lake (called Marian Lake by King after his half sister). The nature of the terrain and the presence of the lake demonstrated to King that this region had undergone glaciation in the Ice Ages. (Photograph by John Bridgman)

ment vouchers were not accepted, only gold would purchase needed materials. This use of coin required another layer of bureaucratic control.

King tried whenever possible to delegate this task to others, but invariably it reverted back to his responsibility. If the vouchers were made up too hastily, the accountants at the headquarters of the Corps of Engineers were sure to find the tiniest irregularities. They then cited from the book of regulations how the vouchers need be amended. The specific dates that horses were out to pasture had to be certified, the word "mileage" was to be replaced by "transportation," and the specific dates and nature of all services had to be spelled out.[56] King found himself weighed down by these bureaucratic trivia, but to obtain his funding he was obliged to comply.

The survey met again at Humboldt Wells, near the headwaters of the Humboldt River, by mid-September 1868. As before, separate parties moved out to distinct areas. Arnold Hague worked the country to the east, following the railroad around the north side of Great Salt Lake. Here at Promontory Point, in less than a year, the Cen-

FIGURE 7.27.   Clarence King, looking east at the Shoshone Falls of the Snake River in Idaho in 1868. The falls, 190 feet high, are carved in trachyte, a massive rock more favorable to the production of high scarps and falls than the thinner lava flows of basalt that cap it, and extend up into the unbroken lava plain on the horizon. King considered this one of the three great waterfalls on the continent, the others being Niagara Falls and Yosemite Falls. (Photograph by Timothy O'Sullivan; King, 1878)

tral Pacific Railroad pushing east would meet the Union Pacific pushing west. Emmons paralleled Arnold Hague's path on the north to fill out the northern part of the project area. Gardner made the long trip west to Wadsworth, on the Big Bend of the Truckee, to make astronomical observations, then went on to Salt Lake City.

King took a group still farther north, and there was drawn to the massive Shoshone Falls of the Snake River, in Idaho. This he considered—along with Yosemite Falls and Niagara Falls—to be one of the three great waterfalls of America. The region is markedly north of King's survey area, but he justified the visit to the falls because of its great geological interest, and because it demonstrated so dramatically the nature of canyon cutting though hard lava rock. King noted that "No sheltering pine or mountain distance of up-piled Sierras guards the approach to the Shoshone. You ride upon a waste,—the pale earth stretched in desolation. Suddenly you stand upon a brink, as if the earth had yawned. Black walls flank the abyss. Deep in the bed a great river fights it way through labyrinths of blackened ruins, and plunges in foaming whiteness over a cliff of lava."[57] The river is some 600 feet below the plain, and the top

Field Personnel in U.S. Geological Exploration
of the Fortieth Parallel

Field Season	1867	1868	1869	1870	1871	1872
Map Sheet	V	IV	III	III, II	II, I	I
Activities	Begin survey Nevada	Nevada Comstock Lode	Salt Lake Wasatch Mtn. Railroad opens	Mt. Shasta Nevada	SW Wyoming Mineral Industry False Mt. Whitney	Diamond hoax Mountain-eering
Geologist	C. King	C. King	C. King	C. King	C. King	C. King
	J. Hague	J. Hague	J. Hague	J. Hague	S. Emmons	S. Emmons
	A. Hague	A. Hague	A. Hague	A. Hague	A. Hague	A. Hague
	S. Emmons	S. Emmons	S. Emmons	S. Emmons		
Topographer	J. Gardner	J. Gardner	J. Gardner	J. Gardner	J. Gardner	J. Gardner
	F. A. Clark	F. A. Clark	F. A. Clark	F. A. Clark	F. A. Clark	F. A. Clark
	H. Custer	H. Custer	N.L. Davis	A. D. Wilson	A. D. Wilson	A. D. Wilson
		A. D. Wilson	A. D. Wilson			
Photographer	T. O'Sullivan	T. O'Sullivan	T. O'Sullivan	C. Watkins		T. O'Sullivan
Artist			G. Munger	G. Munger		A. Bierstadt
Botanist	W. Bailey	S. Wilson				
	S. Wilson					
Zoologist	R. Ridgeway	R. Ridgeway	R. Ridgeway			

FIGURE 7.28. Chart listing the scientific and technical personnel of the U.S. Geological Exploration of the Fortieth Parallel, initiated by Clarence King in 1867 and headed by him until its termination in 1879. The listing shows the activities and technical personnel engaged during the six years of survey fieldwork. The survey was funded for another six years, during which time a more limited staff compiled maps and wrote up results.

of the falls is reached by descending 400 feet to a broad bench, below which the main cataract falls 190 feet. The party camped on the bench and King placed his tent at the edge where he had a dramatic view. "From my door I looked over the cataract, and, whenever the veil of mist was blown aside, could see for a mile down the river. . . . At the very brink of the fall a few twisted evergreens cling with their roots to the rock, and lean over the abyss of foam with something of that air of fatal fascination which is apt to take possession of men."[58] For ten days the group worked in this region, investigating the erosional and volcanic features and studying the rock layers that are so well exposed in the canyon.

By the middle of October, the survey reassembled in Salt Lake City, where the camp men and escort were dismissed. All had a chance to meet Gardner's new bride Josephine, whom he had married September 7 in Oakland, California. King remarked that she was "as charming a little recent vertebrate as was ever collected."[59] The bridal couple was heading east to meet his family and friends and to set up housekeeping.

Equipment was put into storage, livestock was sold or put out to pasture, and the main scientific party boarded the Union Pacific at Green River City, Wyoming, for the trip east. From now on, travel between east and west, by rail rather than by sea, would be much quicker. The corps was weary after having spent eighteen months in the field, much of it under primitive camp conditions. King requested from General Humphreys a month's vacation for all hands, and it was promptly authorized. Marryatt, who had become such a sterling addition, was retained by the Survey and also went on to Washington with the others because "He has learned the manipulation of our collections, and will far more than save his pay in handling our material besides acting as messenger and taking care of our office rooms."[60] Marryatt "the man of all work" had also assumed the position of King's personal valet, but King, after being admonished by the auditors for using the title "servant" was careful how he characterized Marryatt's duties.[61]

With surveying within the state of Nevada essentially completed, King and Gardner were pleased with progress during this second field season. In their march east they had completed most of the 100-mile-wide strip that lay in the Great Basin—that part of the continent with no exterior drainage. The topography had been completed in two and a half map sheets—of the five that would delineate the total area of the survey—and the geology of most of this area was blocked out.

CHAPTER EIGHT

TRUE ICE AND FALSE SUMMIT

We climbed an ice-crag together; all around rose strange, sharp forms; below, in every direction, yawned narrow cuts, caves trimmed with long stalactites of ice, walls ornamented with crystal pilasters, and dark-blue grottoes opening down into deeper and more gloomy chambers, as silent and cold as graves.
—*Clarence King,* Mountaineering in the Sierra Nevada

In December 1868 King rented an office in Washington, D.C., at a rate "not to exceed $75 per month." He also had to request permission through General Humphreys to purchase each item of furniture and equipment, including, for example, one broom, two waste baskets, and ten tons of coal.[1] Gardner assumed charge of the day-to-day routine, and it was to him that permission was granted to obtain the necessary drafting supplies.[2] Work went forward on the topographic maps, and the other scientists organized their notebooks and specimens and began writing up the results of two seasons of fieldwork. James Hague and Samuel Emmons, who preferred to work in their homes, departed for Boston, and King visited Hague there to help push forward the volume on the mining industry. The plan was that Hague would continue office work during most of the coming field season, the hope being that the published volume would give King a trump card to play at the next appropriation hearings. Arnold Hague worked in his Yale laboratory on the chemical analyses of the Comstock ores. His interest in the composition and character of the ore-bearing minerals would lead to improving the efficiency of the ore treatment process. Enthusiastically, King wrote Humphreys that " . . . at first survey of results, it appears that we have discovered the great error of the silver process, and by a slight variation of the chemical conditions we have succeeded in raising the percentage of yield from 64 and 66 percent to 93 and 95 percent."[3]

FIGURE 8.1.   Meeting of locomotives from the Central Pacific and Union Pacific railroads at Promontory Point, Utah, where the golden spike linking the rails was driven on May 10, 1869. At this spot Union Pacific Irishmen laid the next to last rail, and Central Pacific Chinese men laid the last rail. The two men shaking hands in the middle are the chief engineers for the two railroads, and the two men hoisting bottles from each locomotive are the locomotive engineers. The previous cross-country transport by wagon, which took months, was now reduced by rail to 4 days, 4 hours, and 40 minutes. (Courtesy of Department of Special Collections, Stanford University Libraries)

King's mother was ailing, however, and he spent the month of April with her in Newport. It was clear that she was not happy with her son's engagement to Miss Ellen Dean, and this weighed heavily on King. He remained in Rhode Island until it was time to take to the field again.[4]

The 1869 field party was little changed from that of the previous season except that Timothy O'Sullivan departed for a Navy expedition to Panama, and N. L. Davis replaced Henry Custer in the topographic department. Most of the men arrived by train at Salt Lake City less than a week after the joining of the railroads on May 10, 1869. It was at Promontory Point, northwest of the city, where Dr. Thomas Durant,

FIGURE 8.2. King and Gardner sit on either side of a tripod of rifles and a barometer in camp near Salt Lake City in the summer of 1869. James Marryatt, King's cook and valet, is on the right. All three men are formally dressed for dinner, a custom King honored in the field whenever possible. (Photograph by Timothy O'Sullivan; U.S. Geological Survey)

vice president of the Union Pacific Railroad, and Leland Stanford, Governor of California (and one of the four heads of the Central Pacific Railroad), had symbolically driven the last spikes securing the rails to the ties. Durant had used a silver spike and Stanford, a gold spike. Twenty-two years later, in 1891, Stanford would endow a university adjacent to Palo Alto, California, to honor his deceased son. Its first class (which included future President Herbert Hoover) would graduate in 1895.

Most of the survey's livestock had wintered well, but getting the outfit together—much of the field equipment had disappeared over the winter—proved to be an arduous task. With the permission of Brigham Young, King set up camp above Salt Lake City, on the terrace that marked the high-water level of Pleistocene Lake Bonneville. That elongated, northerly trending ancient lake was some 330 miles by 135 miles, compared with the present Great Salt Lake, which spreads just 75 by 65 miles. Since 1850 the modern lake had risen about 9 feet, owing to a series of wet winters, and the sur-

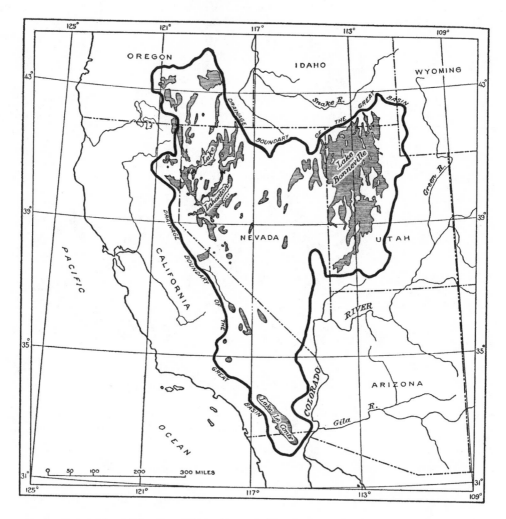

FIGURE 8.3.   Map of the Great Basin (bounded by the heavy line), the broad area with no drainage to the sea that includes most of Nevada and parts of California, Oregon, Idaho, Wyoming, and Utah. All rivers and streams in the region flow into desert sinks, the largest of them Great Salt Lake, where the water is lost by evaporation. Previously, during the Pleistocene Epoch, these lakes were much larger, as shown by the gray tone. The ancestral Great Salt Lake, named Lake Bonneville, is on the east side of the Great Basin, and the ancient lake that includes the present Pyramid Lake and Carson Sink, named Lake Lahontan by King, is on the west side. (Modified from Gilbert, 1890)

vey engaged a boat to map the lake and its islands, and take soundings. N. L. Davis, a new man with naval experience, was placed in charge of this work. Sereno Watson, Robert Ridgeway, and Frederick Clark completed the crew of the vessel *Eureka*.

At the Salt Lake City camp—as at his other camps—King tried to maintain some of the amenities of civilization. He knew that the men's spirits—and productivity—

varied with the quality of the food. King's camps were known for the tastiness and healthfulness of the meals served. He tried to procure the best supplies for the cook, and to make the dining as refined as possible. On occasion, the men were expected to dress for dinner, and King commonly changed from field clothes into evening dress. When questioned on this matter, he replied that "It is very well for you, who lead a civilized life nine or ten months in the year, and only get into the field for a few weeks at a time, to let yourself down to the pioneer level, and disregard the small elegancies of dress and manners which you can afterwards easily resume, because you have not laid them aside long enough to forget them. But I, who have been for years constantly in the field, would have lost my good habits altogether if I had not taken every possible opportunity to practice them. We don't dine this way every day, but we do so whenever we can."[5]

While Samuel Emmons went south to map the desert country west of Salt Lake City, King led a party to the north to search for the outlet of ancient Lake Bonneville. The altitude of the highest terrace, some 300 feet above the present lake, told him that

FIGURE 8.4. Ancient horizontal shorelines at the west base of the Wasatch Range near Farmington, Utah, that record two distinct levels of the ancient Lake Bonneville, ancestral to Great Salt Lake. They were cut by wave action on the margins of that giant expanse of lake water. (Gilbert, 1890)

the outlet must have lain in the north, overflowing through one of the passes into the region drained by the Snake River. (King picked one valley as the likely outlet, but more detailed mapping later by Karl Gilbert identified the actual outlet as Red Rock Pass, at the head of Cache Valley.) The waters at their peak must have thundered through the pass in a cascade rivaling Niagara Falls.[6]

In June, King moved the main camp to Parley's Park, 25 miles east of Salt Lake City. With its cool mountain setting, this camp was a welcome change from the terrace camp at the edge of the desert. Morale ran high in the new camp, and the men were able to supplement their diet with waterfowl, venison, and river trout. The artist Gilbert Munger began working on a series of paintings of the Wasatch Range.

King made frequent business trips to Salt Lake City, but upon his return the men's spirits were always raised by his good humor. As James Hague wrote, "King, always a delightful companion, was especially so in camp. Everybody missed him when he went away and was glad when he came back. If any discontenting grievances, dissentions or difficulties had arisen during King's absence, they all vanished before his

FIGURE 8.5. The Fortieth Parallel Survey party in 1869 riding through lush vegetation in Parley's Park in the Wasatch Mountains, Utah. (Timothy O'Sullivan; U.S. Geological Survey Library)

FIGURE 8.6. Party of the Fortieth Parallel Survey climbing into the heights of the Wasatch Range. The main camp of the survey at Parley's Park was a delightful departure from the dry and dusty desert below, and was used in 1869 as a base for work in the mountains. (From a painting by Gilbert Munger; King, 1878)

genial presence and cheerful spirit as soon as he returned. Many a scanty meal has been made good cheer by his encouraging pleasantries."[7]

By mid-July 1869, the crew of the *Eureka* joined the main party at Parley's Park and was divided among the other parties. The crew had mapped out the great enlargement of the lake caused by the recent wet years when the inflow had exceeded evaporation. They sounded the depth in many places, and investigated wildlife and geology on the islands. The lake work was completed, but along the way they had barely avoided disaster. On two occasions the boat had been caught in heavy squalls and capsized. Once they clung to the hull all night, driven to extreme thirst and nearly blinded by immersion in the concentrated salt water.

King led a squad along the railroad through Echo Canyon and then up the Bear River Valley. Flanking him on the north, James Gardner's party mapped the northern Wasatch Range and then went east to the Medicine Bow Mountains in southern Wyoming. Emmons, on the south, worked in the Wasatch and the Uinta Mountains. In the high country of the Uintas, King observed abundant evidence for glacial action at the headwaters of the Bear River, and noted how it compared with that in the Sierra Nevada and in the East Humboldt Range, Nevada. Coming upon a high peak flanked by cirque-bound lakes, he made the first ascent of the peak and named it Mount Agassiz, after the Harvard professor, Louis Agassiz, an expert on glaciation. He examined the two glacial lakes and named them for two young girls, Jan and Lall, friends of his sister Marian. He composed a poem for them and included it in the 1870 Christmas book that he gave to the three youngsters.[8]

Early in the summer King found time to take his fiancée, Miss Dean, back east to Rhode Island to meet his mother. But after that trip the engagement was abruptly and unaccountably broken off. Gardner, lamenting the fact that he was so distant from his own new bride, wrote his mother from the camp at Parley's Park to "Please say nothing to anyone about Clare's engagement unless to Mrs. Howland [King's mother]. She feels terribly at its being broken for she admired and loved Ellen's noble qualities."[9]

King's mother's dominant nature, coupled with King's growing infatuation with dark-skinned "primitive women"—his head was easily turned by the pretty Indian girls he had met in the West and the tropical beauties of Central America—may both have been factors in this decision. In later years King remarked that "I would never marry a woman anyhow, *just because I said I would.* That is the poorest possible reason men or women can ever have for marrying each other. People who marry without any better reason than that must surely come to grief."[10] Was he simply parroting his mother's words? Whatever the reasons, Deany returned home to the West Coast alone, and remained a spinster the rest of her days.

During the summer's work the survey's crews made important observations on the extensive coal deposits in the Weber Basin, the Bear River Basin, and the west half of the Green River Basin. James Hague arrived in the field and studied gold-silver mines and coal deposits in Colorado. Gardner occupied triangulation points in the high peaks, but by August he had to backtrack to map the terrain west of the Wasatch that had not been completed in previous work. He lamented about "the burning heat of those waterless plains," and wrote "it is very hard to come from the pure brooks to these half poison springs of the desert."[11]

Through the whole summer, Gardner passionately missed his wife of less than a year, and in his letters he mentioned the places in the Rockies they had visited together the previous summer: "At Main Camp. *Parley's Park.* This is where we took dinner the first day out of Salt Lake. In the next tent is a great pile of letters from you locked up, but Palmer and Clare are in the City and will not return till tomorrow. To keep down my impatience I shall climb a peak."[12]

FIGURE 8.7. Clarence King outfitted in buckskin field attire and leggings, sitting on a rock at the shore of Uinta Lake, with a mercury barometer slung over his shoulder. (Photograph by Timothy O'Sullivan; King Memoirs, 1904)

Josephine Gardner suffered from ill health, and from near Salt Lake he wrote her that "I only wish that I could know that your body was doing as well as your mind but I fear you are not able to do much for its development. Oh Darling I am camping at Tuilla on the same spot where we spent that delightful day and evening. The same waving corn fields and in the foreground the same green and yellow meadows stretched beyond to the purple lake shores and the placid blue water shading to a landless horizon in the distance between the mountain islands that stand so sharp and dark against the amber sky. How lovely in itself. How hallowed with sweet associations."[13]

"As I pause for a few days from hard physical labor the whole desolation of this sundered life rolls over me. Oh God, I cry, strengthen me from despair! The blows of my hammer on the rocks, the buzz of a brain busy with intellectual philosophy, will drown the ceaseless moan of this lonely soul; but the hours of rest must come, and then the grief. How must it be with you my poor wife who have to be still so much listening to your sad heart's throbbing! Thank God we both have mental activity."[14]

"Tomorrow will be our anniversary Darling. I can thank God that you are far dearer to me now than then. May each succeeding year come freighted with an equal increase of love and all its beautiful fruits! A thousand blessings rest upon you my Sweet Love, My Life, My All . . . From you alone do I get that sympathy without which life is blank. I feel as if I am alone in the world with you. All the rest are strangers from whom I must keep the knowledge of my inmost soul. Oh if I could clasp you Darling."[15]

Later in August Gardner made astronomical observations at Salt Lake City and invited Brigham Young, who was interested in this work, to visit the observatory.[16] The two had opportunities for long religious discussions during the project. Gardner found that " . . . his mind dwells constantly on political economy. There is no evidence of any Idealism in his nature. It is not the lofty ideal standards toward which the very few strive and the many are dragged along, that make an impression on him. He sees distinctly the *actual average man*, the standards and motives he can appreciate and the resulting morality of life. The mass of people he believes need somebody to do their religious, political and social thinking for them." Gardner wrote that

FIGURE 8.8 (*opposite*). Posed photograph of King taking a break while roping down a rocky crack in the Uinta Mountains. It is clear that the leather barometer case on his shoulder is empty because it is bent. (Timothy O'Sullivan, 1869, Rare Books Division, The New York Public Library)

Young declares, "Here is a Christian world holding what they call high standards. . . . For two thousand years they have preached that man ought to be satisfied with one woman and the result shows that the average man *cannot* be satisfied with one. That is nature. Therefore religion ought to sanction it. For religion should be possible to all. The Christian religion has not met the wants of the ignorant masses. Let us adopt the standards to them in the form of a new church where those that have brains shall think for those that have none, and so direct their lives and labor as to make them happier and more productive. Riches are destructive to most people. Only the few have the mind and character to use them rightly. The masses are happiest with just a fair living earned by hard physical labor."[17]

In describing Mormon women to his wife, Gardner wrote "This summer's experience has taught me to select by expression of face Mormon wives from gentile with almost absolute certainty. A depressed, unsatisfied, and where there is elevation of character, a broken-hearted look, goes through me with a pang. The men are more contented. In their beastly satisfaction they have lost consciousness of a higher life and perish without an aspiration beyond material prosperity. Until lately I have not known how many divorces there are here. Cases are constantly occurring of the first wife leaving her husband on account of neglect after the coming of other wives."[18]

Preparations were made to finish the fieldwork for the season. By late September, the main party returned to Salt Lake City, where some of the worn equipment was auctioned off, the camp men were released, and part of the scientific staff departed by train for the east. Other squads moved west to field-check questionable outcrops and fill in holes in the mapping. The group then disbanded at Argenta, Nevada, 250 miles west of Salt Lake City, most going east, while James Hague went to Virginia City in western Nevada to complete work on the Washoe Mining District. King went on to San Francisco on the now completed railroad and began working on his part of the mineral-deposit study.

After returning east in December 1869 King again rented an office in Washington, D.C., and over the winter the topographic crew set to work reducing the abundant astronomical observations. The maps were brought up to date. The geology work fo-

FIGURE 8.9 (*opposite*). Nine men of the Fortieth Parallel Survey scrambling over a rock face, practicing climbing skills, examining the rock, and apparently enjoying themselves. The man at upper right is Clarence King, passing down a barometer case. This photograph was taken at the same time and place as the previous photograph. (Timothy O'Sullivan, 1869; Yale Collection of Western Americana, Beinecke Rare Book and Manuscript Library)

FIGURE 8.10. Mount Agassiz and glacial Lake Lall in the Uinta Mountains. King named the mountain—carved out of the Carboniferous Weber quartzite—after the Harvard professor from whom he had heard lectures on glaciation. He named the lake after a girlhood friend of his sister Marian, and alluded to its glacial origin in a poem he wrote for a Christmas gift book. (From painting by Gilbert Munger; King 1878, 1870, and Appendix S)

cused on the mining industry volume, and biologist Robert Ridgeway was nearing completion of the zoology volume.[19] Still, the six years of almost constant fieldwork, living under primitive conditions, had begun to tell on King, and he determined to spend more time this next summer in the office, and to live the good life, even though scarcely more than three of his five map sheets were completed.

All the while, King conferred with scientists and explorers from every quarter. He heard a lecture by John Wesley Powell, who had just completed his epic exploration, the first boat trip down the Colorado River. He submitted collections of fossils to Fielding Meek, the Smithsonian Institution paleontologist who had described fossils from the collections of the surveys of both Whitney and Wheeler. He prepared rock specimens for microscopic examination, and ordered chemical analyses of rocks and of precipitates from saline lakes and hot springs. Long walks and horseback rides with Samuel Emmons and James Gardner helped him hold an even keel, but the limitations of Washington soon became apparent. The oppressive summer heat, the lack of a good scientific library, and the distance to the laboratories at Yale made the Washington office less than adequate. Accordingly, he moved to New Haven.

King also took time to draw upon his copious notes to write up some of his experiences for a general popular audience. His superb powers of observation and description served him well, and he first wrote up a piece on the Shoshone Falls of the Snake River that he had visited in September 1868. This was published in October 1870 in the *Overland Monthly* magazine, edited by the writer Bret Harte, a close friend.

As planned, the volume on mining industry, completed by James Hague, was the first volume of the Fortieth Parallel Survey to be published, appearing in 1870 (although it was designated Volume III).[20] It was an exhaustive treatise on the mineral industry of the west, offering a complete scientific and technical description of the Comstock Lode and a large number of precise drawings of mining and milling equipment and the like. King wrote the sections on the geology of the Comstock Lode and on the Green River Coal Basin. A separate accompanying atlas presented a series of sections through the Comstock mines, but what was most innovative were the three geologic maps of mining districts distinguishing different rock units in bright primary colors. Moreover, the topography on the maps was depicted not by the finely penned hachures that had been used almost exclusively in prior publications, but by so-called *grade curves*, lines connecting points of equal elevation now called *contours*. The vertical interval between the curves was 50 feet on two maps of the mining districts and 300 feet on a map of the entire Toiyabe Mountains. At this early use of the contours, they were not elevation-labeled, and no other elevation data appeared on the maps.

When the volume and atlas appeared, they were received enthusiastically by the scientific community. General Andrew Humphreys was surprised to find that the demand exceeded by three times the number printed. Both the volume and the maps were eagerly examined by those involved in other western surveys, and many of the elements, techniques, and ideas were adopted by others. James Hague left the survey shortly after publication to become a private mining consultant.

While comfortably working on his major report on the systematic geology of the western Cordillera, King received a telegram from General Humphreys ordering him into the field to resume survey work. Apparently, new congressional appropriations earmarked for investigations in the West required that some work be done this calendar year, even though it was already late in the season. King reluctantly accepted, but shaped the short season into a venue that was of particular interest to him. In short, he wanted to work on the Cascade volcanoes, especially his first love, Mount Shasta, and that would be the focus of his work.

King hastily began organizing for the new campaign of fieldwork. While eating breakfast, served as usual by his valet, Jim Marryatt, he received a telegram from an old acquaintance, a San Francisco preacher. The clergyman had met a woman who had heard that her long-lost son Jim was employed by King, and she was seeking information about him. King immediately wired that Jim indeed was with him, and that they had planned a trip soon to San Francisco by train, but King would send Jim ahead. When King arrived in San Francisco August 12, 1870, the first visitors to his hotel were Jim and his mother. "As she entered the room and met King face to face, recognizing and greeting him immediately with vigorous expressions of surprise and pleasure, she exclaimed abruptly: 'Well! I declare! And how's the baby?' The woman who had cared for and served as wet nurse for King's baby in her cabin at Panama was Jim's mother."[21]

In San Francisco, King assembled his party, which consisted of geologists Arnold Hague and Samuel Emmons; clerks O. L. Palmer and Albert Clark (who would serve also as barometric observers); and topographers Frederick Clark and Allen Wilson. King also engaged the Yosemite-famous photographer Carlton Watkins and invited the landscape painter Gilbert Munger as an unpaid expedition guest. Jim Marryatt also accompanied the group.

King wrote General Humphreys, justifying this project by pleading that "special geological problems connected with former work seemed to demand a thorough examination of the origin, source, and mode of occurrence of the immense system of volcanic materials and disturbances which form the northern and western margin of the Survey of the 40th Parallel. Much of the fertility of the northern portions of California and Nevada, many of the most important silver deposits, and the most grave of the unsolved questions of Cordillera geology lie in this cordon of volcanic rents. Time, expense, and the arid character of Nevada deserts making it unwise to attack them from the Great Basin side, I came to California, and after an earnest request to General Schofield, obtained gratis an entire outfit, saving thereby almost ten thousand dollars."[22]

Arnold Hague and Allen Wilson went on ahead to investigate Mount Hood, overlooking the Columbia River in Oregon. King's destination was Mount Shasta—his original stimulus to come west in the spring of 1863. Dana's lectures and Brewer's letter were still vivid in his mind, and he had seen but not climbed the peak while with William Brewer in 1863. The team departed from San Francisco August 27, 1870, by steamer for Sacramento, and thence by rail to Chico, 75 miles north. Allen Clark brought 18 government mules over from Camp Halleck, Nevada, and met them en route.

FIGURE 8.11. Looking north toward Mount Shasta from a point 25 miles south, on the upper Sacramento River. Seven years after he first saw the mountain, King finally climbed the peak, in 1870. On that climb his party spent two nights above 12,000 feet examining the upper reaches of the giant volcano. King excitedly reported the discovery of several glaciers on the mountain, deemed an important finding since all authorities up to that time had stated that no active glaciers exist in the United States. (Abbot, 1857)

The Shasta contingent rode north up the Sacramento Valley, where King, with an art critic's eye, described the full palette of the landscape: "Miles of harvested plain lay close shaven in monotonous Naples yellow, stretching on, soft and vague, losing itself in a gray half-luminous haze. Now and then through more transparent intervals, we could see the brown Sierra feet walling us in to eastward, their oak-clad tops fainter and fainter as they rose into this sky. Directly overhead hung an arch of pale blue, but a few degrees down the hue melted into golden gray."[23]

At length, they came within sight of the great mountain. King excitedly related that "At last, through a notch to the northward, rose the conical summit of Shasta, its pale, rosy lavas enameled with ice. . . . From that moment the peak became the center of our life. From every crest we strained our eyes forward as now and then, either

FIGURE 8.12. Camp at base of Mount Shasta, 1870. Painter Gilbert Munger is at work at his easel, topographer Frederick Clark is adjusting his transit, and Clarence King is lounging on the grass. Photograph is by Carlton Watkins, whose buggy is in the back, on the left, with a tripod on top. (Courtesy of Department of Special Collections, Stanford University Libraries)

through forest vistas the incandescent snow greeted us, or from some high summit the opening canyon walls displayed grander and grander views of the great volcano. It was sometimes, after all, a pleasure to descend from these cool heights, with the impression of the mountain upon our minds, to the canyon bottom, where, among the endlessly varying bits of beautiful detail, the mental strain wore off."[24]

In short order, they made camp on the west side of Mount Shasta, at the ranch of Justin Hinkley Sisson, who operated a successful inn and tavern. Sisson settled in the area in 1853, opened a popular wayside inn, and became the resident expert and guide for Mount Shasta. Packs were made up, but Emmons wrote that photographer Watkins' equipment was "about four times the amount [O']Sullivan used to carry, and took up most of the load of our 4 pack mules, so there was very little room left for grub. King had to do most of the packing, and the camp pots were carried on the pommels of our saddles. Sisson led us by a roundabout trail through timber and chaparral some 12 miles to the edge of the timber on the SE slope of the mt."[25]

They took the mules as far up as possible, to about 9,000 feet, and from there the party, consisting now of King, Emmons, Frederick Clark, Albert Clark, and the guide

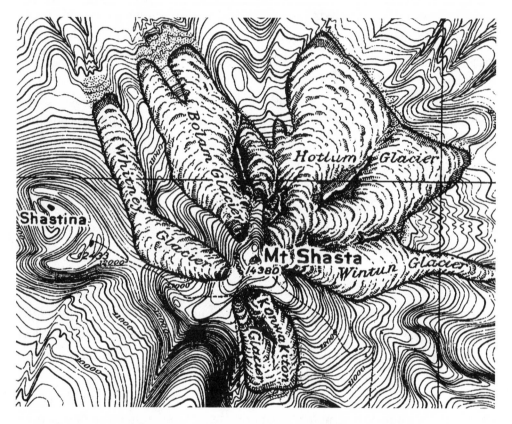

FIGURE 8.13. Map of the upper reaches of Mount Shasta, showing the five glaciers mantling the summit region. The 1870 King party climbed Shastina, the parasitic cone on the west flank of the main peak, ascending from the southwest map corner, and camped on the Shastina Crater rim, from where they spotted the westernmost glacier. King generously named it the Whitney Glacier after his former chief, Josiah Whitney, the director of the California Geological Survey, and proclaimed it to be the first known glacier found in the United States. The climbing party took the route (dashed line) along the Shastina-Mount Shasta saddle to the Shasta summit, camping below the summit the second night. They then descended on the southeast route—that taken by Whitney and Brewer in 1862. That trail affords no good views of the glaciers, apparently explaining why the Whitney party did not see them in 1862. The distance from the high point of Shastina to the peak of Mount Shasta is 2.4 miles. (U.S. Geological Survey 1897 quadrangle map)

Sisson, made up their packs and struck out on foot. They crossed a ridge and headed up a broad gulch toward the western peak, Shastina, some 2,000 feet lower than the main summit. They carried only "fur bags and two days grub of cold venison and bread" and climbed to the rim of Shastina's crater at an elevation of 12,500 feet. Sisson, who had carried up a heavy load of firewood for them, threw it to the ground, saluted, and made his way back down the mountain.

Emmons reported that they "found a little spot about six ft. square, tolerably level under the highest part of the rim, where we made camp by leaving our packs there, and spent the afternoon in working up the crater, the two Clarks topographically, King and I geologically. We discovered a fine glacier between the north side of the crater and the main mass. . . . Whitney and his whole Survey had made the ascent 8 years previously to a day (Sept. 11) and reported that there were no glaciers . . . we prepared our sleeping places by clearing away the larger stones as much as possible, and building a little wall about 2 ft. high around us to break the wind. There making a little fire from some small wood we had brought up with us, we had a nice supper of hot coffee, toasted bread and venison, with a little bacon (the latter I much preferred at that altitude, but unfortunately we had but little). The night was cold, but we managed to pass it pretty comfortably, King and I put our bags inside of each other, getting in together for the warmth: the rocks underneath were very hard, however."[26]

In the morning they crossed into the saddle connecting Shasta and Shastina and began the ascent of the main peak, and from there spied two more glaciers on the northeast side. Emmons noted that his pack "was now very heavy, having the long barometer, my overcoat, and some specimens in addition to what the others carried, 30 lbs I guess at least. We had a very hard climb of four hours over a steep debris slope of loose rocks and sand, which slipped under one at every step, so one could never count on a sure footing, made still more tedious by having to wait for the Clarks, one of whom was climbing his 1st mountain, the other in my opinion a poor mountaineer. The rest of the way alternations of very slippery ice and debris slopes, brought us to the summit about four P.M. where such a wind was blowing it was ticklish work getting on to the highest point . . . we remained till sunset which was the finest thing I ever saw in my life. You may imagine what an extended view we had, when you considered that within at least 100 miles there was no mountains within 5000 ft. of our height. The golden sunset colors extended equally all around the horizon . . . the shadow of the mountain, an immense pyramid of shade, traveled slowly, and yet at a really great speed over mountains and valley to the east of us, away out into Nevada, and there gradually rose up against the sky to an altitude of 20°, and gradually disappeared."

Emmons continued, "We were chilly enough by this time for the thermometer marked 28° (F), and the wind was blowing a small gale, so we hastily descended to [a flat] about 100 ft. below the summit where there is a volcanic spring sending forth sulphurous steam and searched for a shelter from the wind. This was not so easy to find, as the wind swept up from both sides: so we selected a sandy spot, and built ourselves a simple enclosure of stones, but it was bitter cold all night, and the wind blew so that it was with the greatest difficulty we could heat our water to make coffee."[27]

In King's version, "When we sat up for our cup of coffee, which Clark had artistically concocted over the scanty and economical fire, the walls sheltered our backs; and for that we were thankful, even if the wind had full sweep at our heads and stole the very draught from our lips, whirling it about north forty east by compass, in the form of an infinitesimal spray. The zephyr, as we courteously called it, had a fashion of dropping vertically out of the sky upon our fire and leaving a clean hearth. For the space of a few moments after these meteorological jokes, there was a lively gathering of burning knots from among our legs and coats and blankets."[28] That was indeed a

FIGURE 8.14. Whitney Glacier heading in Shasta's western cirque, near the saddle between Mount Shasta (center) and Shastina (out of view on right). It was this view that excited King in 1870. He reported this to be the first glacier discovered in the United States. (Photograph by Carlton Watkins; U.S. Geological Survey Library)

FIGURE 8.15. A close view of the deeply crevassed part of the Whitney Glacier shown in the previous photograph, with man holding an alpenstock in the foreground. (Photograph by Carlton Watkins; U.S. Geological Survey Library)

cold night, despite the warmth of sleeping bags made of wildcat fur, and in the morning each played the waiting game until finally Fred Clark made the coffee. After getting thawed out by the sun, they struck directly down the mountain on the south side and arrived at camp in about 5 hours. King named the first ice sheet that they discovered—heading in the saddle between Shasta and Shastina—Whitney Glacier in tribute to his old chief (the observer who had maintained it did not exist).

Back at the base camp, they were pleased with the images executed during their absence by Munger. Emmons wrote that "The next day a council of war was held in which it was decided that in view of the lateness of the season, Mt. Baker, being the farthest north should be given up, and Mt. Pit, a smaller volcano in Southern Oregon substituted, and King gave me the choice of finishing Shasta, or going immediately North and doing Rainier, and coming back to Pit later. Though I felt that Shasta was probably the finest thing scientifically, Rainier being unknown, no one ever having succeeded in reaching it, yet I could not give up the chance of seeing an entirely new country and chose the latter. King said he calculated to finish Shasta in about ten days, and would then join me as he wished to make the ascent with me for the sake of his Atlantic articles. So I started that same afternoon, Charley driving me over to Yreka, 38 m. distant, whence I took the stage for Portland, Oregon, a weary ride of three days and nights over a terrible rough road."[29]

Next, King and Fred Clark headed out for a week, working along the lower skirts of the Mount Shasta cone. On the east side of the volcano they worked up McCloud Creek to the terminus of a large glacier, and then scrambled up on the ice. The lower part of the glacier was covered with a thick layer of broken rock, but at intervals, where meltwater streams emerged, great caverns were carved back in the ice. About a mile up on the glacier, they encountered a crevasse zone where tumbled blocks of ice lay chaotically about. King wrote that "We were charmed to enter this wild region and hurried to the edge of an immense chasm. It could hardly have been less than a thousand or twelve hundred feet in length. The solid white wall of the opposite side—sixty feet over—fell smooth and vertical for a hundred feet or more, where rough wedged blocks and bridges of clear blue ice stretched from wall to wall. From these and from numerous overhanging shelves hung the long crystal threads of icicles, and beyond, dark and impenetrable, opened ice-caverns of unknown limit. We cautiously walked along this brink, examining with deep interest all the lines of stratification and veining, and the strange succession of views down into the fractured regions below."[30]

They camped near the glacier, and then after a day's march reached the main camp and rejoined their comrades. King now decided to return south, aware that Emmons expected him to join the group on Mount Rainier. On the return to Chico, King's party paused at the same lava tube (Pluto's Cave) that Brewer and King had visited in the fall of 1863. King noted that "Fresh-lava froth and smooth blister-holes lined the sides. Innumerable bats and owls on silent wing floated by our candles, fanning an air singularly still and dense. . . . We then repeated an experiment, formerly made by Brewer and myself, of blowing out our candle to observe the intense darkness, then firing a pistol that we might hear its dull, muffled explosion . . . we felt, as we walked and climbed back to the opening and to daylight, as if we had been allowed to travel back into the volcano age."[31]

When they arrived at Chico, King could not contain his excitement and wrote General Humphreys that "We completely upset the ideas of Humboldt and of Fremont concerning the mountain itself, and have made the somewhat startling discovery of immense existing glaciers. This is the more surprising when we consider that Whitney, Brewer, Dana, and Fremont all visited the peak without observing them, and that Whitney, Dana, and Agassiz have all published the statement that no true glaciers exist in the United States. May I ask that this be kept private until my return.... My plans are all working well and the party continues in good health notwithstanding the terrible physical strain I have called on them to endure."[32] King's party next extended the exploration 60 miles northeast of the Lassen Peak area and worked on volcanic problems on the Madeline Plains, before crossing the border into Nevada.

Meanwhile, Emmons took the stage to Portland and went up the Columbia River, where, fortunately, he met Arnold Hague and Allen Wilson, who had just completed surveying Mount Hood and were heading for Mount Adams. They had indeed discovered an extensive glacier system on Mount Hood. Arrangements were then modified. Emmons would take Wilson and nine government mules and one bell mare on his excursion to Mount Rainier, where he knew that transport would be difficult, while Arnold Hague proceeded to Nevada.

Upon returning to Portland, they learned that Mount Rainier had just been climbed for the first time! Emmons lamented that "I was greatly disappointed therefore on my arrival at Portland to learn that its summit had been reached by Messrs. Stevens and Van Trump of Olympia (the Capitol of W. T. [Washington Territory]) who published an article in the papers, giving a most discouraging account of the dangers and hardships they had gone thro', and everyone assured me that it was very doubtful if I could get in at this late season of the year."[33]

In Olympia, their next stop, they met Hazard Stevens, who gave them detailed information on the route he had taken up the mountain, but again cautioned them about the lateness of the season. The small party continued on—not to be discouraged by this recurring advice. Emmons writes, "Monday after getting some camp pots, and some roughly made ice creepers, we started about one for Yelm Prairie 25 m. to the east, reaching the ranch of [James] Longmire, one of the old settlers, whom we wanted to secure as guide, about sunset. . . . Longmire was very loath to go; he had already been across the mts. twice that season, once for himself, once with Stevens, and the hardships nearly made him sick every time he went. I talked and persuaded, but it was nearly noon the next day before I could make him decide to go."[34]

The party rode several days through the forest, often beset by rain, and eventually worked up the Nisqually River to its junction with the Paradise River, and attempted to move the mules up the valley, thick with tall timber and studded with rocky outcrops. At this point, a mishap with the pack train proved to have serious consequences, as Emmons reports: "Having fallen a little behind, I came hurrying up to find the two pack mules perched like goats, all four feet together, and facing me on a pile of immense boulders, which they had crossed halfway, and there becoming frightened had turned about, and didn't dare to go either way. I tried in vain to urge them on, and finally had to call Wilson back to my aid; but the mules were obstinately determined not to go ahead the way the other animals had gone, and finally one jumped among the rocks, slipped and wedged himself in between two masses bigger than himself; he made such violent efforts to extricate himself we could not get near him, though we were afraid he would break his legs; he finally got out, lost his balance from the weight of his pack, and rolled over down the rocks, bringing up luckily against a fallen tree, his feet in the air and his whole weight resting on the box containing our camp pots and grub. We hauled these out fortunately without damage, but to get him on his feet again was no easy task, for as he was he couldn't assist himself; we had to call Longmire back, and he being pretty strong, by putting ropes round [the mule's] head and tail, we managed to haul him uphill far enough for him to right himself; we then packed him up again, mended the path somewhat and got them over the rocks.

"I put on my barometer, which I had laid aside during this operation and we resumed our march. Scarcely fifty yards further on crossing another pile of broken rock which extended nearly down to the stream, the other pack mule slipped down; seeing that in recovering himself he would be likely to fall the other way and roll down over the rocks, I rushed forward to stop him, when just as I was below him over he came rolling down right upon me. I jumped out of the way as best I could, but he kept on rolling and finally lodged between two big rocks right in the middle of the slope. We took off his pack, and tried to make a way out for him. But after lying quiet a few moments he jumped clean out into the air, seeming bound to kill himself, and it was a wonder he did not, for he must have gone down fifty feet before he stopped, landing finally on his head; we got him out, somewhat cut up, but no bones broken, got him up the hill again and packed him up. I now examined my barometer, which I found broken, and from the state of my leg afterwards concluded I must have gotten a fall among the rocks in trying to get out of his way. This was very disheartening," and that night Emmons was struck by the impact of the loss of the barometer: "It was rather a dismal night for me, for I was feeling very weak from a chronic diarrhea, which had been on me for several days past, brought on partly by the wet and cold, and the means of measuring the mountain now being destroyed, if anything should happen to prevent King's coming."[35] Without a barometer, the work would be rudimentary, at best.

Realizing that this route was not feasible, Emmons, Longmire, and Wilson returned to the Nisqually River and worked up to its head at the magnificent Nisqually Glacier, which presented a 500-foot-high wall of ice at its snout, but again could find no easy route up onto the mountain. A long trek downstream brought them to the Cowlitz Valley, which took them finally to a campsite on Backbone Ridge, overlooking the Cowlitz Glacier. Here they decided to wait for King, who was still expected and would have a replacement barometer and more provisions. While waiting, they returned down the valley and made excursions along the base of the volcano to explore the Nisqually and Paradise Valleys to the west and then up the east side to beyond the White River on the north side. But provisions were low, and for several days they had subsisted on only a small cup of flour each per day. On returning south they met a group of Indians who had just killed a mountain goat. Emmons wrote, "That evening they brought it into camp and after some bargaining I got the whole of it for $3.50. I should think there was over 75 lbs of meat. At first the meat was a little tough and had a slight goaty flavor, but after keeping several days it was delicious, something between beef and mutton. I don't think I ever ate more delicious steaks than those we broiled from its hams; it lasted us two weeks, but we didn't waste any, stewing what wasn't fit to fry or broil."[36]

They then measured out a baseline in flat country to serve as a basis for the triangulation of the mountain, and measured angles to the summit. It would be much easier on a later trip to determine the elevation of the baseline and from that calculate a fairly precise elevation of the peak, without climbing it. They had now spent 20 days on the mountain. After waiting out a four-day gale, and resigned to the fact that King was probably not coming, they established a high camp on the west side of the Cowlitz Glacier at a gnarled pine, the highest firewood available. Longmire did not climb to the camp, but decided to return to Yelm Prairie. Because of the lateness of the season and what appeared to be an impending storm, Emmons and Wilson committed themselves to a summit attempt the following day.

At four the next morning, October 17, 1870, they began climbing across ice and rocky outcrops by moonlight. As Emmons wrote, "The surface was rough, but frequently from the melting and refreezing on this surface quite glassy, but using one of the legs of Wilson's tripod as an alpine staff, I could make a pretty regular progress; we crossed several other crevasses, fortunately not so wide, but that we could find bridges instead of making long detour; but it was very ticklish work after all, for the wind was now blowing violently; and when the strong gusts came we had to stop and brace ourselves against it, for had we once lost our footing we would have slid down this icy slope like the wind, and shot out over the precipices below, if we had not fallen into any of the crevasses. At length we came in sight of some rocks peering out of the snow above us; this was the beginning of the end, we pushed on faster and soon stood on the edge of the crater which forms the summit of the mountain, a remarkable regular circular basin about 1/4 of a mile in diameter, the interior filled with snow and ice to within about 50 feet of the rim, which is abruptly escarped on the inside, and on the outside a very steep debris slope down to the ice, which clothes the whole side of the mountain. It was just 1 o'clock when we reached the highest point of this rim which was on the interior side. Two separate peaks not more than a few hundred feet lower than this, but apparently a mile or two distant, the one N.W. the other S.W., were separated from us by broad valleys filled with ice, that formed the head of glaciers descending east and west. About 1/4 of a mile to the west of the crater rim was a portion of a second rim, almost concentric with this only the sharp upper edges of these rims peered out from the eternal covering of ice. The violence of the wind was beyond anything I had ever experienced, and the cold was intense: my buckskin gloves which got wet on the way up were frozen stiff, and the ends of two of my fingers, which were exposed by holes in them were partially frost bitten. I longed for my overcoat, but consoled myself with the reflection that several overcoats would have been insufficient to keep me warm. We descended into the crater, all along the interior of whose rim were little jets of steam in a vain search for a sheltered spot; finding it impossible to warm up, Wilson divided his lunch with me, and using the cup to my flask, I melted some [snow] and warmed the resulting water, so that we had a little sip of hot brandy and water, and then proceeded to work, for we were convinced that it would not be safe to remain later than 3 o'clock. Wilson went out to a little hogback of glare ice which formed the very highest point to set up his instrument, but the wind lifted it up so that he could not take his hands off it for fear it would be dashed to pieces; just then a stronger gust came which took his feet out from under him so that he sat down and gracefully slid off this slippery peak. The only observations he could get were from points where he was sheltered by the rocks, however the top of the mountain was so broad and sloped off so gradually at first, that the observations from it were not of much account topographically. By then I had examined every thing within my reach, tho' the N.W. and S.W. peaks were too distant to visit in that time. We now commenced the descent."[37]

The climb down from the summit was slow and dangerous. They reached camp by starlight, thus completing the second ascent of Mount Rainier, and the first one-day ascent of this highest of the Cascade volcanoes.

King and his party, having abandoned hopes of joining Emmons at Rainier, continued on from the Lassen area to Nevada and completed the season there. Word

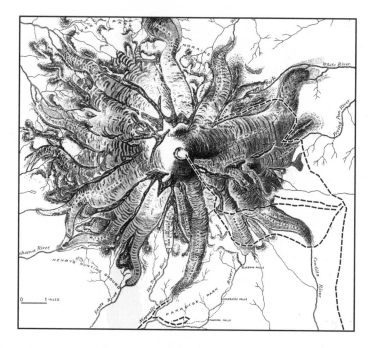

FIGURE 8.16. Map of Mount Rainier showing routes (dashed lines) taken by Samuel Emmons and Allen Wilson in 1870. After exploring the south, east, and northeast flanks of the mountain, they finally reached the summit in one long day, October 17, ascending from the southeast between the Paradise and Nisqually Glaciers. Theirs was the second ascent of the mountain, the first having been made by Hazard Stevens and Philemon Van Trump two months earlier, on August 18 (Haines, 1962; modified from map by H. M. Sarvent and F. F. Evans, 1896, as published in Russell, 1898)

reached them there that Gardner's daughter, Florence, was born in New Haven, November 16.

The party scattered, and in December, on trips to Harvard and Yale, King discussed with his colleagues the significance of the newly discovered glaciers in the west. The fact that others had claimed to have discovered glaciers previously did not diminish the significance of King's careful work. He gave a talk on glaciation for the Connecticut Academy of Sciences, and Dana, editor of the *American Journal of Science*, begged him to write an article for the magazine. A scientific article published in March 1871 included sections on the glaciers of Mount Rainier, by Emmons, and on the glaciers of Mount Hood, by Arnold Hague. King described the five glaciers of Mount Shasta, which attain lengths of 4 to 5 miles. Emmons reported his team had found ten glaciers up to 10 miles long on Mount Rainier, and that at least half as many more were hidden by the mountain. Hague found three glaciers, up to 2 miles in length, on the south side of Mount Hood, all heading in a breached crater.[38] This work inaugurated the scientific study of active glaciation in this country.

During the winter, King revisited his notebooks and wrote several articles for the popular press. From May to November 1871, he published six articles in the *Atlantic Monthly* on his Sierra experiences, and one more, in December in the *Atlantic*, on Mount Shasta. He added to these pieces and in February 1871 reached an agreement with the publisher James R. Osgood to combine them into a book.

King was of the opinion that some of the best science to be accomplished in the West could be realized by concentrating on the great volcanic cones of the Northwest. He had found impressive glacier systems on three of them, and he knew that a systematic study of the whole chain would contribute to our knowledge of past climates as well as provide a hint of what was to come. Moreover, he felt that to continue the belt of mapping he had begun along the 40th parallel would be less productive than the part he had already completed, because other scientists, especially Ferdinand Hayden, had already skimmed the cream from the geology of the Rockies.

But the plan was not received well by General Humphreys, who ordered King to complete the original plan to map and explore " . . . a belt of country extending from the 120th meridian eastward to the 105th meridian, along the 40th parallel of latitude with sufficient expansion north and south to include the lines of the Central and Union Pacific railroads."[39] Regarding King's proposed volcano project, he noted that interesting though it was, it could " . . . hardly be considered authorized under any existing act or appropriation" and that he did "not feel justified in recommending to the Secretary of War that a Revenue Steamer be sent to Alaska for the purpose of examining Mount St. Elias."[40] King dutifully abandoned his plan and geared up for more fieldwork in the eastern extremities of the Fortieth Parallel area.

By early June 1871, the survey party was in camp near Fort Bridger in southwest Wyoming. Parties under Arnold Hague and Samuel Emmons set out to map the country between the Green River and the Front Range in Colorado and Wyoming. After seeing the fieldwork underway, King made a trip to San Francisco to obtain additional supplies and hire packers. While there, he stole a march on General Humphreys and took the opportunity to make another attempt on Mount Whitney. No doubt his interest was quickened by correspondence from Charles Hoffmann, who had made new measurements in the summer of 1870 on the position of the mountain, as viewed from Owens Valley east of the Sierra. Hoffmann would use these measurements in preparing his topographic map of the central part of California, which was published in 1873. But unbeknownst to him (and to King), the angles from

FIGURE 8.17.   The staff of the California Geological Survey in about 1870. From left to right: William H. Pettee, Josiah D. Whitney, Alfred Craven, Watson A. Goodyear, Carl Rabe, and Charles F. Hoffmann. All but Pettee played a role in the Mount Whitney saga. Hoffmann (topographer) was on the 1864 Brewer expedition that identified and named Mount Whitney, honoring the director of the survey. Craven (assistant topographer), Goodyear (geologist), and Hoffmann were on the mapping expedition of 1870 to Owens Valley that incorrectly identified and surveyed Sheep Mountain (now Mount Langley) as Mount Whitney. In July 1873, Goodyear rode a mule to the summit of Sheep Mountain and reported that the true Mount Whitney was about 5 miles to the north. Rabe (cook and topographic assistant) was in the 1873 party that made the third ascent of the true Mount Whitney, and made the first barometric measurements of its height. (Courtesy of the Bancroft Library, University of California, Berkeley)

Owens Valley were taken on the wrong mountain, so that the supposed Mount Whitney ended up on the map some four to five miles south of its true position.

During a jolting three-day stage ride from Carson City to Lone Pine, King noted that "The Sierra, as we traveled southward, grew bolder and bolder, strong granite spurs plunging steeply down into the desert; above, the mountain sculpture grew grander and grander, until forms wild and rugged as the Alps stretched on in dense ranks as far as the eye could reach. More and more the granite came out in all its strength. . . . Here and there a canyon-gate between rough granite pyramids, and flanked by huge moraines, opened its savage gallery back among peaks."[41]

FIGURE 8.18. If the weather had not been cloudy when King climbed the false Mount Whitney (Mount Langley) on a stormy day in June 1871, he would have had this view of the true higher Mount Whitney five miles northwest. Instead, he believed he had climbed Whitney and happily proclaimed to the press his success in climbing the nation's highest peak. (Sketched in 1875 by William A. Cowles when with the Wheeler survey; Wheeler, 1889)

When the coach reached its destination, King "left a Green barometer to be observed at Lone Pine, and carried [a] short high-mountain instrument, by the same excellent maker."[42] In Lone Pine, King gained a companion, Paul Pinson, and the two proceeded west through a range of low hills, where King noted that "the granite was riven with innumerable cracks, showing here and there a strong tendency to concentric forms, and I judged the immense spheroidal boulders which lay on all sides, piled one upon another, to be the kernels or nuclei of larger masses."[43] This is a clear description of the spheroidal weathering of granite bedrock in the Alabama Hills, a small fault-block range that protrudes above the great debris slope rising westward to the Sierra Escarpment.

Taking a route he expected would bring them to Mount Whitney, King was guided by the erroneous position supplied by Hoffmann. This position was based on two 1864 magnetic bearings (by Hoffmann from Mount Brewer and by King himself from Mount Tyndall), and on Hoffmann's 1870 bearings from Owens Valley, which were erroneously sighted not on Mount Whitney, but on Mount Langley (called

Sheep Mountain at the time). King and his companion began climbing a "southern canyon," probably Tuttle Creek, but soon encountered stormy wet weather. They made camp at nightfall in an alpine grove under an overhanging rock at 10,000 feet. After a meal of beef, toast, and tea, they bundled up in their overcoats for the night before a blazing fire.

The next morning, June 22, 1871, dawned clear, and they strode up a glaciated valley toward timberline. As they ascended, a mist began to develop, and toward the top of the great mountain they found themselves largely in clouds, denied a clear view of the surrounding peaks. At the summit they found a small cairn in which was fixed an Indian arrow pointed west. King was overjoyed seemingly to have finally reached the summit of the peak that he had failed to attain on two previous occasions. In reviewing the climb he noted that "Only at the very crest, where ice and rock are thrown together insecurely, did we encounter any very trying work. The utter unreliableness of that honeycomb and cavernous cliff was rather uncomfortable, and might, at any moment, give the death-fall to one who had not coolness and muscular power at instant command. I hung my barometer from the mound of our Indian predecessor, nor did I grudge his hunter pride the honor of first finding that one pathway to the summit of the United States, fifteen thousand feet above two oceans."[44] Assuming that only Indians had climbed the peak before, he left at the summit a half-dollar on which was inscribed his name as a record of his "first ascent" of Mount Whitney. On his return to Lone Pine, he proclaimed his success to the local press and described how the highest mountain in the United States had finally been conquered. The altitude that King measured for Mount Whitney, 15,000 feet, was perpetuated on later maps. It would be two years before others discovered that King had climbed Sheep Mountain, not Mount Whitney.

King next took the train back east so he could supervise the printing of *Mining Industry*, the first volume to be published under the auspices of the Fortieth Parallel Survey. King noted that "Volume III has been first prepared and published, because its subject, Mining Industry, is most directly applicable to the material development of that great extent of mountain territory opened up by the Pacific Railroad."[45] He prepared a lengthy list of recipients for the volume, including scientists, managers, politicians, and libraries in Europe and America. This task completed, in August, he returned west by rail to rejoin the survey.

Mining Industry was published as a handsome volume of some 650 pages with an accompanying folio of 14 atlas-plates of maps and sections of mines and mining districts. James Hague was the principal author, his work concentrating on the engi-

FIGURE 8.19. View southeast across Mount Whitney (W) to Mount Langley (L), showing the similarity in shape of these two mountains. Clarence King climbed Langley in 1871 in cloudy weather, believing it to be Mount Whitney. He wrote about his success in climbing the highest peak in the United States in his book *Mountaineering in the Sierra Nevada*, published in 1872. In 1873 the true Mount Whitney was climbed by a group of fishermen from Lone Pine, and King retracted claims of his mistaken first ascent in a second edition of his book. (U.S. National Park Service photograph by François Matthes)

neering and economic aspects of various mines, especially Nevada's Comstock Lode. He included many plates detailing mining and milling machinery and methods.

James Hague also wrote a section on the mining districts of Nevada, Utah, and Colorado. Arnold Hague included an essay, supported by numerous chemical analyses, on the chemistry of the Washoe process of reducing the Comstock ores. Clarence King wrote sections on the comparative geology of mineral deposits of all the mines in the Fortieth Parallel area, and also a section on the geology of the Comstock Lode based on extensive surface and underground examination.

King also included an article on the Green River Coal Basin, supported by an analysis of recovered fossils by Fielding Meek. The strata bearing these coal deposits began to be laid down in a Cretaceous marine environment that merged upward into a Tertiary freshwater environment. King states that "Our knowledge of the formation is now so well advanced that it can be said with perfect safety that the series contains a practically inexhaustible supply of coal. Beds from 7 to 25 feet in thickness are discovered at intervals over 500 miles, and from their ordinarily gentle dips may be mined with unusual ease." He noted that the Pacific Railroad Company owned a checkerboard of alternate square-mile sections in the coal country, except where Mormon settlers had made claims prior to the railroad surveys. He continues "That the land policy, however, of the Mormon Church having been arbitrary and peculiar, it is difficult to say where the final ownership of these lands is vested. The paradox of a community claiming land under a government against whose laws they rebel, casts a shadow over all their titles."[46]

The *Mining Industry* volume was well received, and requests were received for more than three times the number printed. Reviews by experts in the *North American Review* and the *American Journal of Science* were favorable. This, the first tangible product of the Fortieth Parallel Survey, helped pave the way for increased Congressional support.

Prior to the 1871 field season Samuel Emmons had invited his boyhood friend Henry Adams out to visit him in the field, in Wyoming. Adams, the grandson and great-grandson of presidents, was a professor of history at Harvard and editor of the *North American Review*. Because of the sedentary lifestyle of his university position, he enjoyed traveling during the summer, and decided to indulge his interest in natural history, as well as hunting and fishing, with a trip to the West.

Upon arriving in Denver for the field season, King took a light buggy over rough roads and trails to the Long's Peak region, where he intended to join up with Arnold Hague's party. He found lodging at Estes Park in a rough cabinlike inn that provided a single room and bed for guests. Long after dark, a man who had been fishing came to the cabin alone asking for dinner and a place to stay. It was Henry Adams, and here he met Clarence King, who seemed a kindred soul. Adams later wrote in his third-person style that "King had everything to interest and delight Adams. He knew more than Adams did of art and poetry; he knew America, especially west of the hundredth meridian, better than anyone. He knew even women; even the American women; even the New York women, which is saying much. Incidentally he knew more practical geology, than was good for him, and saw ahead at least one generation further than the text-books. . . . His wit and humor; his bubbling energy which swept every one into the current of his interest; his personal charm of youth and manners; his faculty of giving and taking profusely, lavishly, whether in thought or in money as though he were Nature herself, marked him almost alone among Americans."[47]

The two men talked late into the night before the fire, and then they shared the only bed, where they continued to talk nearly to dawn. Thus began a friendship that lasted the rest of their lives. The two visited Arnold Hague on Long's Peak, and then went on to Bridger Basin where Adams joined his old friend Emmons in the high Uinta Mountains and spent the next two weeks with him.

King, meanwhile, went to Cheyenne, Wyoming, to meet N. R. Davis, the former assistant who had been in charge of the boat *Eureka* on Great Salt Lake. Davis had meanwhile become a stockman on the Wyoming plains, where ranchers made good use of the abundant feed for beef cattle, which were then sent by rail to the stockyards in Chicago. Davis had a ranch on Owl Creek in Colorado, not far south of Cheyenne. This business of running cattle on the open range had an obvious potential for profit, and King invested a modest sum in the business, leaving all the operations to Davis.

Under Davis' management, the enterprise prospered, and by the summer of 1872, King had made a 25 percent profit on his investment. To help expand the business, he looked for more investors, and did not have to look far: Gardner, Emmons, and F. H. Sheldon (a topographic assistant on the survey) were eager to invest their savings, and came up with $15,000 between them. They agreed that new cattle would be purchased with this money, the cattle to be branded separately and run with the main herd. (After a five-year period the investors would realize a 50 percent return on the current value of their share of the cattle.)

After the initial Cheyenne dealings, King had rejoined Arnold Hague's group in North Park, but found that the topographic work had come to a standstill because of a pervasive haze—caused in part by forest fires—that limited instrumental observations. They would simply have to concentrate on geologic mapping and wait until rain and snow cleansed the atmosphere.

King rejoined Emmons' party in late September 1871, in the northern Uinta Mountains, to examine key geologic features and to complete parts of the range not yet visited. They went through Brown's Park and studied the steep walls of the canyon of Ladore, where grand layers of rock were exposed where the Green River cut through the range. After enduring a snowstorm, they went on to the Yampa River, crossed it at the junction with the Little Snake River, and worked the country to the headwaters of that stream.

A second storm nearly forced the close of the season, but while crossing a desolate region of badlands they surprised a grizzly bear and immediately gave chase on horseback for sport. Progressively, the region became more rugged, until the horses could no longer navigate the maze of steep gullies, some with nearly vertical walls. King, Allen Wilson, Samuel Emmons, and two soldiers finally ran the grizzly to ground. Its tracks led into a narrow cave formed where a stream had undercut a canyon wall and breached into another ravine.

Samuel Emmons reported that "Various attempts at dislodgment by smoking, etc., were unsuccessful; and finally King, who had poked his head far enough in at the upper end to see in the dark, said he could distinguish the animal's eyes, and would go in and shoot him. . . . King wriggled himself into the little hole at the upper end until he was far enough in to raise his body on one elbow and put his rifle to his shoulder. Even then he could not distinguish the form of the bear; but he could see the gleam of its two eyes and feel its hot breath. Nor could he, at first, distinguish the sights of his rifle; but, after accustoming himself somewhat to the darkness, he aimed as best he could between the eyes, and fired. The big soldier that had been stationed for that purpose behind him, at once dragged him out by the heels, and in his excitement, kept on dragging long after he had got his man out. As a result, King's face was badly scratched in the sand."[48] When the bear was pulled out into the sunlight it was discovered that King's aim was true; his shot had penetrated the beast's brain.

At length, bad weather heralded the end of the 1871 season. The party retreated to Fort Bridger on November 2, and from there traveled by rail to San Francisco for winter quarters.

As the year waned, Gardner's wife Josephine, suffering from the effects of consumption, became increasingly unable to care for her infant daughter.

CHAPTER NINE

AN UNPARALLELED FRAUD

Rocks rich in gems and mountains big with mines
Whence many a bursting stream auriferous plays
—James Thompson, "The Seasons"

By the end of his twenties in 1871, Clarence King had already risen to national prominence. He had led a successful government survey that by then had published the first
of several volumes to come, a major work on mining in the West. It included an exhaustive description of the fabulous Comstock Lode, the silver strike that largely fi-
nanced the Union efforts in the Civil War. He was the first to discover glaciers in the
United States, and was acclaimed as the first to climb the highest peak in the nation.
Along the way, he had published a series of popular essays in a widely circulated magazine, the *Atlantic Monthly*, describing his adventures in the mountains of the West,
and these would soon be combined into a book. The year 1872 would bring more ac-
colades, but three other experienced explorer-mappers were steadily moving their
own surveys into the same busy arena.

In early January 1872, James Gardner's wife Josephine died of tuberculosis in
Oakland, California, after a three-year marriage. Daughter Florence, less than 14
months old, also suffered from the disease, but she would recover. After Josephine's
death, Gardner took Florence east, where his mother could raise her. Gardner missed
his daughter, and in June wrote his mother from Wyoming about his encounters with
wild goats: "If it were not so far I should bring home a young one to tame for Florence. When the time comes that she begins to desire to ride the pigs think how much

FIGURE 9.1.   Kilauea Crater, Hawaii, in 1840 when examined by geologist James Dana with the U.S. Exploring Expedition. The crater looked much the same in 1872 when visited by Clarence King and Arnold Hague. They studied molten lava within the crater, and examined the broad ledge (called the Black Ledge) about 600 feet beneath the rim of the crater, which marks a high lava level. The bottom of the crater, in which a circulating lava lake is commonly active, fluctuates in height beneath the ledge. (Etching by J. Drayton; Dana, 1890)

more amusing it would be to caper about on one of these lively animals. A friend of mine had one that used to run up his great chimney and out onto the roof then jump to the ground. Well you may kiss the little bird for me."[1]

King continued to suffer intermittently from ill health, perhaps brought on by the hardship of the late season's fieldwork. Early in the year he decided to take time off for a vacation in Hawaii, no doubt inspired by the Yale lectures of James Dana, who had visited the islands in 1840 as part of the U.S. Exploring Expedition under the command of Lieutenant Charles Wilkes. King, with Arnold Hague, took passage from San Francisco for Hawaii in February, and in justifying the vacation time to General Humphreys, he wrote: "My reason for asking this absence was that both Mr. Hague and myself were seriously run down by long and arduous work."[2] Gardner was left in charge of the office.

They sailed by steamer to Honolulu, then directly to Hilo on the big island of Hawaii, aboard the inter-island paddlewheel steamer *Kilauea*. There they studied the ongoing volcanic activity at Kilauea Volcano, where a molten, red-hot lava lake was actively circulating within the firepit Halemaumau. They pondered the flow of small streams of red-glowing lava, and studied the marvelous forms of new black lava immediately after it had cooled and solidified. Here one could *see it happen*. There was no doubt how the features of the lava formed, features that the two geologists had studied on ancient lava flows in California and Nevada.

King enjoyed the Hawaiian people and was eager to learn more about them. He talked to the natives in their villages and jotted down observations in his notebook. He delighted in swimming in the surf and testing his strength against that of the natives. King and Hague joined the Hawaiians in feasts, and King reveled in watching the young people ride the swift current of a stream near Hilo, "Resigning themselves to the resistless current, their folded feet tapering like arrowheads, their hands clasped high above them, they stretched their lithe length in ecstasy as they sank into the curved crest of the cataract and shot down with the descending flood, a flight of shadows over the shimmering surface of a screen. The wave clothed them in its limpid garment; they were as spirits in their native elements, a denser part of it fashioned in the image of their maker, that anon dissolved, as it were, only to flash again in spurts of phosphorescent flame adorn that crystal column; naiads they were, and nereides, and water sprites and angels in liquid amber, as they vanished into the depths below."[3]

Years later, King's artist friend John La Farge told of King's interest in these visions, "Pretty girls, with arms thrown out and bodies straight for balance, their wet clothes driven tight to the hips in the rush of water had a look of gold against the gray that brought up Clarence King's phrase about Hawaii and the 'old-gold girls that tumble down waterfalls.' In the plunge and the white foam, the yellow limbs did indeed look like goldfish in a blue-green pool."[4] King found himself more attracted to these golden girls in a state of nature than he was to the stylish Victorian women of his own social stratum. He lusted for a spontaneous natural lover, unfettered by the mores of his own class that seemed always to preclude abandonment to passion. As Henry Adams wrote, "He loved the Spaniard as he loved the Negro and the Indian and all the primitives because they were not academic."[5]

While King and Hague made the most of their Hawaiian vacation, King's book *Mountaineering in the Sierra Nevada* was published. The book, primarily a collection of his *Atlantic Monthly* articles, was based mainly on his adventures in the Sierra Nevada with the California Geological Survey. It was largely factual, but rendered very readable by its captivating adventures (some perhaps a bit exaggerated), and by vivid descriptions of the country and insightful portraits of local people, often speaking in dialect. It included chapters on the great mountain range and its forests, the

FIGURE 9.2.   West bank of the North Platte River near Fort Fred Steele, not far from
Rawlins, Wyoming. The fort was maintained by the U.S. Army from 1868 to 1886 to protect
the Union Pacific Railroad from attack by Indians, and was a supply and rendezvous point
for King's Fortieth Parallel Survey during the final years of fieldwork in the eastern project
area. Timber floated down the river from the Medicine Bow Mountains was cut into ties for
use on the railroad (note the stacks on the left). (William Jackson photograph; U.S.
Geological Survey Library)

austere, treeless beauty of the Sierra high country, discovery of Mount Whitney, the
first ascents of Mounts Tyndall and Whitney, the glories of the incomparable
Yosemite Valley, and tales of mountain men, settlers, Indians, and desperados. Two
chapters describe the Mount Shasta region, and recount the ascent of that magnificent volcano and King's rambles over and around the nation's first known glacier system. His vivid description of nature in all of its scenic diversity bespoke the singular-
ity of his training in art and photographic memory. The spirited chapters recounting
his interactions with local settlers and natives reveal his sensitivity and his genuine interest in all of humankind.

    The book became popular overnight. As the historian Therman Wilkins wrote,
"The whole of *Mountaineering* was so steeped in the flavor of California that its iden-
tity as 'local color' was quickly perceived, and the sketches were linked with land-

marks of regionalism like Harte's stories of the Mother Lode. But neither King's local color nor his evident romantic tendencies could obscure his book's position as an original of American realism."[6] The book went through more editions in England than in the United States, and was generally regarded there as the best book of its kind that had been written.[7]

King and Hague returned to San Francisco on March 26, 1872, and on April 28 three parties were dispatched for the field, under the charge, respectively, of Samuel Emmons, Arnold Hague, and James Gardner. Emmons and Hague proceeded to Winnemucca, Nevada, Gardner having been delayed in New York, arranging for his daughter's care by his mother. Frederick Clark assumed charge of the topographic crew until Gardner was able to join them with men and animals at Fort Steele, Wyoming. The topographers spent most of the season in the easternmost of the designated survey's quadrangles, north of the North Platte River. They measured a base-

FIGURE 9.3.   The train station at Sherman, Wyoming, in the 1880s, at the crest of a broad plateau-like summit about 33 miles west of Cheyenne. This station, at 8,271 feet above sea level, is the highest on the entire railroad, and was the site for the easternmost astronomical station within King's survey area. (William Jackson photograph; U.S. Geological Survey Library)

FIGURE 9.4. An astronomical station set up for the determination of latitude and longitude in the late 1860s. The instrument on the left is an astronomical transit by which longitude was determined by measuring the exact time that a given star passed across a north-trending line through the station. The time was measured either by the chronometer in the man's hand or by a telegraph connection to a precise clock. The instrument on the right is a zenith telescope, which measured the elevation above the horizon of given stars at a fixed time to determine latitude. All measurements were repeated nightly for weeks to increase precision. The astronomer is probably James Gardner. (Photograph by Timothy O'Sullivan, U.S. Geological Survey Library)

line between Fort Steele and Rawlings and established the stations necessary to tie it to the main triangulation net. When the snow melted in the high country, they went into the Medicine Bow Mountains, surveyed that range, and marched on to the Laramie Plain and the Rabbit Ears Mountains. During September and part of October they worked in the high mountains north of Long's Peak, and in the drainages of the Platte, Grand, Cache la Poudre, and Big Thompson rivers.

Early in October, Gardner rode to Sherman, Wyoming, to make astronomical observations at the Coast Survey longitude station on the railroad. Satisfied at length with his weeks of observations—all using telegraphed time—he traveled 800 miles west, by railroad, the entire length of the Fortieth Parallel Survey project area, to Verdi, Nevada, near the California border. There, he and Professor George Davidson of the Coast Survey made similar astronomical observations—again using telegraphed time signals from Washington or Salt Lake City—for determination of longitude. For these measurements they employed an astronomical transit, a telescope set up so as to sweep the heavens up and down only along a precise north-trending line, i.e. the meridian. As each of a series of known stars passed across the vertical crosshair, their passage time was measured to an accuracy approaching 1/100th of a second. The same kind of time measurement was done for the same stars at another eastern observatory positioned at known longitude. From the time difference between the meridian transits of the selected stars at each of the two sites, the longitude difference of the unknown (western) site could be determined relative to that of the known (eastern) site. Dozens of such measurements had to be made on each star over a period of weeks, so that a large body of data could be appraised and averaged. The processing of large amounts of numerical data of this kind led to some of the first systematic studies of the theory of error.

The longitude measurements from Sheridan, Wyoming, Verdi, Nevada, and the Salt Lake Observatory, Utah, situated midway between the other two, provided the longitude control needed for the entire survey. With the astronomical observations complete, Gardner went on to San Francisco and spent the next month and a half reducing his data and compiling maps.

Meanwhile, Samuel Emmons worked north of the Humboldt River in central Nevada, in a block of land extending past Elko to Humboldt Wells. As King reported to General Humphreys, "The object of this work was to enable us to carry our second block of work farther north than we had originally planned, in order that the geological sections drawn through the whole belt of surveyed country might lie on a great circle, thus bearing an important relation to the questions in sphericalorography" [mountains on the globe].[8] Samuel Emmons arrived by rail at Fort Steele by the middle of June and investigated the drainage of the Muddy River to its junction with the Snake. He then traveled to the summit of the Grand Encampment Mountains, where he met Gardner's party. On October 1 he left his own party under the command of Allen Wilson and went by rail to Austin in central Nevada to measure the thickness of geologic sections, and then met King at Fort Bridger. Wilson was joined by the photographer Timothy O'Sullivan, and they ended the season crafting a series of photographs of the Cherokee Bad Lands, as well as the great canyons of the Green and Bear Rivers, which had cut giant canyons through the Uinta and Escalante ranges.

Arnold Hague worked south and east of Winnemucca examining mining operations at Eureka, Mineral Hill, Hamilton, and Spruce Mountain before taking the railroad to meet King at Toana (somewhat west of the present Wendover, Utah). He focused on the relationship of the older geologic formations (Paleozoic and Triassic) to the silver deposits. Hague went by rail to Ogden and from there rode into the drainage of the Bear River, eventually to join forces with Gardner's group. This collective effort by the several parties of the survey completed virtually all of the remaining fieldwork in the Fortieth Parallel Survey project area by the end of the season. The region had been intensively covered, and the men were intimately familiar with the terrain.

After the Hawaiian interlude, King set off in April to investigate glaciation in the Sierra Nevada, between the Fresno and Merced Rivers, but was unable to accomplish much so early, owing to a heavy snow pack. His two assistants remained in the range, intent on moving into the higher country when the snow melted. King, meanwhile, made a tour of the Fortieth Parallel Survey groups working in Nevada and Wyoming. Returning then to San Francisco, he found the mining world agog over reports that diamonds had been discovered at an undisclosed spot in the West, reportedly in Arizona.

This frenzy had been set off early in 1872 when two prospectors deposited a bag of raw diamonds in a San Francisco bank. William Ralston, a director of the Bank of California, and a group of businessmen he assembled quickly took interest in the find, found the prospectors, and urged them to take representatives of the group to the gem locality. They agreed on condition that the men be blindfolded during the journey so that the find's locality would remain secret. The trip was a long one. After travel on the Union Pacific Railroad, the agents were conducted on a four-day trek on horseback through canyon country to the prospect. There diamonds, rubies, and other precious stones were found in abundance. Retracing their steps to the railroad, at an unknown station, they traveled back to San Francisco, and reported on their stunning findings.

Later, the same two miners, having worked the prospect further, returned with a bag of stones. Asbury Harpending, a friend of Ralston's, met the miners who "were travel-stained and weather-beaten, and had the general appearance of having gone through much hardship and privation." Harpending brought the men to his house, where his associates had gathered. "We did not waste time on ceremonies. A sheet was spread on my billiard table, I cut the elaborate fastenings of the sack, and, taking hold of the lower corners, dumped the contents. It seemed like a dazzling many-colored cataract of light!"[9]

Samples were sent on to New York, where Charles Tiffany examined the gems and declared them to be "a king's ransom." Being cautious, the syndicate then hired Henry

Janin, a well-respected mining engineer and friend of Clarence King. As before, Janin
and his inspection party were blindfolded at critical junctures, and efforts were made
to confuse such spies, from outside the San Francisco group, as might have been
watching. When the party finally reached the site, Janin was convinced of the authen-
ticity of the occurrence, and he too verified the presence of a rich deposit of precious
stones. On the basis of his report, "The syndicate purchased the claims for about

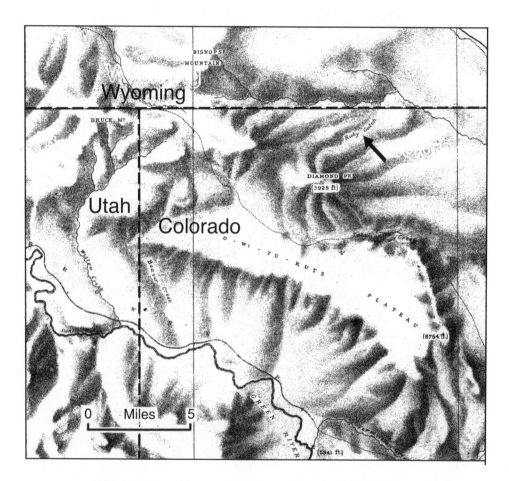

FIGURE 9.5.   Map of the common boundary area of Wyoming, Utah, and Colorado
where the fraudulent salting of diamonds and other gems was uncovered by King's party in
November 1872. After riding 150 miles from Fort Bridger in freezing weather, King's pack
train reached the supposed mine site at Ruby Gulch, north of Diamond Peak in Colorado,
about one mile from the Wyoming line (arrow). They quickly ascertained that the diamond
field—previously authenticated by several parties of experts—was actually a hoax. Gems
had been scattered about and dropped in holes poked in the ground. (Modified from a small
part of the topographic map of Atlas Sheet II; King, 1876)

$600,000, stocked a company for $10,000,000, as I believe in good faith, and the excitement was at fever heat from New York to San Francisco."[10]

In August, King left San Francisco again for Fortieth Parallel Survey business, and spent three weeks at mining camps in Nevada. A month later, he again crossed the Sierra near Yosemite to Owens Valley, where, as planned, he met his friend Albert Bierstadt, a celebrated landscape painter. They traveled up Bishop Creek and met King's glacier-study group in the High Sierra, joining them for several weeks in the vicinity of Mount Humphreys and the Evolution Valley. Here King traced moraine systems left behind by the melting of past glaciers. The barometric altitudes of these ancient ice rivers would record climate history. Bierstadt sketched and painted.

Returning at length to Owens Valley, the two observed the effects of the powerful earthquake that had occurred near Lone Pine on March 26. All buildings in the small town were destroyed, and 27 people had been killed, primarily by the collapse of adobe buildings. They then reentered the range at Kearsarge Pass, west of Fort Independence, and retraced in reverse the trail the pioneering Brewer Party had taken in 1864. Bierstadt filled his sketchbook with drawings of the mountains. After riding the treacherous, rocky trail down Bubbs Creek to Kings River Canyon, they emerged from the mountains at Visalia, where King and Bierstadt took the train back to San Francisco.

By then, the diamond fever in San Francisco was raging higher than in April. But even though the diamond discovery site was reported to be in Arizona, Allen Wilson and others from the King survey who had been working in Wyoming and along the railroad during the summer noticed that several suspicious parties had left the train in a certain sector and later reboarded. The surveyors believed they were those who visited the diamond prospect; they had left the Union Pacific Railroad in Wyoming between Green River and Rawlins.

Wilson, Emmons, and Gardner assembled in San Francisco in the fall, and while waiting for King to arrive they began piecing together information on the possible site of the diamond fields. It was clear that the discovery must lie between the Green and Yampa Rivers, because reports placed the rail offloadings between those two streams, and both would have been difficult to cross at the time the fields were visited. The geologists themselves had worked this country during the summer and were intimately familiar with it.

Corroborative information was obtained through casual talks with selected people in mining circles. Three different parties had been to the site, and from them the geologists learned something of the availability of timber and water, the lay of the land, and the general appearance of the nearby mountains. Such seemingly innocuous information was particularly meaningful to those who knew the country well. When King returned from the field, his men convinced him that they knew the site's location beyond reasonable doubt and asked to visit it immediately. They believed that it lay in their map sheet Number II, near the point where Utah, Colorado, and Wyoming meet. King not only agreed but eagerly joined them. Quickly putting together some equipment, including sieves and a diamond point to test the gems, King, Wilson, and Emmons departed the next day by railroad for Fort Bridger, Wyoming. Gardner remained in San Francisco to complete work on the maps, now that the topographic fieldwork was done.

King's party stopped at Fort Bridger, where Wilson had left the camp outfit and animals for the winter. After several days assembling equipment, a party of six, including two packers and a cook, headed south over sagebrush hills and open country to northernmost Colorado. The weather was bitter cold, reaching subzero temperatures Fahrenheit, with a cold wind and fresh snow on the ground. When crossing streams, ice balled up on the mules' legs and "rattled as they went like rude castanets."[11] After 150 miles on the trail Wilson reported that "On the afternoon of the fifth day [November 2] we came to a small spring. I knew that we were near the place that I thought was the supposed diamond field, and suggested to Mr. King that we halt and tell the packers to camp, and then proceed ourselves to investigate further, as we did not wish the men to know what we were about, thinking that if we were to be fooled, the fewer who knew of it the better."[12]

They climbed a mesa (called Table Rock) capped by beds of sandstone, and before long found some recently planted posts, staking out the ground as a mining claim. Indistinct boot tracks indicated where former visitors had walked. Carefully searching the ground, they began finding rubies, and by the time the sun had gone down they had several rubies (actually pink garnets) and three stones proved to be genuine diamonds, when tested with the diamond point. There was no doubt that gems were really present. They celebrated that night around the campfire. They were pleased that under such difficult circumstances they had pinned down the site of the elusive diamond field, and that they had verified the presence of gems.

The next day they expanded the search and began a systematic study of the entire area with unforeseen results. Surface soil and sand were collected from more than thirty sites around Table Rock. The location and nature of all gem finds were mapped. The samples were screened and washed. Four pits were dug in the ravine—which they called Ruby Gulch—on the north side of the mesa, and several tons of debris from the pits were sieved and systematically examined. Not only were four types of diamonds found, but they were associated with rubies, sapphires, garnets, amethysts, spinels, and emeralds, an association that is highly unlikely in nature. Many of the gems were found in recently disturbed ground and in holes apparently poked by a stick. None were found below the surface in undisturbed ground. Those lying on exposed bedrock would long ago have been swept downhill by the natural processes of wind and rain.

The work convinced the geologists that *the gems had been salted*—that the so-called diamond field was a carefully engineered hoax. As the team was leaving the site on their last day, a party of prospectors arrived, men who had apparently followed King's party into the site on the long ride. King told them of the fraudulent nature of the prospect, but realized that he would have to report the plot as quickly as possible before others were misled and mischief done. Before daylight the next morning, he and Allen Wilson slipped out of camp and headed cross-country directly for the railroad, toward a point considerably east of where they had departed, and a much shorter ride to the railroad. Samuel Emmons, with the camp men and pack train, took the much longer route back to Fort Bridger, where they would again prepare the equipment for winter storage and put the stock out to forage. King and Wilson's trail was tortuous over badland country, but without the pack animals they were able to travel quickly. They rode all day and long into the night, and then good fortune smiled on them: they saw the light of the train as they approached the tiny station of Black Buttes. They boarded the train, put the stock in a boxcar, and headed for San Francisco.

Reaching the city during the evening of November 10, King spent the night preparing a report on his survey. He delivered it the next morning to the San Francisco and New York Mining and Commercial Company, the company holding options on the property. He reported to the board of directors that "the new diamond fields, upon which are based such large investment and such brilliant hope, are utterly valueless, and yourselves and your engineer, Mr. Henry Janin, the victims of an unparalleled fraud."[13] King emphasized the skill of the deception "partly to soften criticism of his friend, engineer Henry Janin, and perhaps also unconsciously to emphasize his own skill in the detection."[14]

The directors were convinced, but they stalled for time. They were determined to keep the hoax secret until there was an absolute confirmation of the worthlessness of their property. King kindly agreed to accompany Henry Janin on a second visit to the Colorado site, and a party was hastily organized for the long and arduous trip. Upon reaching the site with no little hardship, Janin was quickly convinced of the hoax, and upon their return to San Francisco on November 26, both King's letter and one by Janin confirming King's conclusions were published in the San Francisco press.

As the fraud unraveled, it was discovered that one of the prospectors first got the idea for the hoax when in London, where he purchased a bag of uncut small inferior diamonds used for drilling. These were salted with other cheaper stones on the sandstone terrain at the Colorado site, which was believed to be similar to the sand and gravel setting of a Brazilian diamond occurrence. During the time of the first examination of the property, larger diamonds and gems were surreptitiously added to the sampled material taken for testing.

Although reports vary, the miners received approximately $600,000 for their prospect, paid from the more than $2,000,000 raised by the sale of stock by the promoters. When the fraud was exposed, the stockholders were refunded, and Ralston and his partners suffered the loss paid to the prospectors, as well as that for trip expenses to the site. One prospector disappeared, and the other eventually surrendered $150,000 of his ill-gotten gains.

Because of his rushed schedule in the weeks of the diamond incident, as well as the sensitive nature of the entire issue, King had been unable to notify General Humphreys as the fraud unfolded. Immediately after the hoax became public, he telegraphed the general,[15] and then followed with a lengthy letter giving the details. Humphreys responded more than a month later, writing that the Corps of Engineers should have been notified first. His was the typical bureaucrat's lament that "The most judicious course, and one more strictly in accordance with the regulations and custom of the service (which are founded upon long experience) would have been for you to have made to me immediately a brief official report of the examination, with your views and conclusions; to have requested authority to publish the official report, to have mailed it at the first Post Office, and to have awaited in San Francisco, the communication by telegraph of the authority to publish, which could have been so worded as to give no one any clue to its meaning. This would not have led to any material delay in making the information public, and would have been in conformity to the established order by which the Engineer and War Departments are the first to be informed of the results of their operations."[16] King was not dismayed by this rebuke. He was guided by the code: for an honorable man, forgiveness is much easier to get than permission. From most quarters, King received high praise for his part in uncovering the diamond swindle, and was hailed as an honest public servant.

At the close of 1872 the principal part of the fieldwork for the geologic exploration of the 40th parallel had been completed, and King was perhaps at the zenith of his popularity. He was widely recognized for his leadership of the western survey, which had produced a major work on mineral deposits, and for his discovery of the first active glaciers known to exist in the United States, the first ascent of the highest

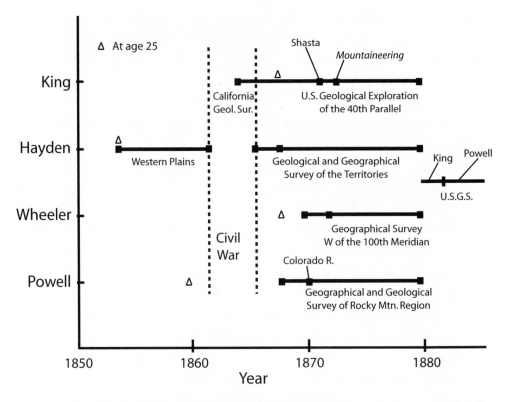

FIGURE 9.6. A chronological outline of the four principal government surveys initiated after the Civil War, with their leaders. The four surveys were terminated in March 1879, and replaced by the newly created United States Geological Survey. The U.S. Army Corps of Engineers had supported King's U.S. Geological Exploration of the Fortieth Parallel. Hayden's modest effort before the Civil War had been funded by various patrons and learned societies, by the U.S. Pacific Railroad Survey, the U.S. Army Corps of Engineers, and the Smithsonian Institution. After the Civil War his Geological and Geographical Survey of the Territories was supported largely by the U.S. Department of the Interior. Wheeler's work with the U.S. Geographical Survey West of the 100th Meridian was funded and managed by the U.S. Army Corps of Engineers. Powell's early surveys, after the Civil War, were staffed by students, volunteers, and relatives and funded from a wide variety of sources, including museums and colleges in Illinois and four railroad companies. He was authorized to draw rations from frontier U.S. Army camps. After his 1869 success in running the Colorado River, he established the U.S. Geographical and Geological Survey of the Rocky Mountain Region, with funding from the Smithsonian Institution and the Department of the Interior.

peak in the country, his integrity in uncovering the fraudulent claim of a diamond discovery, and much else, and his popular book *Mountaineering in the Sierra Nevada* was receiving widespread acclaim.

During the early years of the Fortieth Parallel Survey three other major surveys had begun operations in the West. They each had started in different areas but were beginning to encroach on one another. All were funded by the government, all were directed by remarkably able leaders, and all explored, mapped, and made important collections over broad areas. The earliest was that led by Dr. Ferdinand V. Hayden, who conducted surveys in Nebraska, the Dakotas, Wyoming, and Colorado under the auspices of the Smithsonian Institution, General Land Office, and later the Department of the Interior. In 1869 Major John Wesley Powell made his historic initial expedition down the Green and Colorado Rivers and later continued work on the Colorado Plateau. Lieutenant (later Captain) George Wheeler commanded the U.S. Army Geographical Surveys West of the 100th meridian in Nevada, Colorado, Arizona, and California.

Hayden, born in Westfield, Massachusetts, in 1829, grew up on a farm and worked his way through Oberlin College, Ohio, where he got a reputation as a hardworking, single-minded student. He took a deep interest in geology, and a fellow student, John Newberry, convinced him to seek study under James Hall, a noted paleontologist at Albany Medical College, New York. Hayden went on to receive an M.D. there in 1853, a degree that was a common entree into natural science at the time. He studied primarily with Hall, who was also funded in part by the Pacific Railroad Surveys. Upon Hayden's graduation, Hall offered him a spot on a collecting trip to the rich fossil beds of the Dakota Badlands. Hayden jumped at the chance and, joined by the paleontologist Fielding Meek, traveled up the Missouri River by steamboat. From Fort Pierre, South Dakota, they trekked cross-country to the Badlands and were able to conduct a successful collecting trip despite hardship and several setbacks. The trip proved to be the springboard from which he launched his life's work.

The next two years, 1854 and 1855, Hayden, on his own (because of difficulties with Hall), obtained limited funding from patrons and learned societies and conducted two more expeditions to the terrain drained by the upper Missouri and Yellowstone Rivers.[17] In collaboration with Meek he collected and described important fossil material from the Cretaceous beds of the mid-continent region. Hayden continued these collecting trips and by 1857 he had amassed enough material that, by drawing on Meek's expertise, he was able to construct a systematic relationship among the units of sedimentary rocks. This stratigraphic model depicted the succession of rock layers in the West, showing their ages and correlation from place to place, on the basis of their contained fossils. In this model, Cretaceous strata containing dinosaurs and ammonites were subdivided into a meaningful sequence of units that could be recognized over great distances.

Subsequent work in younger Tertiary rock sequences revealed evidence for the existence of large freshwater lakes in the Dakotas during the Eocene Epoch. Hayden came to know these fossil-bearing beds intimately and developed an uncanny skill in collecting the best material. He shipped a large number of Tertiary vertebrate fossils to Professor Joseph Leidy at the University of Pennsylvania. Leidy described these fossils, which included animals now extinct in North America but still present in other parts of the world, such as camels, small horses, rhinoceroses, and elephants. This evidence of a rich record of ancient mammals became important in supporting Charles Darwin's theory of organic evolution, which was published in 1859.

With the onset of the Civil War, Hayden joined the Army as a Surgeon of Volunteers, and served until 1866. At war's end he resigned his commission and without hesitation went back to fieldwork in the Dakota Badlands, but now with better funding. In 1867 he was appointed Professor at the University of Pennsylvania, and through the good offices of Spencer Baird, Director of the Smithsonian Institution, for whom Hayden had previously collected fossils, was able to make use of money earmarked by Congress for a geological survey of the new state of Nebraska. The General Land Office in the Department of the Interior administered this program. This government-sponsored work was initiated the same year as King's geological exploration of the 40th parallel.

Hayden's program began with a detailed look at all the resources of Nebraska, but did not omit examination of other geologic features that interested him. His annual reports included much practical material, including the location of coal and limestone beds, the availability of timber, and the growth of crops, grass, and orchards. The reports were quickly produced, written in a popular, nontechnical manner that praised the benefits of the land, so as to encourage immigration and settlement. His work was dependable and well received, and each year the government increased his appropriation.

The area of his project, by then called the United States Geological Survey of the Territories, enlarged and spilled over into Kansas, Colorado, and Wyoming, imping-

FIGURE 9.7 (*opposite*).   Ferdinand Vandiveer Hayden, one of the first geologists to work in the West, began surveying in the Missouri Basin and northern plains with the paleontologist Fielding Meek in 1853. He later became the leader of the U.S. Geological Survey of the Territories funded by the U.S. Department of the Interior. He considered himself the prime candidate for the directorship of the new U.S. Geological Survey in 1879, when all the federally funded western survey programs were combined into one bureau. (Photograph by William Jackson; U.S. Geological Survey)

FIGURE 9.8.   Liberty Cap, a travertine spire deposited from a localized hot spring in
Yellowstone National Park, which was systematically explored and mapped by the Hayden
survey in 1871 and 1872. The column, more than 50 feet high, occurs in the Mammoth Hot
Spring region. (Photograph by William Jackson during the 1872 expedition; U.S. Geological
Survey)

ing upon territory designated for King's Fortieth Parallel Survey. In 1869 William
Henry Jackson, considered by some the greatest Western photographer, joined Hayden's survey. Hayden's annual report of 1870 included many of Jackson's photos, as
well as commissioned articles by a host of scientists, including John Newberry on ancient lakes, Joseph Leidy on vertebrate fossils, Cyrus Thomas on agriculture, Fielding
Meek on invertebrate paleontology, James Hodge on Tertiary coal deposits, and Edward Cope on fossil fish. The volume was uneven and not carefully integrated, but
Hayden justified these shortcomings by his rapid schedule of publication, which
made available to the public in the shortest possible time a great amount of information from many experts.

By 1871, Hayden's appropriation had risen to $40,000, and he undertook an ex-
pedition to map and study the Yellowstone Basin. His party consisted of 34 men and

seven wagons, and included two men considered the best in their professions for generating images of such scenic regions: the photographer William Henry Jackson and the painter Thomas Moran. The historian William Goetzmann wrote, "Moran always believed that he was painting the truth in nature, but his primary achievement went beyond simple depiction and deserves greater attention today. He painted, quite literally, the sublime psychological reality of the West, in which if a mountain was larger than life, a cloud formation somewhat overdramatic, and the rainbows seemed artificial, still it all added up to a portrayal of the impact of the magnificent scenery on those who were viewing it for the first time."[18]

The party investigated the multicolored pools of Mammoth Hot Springs, visited the falls of the Yellowstone River, and launched a collapsible sailboat on Yellowstone Lake, by which they explored the lake and mapped its many irregular arms. They examined several thermal areas, including Firehole and the Upper and Lower Geyser Basins. Hayden made the first systematic geologic observations, and Jackson took many photographs of the seemingly endless variety in this, the world's most active geothermal area.

Hayden distributed photographs and descriptions of this wonderland to every influential person at hand, not only to promote himself and as a strategy for future funding, but also because of his interest in preserving this remarkable region from homesteading and commercial development. In conjunction with the Northern Pacific Railroad and other groups, he lobbied for a Yellowstone National Park, to be modeled after the California state park at Yosemite. Congress and President Grant designated the Yellowstone region as the first U.S. National Park, March 1, 1872, and for many people, Hayden's name was closely linked to this grand accomplishment.

Hayden's expedition of 1872 was larger still, with 61 men divided into two groups: one, headed by Hayden, to continue the Yellowstone work; the other, led by James Stevenson, to examine the Snake River Plain and the Teton Range. Stevenson reported a first ascent of the Big Teton (Grand Teton), which he explained was renamed "Mt. Hayden by our party, in default of any previous specific title, [and] was found by angular measurement, from well-determined barometric bases, to be 13,858 feet high."[19] In 1898 a party led by William Owen climbed the Grand Teton and determined that Stevenson had not reached the summit and had fabricated his account of the upper reaches of the mountain.[20]

Hayden's topographic mapping in his earlier surveys was rudimentary, but on this expedition he included four young topographers, two of whom, Henry Gannett and Arthur Holmes, later developed distinguished careers. Gannett received his training at Harvard under the instruction of Charles Hoffmann, from the California Geo-

FIGURE 9.9.   John Wesley Powell lost his right arm in the Civil War but went on to
organize and direct the first study of the Colorado River System. In 1869, after many
hardships, he and five other adventurers explored the length of the Green–Colorado River,
which they ran in small boats. He also initiated the study of Native American culture in the
Southwest and became the first Director of the Bureau of American Ethnology. Powell
served for 13 years as second director of the United States Geological Survey after Clarence
King's short tenure of less than 2 years. (U.S. Geological Survey Library)

logical Survey, and later became chief topographer of the U.S. Geological Survey.
Holmes, a man of many talents, moved into the fields of geology and anthropology,
and later became a world-class artist. He had the ability to sketch panoramas of vast
areas in an aspect both beautiful and natural, but subtly emphasized geologic strata
and structure as well. As Goetzman wrote, "His artistic technique was like no other's.
He could sketch panoramas of twisted mountain ranges, sloping monoclines, escarp-
ments, plateaus, canyons, fault blocks, and grassy meadows that accurately depicted
hundreds of miles of terrain. They were better than maps, and better than photo-

graphs because he could get details of stratigraphy that light and shadow obscured from the camera."[21]

Gannett tells of climbing a Yellowstone peak in July 1872 with Ferdinand Hayden and assistant topographer Alexander Brown. During an approaching thunderstorm he related that "I was above the others of the party, and, when about fifty feet below the summit, the electric current began to pass through my body. At first I felt nothing, but heard a crackling noise, similar to a rapid discharge of sparks from a friction machine. Immediately after, I began to feel a tingling or prickling sensation in my head and the ends of my fingers, which, as well as the noise, increased rapidly, until, when I reached the top, the noise, which had not changed its character, was deafening, and my hair stood completely on end, while the tingling, prickling sensation was absolutely painful. Taking off my hat partially relieved it. I started down again, and met the others twenty-five or thirty feet below the summit. They were affected similarly, but in a less degree. One of them attempted to go to the top, but had proceeded but a few feet when he received quite a severe shock, which felled him as if he had stumbled."[22] The three judiciously began to descend the mountain, thereafter known as Electric Peak.

Despite their qualifications, the young topographers assigned to the 1872 survey did not produce any high-quality regional maps, both because of their inexperience and because Hayden had not appreciated the levels of organization and management that such an endeavor required. He then realized that he needed someone already expert in the art of topographic mapping. His wish was soon satisfied when he was able to entice the most qualified young topographer in the nation to join his survey.

John Wesley Powell's upbringing was not unlike that of Hayden's. He was born in 1834 in western New York State and grew up on a series of farms managed by his father, who was also a Methodist preacher and part-time tailor. In 1841 the family moved to Ohio, and in 1846 to a farm in Illinois. Powell was an eager learner, despite the indifferent quality of the country schools he attended. While in Ohio he came to know a neighbor farmer and natural philosopher, George Crookham, who had a museum filled with natural specimens and Native American artifacts, and was acquainted with other scientists, including the Ohio State Geologist, William Mather. Crookham was happy to provide instruction to any young men who sought it. He had them read the classics and perform experiments in his homemade chemical laboratory, and he introduced them to natural history on extensive field trips. Wallace Stegner wrote, "The influence of Crookham was crucial and definitive: it was an influence calculated to make young Powell a leading citizen of some rural Athens, a member of the debating club, a lecturer on Lyceum circuits, a pillar of the crude structure that learning was building in the wilderness."[23]

Powell became a schoolteacher in a country school in southern Wisconsin and began a cycle of teaching in a series of schools in Illinois to support himself while attending colleges for brief periods. He attended Illinois Institute (Wheaton College), Illinois College (Jacksonville), and, for one term, Oberlin College, Ohio, never able to attend a college for more than a year at a time. His interest in natural science led him to find the time to take lengthy field trips to collect plants, minerals, and fossils. Presaging his epochal expedition on the Colorado, he also became an accomplished boatman, traveling by skiff down the Mississippi from Minneapolis to New Orleans in 1856 and down the Ohio River from Pittsburgh to St. Louis, in 1857. In 1858 he descended the Illinois River to its mouth and then rowed up the Des Moines River to Raccoon Creek.[24] By 1860 he became principal of public schools in Hennepin, Illinois, traveled a circuit to give lectures on natural history, and was elected secretary of the Illinois Natural History Society.

At the outset of the Civil War, Powell enlisted as a private in the 20th Illinois Volunteer Infantry and quickly rose to the rank of sergeant and then lieutenant. During a furlough from working on fortifications as an engineer he married his cousin, Emma Dean. Upon returning to Army duty, he was appointed commander of an artillery battery, and in the battle of Shiloh he occupied a position in the center of the line that held back the confederate forces until General Grant could reform his army. It was here that Powell lost his right arm after it was smashed by a rifle bullet. Despite this crippling injury he participated in the siege of Vicksburg, the Nashville campaigns, and General Sherman's march on Atlanta.[25]

Powell returned to Wheaton after the war and took a post as a Professor at Illinois Wesleyan College, where he taught a course in natural science, including geology. He loved field excursions and made them an important forum for instruction in his classes. The desire to explore still farther afield drove him to seek support for a state natural history museum in Bloomington. He was successful in raising funds from Illinois Wesleyan College, Illinois Normal University, the Illinois Natural History Society, and eventually the state legislature for the establishment of a museum with a grant of $1,500. Powell was appointed Curator, and made sure that $500 was earmarked for a collecting trip to the Rocky Mountains. Drawing still further on his remarkable persuasive skills, he obtained additional backing for this venture from Illinois Industrial University, the Chicago Academy of Sciences, and four railroads, including the Union Pacific. Because of his acquaintance with General Grant, he received authorization to draw rations at cost from Army posts and be assigned a military escort out of Fort Laramie, Wyoming.[26]

FIGURE 9.10. In 1869 John Wesley Powell led a party that descended by small boats nearly a thousand miles down unexplored gorges of the Green and Colorado Rivers. This journey through the Grand Canyon of the Colorado was one of the great epic feats of western exploration. (Powell, 1875)

Powell's field party was made up of students, amateurs, teachers, and family members, including his wife Emma. They assembled June 1, 1867, at Council Bluffs, Iowa—at about the same time that King was assembling his corps in California for the first season of work on the Fortieth Parallel Survey. Powell arrived in Denver a month later, and his crew of naturalists explored and collected in Middle and South Park, climbed Pike's Peak, visited the active mining camp of Central City, and shipped a full load of natural history specimens home.

Again in 1868 Powell exercised his skill in organizing and managing an expedition. This one, too, though quite different in character, was supported from a variety of Illinois sources, supplemented with federal government supplies for a party of 25 men, obtained with the aid of General Grant and Illinois congressional members. Powell set up camp in Middle Park, Colorado, and explored the nearby mountains.

But Powell had more ambitious plans. He prepared to strike out for western Colorado, to the White River, and there to spend the winter and prepare for an audacious trip the following summer—to go by boat down the Green to the Colorado River and run the Colorado to its mouth. They wintered over in three cabins on the White River, 150 miles above its junction with the Green River in northeastern Utah. In the spring, with snow on the trail, they traveled through Brown's Hole to Fort Bridger and took the Union Pacific line to Chicago. There he arranged for a boatbuilder to build four stout boats, three 21 feet long of oak and one 16 feet of pine. The lighter one would serve as a pilot boat to scout the way. The boats were tested on Lake Michigan, and Powell went to Washington to negotiate further appropriations for government supplies.

With business completed, Powell assembled a party of nine adventurers and headed by rail, the boats secured on a flatcar, to Green River, Wyoming. After a few weeks of training and assembling supplies, the four boats left Green River May 24, 1869, on their epic voyage down the Green and Colorado Rivers. On June 7 they lost one boat in Ladore Canyon in the Uinta Mountains when it struck a large rock broadside and broke in two. Most supplies were lost, but some items were retrieved from a compartment in the wreckage. In about two months, after experiencing many rapids, the loss of the boat, and the departure of one man on a side trail, they had traveled 538 miles to the junction of a larger river entering from the east—it was the Grand River, now called the Colorado.[27] Below this confluence, the combined river was then (as now) called the Colorado. On August 10 they reached the point where the muddy waters of the Little Colorado River joined the main river. Downstream, the canyon walls became higher and steeper and the river more formidable. As they prepared to enter the Grand Canyon, Powell wrote, "We are ready to start on our way down the Great Unknown. . . . We have an unknown distance yet to run; an unknown river yet to explore, what falls there are, we know not; what rocks beset the channel, we know not; what walls rise over the river, we know not."[28] From that point, 250 miles of the river still awaited them.

The three boats encountered ever-rougher rapids, and in places they gained passage only by struggling along the rocky shore while lowering the boats by rope through the heaviest rapids. As they proceeded down the canyon the rocks on the canyon walls beside them became older, where the river had cut ever deeper into the layered sequence. They passed even the Cambrian strata, which bear the oldest known fossils, and beneath which the ancient crystalline granite and schist—designated simply Precambrian—lay exposed in a narrow and forbidding canyon cut by the river. The precipitous walls of this inner canyon became steeper and higher until only a small window of sky remained. Beyond several of these granite gorges, the overlying sedimentary rocks dropped again to river level, but now another menace confronted them.

Young lava outpourings had left shoals and blocks in the river, creating seemingly impassable rapids. When a particularly formidable rapid loomed in their path, three of the men declared they had had enough and refused to go on. They demanded to leave the expedition and climb out of the canyon, up a tributary gorge later called Separation Canyon. They preferred to take their chances on an overland route, rather than commit their fate to the river. The trio could not be dissuaded, despite Powell's strong entreaties. The next morning the party divided—the three to climb out of the canyon on foot and the six to run the river in the remaining two boats.

Wallace Stegner provides a graphic account of the trials of this rapid. "The river seized them. They shot down a hollow, up a wave, past a rock half buried in the foaming water. The oarsmen pulled madly at the clumsy oars—a job of enormous difficulty in a boat leaping through waves at a speed of twenty miles an hour, tossed now up, now down, the water falling away suddenly so that the oarblade bites air, then surging up to bury the oar to the handle. To hit a hidden rock with an oar was to risk shattering it or having it driven into the oarsman's body; to catch a crab was to lose all chance of control. They rowed as the river had taught them to row, pulling hard for the tongue of the second fall. There the boat was all but snatched from under them. They shot down the fall and burst into the great back-cresting waves at its foot. Instantly they were full of water, but half swamped they still rowed like madmen, pulling across the current. The wild pile-up of water against the righthand rock caught them only partially. They raced up the sloping wall of water, fell away to the left, down into a hole, and were through into the diminishing tailwaves. The whole rapid had taken perhaps a minute."[29]

These rapids proved to be their last serious obstacle. Within three days, on August

FIGURE 9.11.   Lieutenant George Wheeler, who commanded the U.S. Army-sponsored Geographical Surveys West of the 100th Meridian. His well-funded mapping program sought to maintain the preeminence of the military in conducting exploration and mapping in the West. The funding for his survey was increased after his spectacular 1872 trip, traveling 50 miles up the Colorado River into the lower Grand Canyon. Much of this progress required arduous roping of the boats upstream against the fierce river current. (U.S. Geological Survey Library)

30, 1869, two battered boats and a ragged, but jubilant, crew of six came upon a Mormon settlement. Powell and his party had traveled nearly one thousand miles in 97 days, making the first transit down the Green–Colorado River System, thereby unmasking the largest area of *terra incognita* remaining in the West. The three men of the overland team who had climbed out of the canyon were killed by Shivwits Indians.

Upon returning east, Powell set off on a well-received lecture circuit, describing his adventures on the river and providing the first account of the geography of this isolated region. Because of his expedition's success he was able to convince Congress to support further surveys in the plateau-canyon country and received an appropriation of $10,000 for his "Geographical and Topographical Survey of the Colorado River of the West." He began preparing for another assault on the river, and late in the summer of 1870 traveled again to the West, this time with the plan of making extensive topographic surveys of the plateau country through which the river ran. In May 1871, three new boats, their design improved over those of 1869, set off from Green River, Wyoming. The trip was beset with difficulties, however, and the party finally left the river in December for winter quarters at Lee's Ferry, above the Grand Canyon proper. During that winter much of the party was engaged in topographic mapping from a base at Kanab, Utah.

The next summer, the party got a late start at Lee's Ferry and floated down into Marble Canyon, where high water made the river more treacherous than it had been in 1869. Powell was cautious, and diverted the expedition at Kanab Canyon, declining to run the river through the main part of the Grand Canyon. They hiked out of the canyon and continued exploration and mapping of the plateau country until December 1872.

Ever since Powell's encounter with natives during the winter of 1868–69 while camped on the White River—preparing for the next season's exploration of the Colorado River—he had developed an abiding interest in the Native Americans. The local Indians, the White River Utes, were a fascinating subject for study. He traded with them for a wide variety of cultural objects: pottery, beadwork, buckskin clothing, moccasins, and ceremonial items. He also studied their language and made vocabulary lists. This endeavor launched a lifelong interest in cultural anthropology—then called ethnology. The trade items he had accumulated became the core of the Native American collection at the Smithsonian Museum.

Powell continued his exploration of the plateau country, and expanded what was now known as the U.S. Geographic and Geological Survey of the Rocky Mountain Region, a program funded by the Department of the Interior, dispatching several parties for fieldwork in different areas. In 1874 the geologist Clarence Dutton joined Pow-

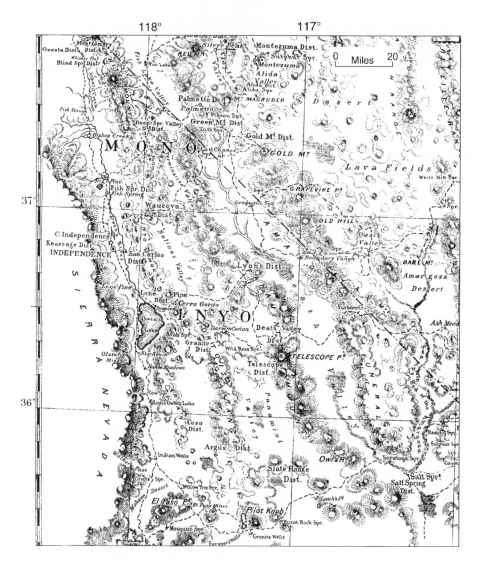

FIGURE 9.12.   Part of Wheeler's preliminary map of his survey that investigated mining camps in eastern California and Nevada, largely working out of Camp Independence at the east base of the Sierra Nevada. They then mapped Death Valley in midsummer, where two party members were lost, and then moved east to explore and map the lower part of the Colorado River. This map was rushed into publication so as to provide justification for continued military funding for the survey. (Wheeler, 1872)

ell's survey, and late in the year Grove Charles Gilbert left the Wheeler survey to join his survey.

In 1877 Powell published two volumes on American Indians, one on *The Tribes of the Extreme Northwest* and one on *The Tribes of California*. He also collaborated with

Joseph Henry of the Smithsonian Institution on a *Manual of North American Ethnography* to guide his workers (and other anthropologists) in collecting information on the Indians. In this endeavor time was limited—the Native Americans were fast disappearing.

George Montague Wheeler was born in 1842, the year King and Gardner were born, in Hopkinton, Massachusetts. He gained entry into the U.S. Military Academy at West Point with the assistance of a western legislator, and ranked sixth in his graduating class of 1866. Having shown great aptitude in mathematics and engineering, he was selected for the Corps of Engineers, sent first to San Francisco to work on coastal defenses, and then to conduct a survey of Point Lobos, near Monterey, California. There he came under the tutelage of Colonel Robert Williamson, who had supported King's effort to obtain funding for the Fortieth Parallel Survey. In 1869 Wheeler was assigned to head a reconnaissance from Camp Ruby in east-central Nevada, northeast of Elko, with the mission of investigating much of Nevada and western Utah. This survey resulted in a map and short report, both published late in 1869.

In 1871 the Army Corps of Engineers expanded its survey mission and established the United States Geographical Survey West of the 100th Meridian, with Lieutenant Wheeler in charge. This survey was created by General Humphreys essentially to counter the growing threat to the military of the civilian-based surveys conducted under the Department of the Interior. The Army had considered the surveying of the West as an integral part of its domain, as pioneered by Captains Meriwether Lewis and William Clark across the continent from the Missouri River to the Pacific, by Lieutenant John Fremont in the mountain West, and by officers of the Corps of Engineers, including A. A. Humphreys, R. S. Williamson, E. G. Beckwith, J. W. Gunnison, W. P. Blake, J. C. Ives, and A. W. Whipple, working on the various surveys of a railroad route from the Mississippi River to the Pacific Coast.

Wheeler was directed to prepare maps of the area south of the Central Pacific Railroad (thus south of the region of King's survey) in Nevada and Arizona. He was also commanded to note the numbers and disposition of the Indians, to survey potential rail and road routes, to describe the mineral deposits, climate, and vegetation, and to note the availability of wood and water along the way. In order to formulate these maps, the expeditions were charged with determining as accurately as possible, by astronomical means, the latitude and longitude of principal points within the assigned area.[30]

Wheeler, though deeply imbued with the long heritage of military-sponsored programs of exploration in the West, realized that the Congress expected more from these surveys than simply military-style maps. In 1871 his surveying party upgraded its scientific investigations and enlisted well-qualified surveyors and scientists from civilian backgrounds. He was most fortunate when he hired Grove Karl Gilbert, a young scientist who would become perhaps the most imaginative and productive geologist the country has ever produced. He also enticed the photographer Timothy O'Sullivan to leave King's Fortieth Parallel Survey and join his corps. Wheeler had another agenda; he had a personal interest in discovering and developing, for personal gain, promising mineral prospects.

The expedition began on the railroad line at Halleck Station in central Nevada northeast of Elko and traversed to eastern California via Carlin, Eureka, and Belmont. The party visited sites along the east front of the Sierra Nevada from their base at Camp Independence, 20 miles north of Lone Pine. Astronomical measurements were made at the camp, with longitude determined by measurement of lunar culminations. This work led to the preparation of a preliminary map published in 1872. Wheeler drove his party into the mapping of Death Valley in July at temperatures exceeding 120° F. Two men disappeared; one was found dead, the other deserted.

Wheeler's party then moved on to the lower Colorado River at Camp Mojave in mid-September (where King and Gardner had first crossed the river in their near fatal Arizona exploration of 1866). His plan was to take boats upstream as far as possible, so as to establish the head of navigation on the river. Separate groups went cross-country to establish supply bases at points where the river could be reached. Wheeler's river party consisted of six mappers, six boatmen, six soldiers, and thirteen Mojave Indians, all using three riverboats and a barge. The barge was sent back when the river became too difficult. Wheeler was in charge of the first boat, O'Sullivan the second, and Gilbert the third. They worked up the river past the Big Bend to the mouth of the Virgin and Grand Wash. Two boats capsized at Vernal Falls, and on October 11 Wheeler's boat was destroyed as it was being roped up a cascade, later called Disaster Rapids.

Wheeler's report of this accident noted that "All the boats were brought up and lines thrown ahead. This rapid seemed long but not dangerous, however, but the first boat going into it proved differently. The first dash filled the boat with water, the second swamped it, and in this way the lives of two boatmen were endangered. The boat ran back against the rocks almost a perfect wreck, and its contents were washed down below the overhanging rocks. A stout case containing my most valuable public and private papers and data for a great share of the season's report, which for the first time had not been taken out of the boat at a portage, was lost, as well as valuable instruments, the astronomical and meteorological observations, and worse than all, the entire rations of that boat."[31]

Travel up the river with the two remaining boats steadily slowed as the rapids increased in frequency. By October 16—the time that they were scheduled to reach a land supply party at Diamond Creek—the food was nearly exhausted, and Wheeler was forced to halve the rations for the party. The two boats continued upstream, requiring frequent lining up the rapids, and finally reached Diamond Creek and fresh provisions at nightfall on October 19, 1871. They had forced their way 222 miles upstream from Fort Mojave, and 50 miles up the Grand Canyon. Diamond Creek was 13 miles upstream from Separation Creek, the point where Powell's party had divided three years earlier, and three men had climbed out of the canyon on foot.[32] Wheeler's expedition established the limit of navigation up the lower Grand Canyon, and it certainly demonstrated the pluck of the leader and his men. During the return, three members of the party traveling overland by stage, including the chief topographer, were fired upon at point-blank range by Apaches and killed.

Part of the survey party then went on to Fort Whipple in Arizona, but Wheeler and a second group traveled west to a promising mining site, 30 miles east of the California line, where they staked 30 mineral prospects. After returning to Washington, in early 1872, Wheeler formed the Lyons and Wheeler Mining Company for profit. The company incorporated these new prospects, as well as other lodes and veins that had been investigated during the course of his mapping ventures.

Emboldened by the accomplishments of his survey, Wheeler next proposed a plan for the systematic mapping of all territories west of the 100th meridian, to be carried out by the Army. He estimated that the survey (at a scale of 8 miles to the inch or 1:500,000) would require 15 years at a cost of about $2.5 million. Congress, encouraged by the accomplishments of the 1871 expedition, generally approved the concept. Two parties fielded by Wheeler in the 1872 season mapped 50,000 square miles in the contiguous region of Nevada, Arizona, and Utah. During the 1872 season, however, Wheeler's survey encroached on part of the region being mapped by John Powell's survey, and in the 1873 season he duplicated some of the mapping by Ferdinand Hayden's survey in Colorado. It would not be long before the public and the politicians took notice of this duplication.

CHAPTER TEN

PUSHED WITH THE UTMOST VIGOR

Then skeletons of men,
Of beasts, behemoth and leviathan,
And elephants and eagles and huge jaw
Of nameless monster.
          —*John Keats, "Endymion"*

With the Survey's fieldwork essentially completed, Clarence King's scientific party remained in the office during 1873. Most of the Survey worked in the offices in Washington and New York, but King, because of ill health, spent the winter in San Francisco. He brought his mother and her children to California and obtained a house for them across the Bay in Oakland. He wrote Samuel Emmons, "My mother is extremely delicate and altogether the family gives me pretty constant anxiety. As for myself I feel rather worn out but hope with the leave of absence I have (from Feb. 1st to April 1st) I shall be all right and ready to plunge into the geology strong and deep."[1] Despite the realization that the urgency of his duties beckoned him east he remained in San Francisco, working on reports and pushing the work forward on the atlas. In April he wrote again, "I cannot express the sorrow and mortification it has been to me to remain here and leave you fellows at such loose ends. Family trouble and misfortune cannot be anticipated or prevented. It comes like a shadow and darkens our days most painfully. I have sought to do my duty and hope I have saved my mother from a decline but the sense of being absent from my post has galled me from morning to night."[2] He returned east in June.

The scientists settled in for office work, examined their notes and collections, compiled data, analyzed materials in the laboratory, and in due course wrote up descriptions and interpretations of the landforms and rock layers of the project area.

King was well aware of the impending reality that the primary product and justifica-tion of the Survey's six years of fieldwork, with all of its attendant costs, would be the published work. He had been optimistic that this phase of the work could be accom-plished in two years, but five years would pass before all reports and maps were fin-ished and published.

Laboratory study undertaken in two areas supplemented the field and map work. Arnold Hague set up a chemical laboratory and proceeded to analyze the waters and precipitates collected from the saline lakes, hot springs, and evaporite deposits. His group also analyzed the silicate rocks to aid in their classification and constrain their origin. Samuel Emmons traveled to England to select and purchase a polarizing mi-croscope. In Germany he reviewed the latest techniques for studying rocks in thin section, in which ultrathin slices of rock were examined microscopically under po-larized light. His discussions of the Survey's remarkable collections convinced Pro-fessor Ferdinand Zirkel, a leading microscopist at the University of Leipzig, to come to New York to oversee the microscopic examinations. Zirkel's volume on the micro-scopic description of Fortieth Parallel rocks would foster the new discipline of mi-croscopic petrography in American science.[3]

During the winter following the 1872 field campaign, James Gardner completed the compilation of the topographic maps of the Fortieth Parallel Survey in the Washing-ton, D.C., office. The mapped area yielded a strip of five rectangles, each 107 miles wide, that reached from California across Nevada, Idaho, and Utah into Colorado and Wyoming, a span 800 miles long west to east, that encompassed some 88,000 square miles. The maps were drafted at a scale of 2 miles to the inch, and photographically reduced to 4 miles to the inch for printing. The final map sheets, if laid out in se-quence, would form a strip nearly 17 feet long. The rectangles were designated from east to west: I, Rocky Mountains; II, Green River Basin; III, Utah Basin; IV, Nevada Plateau; V, Nevada Basin.

Each of the map sheets was drafted and printed in two formats at the same scale: one map shows cultural and natural features, with topography depicted by a shaded relief system as if obliquely illuminated from the west; the other map presents geo-logic formations in color, with topography depicted by elevation contours (which King called *grade curves*). The contours were constructed at constant elevation with a separation of 300 vertical feet, but they were not labeled by elevation. They served to portray all of the topographical information obtained from barometer elevations, sketches, and slope angles.

Nonetheless, these two methods of representing elevation were innovative departures from the ancient system of utilizing tiny, downslope-directed lines called *hachures*. The prior Goddard and Hoffmann maps, as well as Gardner's Yosemite map, had all made use of hachures. And such contoured maps as had previously been made had generally been restricted to small areas. The method of the Fortieth Parallel Survey maps thus represented one of the first systematic uses of contours in America over such a large area.

The Survey made precise determinations of latitude and longitude at three primary stations, employing astronomical methods: one at Verdi (14 miles west of Glendale, Nevada) at the west end of the mapped belt, another at Salt Lake City in the middle of the belt, and a third at Sherman (30 miles west of Cheyenne, Wyoming) at the east end of the belt. The three stations were all on the railroad and the telegraph line, and thus had access to telegraphed time for longitude determination. Gardner also determined latitudes at five other stations by zenith telescope, and the azimuth of Polaris was observed astronomically at 21 other stations, as an additional check on determinations of true north. This redundancy was employed both to refine the maps and to discover such observational and computational errors as may have arisen.

The average length of triangle sides—that is, the length of theodolite sightings—was about 70 miles over most of the primary triangulation net. "From Peavine Mountain (long. 120°00′) to Medicine Butte (long. 111°00′) the average error of closure, after reduction for spherical excess, was 13″ [13 seconds of arc]; from Medicine Butte to Separation Peak (long. 107° 30′) the average error of closure was 80″ [80 seconds of arc]; from Separation Peak to Sherman (long. 105°30′) the average error of closure was 150‴" [15 seconds of arc].[4] Thirteen seconds of arc is 0.0036 degree, equivalent to 23 feet at 70 miles—certainly an acceptable error for a map covering such a vast area.

King describes the preparation and printing of the topographic maps in a report to General Humphreys: "The ten crayon-shaded sheets which constitute our series of topographical maps have all been pushed with the utmost vigor; five are already completed, and the remaining five now in an advanced state of preparation will be done by the first of December [1875]. Each of these maps will receive impressions from three separate stones; one, upon which are engraved lines, including projections, boundaries, borders, lettering, rivers, &c.; a second upon which are shaded in lithographic crayon all the hill work; and a third which will carry a faint tint over plateaux and level lowlands besides emphasizing certain features in the mountain topography. All the minutiae of production of this series even to the 'pulling' and seasoning of the paper has been attended to and the printing necessarily slow for the need of great evenness of press work will be begun as soon as the present damp weather is over, and carried steadily on to completion."[5]

Although the analysis of the scientific work—the geology, microscopic petrology, chemistry, biology, and paleontology—would take several more years, Gardner's primary responsibility to the Survey was finished. By this time in his career, he had mastered the science and art of mapping. His practical experience included laying out fortifications on San Francisco Bay with the Army Corps of Engineers, an apprenticeship with Charles Hoffmann in the previously unmapped southern Sierra Nevada, reconnaissance mapping in Arizona, and preparing the first map of Yosemite. But his six years as chief topographer with the Fortieth Parallel Survey had honed his professional skills, and he considered himself the best topographic mapper in the country. It was largely through his efforts that the essential linkage of concurrent topographic and geologic mapping was established for the subsequent western surveys.

Gardner now had time to think about his future. He had been closely—even intimately—associated with King since their high school years. During this time he had always maintained a brother-like relationship with King and had served as second in command of the Fortieth Parallel Survey. But he, unlike King, had no other close friend. It was clear that they were very different people. King's ebullient good humor, love of people, and outgoing character made him a born leader, a man who attracted others. Gardner, in contrast, was more serious, introspective, detail-oriented, and deeply spiritual. He now had, as well, a special responsibility—an infant daughter with no mother. Gardner decided that his future lay in breaking the close ties with his friend and striking out in a new direction, where he might play a more independent role.

At this time he was offered a position as topographer with Hayden's survey. It was obvious to him that topography was an integral element in these surveys of the West and was underappreciated. Without good maps to serve as a framework for all other scientific work, subsequent explorations would be of lesser value. He negotiated with Hayden and was assured that his place in the survey would be second only to Hayden's, not with the title topographer, but with the more imposing title of geographer.

Dr. Ferdinand Hayden, who headed up the U.S. Geological and Geographical Survey of the Territories, had completed two seasons in the Yellowstone region and decided to move his operations to a more accessible region, because, as he wrote, "The Indians, also, are in a state of hostility over the greater portion of the country which remains to be explored."[6] Hayden planned to move his field of investigation to Colorado, and requested $100,000 for this work. Keenly aware of criticisms leveled against him earlier for inadequate topographic mapping, he set his sights high and enticed Gardner to direct this work. With the matter thus settled, Gardner wrote to King in San Francisco that he was leaving the Fortieth Parallel Survey. He had decided

to accept an offer, with higher pay, to undertake a mapping program in a large area in the central Rocky Mountains, principally in Colorado.

King was angry and troubled that his best friend and "brother" would desert him and move on with a competing group. The fact that Hayden's survey was funded by the Department of the Interior, not the Army Corps of Engineers, made the defection doubly repugnant to him, and he wrote Gardner that "Now of Hayden I know but little except that his geology is hopeless and his private character bad. You cannot fail to be more or less connected with him in the public mind and I feel altogether certain that his future will be *bad,* for his science is weak and ignorant and men of his character sooner or later have the mask of position torn off. . . . Do not disguise from yourself the fact that H is a selfish and Christless man."[7] Gardner nevertheless forged ahead, and his change in affiliation ended the close association the two men had maintained for 17 years, from their first meeting as boys at Hartford High School. Although they would remain lifelong friends, the magic connection of the former years was gone.

Spurred on by King's description of climbing Mount Whitney in his mountaineering book, others were drawn to "the highest peak in the nation." During an attempt to re-climb it, a curious issue unfolded. Watson Goodyear was a geologist with the California Geological Survey and a graduate of the *Yale Scientific School.* He had been with Hoffmann in 1870 in Owens Valley when the position of Mount Whitney had been incorrectly identified and triangulated. In 1873, two years after King's celebrated success, Hoffmann published his map of the entire central Sierra Nevada, which incorporated that inaccurate location of Mount Whitney. Guided by the map, Goodyear and a companion climbed the mountain in July 1873 and found they were able to *ride mules* to the summit of "King's mountain."[8] Goodyear then made a startling announcement, in a talk at the California Academy of Sciences in San Francisco. He had found King's inscribed silver half dollar on the summit, yet saw a peak five miles to the north that was considerably higher. This higher peak was the one seen in 1864 from Mount Brewer by the Brewer party, and the one the party had named Mount Whitney at that time. King

FIGURE 10.1 (*opposite*). John Muir at 55, perhaps California's most famous historic figure. He climbed Mount Whitney up the precipitous east side in 1873, just two months after it was first ascended. Muir's love of the mountains and his tireless conservation efforts helped to preserve Yosemite and Sequoia as national parks. Curiously, King and Muir, despite their many common interests, never met. (Courtesy of the John Muir Historic Site, Martinez, California) had not seen the higher mountain to the north in 1871 because of cloudy and stormy weather. *He had mistakenly climbed the wrong mountain.* The mountain that King climbed and took to be Mount Whitney was locally called Sheep Mountain, was later called Mount Corcoran, and is now named Mount Langley.

Later in the summer of 1873, several other parties, spurred on by Goodyear's announcement, contrived to make an attempt on the true Mount Whitney. On August 18 a group of Lone Pine residents, Charles D. Begole, Albert H. Johnson, and John Lucas, made the first known ascent of Mount Whitney, which they approached from the west. They called the mountain Fisherman's Peak. Later in August a second party, consisting of William Crapo and Abe Leyda, climbed the mountain, and on September 6 a third ascent was made by Crapo, William L. Hunter, Tom McDonough, and Carl Rabe.[9] Rabe, who had been employed as a cook by the California Geological Survey, had learned about the handling of surveying instruments as an assistant topographer. He had therefore been entrusted with a barometer, which he carried to the summit during this ascent. An identical mercury barometer was set up in the town of Lone Pine, and readings were made every half hour during the day, so that corrections could be made later for natural weather-related variations in air pressure. When the readings were compared, and corrections applied, the summit's altitude was made to be 14,898 feet (somewhat higher than the presently accepted altitude of 14,491 feet).

The only fieldwork planned for the Fortieth Parallel Survey that year was a geologic reconnaissance by King partly in the White Mountains of western Nevada and adjacent California during September to December. The work was to study Archaean formations—sedimentary beds that are so old that they were laid down at the dawn of life and contain no fossils.

However King, having read Goodyear's report after arriving in San Francisco, decided to have another attempt at Mount Whitney. He later reported to General Humphreys, "I therefore determined to ride across the Sierras, taking the peak in my way to the White Mountains, knowing that I could do so almost as quickly as I could go round by stage and rail. Accordingly the day after arriving in San Francisco, being the 10th of September, I went by rail to Visalia, procured a couple of men and horses and continued on the same day, reaching the Sierra summit on the Hockett trail on the 14th. Here I was taken violently sick with dysentery and lay on my back in great prostration for a week. Recovering almost as suddenly as I had been attacked, I devoted two days to the measurement of the mountain."[10]

He and Frank Knowles, a settler in the Tule River region, finally climbed the mountain from the west on September 19, 1873, one month after the Lone Pine group's first ascent. In the second edition of *Mountaineering*,[11] King added a 16-page section in which he described his belated climb of the mountain and admitted his mistaken identification of 1871, which was attributable both to cloudy weather during the ascent and to magnetic aberrations that had affected his compass reading from Mount Tyndall in 1864. He eloquently (but somewhat sarcastically) stated in referring to his climb of 1871, "My little granite island was incessantly beaten by breakers of vague impenetrable clouds, and never once did the true Mount Whitney unveil its crest to my eager eyes. Only one glimpse and I should have bent my steps northward, restless till the peak was climbed. But then that would have left nothing for Goodyear, whose paper shows such evident relish in my mistake, that I accept my '71 ill-luck as providential. One has in this dark world so few chances of conferring innocent, pure delight."[12]

King absolved Hoffmann of all blame in the matter, and noted that the incorrect mapped position of Mount Whitney had resulted partly from the erroneous magnetic bearing that he had measured from the summit of Mount Tyndall in 1864. This

FIGURE 10.2. Flowers from the Fortieth Parallel Survey project area described by Sereno Watson. His comprehensive volume on the botany of the Fortieth Parallel region contained 25 full-page plates of drawings of plants, and was quickly recognized as a classic in the field. (Watson, 1871)

incorrect reading, which apparently resulted from a local magnetic anomaly on the summit of Mount Tyndall, had in turn misled Hoffmann in his identification (and measurement) of the supposed Mount Whitney as seen from Owens Valley in 1870. The mislocation was recorded on two maps, those by Hoffmann of 1873 and by Wheeler of 1874, which were published before the error came to light. Hence, King's incorrect compass reading from Mount Tyndall in 1864 had come back to haunt him. It led to Hoffmann's incorrect angular measurement from Owens Valley in 1870, which was then incorporated in the information Hoffmann supplied to King, who then went on to climb the wrong mountain in 1871.[13] King was entirely open in accepting the responsibility for these errors. He was a man who made friends when he won and when he lost.

King described his feelings at the real summit in his inimitably colorful prose: "This is the true Mount Whitney, the one we named in 1864, and upon which the name of our chief is forever to rest. It stands, not like white Shasta, in a grandeur of solitude, but about it gather companies of crag and spire, piercing the blue or

FIGURE 10.3.   Images of greatly magnified rock specimens made by Ferdinand Zirkel, who returned with Samuel Emmons from Germany to aid in the study of rocks collected in the area mapped by the Fortieth Parallel Survey. Zirkel introduced the latest developments in the microscopic study of rocks to this country. Drawings show two types of lava: *right*, rhyolite from northwest of Wadsworth, Nevada, showing large crystals (quartz and feldspar) in a groundmass of fluidal bands, and *left*, basalt from the lower Truckee Valley, Nevada, showing lath-shaped feldspars and small equant augite crystals, with a few large fractured crystals of olivine. Diameter of field of view is five millimeters. (Zirkel, 1880)

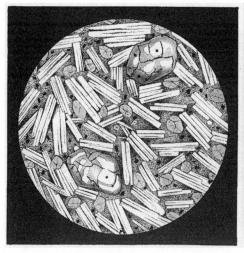
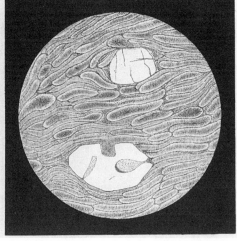

FIGURE 10.4. Fossil shells from the Fortieth Parallel project area. *Left*, spiral-shaped Upper Triassic ammonites (about 210 million years old) from the West Humboldt Range, Nevada (Meek, 1877). *Right*, Lower Carboniferous brachiopods (about 340 million years old) from Dry Canyon, Oquirrh Mountains, Utah (Hall and Whitfield, 1877). Paleontologists quickly discovered that many of these fossils were of the same genus as those found in well-recognized sequences of layered rocks in Europe. They therefore were able to utilize the fossils as a powerful tool in correlating and dating rock units across and between continents.

wrapped in monkish raiment of snow-storm and mist. Far below, laid out in ashen death, slumbers the desert. Silence reigns on these icy heights, save when scream of Sierra eagle or loud crescendo of avalanche interrupts the frozen stillness, or when in symphonic fullness a storm rolls through vacant canyons with its stern minor. It is hard not to invest these great dominating peaks with consciousness, difficult to realize that, sitting thus for ages in presence of all nature can work, of light-magic and color-beauty, no inner spirit has kindled, nor throb of granite heart once responded, no Buddhistic nirvana-life even has brooded in eternal calm within these sphinx-like breasts of stone."[14]

This same year, in October 1873, John Muir—carrying, and misled by, the Hoffmann map—and apparently unaware of the several ascents of the true Mount Whitney, mistakenly climbed Mount Langley and from its summit noted the higher peak to the north. He attempted to traverse to it, but was thwarted by high intervening ridges and deep canyons, and spent the night blanketless, dancing on the ridge to keep from freezing. The next morning he turned back and returned to Lone Pine, but

FIGURE 10.5. Fossilized head and neck of a
great wingless diving bird (*Hesperornis regalis*;
about 70 million years old) that was found in
Middle Cretaceous strata of Kansas and Colorado
by Othniel Marsh. This toothed bird was one of the
300 vertebrate species that Marsh described, out of
1,000 extinct animals found from 1868 to 1880 in
the United States that now reside in the Yale
Peabody Museum. This wealth of fossil material
provided tangible evidence for Darwin's theory of
evolution. (Marsh, 1880)

with bulldog tenacity headed again for the true mountain. Muir climbed Mount
Whitney solo up the forbidding east wall and reached the summit a few weeks after
King's ascent.

    After his belated conquest of the true Mount Whitney, King went on to examine
the ancient rocks of the White Mountains of eastern California. But when at Bishop,
California, below the Sierra Escarpment, he was struck again for a week by the same
illness that had plagued him in the Sierra. Courageously, King continued his examinations of mining districts in Nevada, testing his ideas on the relationship between
mineral deposits and the geologic age of their host rocks. But the illness continued to
torment him. He suffered for five days in the hospital in Pioche and was ill for three
more days in Eureka. After returning to San Francisco to testify in a lawsuit stemming

from the diamond hoax, he departed by rail on December 6, 1873 and arrived in New York on the morning of December 13.

The published volumes from the Fortieth Parallel Survey came out one by one, and not in numerical order. Volume III on *Mining Industry*, prepared primarily by James Hague, was first in 1870, and it was followed closely by Volume V on *Botany*, by Sereno Watson, in 1871. Volume VI on *Microscopical Petrography* [the study of rocks], by Ferdinand Zirkel, was published in 1876, and Volume II on *Descriptive Geology*, by Arnold Hague and Samuel Emmons, appeared in 1877. Volume IV, a composite of three reports, two on *Paleontology* respectively by Fielding Meek, and by James Hall and Robert Whitfield, and one on *Ornithology* [birds] by Robert Ridgeway, was published in 1878. Volume I on *Systematic Geology*, by Clarence King, published in 1878, was the general wrap-up of all the studies. A latecomer was Volume VII, *Odontornithes: Extinct Toothed Birds of North America* by Othniel Marsh, which appeared in 1880. This irregular order resulted from King's desire to emphasize geology by including it in the first three numbered volumes. Historians have noted that the appearance of the first volume, "*Mining Industry*, and the King survey goals, organization, and field methods served as both model and standard for the other three Federal surveys of the western territories."[15] It proved to be propitious that nearly all of these handsome volumes were in print when final negotiations to select a director for the new combined western surveys began.

The Map Atlas of the Fortieth Parallel Survey was published in 1876, and no atlas of such scope and accuracy had ever been seen in the country before. The geodetic and topographic base for the atlas was a major achievement in James Gardner's career. The geologic maps utilize bright colors to distinguish some 26 separate geological units ranging in age from the most ancient (Archaean) to the most recent basin-filling sediments. Young volcanic rocks are separated by color into seven compositional types. The areas and shorelines of ancient lake basins and the extent of ice-age glaciers are also set out on the maps.

In addition to the twenty large map sheets in the atlas (two topographic and two geologic for each of five rectangles) there are remarkable geologic-topographic cross-sections in vivid colors keyed to every map sheet that show the rock units in profile down to a mile or more below the surface. A general cross-section depicts the regional geology across the entire 800-mile length of the survey.[16]

Gardner was generally pleased with the final lithographic printing of the maps. He was ever cautious and stated that because of the large region covered and the lack of previous mapping, it was of lesser precision than the products of some European

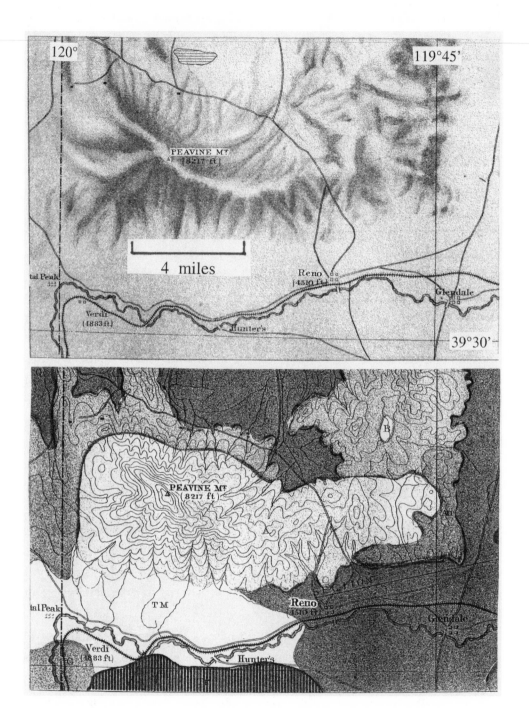

120°   119°45'

PEAVINE M?
(8217 ft)

4 miles

tal Peak

Reno
(4510 ft)

Glendale

Verdi
(4883 ft)

Hunter's

39°30'

PEAVINE M?
(8217 ft)

B

tal Peak

T M

Reno
(4510 ft)

Glendale

Verdi
(4883 ft)

Hunter's

mapping programs. He noted that the maps show "the general contours and elevations of the mountains and plateaus, the drainage-systems, roads, towns, &c., with
such accuracy that errors in relative positions and distances between points should
not be apparent on the given scale."[17]

King had moved to a brownstone house on Fifth Avenue in New York in 1875, and had
begun in earnest to write reports, edit the reports of others, and usher through the
press the several volumes of the survey. Along the way, he began writing *Systematic
Geology*, the final volume and overall summary of the Fortieth Parallel Survey. In this
enterprise, he was fortunate in meeting a young reporter named Edgar Bronson who
knew shorthand. King quickly hired him, and the book proceeded with King dictat-
ing and Bronson taking shorthand and later transcribing the manuscript. This routine continued for three years as King submitted the manuscript to the printer piece-
meal and then often retrieved it for revisions—a process that continued on into 1878,
the year of publication. King was, as always, enthusiastic but overly optimistic about
his material, and he tended to submit it before final revisions had been effected. One
of the editors at the Public Printing Office wrote him, "If you want your work hurried
up, please see to it that your manuscript copy is nearer what you want it when sent to
this office. The part just returned this morning is perfectly terrible. The additions and
erasures you have made cause more than *double* work. In fact when the book is completed it will be found to have cost nearly or quite twice as much as it ought. Isn't
there *some* way to prevent this extravagance?"[18]

King's final product, *Systematic Geology*, is a magnificent volume organized his-
torically according to the ages of the rock units. In the introduction King states that
"It has rarely fallen to the lot of one set of observers to become intimate with so wide
a range of horizons and products. Embracing within its area a pretty full exposure of

FIGURE 10.6 (*opposite*).   A part of the Atlas of the Fortieth Parallel Survey area. The area
shown is the southwest part of Sheet V, which includes the California state line (left) and the
town of Reno, Nevada (bottom center). The topographic map (top) shows shaded
topography as if obliquely illuminated from the west. The geologic map of the same area
(bottom) shows topography by unlabeled contours with a vertical interval of 300 feet and
only a few scattered measured elevations. The geologic units represented (in color on the
original) are: white, Tertiary sediments; white with letter "B," basaltic lava; light gray,
Archaean (very ancient) crystalline rocks; medium gray, granite; dark gray, young
unconsolidated sediment; dark gray with vertical ruling, trachyte, a volcanic rock. The width
of the maps is 16 miles. (King, 1876)

the earth's crust from nearly the greatest known depths up through a section of 125,000 feet, taking in all the broader divisions of geological time—a section which has been subjected to a great sequence of mechanical violence, and can hardly fail to become classic for its display of the products of eruption—this Exploration has actually covered an epitome of geological history."[19]

The volume is illustrated not only with many of Timothy O'Sullivan's outstanding photographs, but also with color lithographs of several of Gilbert Munger's paintings. It begins with the Archaean (Precambrian) rocks, those most ancient rocks that are commonly metamorphosed and recrystallized across time, thus displaying little of their original structure and wholly lacking in traces of life. It then proceeds through the successively younger rock units from the Paleozoic (ancient life) and Mesozoic (middle life) to the Cenozoic (recent life) geologic eras. Determinations of fossils, which contributed significantly to the establishment of the age groups, were made primarily by paleontologists Fielding Meek, James Hall, and Robert Whitfield. The outcrop areas for each of the major age groups are displayed on several foldout, two-page colored maps of the entire Fortieth Parallel Survey area. The twelve colored geologic maps reproduced in the volume are simplified, reduced-scale versions of the much larger geologic maps in the Atlas.

Great advances in both chemistry and geology were prompted by the appearance of new scientific tools, which facilitated the ordering of information into more readily understandable and more broadly applicable form. One view holds that chemistry emerged in the early nineteenth century as an experimental science, and lost its old association with natural history, as a result of the invention of the sign system of chemical formulas by the Swedish chemist Jacob Berzelins.[20] The historian of science William Glen has noted that in much the way chemistry had progressed, at about the same time, geology attained a more scientific footing, expanded, and moved beyond its old status as a branch of natural philosophy. This shift was triggered when the first precise geologic maps appeared in England. Likewise, the colored geologic maps of the Fortieth Parallel Survey, each overlaid on a precise topographic base showing elevation by contours, provided a firm new basis by which to test geologic musings. These maps were widely emulated by the other ongoing surveys and clearly elevated Earth science to a new level in this country.[21]

In the letter of transmittal of the volume to General Humphreys, King mentions that "For the freedom of action you have always granted me, for your generous bestowal of every needed facility, and above all for your wise and just guidance of the general plans of the work, I beg to offer my warmest thanks. That which a student of geology most earnestly longs for, I have freely received at your hands, and whatever value this Report may possess, either as a permanent contribution to knowledge or as a stepping-stone worthy to be built into the great stairway of science, I feel that the honor belongs first to you. For those who are to continue the arduous labor of American field-study, I can wish no happier fortune than to serve within the department which you command."[22]

Systematic Geology was a remarkable synthesis of geological information on the vast area of the Fortieth Parallel Survey reaching across nearly half a continent. In it was compiled data on the nature and age of all the sedimentary rock sequences, the structural dislocations that they had undergone since deposition, the areal extent, and compositions of, the plutonic and volcanic igneous rocks, the extent of glaciation during the Ice Ages, and the regions occupied by, and water compositions of, the giant ancient lakes during the humid periods of glaciation. The historian K. R. Aalto has declared that the volume is "one of the great scientific works of the late nineteenth century."[23]

During this time King led an active social life. He dined out with the rich and cultivated, and was always an honored guest at dinner parties, owing to his sparkling conversation and good humor. He joined several prestigious men's clubs, including the Round Table Club, the Knickerbocker Club, and the Century Club. John Hay, who sponsored him for membership in the Century Club, had been an assistant to President Lincoln and had served the State Department in several legations in Europe. Hay, a brilliant writer, would eventually become Secretary of State under President McKinley. King would remain a lifelong friend.

Because of the broad range of his interests, King was a constant joy to his associates. Fellow Century Club member Edward Cary wrote, "It was at question to foresee at what point his tangential fancy would change its course. From the true rhythm of Creole gumbo to the verse of Theocritus, from the origin of the latest *mot* to the age of the globe, from the soar or slump of the day's market to the method of Lippo Lippi, from the lightest play on words to the subtlest philosophy, he passed with buoyant step and head erect, sometimes with audacity that invited disaster, often with profound penetration and with the informing flash of genius. . . . Intense, restless, wide-reaching, nourished by much reading, trained in the exercise of an exact and exacting profession, stimulated by commerce with many lands and races, it played incessantly on the topic of the moment and on the remotest and most complex problems of the earth and dwellers thereon."[24]

King at this time began supplementing his income by investigating private mineral deposits, writing reports intended for investors, serving as an expert witness in mining lawsuits, and forming companies for the purpose of operating mines. Such activities, which inherently mixed private investigations with funded government work, were not illegal, but they naturally diverted his energies from the national surveys at hand.

King in fact took leave from survey business July 1–Nov. 1, 1877 in order to join his business partner N. L. Davis in Wyoming for a major roundup and tallying of the cattle. The five-year period was up, and the time had come for a complete assessment of the state of the commingled herds, including those in which Emmons, Gardner, and Sheldon had an interest. Some 1,500 steers were shipped to Chicago by rail, and an independent stockman was selected to oversee the roundup. After the cattle were purchased by Davis and King, Emmons, Gardner, and Sheldon realized about a two-fold growth in their investment. Gardner, much pleased, wrote, "We were thoroughly satisfied with the way in which the trust was executed."[25]

King delivered the commencement speech at the Yale Sheffield Scientific School, June 26, 1877. Speaking on catastrophism and evolution, he introduced his talk with a typical Kingian flourish, "If I turn from the far greater and more attractive achievements of others, from the wealth of literary and philosophic materials which press forward for utterance, and bring here something which I have reached myself, it will afford you a more intimate interest. I have hoped, too, that other graduates might feel as I have, and that year by year men might stand here, fresh from the battle-field of life, out of the very heat of the strife, to tell us of their struggles, and hang the shields they have won along the walls of this temple of science."[26]

His stance was to question the doctrine of uniformitarianism, a concept of enduring influence formulated by James Hutton in 1785. This theory, a guiding tenet of geologists, holds that the present is the key to the past, that the everyday processes of erosion and sedimentation when extended over the vast reaches of geologic time can produce the rock units and the landforms we see today. Uniformitarianism was considered compatible with Darwinian evolution by natural selection, which envisages generally slow processes that, over long time periods, generate the changes and diversity of the plant and animal worlds.

King, on the other hand, maintained that "the interaction of energy and matter which make up environment should, from time to time, burst in upon the current of life and sweep it onward and upward to ever higher and better manifestations. Moments of great catastrophe, thus translated into the language of life, become moments of creation."[27]

King's was not a popular notion, and his talk was not well received by the scientific community, but it clearly demonstrated his independent bent. The address, interestingly, was not published in the *American Journal of Science*, which was based at Yale and edited by James Dana, but instead appeared in the *American Naturalist*. King's entry into this debate was neither the first nor the last. Today, the pendulum is swinging toward general acceptance of elements of the catastrophist view. For example, it is well accepted that major meteoritic impacts and episodes of massive volcanism have assaulted the Earth across the eons with catastrophic results, thus shaping and accelerating physical and biologic evolution. Many of these catastrophes have been shown to occur at the boundaries of the great geologic eras and periods, boundaries that were originally discovered and defined because they marked the time that major extinctions and changes occurred in plant and animal life.[28] The debate, fueled by new discoveries and fresh interpretations, continues.

King also struggled with the enigma of the origin of the vast Basin and Range Province, which includes about 25 north-trending blocky mountain ranges standing along his primary cross-section from the Sierra Nevada to the Wasatch Front in central Utah. His maps in the 1876 Atlas show virtually no faults or fractures along which the mountain ranges might have been uplifted or tilted, but they do show the axes of major folds in the layered rocks. How did these ranges form? He first interpreted the structure as resulting exclusively from the folding of strata, as had been so amply and elegantly demonstrated in the folded Appalachian Belt of the eastern United States. Regarding the Nevada mountains, he stated in 1870 that "These low mountain chains which lie traced across the desert with a north-and-south trend are ordinarily the tops of folds whose deep synclinal valleys are filled with Tertiary and Quaternary detritus."[29]

Grove Karl Gilbert and John Wesley Powell, however, emphasized the importance of uplift of the ranges along bounding faults. Gilbert wrote in 1875 "In the Appalachians corrugation has been produced commonly by folding, exceptionally by faulting; in the Basin Ranges, commonly by faulting, exceptionally by flexure. . . . The former demand the assumption of great horizontal diminution of the space covered by the disturbed strata, and suggest lateral pressure as the immediate force concerned; the latter involve little horizontal diminution, and suggest the application of vertical pressure from below."[30]

King recognized the existence of major faults that had dislocated earlier folded strata.[31] In *Systematic Geology*, he remarked that "The two grandest fault-lines shown in the Great Basin are those which define its east and west walls."[32] Here he refers to the east front of the Sierra Nevada and the west front of the Wasatch Range. King did not show a single fault on the geologic maps of the 1876 Atlas, or in the generalized maps of the *Systematic Geology* volume. He did, however, portray seven normal faults in the generalized cross-sections that accompanied the maps in the atlas. He modified his surmise about the primary importance of folding and instead concluded that two epochs of mountain building had occurred, such that "The frequency of these monoclinal detached blocks gives abundant warrant for the assertions of Gilbert and Powell that the region is one predominantly characterized by vertical action; yet when we come to examine with greater detail the structure of the individual mountain ranges, it is seen that this vertical dislocation took place after the whole area was compressed into a great region of anticlinals [upward folds] with intermediate synclinals [downward folds]."[33]

Because he emphasized the folding of strata, however, King concluded that the area of the Basin and Range Province has contracted in area. He states "From what I have seen in the Fortieth Parallel field, I am confident that the whole area has suffered a linear diminution of ten per cent."[34] Gilbert concluded that the ranges were formed by differential vertical uplift with no mention of horizontal contraction or extension. It was only later that modern workers realized that the entire area had undergone regional extension, and that tension-induced faulting greatly predominates. Modern workers estimate that during the past 17 million years the entire Basin-Range Province has been extended or stretched in an east-west direction by 25 to 40 percent of its former extent.[35]

ROCKY TRIANGULATION

My joy was in the wilderness to breathe
The difficult air of the ice mountain top
Where the birds dare not build nor insects wing
Flit o'er the herbless granite.
　　　　　　—Lord Byron, "Manfred"

When James Gardner joined Hayden's survey to tackle the topographic mapping of the Central Rocky Mountains, he faced new difficulties, many of them more challenging than those encountered in the desert country. Much of the region was remote and rugged, all but unknown. Colorado has the highest average elevation of any state, and presents scores of mountain peaks exeeding 14,000 feet. The lower reaches of these ranges were heavily forested, with much downed timber, making travel almost impossible on horses and difficult on foot. Supply centers were far apart—not spaced along a railroad—and hostile Indians controlled broad sectors. Matured by the hard schools of the Mount Whitney region, Yosemite, and the Fortieth Parallel country, he knew that preparation of a credible topographic map of the Central Rocky Mountains would be a daunting effort. Moreover, funding was not as liberal as had been hoped. Hayden had expected $100,000 for the season, but received only $75,000.[1] (Pressure from the Army had led Congress to minimize funding for the rival civilian surveys, thus allowing the Army to retain as much of the western work as possible.)

In defining his role in the new work, Gardner emphasized the importance of an accurate map, since information gathered by the survey would be meaningless without precise locations. The geologists of course had the notion that anyone could make a base map, and that real science came into play in identifying and classifying the

rocks, establishing their age sequence and structure, and identifying mineral deposits—all with the goal of unraveling the geologic history of the region. In order to
garner the respect due him, Gardner had his position formalized as Geographer
rather than Topographer, a title that purportedly signified his important cartographic
responsibilities. But Hayden was an autocratic leader and wielded a heavy hand in his
management of the survey. The report of the Geographic Department was respectfully submitted by James T. Gardner, Geographer, to F. V. Hayden, Geologist-in-
Charge, U.S. Geological and Geographical Survey of the Territories.

If the altitude of key points in the map area, from settlements and streams to the
loftiest peaks, were to be measured precisely, a solid elevation basis had to be established. As his first task in the spring of 1873, Gardner set out to assemble all the information concerning the elevation of Denver above sea level. The problem was simple
but profound: Denver lies in the middle of the continent, more than 1,000 miles from
the sea, and sea level is the fundamental elevation datum. He quickly found that, lacking any elevation base points, the primary source of data available to him was the leveling surveys made on the various railroad lines reaching from the East Coast and the
Great Lakes ultimately to Denver. The elevation of the sea is established by lengthy
measurements of water level at tide gauges on the coast, and the various leveling survey lines were tied into these gauges. Gardner found that "The height of Denver above
the sea had been variously reported at from 5,043 feet to 5,303 feet, and the spirit-level
lines of the K.P. and U. P. R. R. [Kansas Pacific and Union Pacific Railroads] seemed
to differ by 200 feet. Believing that any such large discrepancies between spirit-level
lines must be due to false reports and errors in joining the different links of these long
chains to the sea, I determined to reconstruct all possible lines of levels from the
ocean to the Rocky Mountains, using only official reports by engineers, and checking
them by personal examination of their note-books and working profiles wherever
practicable."[2]

He therefore visited the railroad engineer offices in Denver, Omaha, Lawrence,
Kansas City, St. Louis, Chicago, Cleveland, New York, and Philadelphia. At each site
he examined the original notebooks and profile of the leveling survey, and compared
the elevations of different companies, at points where the railroad lines crossed or
served the same depot. In addition, he compared data with those of other groups and
agencies, including the Post Office Department, the Smithsonian Institution, and the
Chief Signal Officer of the U.S. Army. He found many errors and discrepancies in the
data, including simple errors in calculation and copying, differences in official reports
of the same railroad or canal, and problems in finding the endpoints of a given line,
and in connecting them with the mean surface of the ocean.

Gardner gauged the reliability of the data by a series of tests that included the time of the last survey, how it compared with previous surveys, how many connected lines were included, and how various surveys were connected. His painstaking evaluation of these data proved worthwhile. Good agreement was found for the elevation of the Denver Railroad Depot, as determined by two independent surveys. The elevation of the depot on the track of the Kansas Pacific and Denver Pacific Railroad was determined at 5,196.58 feet above sea level, which agreed remarkably well with the elevation on the track of the Denver and Rio Grande Railroad at 5,197.58 feet. It was these numbers that eventually led to Denver's familiar nickname of the Mile High City.

With this altitude reliably established, his team then set up, and measured, the elevation of a series of primary elevation stations on major roads with cistern (mercury) barometers. Repeated reading and transport of the barometer between the Denver depot and each of these stations verified the elevations. In this way the team obtained a body of measurements from which to establish station elevation averages and deviations from these averages. Next, they tied the individual survey barometric observations in towns and on peaks and rivers to these primary elevation stations during a period in which continuous measurements were also read at the primary station. The elevations of inaccessible mountains were determined by triangulation and vertical-angle measurements to the absolute summit of the peaks from points of known elevation.

The next step was to determine the geographic location of the primary points that would control the entire survey. The topographers made a primary triangulation net by constructing a series of linked triangles, each with observation points, generally high peaks, at the triangle apexes. Horizontal angle measurements from the occupied apex to the other triangle corners could then establish their position, and this primary network could be expanded over the area to be mapped. The net of interconnected triangles, despite its precise positioning of all points relative to one another, would at first have no scale and would be at an unknown position on the globe. Therefore, it was crucial to fix with the greatest possible accuracy the precise location—both horizontally and vertically—of a few key points within the area to be mapped. The triangulation net was then hung on those points.

The U.S. Coast Survey had established astronomical observatories at both Denver and Colorado Springs, 75 miles to the south, in collaboration with Hayden's survey. By repeated astronomical measurements of the altitude of reference stars at these stations, their latitude was determined. Longitude was established by measuring the exact time that selected stars crossed the meridian, that is when they moved into a po-

FIGURE 11.1.   Early spring rendezvous camp on Clear Creek, four miles north of Denver, the cottonwoods not yet leafed out. At this first camp of Hayden's survey for the 1873 season, equipment and provisions were assembled and plans for the summer were laid. (William Jackson, 1873, U.S. Geological Survey Library)

sition due north (or south) of the astronomical station. The precise time of crossing was taken from time signals received by telegraph, and under the best of conditions could be as close as a few hundredths of a second. The difference in time that a given star took from its crossing of the meridian in Washington, D.C., as compared to its crossing at Denver, is a measure of how much farther west Denver is than the Washington Naval Observatory. Because the longitude for Washington, D.C., was already known, calculation could establish the precise longitude of Denver.[3]

The survey party assembled at Clear Creek, north of Denver, in May 1873 and was divided into six parties. Gardner had responsibility for the triangulation party that would construct the primary net on which all topographic calculations depended. Three other parties took to the field, each with a topographer, geologist, naturalist, several laborers, and a cook. These were headed up by Henry Gannett, who later would become the first chief topographer of the U.S. Geological Survey; Archibald Marvine from Wheeler's survey; and Allen Wilson from King's survey, who had climbed both Mount Shasta and Mount Rainier in the summer of 1870. The fifth party was William Jackson's photographic team, and the sixth, a supply group under the direction of James Stevenson, which endeavored to keep the scattered field parties provisioned.[4]

Somewhat east of each of the astronomical observatories, Gardner's group laid out baselines on flat ground, well away from the imposing Front Range of the Rocky Mountains. The line near Denver was 6 miles long, 4 miles of which was along the Kansas Pacific Railroad. They measured the line twice; the tape was held at 20 pounds

FIGURE 11.2.   The cook tossing flapjacks over an open fire in a typical camp with sleeping tent in the background. Perhaps stew and biscuits are ready to be served from the Dutch oven. (William Jackson, 1873; U.S. Geological Survey Library)

tension and the temperature was recorded every 5 minutes. These precautions were needed to reduce errors caused by the sagging of the tape and to correct for the thermal expansion of the tape caused by weather fluctuations.

From the stations at each end of the baselines, sighting through a telescopic surveying instrument (theodolite or transit), they measured the angles to a third point in the mountains, which was thus fixed in space at the intersection of the two rays, one from each end of the baseline. In this way surveyors constructed the first triangle of the triangulation network. They repeated the process to all major points in the mountains visible from both ends of the baseline. Survey points on the plain were made visible over a broad area by constructing wooden towers 30 feet high over them. Stone cairns were built on the mountain peaks to mark the exact target points. Where the sightings were too distant to see the stone monuments, angles were made to the topmost spire of the target mountain. To increase the accuracy and provide a check of the triangulation, the instrument was carried to the newly established points so as to measure the angles backward to the original stations at the ends of the baseline. This reversal of sighting improved the precision of the angles and identified mistakes in angle measurement or recording. The telescopic theodolite used for the primary net has an engraved brass disk 8 inches in diameter graduated with 360 lines per degree, that is, 6 lines per minute of arc, or one for 10 seconds of arc. The angle measurements were repeated six times with readings made on different parts of the circle, so as to compensate for instrumental error and to increase accuracy by averaging the measurements.

They then carried the instrument to a large number of primary points—which included Long's Peak and Pike's Peak—and from these summits measured angles to other peaks as far as 100 miles distant. Careful sketches were made of the skyline to keep track of the dozens of peaks visible and measured from a given point, so that they could be correctly identified from the next station on a different mountain and from a different angle. The theodolite and its tripod, weighing about 50 lbs., were carried on the topographer's back for ascents up to 5,000 feet, over the steep terrain. Gardner headed up this primary triangulation, climbed all of the high peaks in the mapped area, and spent most of the summer in the highest parts of the Rocky Mountains.

The observers commonly remained on station after sundown in order to make observations of the North Star (Polaris) so as to independently establish true north and the latitude as a check. All measurements would then be inspected in the office, readings averaged and corrected, and calculations made for atmospheric refraction and curvature of the Earth, in order to establish the position of the points of the primary triangulation net and plot their position on the map.

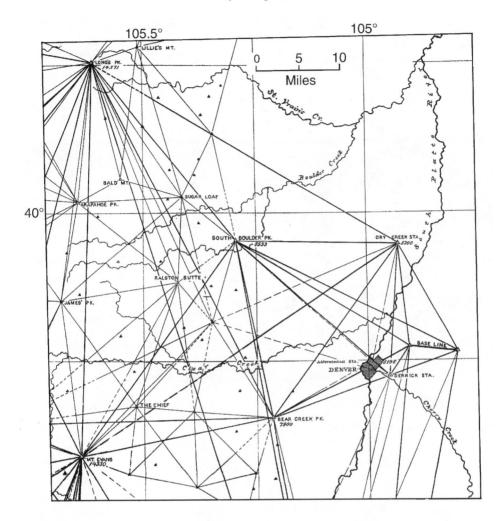

FIGURE 11.3. Part of the triangulation map showing the surveyed lines in Colorado, originally published at 8 miles to the inch. Heavy lines represent the primary triangulation net surveyed by James Gardner, and light lines indicate secondary triangulation by Allen Wilson, Henry Gannett, and Gustavus Bechler. The baseline east of Denver was measured on the ground to provide a scale for the triangle net. Latitude and longitude were precisely determined at the astronomical station in Denver. (Hayden, 1874)

After they had established the first set of large triangles (the primary triangulation net) over a part of the survey area of 12,000 square miles, the other survey parties continued triangulation measurements to locate lesser points between the primary points. The parties working on the secondary net employed smaller, lighter, less delicate, and less precise instruments that could sustain more rugged handling without damage. Then from each of these newly established points the details of the land-

FIGURE 11.4.   Mount of the Holy Cross (14,176 feet) in the northern reach of the Sawatch Range, Colorado, underlain entirely by dark gneissic rock. The cross, formed from snow-filled fissures, is about 1,500 feet high and 700 feet wide. (Photograph by William Jackson, 1873; U.S. Geological Survey Library). The mountain was immortalized in a poem by Henry Longfellow, "The Cross of Snow" (1879), in remembrance of the loss of his wife:

> There is a mountain in the distant West
> That, sun-defying, in its deep ravines
> Displays a cross of snow upon its side.
> Such is the cross I wear upon my breast
> These eighteen years, through all the changing scenes
> And seasons, changeless since the day she died.

scape—towns, ridges, lakes, watercourses, and geologic features—were sighted and sketched on a plane table in their correct positions to flesh out the map.

The triangulations began in the middle of May, and work in the lower country early in the season enabled the crew to become gradually accustomed to higher altitude and the rigors of this activity. Gardner first used a buggy for much of the transport, which helped him break in for the extensive horseback riding that came later. He was also able to travel into Denver in the evening to enjoy the amenities of the town, as he wrote to his mother, "Drove in last night from the camp to dine with the governor of the territory and go to church today. I value church out here far more than in the east. The contrast with the rough materialistic life of the camp is delightful. I come in and take off old buckskin and flannel, and put on a boiled garment (white shirt) and store clothes and feel like myself. If I could only have a little look at you and the baby I should be well contented."[5]

By the end of July the fieldwork had moved into the high mountains, with camps commonly at 11,000 and 12,000 feet, so as to occupy peaks above 14,000 feet. Gardner was pleased with the performance of his assistants and noted that "I am gloriously well and strong, able to lead in every enterprise. I shall have the finest maps that have

FIGURE 11.5.   The hungry crew dining in camp after the rigors of the first ascent of the Mount of the Holy Cross. The trip having taken longer than expected, the rations on the mountain consisted of just two slices of bread apiece for two days. From left: Ferdinand Hayden, James Stevenson, Holman, Jones, James Gardner (in buckskin), William Whitney (brother of Josiah Whitney and professor of linguistics at Yale), and William Henry Holmes (artist and geologist). (Photograph by William Jackson, who also made the ascent with his camera, 1873; U.S. Geological Survey Library)

FIGURE 11.6. Allen Wilson on the summit of Sultan Mountain (13,368 feet), leveling his instrument, and preparing to turn angles on distant peaks. Artist Franklin Rhoda doubles as notetaker. (Photograph by William Jackson, 1874; U.S. Geological Survey Library)

yet been produced outside of the Coast Survey work in this country. I am going to beat my old work all out of sight."[6]

In August, combined survey parties made the first approach to a marvelous peak, plainly visible to the naked eye at 50 miles distance. They first saw it from Mount Evans, and then from Gray's Peak in the Front Range. The Mount of the Holy Cross was some 13,400 feet high and rose 6,000 feet above the surrounding region. It had never been closely approached or climbed. Gardner wrote, "We could not get our animals within many miles on account of fallen timber, and the trip had to be made on foot packing the great 50 pound theodolite while three men carried the photographic apparatus. Expecting to reach the peak and return in one day we only carried a little lunch, two slices of bread apiece. This was all we had to eat for two days of tremendous climbing, while at night we lay on the mountain side without shelter or covering. We succeeded in getting splendid observations and photographs. One large photograph 12 x 14 inches shows the peak culminating in a dark precipice 3000 ft. high on which rests the great White Cross 1500 ft. long as perfect in form as you can imagine. Dr. Hayden worked like a hero."[7] Gardner pointed out that in order to obtain the images of the mountain, "Mr. Jackson, Mr. Coulter the botanist, and one packer, carried 100 lbs. of photographic apparatus for ten hours over rocks and fallen timber and up 4000 feet of the steepest debris slope."[8]

The mapped area encompassed the highest part of the Rocky Mountain System and included the most extensive region of high peaks in the nation. From Mount Lincoln they counted 200 peaks higher than 13,000 feet and 22 more than 14,000 feet. In September they prepared to climb Long's Peak at the east front of the range. Gardner notes that "We are all well in spite of low diet. We have nothing left but flour and beans. Tea, coffee, sugar, and everything else are gone. It will be a week before we reach settlements and get supplies."[9]

In September Anna Dickinson, a journalist, was invited by Hayden to accompany them on the climb of Long's Peak with Gardner's crew. Gardner, a widower, seemed interested in her as a person. He was pleased that Hayden had encouraged her participation on the trip because "She has pledged herself as an advocate of our cause, and she is no mean power to enlist. Dr. Hayden seems to make friends everywhere and I do not wonder, for he is full of good feeling when belligerent power is not aroused."[10]

After the climb, Dickinson compared Gardner and Hayden: "What a pair of heads had that party! Hayden, tall, slender, with soft brown hair and blue eyes—certainly not traveling on his muscle; all nervous intensity and feeling, a perfect enthusiast in his work, eager of face and voice, full of magnetism. Gardner, shorter, stouter,

FIGURE 11.7. High mountains seen from the summit of Sultan Mountain near Silverton, Colorado. Gardner's survey demonstrated that more than 200 peaks over 13,000 feet stand in Colorado, which has the highest average elevation of any state, at 6,800 feet above sea level. (Photograph by William Jackson, 1874; U.S. Geological Survey Library)

with amber eyes and hair like gold, less quick and tense, yet made of the stuff that *takes* and holds on."[11]

Later in the high mountains Gardner shot two mountain sheep to supplement their larder. He related that "I looked from the top over an abrupt edge and saw the wild creatures jumping from rock to rock on the cliff. At a slight noise from me they stopped, looked up, and with two quick shots I sent two of them tumbling a thousand feet down. It was the most delicious meat we have had. You have no idea what attachment one gets for a gun that supplies much needed food."[12]

Back in Denver, after this trip, Gardner had a studio photograph taken with his rifle, buckskin field clothes, long hair, and beard. Later, after a shave and haircut he met in the evening with Miss Dickinson for tea. He relates that when she saw me: "close cropped, white shirted and clad in Weidenfeld's best cut, she bemoaned my changed appearance, especially the loss of what she was pleased to call my beautiful golden hair."[13]

Toward the end of the field season one of the topographic crews encountered another group of mappers in South Park working the same country. It was led by Lieutenant Marshall, in charge of one of Wheeler's main parties. Hayden was angry and had strong words with the invaders over this encroachment by the Army on terrain that he had been authorized to map.

About this time, the growing problem of the duplication of effort by the various government-funded surveys came to the attention of Congress. Hayden and Gardner realized that now was the time to marshal support for the civilian program, in preference to the military surveys. It was certainly to the benefit of the academic and scientific institutions to foster civilian science, and hence help was sought from that quarter. Gardner wrote his old boss Josiah Whitney, then teaching at Harvard, that "It is a great crisis for the science of the country. There must now be decided whether civilians who have devoted years to science are to direct the scientific work of the country. Can you not write an article on the general principles involved and get *The Nation* to print it? I hope Yale and Harvard will speak up nobly in this crisis . . . we shall remember the friends that stand by in this awful struggle."[14]

Whitney responded immediately in May 1874 with a strong letter condemning the quality of Wheeler's mapping, and providing ammunition for Gardner and Hayden

FIGURE 11.8.   Looking across Twin Lakes up the Lake Fork of the Arkansas River in central Colorado. A large extinct glacier that moved toward the front down the Lake Fork heaped up the sinuous ridges (lateral moraines, b) on its sides. The ice pushed forward debris, making the hill on the right with the small trees (terminal moraine) that blocked the drainage and dammed the lake. This is part of one of the masterful drawings by William Holmes that adorn the Atlas of Colorado. (Hayden, 1877)

FIGURE 11.9.   Dismantled wagon ready to be packed over one of the rugged passes of the San Juan Mountains, to be reassembled on the other side. (Photograph by William Jackson, 1875; U.S. Geological Survey Library)

to use against the military-sponsored surveys. He wrote, "In my opinion all of the Engineer work in the Cordilleras is worthless as a finality and only valuable as a preliminary reconnaissance to answer until something better can be had. The recently published maps made under the direction of Lieut. Wheeler seem to me very bad, and entirely behind the present requirements of geographical science in this country."[15]

The Townsend Committee on Western Public Lands of the House of Representatives, chaired by Representative Washington Townsend of Pennsylvania, held hearings in the spring of the year on the problem of duplication of effort among the western surveys. At the meetings, Hayden, Gardner, and Powell directed barbed comments against Wheeler, who lashed out in return. Letters were read citing the backward science and inadequate mapping performed by Wheeler's U.S. Army Geographical Surveys West of the 100th Meridian. Wheeler responded with the opinion that only the military was competent to conduct surveys safely in the West, and that certain questions could not be answered in open session on the grounds that they might compromise sensitive War Department information. The hearings ended in a draw, but they did polarize the differences between the surveys. The committee members judged that a certain amount of overlap, which would lead to a more complete un-

FIGURE 11.10. Geologist Fred Endlich, Franklin Rhonda (Wilson's younger half-brother), and topographer Allen Wilson on muleback. The men are armed and carry equipment in saddlebags, their blankets strapped behind the saddle. Note the large spurs on Endlich, and the cistern barometer in the canvas bag strapped to Rhonda's saddle horn. (Photograph by William Jackson, 1874; U. S. Geological Survey Library)

derstanding of the country investigated, was beneficial. Funding would continue for the four surveys, which was seen to be a minor victory for the civilian scientists, inasmuch as the military had entered the dispute with the notion that all surveys in the West should be under the control of the Army. Wheeler's attempts for the Army to take charge had been thwarted, but the status quo could not be maintained indefinitely, now that the public had become aware of this blatant duplication of effort.

Meanwhile Hayden, with the help of Gardner, sought more support for increased funding for his survey. After a contentious meeting, Gardner reported to his mother, "We have had a grand triumph today. Yesterday it was discovered that the Appropriation Committee was going to cut down our appropriation in a way that would have crippled us very badly. We all went to work on all the friends we could rally and today succeeded in carrying through the Committee the full amount that we asked for. This was a great triumph when everybody else is being cut down. . . . If I had been away we should probably have lost $20,000. I dare not leave here till I see the bill safely in its

passage. It provides for the consolidation of Powell's Survey with ours, and I am now drawing the plans of consolidation for the Secretary of Interior. It is a vitally critical time for I am laying now the foundations for a great permanent Survey of the interior of America which will last many years after I am dead."[16]

During the 1874 field season the work in the high Rockies continued. Gardner, returning to the field, continued to occupy geodetic stations on the highest peaks. "I am thoroughly enjoying the repose of the day after a hard ride and climb yesterday. I rode a trotting mule twenty miles to a mountain and up it as far as mules could go to the edge of snow, then climbed the rocky peak itself 2,000 feet in an hour, and on its summit 14,000 feet high, built a large stone monument. It was four o'clock when we finished work; but we climbed down again to our mules and rode twenty miles back again to camp by 10 o'clock in the evening. . . . I have a French cook who does admirably and we are near a ranch where peas and beets, carrots and new potatoes, milk and butter are always to be had. Our cook too, is a great sportsman and the country abounds in rabbits. From the old ones he makes delicious soup and the young broil like chickens."[17]

Gardner wrote of one hunting encounter that almost seemed inspired by one of King's campfire stories. He told of how during the day in the high mountains he had expended all but two cartridges on ptarmigan (game foul) that ran among the rocks. Then he and two aides spotted a grizzly bear below. Gardner tied up the mule that was carrying the surveying instruments, and the three crept to within fifty paces of the beast. Then two fired, and the wounded bear turned and ran down the mountain. "In a moment we were up and after him, I, the lightest runner, in the lead. On the wounded grizzly plunged, and I dashed after him over snow and rocks for almost half a mile. Suddenly, going too fast to stop or turn aside, I came to the edge of a little cliff, and saw below me—the bear. In the air, as I jumped I flung my rifle-barrel down, ready to shoot and jump again, if necessary. But there was no need. I landed squarely on his ribs, and he never stirred. As we skinned him, working hard at the heavy pelt, I had a strange feeling of danger—danger to the mule, danger to my precious instrument." Gardner climbed back alone to the place where the mule was tethered and af-

FIGURE 11.11 (*opposite*). Italian Mountain (13,379 feet) in western Colorado, named because the dark rock is laced with seams of light-colored intrusive rock giving it a great variety of structure and color, as in Italian marble. On the northeast side, the mass has been pushed up and tilted so that, on the south side, layered sedimentary quartzite beds stand vertically, and in some places are actually overturned by 35°. (Hayden, 1874)

ter resting and appreciating the sunset colors he noticed that the mule was trembling and straining at its rope.

"Beyond over the edge of the sheer western cliff loomed the biggest grizzly that I ever saw, standing up on his hind legs and tottering nearer and nearer to the terrified beast. . . . I had just a moment to think. With only two cartridges I dared not shoot, for his nose was lifted, and in all that huge, furry expanse, only one mark, the small, cold heart would be fatal. Brain or spine I could not hope to touch. The mule I might sacrifice but not my theodolite. Then the thought of the powerful voice of man came over me, and I leaped straight at the bear, with a blood-curdling yell. The effect was uncanny. The big brute dropped cringing and cowered before me, then in panic terror at my waving arms and echoing voice, he turned and fled over the cliff edge, whence he had come. But I was red-angry now and I followed to the top of the steep narrow trail, down which the big coward had plunged. He was fifteen feet below, back half-turned, on a ledge of the rock, and I took aim at the spine as he ran. The bullet ripped a red stripe across the brown fur, but I had overshot the mark by an inch— and, had wasted a cartridge. Worse than wasted! For the silver-tip, brave under the sting of his wounded back turned to charge up the path. The little yellow eyes gleamed hard and bright, coming straight toward me. Instantly I began to reload, and in the little savage brain, the moving of my arms recalled the unreasoning fear of a minute ago. The yellow eyes flickered a moment, then his courage went from him, and again he turned to run. But now he was in good line, and my next shot struck the spine. The shaggy brute fell forward on his head to the edge of the shelf, overbalanced and bounded onto the next ledge, struck and rebounded, and so on for half a mile down the cliffs till at last he lay still."[18]

By September, the weather was beginning to turn cold, but the crystal-clear air was excellent for observations. Gardner wrote to his mother that "For these climbs we rise between three and four in the morning and breakfast by candle light, sitting on the ground in the frosty air with a few coals under the tin plates and cups to keep our food and drink from freezing, for the peaks are already dusted with new snow and the frosts are hard. This does not seem like comfort to eat in the dark wrapped in a great

FIGURE 11.12 (*opposite*).   Studio photograph of James T. Gardner after his survey party of thirteen was attacked by Ute Indians near the Abajo Mountains in southwestern Colorado in August 1875. He is carrying his Sharpe breech-loading, single-shot rifle, and a cartridge belt. The Indians killed two mules and injured others with musket fire, but did not hit any men in the party. To evade the enemy, the men had to abandon most of their equipment, instruments, and provisions, and narrowly escaped injury. (From William Pier Collection) overcoat, but I assure you that with such appetites as we have and such good cooking, I enjoy myself more than at many a meal that had all the surroundings of luxury."[19]

At the end of the 1874 season Gardner wrote, "I am just in and shall in a few days be ready to start east. All of the parties have been very successful and Dr. Hayden seems to feel very happy over the summer's results. The last night in camp we had a bitterly cold hurricane on the open plain. My tent had become weak and tore away in the night, leaving me on the open plain. I got up in my shirt and drawers, rolled the blankets and packed them on my back to a log stable near by and found shelter. It was very breezy work to be trotting around in my night clothes on the prairie, but I took no cold. The exposure that one can endure here is remarkable."[20]

The triangulation continued the following summer of 1875. Gardner described work in the Elk Mountains, of west-central Colorado, to his mother: "While you have been baking under summer heat we have been breaking the ice to wash ourselves in the mountain streams. Our campfires have been delightful. Some of the party sing and we have gone to work to learn a whole series of quartet songs. Both with regard to efficiency in duty and social pleasure my party is everything that could be desired. They can pack, climb, fight or sing as the hour calls for and above all they can endure hardship without murmuring."[21]

They rode from the Elk Mountains back to their supply base in the valley of the Grand River, where the blazing sun and oppressive heat were unwelcome after the congenial air of the mountains. Gardner's team replenished provisions and joined forces with the topographic crew headed by Henry Gannett, and the combined party rode up the Dolores River to work in the region of the La Sal Mountains just across the boundary in eastern Utah. They made camp there on the flank of the main peak at 10,500 feet and took observations from the summit.

They next headed for the Abajo Mountains, some 40 miles to the south. While they were on the trail late in the afternoon a great cloud of dust appeared to their rear and shortly thereafter a band of Ute Indians rode up. The Utes tried to induce the surveyors to camp and trade on the spot, but Gardner decided to ride on to some waterholes about ten miles ahead. Shortly after they resumed the march, the Utes opened fire on the party from the rear.

Gardner, with two men, raced to a ridge on the right of the trail and from that eminence held off the Utes and protected the main party as it moved ahead. A spot was selected to make a dry camp, and pickets were deployed 300 yards out, while the main party tied the stock nearby and erected a barricade with materials at hand, including packs and saddles. The Utes continued firing at the party, injuring one mule, but were generally kept off far enough—thanks to the greater range of the surveyors' rifles—so that no other damage was done.

The shooting finally ceased about midnight. The Indians had probably tired, and realized they were wasting ammunition. At three in the morning the party breakfasted on one-half slice of bread each and a sip of water and began packing up. By this time, thirst had become a major problem for both men and animals. The pack train was no sooner underway than the Indians attacked again and were driven off. They persisted, however, and approached from the sides to fire at the train. To counteract this tactic, Gardner and one man occupied a knoll on the right, and Gannett with another staked out on the left, and in this way they kept the Utes at bay. The Utes kept up a frightful yelping, and one occupied a ridge crest, where he waved a red signal flag to cue the others to the movements of the train. The party, on horseback, moved on slowly, leading the 18 heavily loaded pack animals. Many of the beasts were exhausted, having now gone without food or water for 24 hours.

They next attempted to depart the valley by a side canyon, but that proving too rugged for the exhausted animals, the pack train turned back and continued up the main canyon. Gardner and one companion rode ahead to occupy the high ground and prevent the Utes from crossing over so as to shoot from both sides. The Indians opened fire from the cliffs to the right, where the trail passed over an exposed stretch, but fortunately only one mule was hit.

The situation was now desperate. Gardner noted on their left a low place in the final wall of the 1,000-foot-high mesa, and urged the group up to that gap so they could escape across the mesa. As they wound their way up, the Utes, grasping the tactic, raced ahead to head off the struggling pack train. Gardner wrote, "When three hundred feet from the top a hellish fire was poured at us from a ledge some hundred feet above. Poor 'Jim' a white mule, consequently a good target, fell at the first volley. . . . Several others were hit and each one felt his turn would be next. Volley after volley was poured upon us whenever we were exposed between the trees: finally orders came to halt the train, and all sought safety behind rocks and trees, awaiting events."[22] One of the surveyors wounded a Ute, but it was not determined whether the wound was mortal. As the Indians continued to fire at the main train below the brink, Gardner and two others were able to creep up to the mesa rim, above the Utes firing from a ledge below them. But a second ledge protected the band from above, so they could not be dislodged. While descending to rejoin the main party, they took note of an escape route, a steep and narrow deer trail whereby the party might reach the mesa top with unloaded animals. As a newspaper later quoted a member of the party, "Orders were given to cut the packs loose, and with unwilling hands, deep curses, and tears in their eyes, the boys began the sad work. Some flour, bacon, tea, coffee and a pot were lashed on to two mules—everything else, instruments, grub, bedding and clothing, left. We rested a few moments to gather strength for the fight, for this all had been done under fire, and we knew we must face death at every step. We started, Gardner leading, dragging his mule behind, the rest close after."[23] Strangely, the Utes did not move their position to intercept the party at the rim, perhaps because they thought sharpshooters were still above them. The now lightened stock reached the top without further loss, and the entire train headed out at a fast trot across the mesa. Fear was replaced by disappointment that so much equipment and provisions had had to be abandoned to the attackers.[24]

The Utes followed until dark, intent on preventing the party from reaching water. Eventually, the Indians gave up the chase, and after finding a side trail, the train turned off the plateau and soon found a life-saving spring. Men and animals briefly slaked their thirst and then resumed travel, finally stopping at 11 P.M. The party, as Gardner later wrote, "camped beside an alkaline water hole that night, and a more exhausted set of men never existed . . . nineteen hours in the saddle, nine . . . fighting continually, and nine riding at a hard gait, with one for rest."[25] The water was poor, the meager provisions were nearly exhausted, and the only rest was on the ground under sweaty saddle blankets for warmth during a cold night.

At four the next morning the party was again on the trail and rode a further 50 miles, much of it up and down, crossing steep canyons. The next day they camped early to rest and feed the stock, and then the following day rode 55 miles to reach the first running water in five days, at the Mancos River in southwestern Colorado. A three-hour ride the next morning, August 20, up the river toward the La Plata Mountains, brought them to the mining camp of Parrotstown, near the present town of Mancos. Here, the survey had a supply depot, and they received a friendly welcome from the local miners, as well as from another of Hayden's divisions, headed by artist-geologist William Holmes, which had just arrived from the south. Following a jolly reunion, the weary, famished men devoured a hearty meal.

But their rest was brief, for with the Indians now on the warpath, Gardner was concerned about the two men they had left at the supply camp below the Elk Mountains, the week before. He immediately outfitted a rescue party of six mounted men and four mules, carrying essentials only. All the men but one were armed with breech-loading rifles; the cook insisted on his double-barreled shotgun. The distance to the camp was no less than 280 miles, most of it over mountainous country.

The group left the Mancos Valley on August 23, rode to the head of the San Miguel River, over the high passes of the San Juan Mountains, and down to the valley of the Uncompaghre River. They reached the Gunnison River, rode up that valley, and finally reached the supply camp to find the two men safe. Just a few days before they had been visited by Utes whose intentions had not seemed friendly. Before leaving the supply camp, the full party destroyed everything they could not carry, so as to keep it out of the hands of the Utes. On August 30 they began the long ride back to the mining camp at Parrotstown. On the first evening, they made camp in a beautiful glade beneath towering granite cliffs. One of the party rose and offered thanks to Gardner for his handling of the long episode with the Indians. Those present then signed a formal resolution thanking him for the skill, wisdom, and kindness of his conduct during this affair.[26] Gardner later granted interviews to journalists concerning the Indian attack and subsequent rescue, and the story was picked up by newspapers and publicized across the country. The heroic escape of the surveyors, led by their courageous leader, geographer James Gardner, became big news.

Ferdinand Hayden found the publicity unwelcome, not only because it glorified Gardner while minimizing his own role as director of the survey, but also because it highlighted the danger that the Indians posed to the surveying party. He had hoped to downplay that threat, in his effort to support the concept of management of western surveys by civilian scientists, without interference from the military.

Antagonism also smoldered between Gardner and Hayden over a report Gardner was asked to write about the Cucharas-Trinidad coal field, for the Denver and Rio Grande Railway. When the report appeared, some observers saw this investigation as a misuse of government funds to provide favors to a private corporation. Hayden attempted to sidestep criticism of his survey by blaming Gardner, who reacted to that ploy bitterly.[27] He wrote of Hayden's penchant for taking offense at criticism, leaving Gardner no choice but to wait "till the storm had spent itself, hoping eventually to convince him that I was not seeking to displace him from his position as Chief of the Survey—an idea which seemed ever uppermost in his mind." He wrote further that Hayden was charged with "a very strong current of feeling against me in the Survey: he having informed them that I had sold the whole Survey out and disgraced it. It then seemed to me both undignified to myself and undesirable for the Survey that I should remain longer where I was the object of so much unpleasant feeling. Certainly I could not expect to be useful in such a position. Therefore I handed Dr. Hayden my letter of resignation yesterday, expressing the wish that if it was agreeable to him, I should like to finish the primary triangulation and put the record in an intelligible form, so that the proof of the accuracy of the maps might not be lost."[28] The resignation was accepted.

Gardner worked up the primary triangulation net for Colorado and portions of adjacent territories. The other team members continued their work in topography and geology and compiled all in a handsome atlas of Colorado. The author was Ferdinand Hayden. The atlas, published in 1877, resembled to a remarkable degree, in general layout and style, King's Atlas of the Fortieth Parallel Survey, published the year before.

The atlas offered some refinements not seen in that of the Fortieth Parallel Survey. Although it was at the same scale of 4 miles to the inch, the elevations were depicted by contours with an interval of 200 rather than 300 feet. Moreover, every fifth contour (representing an elevation change of 1,000 feet) was printed with a heavier line, and these bolder contours were commonly labeled by elevation. (In the Fortieth Parallel Atlas the 300-foot grade-curves, as King chose to call them, were unlabeled, and no heavy lines were employed to represent key elevations.)

Moreover, the Colorado atlas contained six of the magnificent pen-and-ink panoramas of William Holmes. These masterful scenic drawings emphasized geologic features in a subtle, yet realistic, manner that was impossible to capture in a photograph. Holmes' panoramas always had an interest point in the foreground, such as a human figure or a gnarled tree.

Early in 1876 Gardner was elected General Secretary of the American Geographical Society with a compensation of $2,000 per year. In July the commissioners of the New York state survey offered him the position of Director, with an annual salary of $4,000.[29] Feeling particularly honored by this appointment, since he had made no application for it, he accepted the position.

CHAPTER TWELVE

A GRAND FUSION

Rare is the institution that escapes the shadow of its founder.
—William Glen

Josiah Whitney was not content to let the issue of multiple overlapping surveys lie fallow. In July 1875, he wrote a major article for the *North American Review*, pointing out that the Hayden and Powell surveys "are duplicates of each other, since to a certain extent there does not appear to be any limit fixed to either of them by Congress so that they shall be prevented from overlapping." He went on to emphasize: "Thus we have two independent geological and geographical surveys over an area of not much less than a quarter of a million of square miles west of the crest of the Rocky Mountains, and it will be noticed that these are both under the control of the Secretary of the Interior, one of them directly and the other indirectly, yet both supported by special grants from Congress. This may appear to be a singular arrangement; but the reader will be surprised to learn that a third geological and geographical survey of the same area is also in progress, under the direction of the Engineer Bureau of the Department of War. This work is usually known as 'Wheeler's Survey' having been in charge of a United States engineer officer of that name. . . . Thus far the field-work of Wheeler's Survey has been almost exclusively carried on in the same region in which Messrs. Powell and Gardner have been employed, and it is evident that this has not been done without design."[1]

Whitney also cited the inability of the Townsend Committee of Congress to solve the problem: "Indeed, the matter has already been up before a committee of Congress, and a very unpleasant altercation had between the officers and employees of the War Department on one side and of the Interior on the other. . . . In point of fact no good has been accomplished by the Congressional investigation; the work is still going on exactly as before." He emphasized that most scientists in the country favored "the continuance of the geographical surveys begun by Mr. Gardner under the direction of the Secretary of the Interior. This was done because, as was clearly shown before the committee, the four maps issued by the Engineer Bureau, as a first installment of the 'Geographical Explorations and Surveys West of the One-hundredth Meridian' were so defective and so far inferior to the work of the 'Fortieth Parallel Survey,' that it seemed inconceivable that, when the public attention was called to the fact, the poorer work should not be stopped and the better allowed to proceed."[2]

Notwithstanding these criticisms, the surveys whose methods had been lagging behind were improving, thereby approaching a certain uniformity. They all began adopting the more precise and reliable methods that had been spearheaded by Clarence King and James Gardner, and the transfer of key personnel among the surveys also helped to elevate standards.

The men who headed up the four western surveys, Ferdinand Hayden, Clarence King, George Wheeler, and John Powell, were survivors. Each was well-grounded in scientific fields, able to manage the complex logistic and personnel problems peculiar to scientific parties operating in isolated areas, and resourceful in working under conditions of physical hardship and the hazards of encounters with dangerously hostile Native Americans. Each had learned to forge a path through bureaucratic mazes to obtain needed support and funding. Any one of them would have been qualified to take on the position of directing a new combined survey, if such were to be the outcome of the ongoing debates.

Each of these veteran field commanders had a college education with an emphasis on science and engineering. King, with his degree from Yale Scientific School, had attended perhaps the most prestigious science school in the country at that time. His primary interests were mineralogy and geology, and he had served a valuable apprenticeship with William Brewer, Charles Hoffmann, and others in the California Geological Survey before organizing his Fortieth Parallel Survey. Hayden had obtained the M.D. degree, which was the usual training ground for natural sciences at that time. He had graduated from Oberlin College, and while there came under the influence of John Newberry and James Hall, who helped him develop expertise with his primary areas of interest—fossils and stratified rock sequences. Wheeler graduated sixth in the 1866 class at West Point. Powell attended several colleges, including Oberlin, and later became a professor at Illinois Wesleyan College, with a special interest in botany.

All but King served in the Army during the Civil War. Hayden was a surgeon, and Powell an artillery officer who had lost his right arm in the Battle of Shiloh, Tennessee, in 1862. After recuperation, he returned to the field to serve as an artillery officer until war's end. Wheeler served out the war as a cadet at West Point.

The most prolific writer was Hayden, who included in his annual reports the latest results of his explorations, often in the form of popularized information for a broad audience. He also produced exhaustive scientific treatises written by collaborating scientists. He drew upon the skills of William Jackson to produce the first large collection of scenic photographs of the West. He was careful to distribute packets of outstanding photographs to his patrons and to helpful politicians, and he was in the habit of hiring as assistants the sons of congressmen or other influential people. He worked closely with paleontologists Meek, Smith, and Whitfield, and he included more scientists from academia in his loosely knit team than any of the other surveys had. Hayden's mapping had been of questionable quality until James Gardner left King's Fortieth Parallel Survey in 1872 and joined his team in 1873, but the 1877 Atlas of Colorado, produced by Gardner, Wilson, and other topographers, and adorned with marvelous panoramas by William Holmes, was considered by some the finest geographic product of all the topographic surveys.[3]

King was more measured in his publication output. He concentrated, as mandated, on high-quality scientific products, and was reluctant to release short summaries and popular reports of work in progress. James Hague's 1870 volume on *Mineral Industry*, with its superb accompanying atlas, clearly set a standard for the other surveys. Thereafter, King strove for excellence over speed. His team was probably of the highest scientific caliber, several having been trained in Europe as well as America. He pioneered the use of chemical analyses of rocks, ores, and waters, and he was one of the first in the country to employ microscopic petrography to study and classify rocks. Because of Gardner's more sophisticated mapmaking techniques, gained during the California work, and through assiduous study of mapmaking methods, the maps of King's survey started off decidedly superior to those of the other surveys, in both accuracy and presentation.

Wheeler, stung by the criticism that his early Army mapping methods were of only reconnaissance quality, quickly improved his techniques and elevated his standards. By chance, he was especially fortunate in taking on Grove Karl Gilbert, certainly the most brilliant American geologist of the time. Thereafter, the methods of Wheeler's fieldwork, mapping techniques, and publication followed the lead laid out by King. Hayden and Powell, too, took advantage of King's pioneering enterprise.

During John Powell's heroic effort in descending the unexplored Colorado River in 1869, survival took precedence over science. But much was learned, and the trip

initiated more detailed study of a vast sector of the Colorado Plateau. By 1875 Powell
had chronicled this epochal voyage, as well as later trips on the river, in a handsome
volume. After Karl Gilbert joined Powell in 1874, the survey staff's professionalism
was assured. Powell also became one of the first scientists in the country to begin a
systematic study of the Native American peoples. Most forward-looking investigators
had by then realized that the rapid immigration of settlers into the West would forever alter this Stone-Age culture.

But Powell was also interested in the special problems of the West brought on by
rapid settlement. He realized that because so much of the region received less than 20
inches of rain per year, it was incapable of supporting the type of agriculture traditionally practiced in the East and Midwest. A quarter section of land—the 160 acres
allotted for an individual homestead—could not support a family. In all of Utah, for
example, only 3 percent of the land was deemed potentially irrigable. Accordingly,
some form of governmental control would be necessary for an equitable planning of
water distribution and land use. In the spring of 1878 Powell rushed into print a report dealing with the western lands in the public domain, and the special problems
that they posed.[4] He urged that the first step in the settlement of this vast territory
should be to classify the land, on the basis of its value for minerals, coal, timber, pasturage, and irrigated farms.[5]

That same spring the problems implicit in the overlapping nature of half a dozen
survey programs—the two active Department of the Interior surveys (Hayden and
Powell), the two of the Army Corps of Engineers (Wheeler and King), as well as those
of the Coast and Geodetic Survey and the General Land Office—came to a head in
Congress. Hayden felt he was the logical candidate for the directorship of a new combined survey. He pointed out that his survey had published 30 books, including annual reports, miscellaneous publications, bulletins, monographs, and 31 maps, in addition to the splendid *Atlas of Colorado*. Powell had produced just eight publications,
including four preliminary reports and four monographs. King, whose survey was by
then complete, had published six monographs and the *Atlas of the Fortieth Parallel
Survey*. Wheeler had been about as prolific as Hayden: 25 books, including annual reports, monographs, special publications, and 36 maps.

In June 1878, the House Committee on Appropriations for the Sundry Civil Expenses Bill directed the National Academy of Sciences to "take into consideration the
methods and expenses of conducting the above surveys and the surveys of the Land
Office, and report to Congress, as soon thereafter as may be practicable, a plan for
surveying and mapping the Territories of the United States on such general system as
will, in their judgment, secure the best possible results at the least possible cost."[6]

When this provision was deliberated, an amendment, offered by Representative Thomas Patterson of Colorado, specified that "the above surveys" be replaced by "all surveys of a scientific character under the War or Interior Departments."[7]

The acting president of the National Academy of Sciences at the time was Othniel Marsh, professor of paleontology at Yale, who had earlier worked with King. He had recently assumed the leadership of the Academy after the death of Joseph Henry, long-time president of the Academy and since 1846 Secretary of the Smithsonian Institution. Marsh quickly appointed a committee charged with making recommendations for the future of government mapping of the territories. The six members of the committee were James Dana from Yale; William Rogers, president of the Massachusetts Institute of Technology; John Newberry, state geologist of Ohio; William Trowbridge, of the Columbia School of Mines; Simon Newcomb, of the Nautical Almanac, and Alexander Agassiz, of Harvard. Marsh was chairman, ex officio.

Marsh had eliminated from consideration any members of the academy who were personally involved with the controversies over management of the surveys. Still, except for Trowbridge, who had attended West Point, most of the committee members were supporters of civilian-dominated science. King, moreover, a member of the Academy, was a personal friend of all the members of the committee, save Trowbridge and Rogers. (He was also associated with Agassiz in his Wyoming cattle business.)

Marsh requested from the Secretaries of both War and Interior that the surveys under their jurisdiction declare their intended mapping plans and funding requests before the next meeting of the Academy, which was to be held November 5, 1878. Those who responded favored business as usual, but each sought an even larger share of the pie. Only Major Powell favored combining all of the surveys into a single agency. He stated that "The prosecution of the work by a number of autonomous organizations is illogical, unscientific, and in violation of the fundamental law of political economy, namely, the law of the division of labor. The work should be unified or integrated by placing it under one general management."[8] He also made available to the members of the Academy committee his 1878 report on the arid lands, which spelled out the necessity for a designated government agency charged with classifying the lands of the public domain.

The final report issued by the National Academy of Sciences Committee on Scientific Surveys of the Territories of the United States was unanimously approved on November 6, 1878, and submitted to Congress December 2. It recommended that the existing exploration and mapping programs of the territories be divided into two groups: those that dealt with land measurement, and those that dealt with geology

and economic resources. The report also recommended that all the existing mapping agencies be placed in two new bureaus within the Department of the Interior. The United States Coast and Interior Survey would include the responsibilities of the old U.S. Coast and Geodetic Survey and would, in addition, perform all the geodetic work across the country, as well as all topographic mapping, both regional and detailed, and conduct the land parceling surveys, previously the responsibility of the General Land Office. The United States Geological Survey would be charged with the study of geologic features and economic resources.

The report was a stunning blow to the Corps of Engineers. Because the two new bureaus would reside within the Department of the Interior, the military would be eliminated from its traditional role of mapping in the West. General Andrew Humphreys—commanding the Corps of Engineers—indignantly voiced his objections and forthwith resigned his position in the Academy. When the report was submitted to Congress, opposition quickly developed. The Secretary of War and General Humphreys both attacked the scheme on the grounds that Coast Survey mapping was inadequate for military purposes. Other representatives strongly supported the retention of the land parceling survey within the General Land Office, as an entity separate from the proposed Coast and Interior Survey.

The Academy report also recommended the appointment by the President of a commission to consider " . . . the codification of the present laws relating to the survey and disposition of the public domain, and who shall report to Congress within one year a standard of classification and valuation of the public land, together with a system of land-parceling survey."[9]

Clarence King began immediately marshaling support of his candidacy for the directorship of the new Geological Survey. At the end of the year he wrote Samuel Emmons, "After covering over the ground very fully I no longer think it necessary to have any letters written against the present incumbent [Hayden?] and that is of course a relief for it is not pleasant to make war. I shall receive the appointment in all probability. I will therefore only trouble you to get letters in my behalf. You could do much good in giving shape to the letters. They should harp somewhat on executive faculty, on a critical familiarity and knowledge as to economical geology and the fact that [a] first class man has sufficient confidence to serve within an organization over

FIGURE 12.1 (*opposite*). Clarence King in polka dot tie. King, the first Director of the U.S. Geological Survey, took the oath of office May 24, 1879, and resigned March 11, 1881. (U.S. Geological Survey Library)

which I should preside. . . . Letters of recommendation should be explicit in urging me for the place, i.e. Director of U.S. Geological Expl. They should be addressed to the President and be enclosed to him as soon as possible."[10]

King wrote Othniel Marsh on January 2 that "I have received a round about and private notice that it is time to put in my credentials. Harvard is going to write a sort of general letter which various professors will sign. Now I am going to get you to confer with President Porter [of Yale] and Brush [professor of mineralogy at Yale] and get up a letter for me at the earliest possible moment which being a Yale letter will be my chief credential. It should, beside any generalities which might read well in my obituary notice, harp somewhat on my fifteen years continuous geological service, twelve being in charge of the 40th Parallel Survey. In geology the main point to be insisted on is that I have practical and intimate knowledge of economic geology. Also that I have enough executive faculty to manage the business. Lastly that my relations to the scientific men of the land are such that I can gain the cooperation of good men. Privately I can tell you and my Yale friends that I shall have Pumpelly, the two Hagues, Emmons, Powell, and Siebert. . . . Besides that, I want a letter of general recommendation for the place of Director . . . to be signed by the members of the Committee of the National Academy who made the report."[11]

King arrived in Washington early in the year and found both Hayden and Powell supporting the bill. King was aware of the awkward position he was in, being a possible candidate for the leadership of the combined civilian-sponsored federal survey while still being funded by the U.S. Army Corps of Engineers. Indeed, the time had come to sever this connection. He forthwith wrote to General Humphreys on January 18, 1879, officially closing his financial accounts and requesting to be relieved of his duties as U.S. Geologist in Charge of the Fortieth Parallel Survey.[12] His resignation was accepted by General Humphreys.

Hayden wrote his friend Sir Archibald Geikie, professor of geology at Edinburgh University, Scotland, requesting a letter of endorsement. "Please write the letter and send to me by return mail for the whole matter will be decided by the 4th of March. All looks well now. My most formidable competitor is Clarence King, who is now rallying his forces and making headway. He has most of the New England and New York influence."[13]

On February 25 the bill was passed by the U.S. House, with an amendment that excluded the public land-parceling surveys from the proposed Coast and Interior Survey. The bill then went to the Senate, where the Committee on Appropriations recommended another major departure from the Academy report—that the reorganizations of the surveys be deleted. Hence, the final bill, enacted March 3, 1879, established the U.S. Geological Survey and the termination of the Hayden, Wheeler, and Powell surveys on June 30, 1879. A key part of the bill follows: "For the salary of the Director of the Geological Survey, which office is hereby established under the Interior Department, who shall be appointed by the President, by and with the advice and consent of the Senate, six thousand dollars; *Provided*, That this officer shall have the direction of the Geological Survey, and the classification of the public lands, and examination of the geological structure, mineral resources, and products of the national domain."[14]

The bill did not resolve the question of which agency would conduct topographic mapping. It did, however, sustain the Academy recommendation that a commission be set up that would "report to congress within one year from the time of its organization; first, a codification of the present laws relating to the survey and disposition of the public domain; second, a system and standard of classification of public lands; as arable, irrigable, timber, pasturage, swamp, coal, mineral lands and such other classes as may be deemed . . . ; third, a system of land parceling surveys adapted to the economic uses of the several classes of lands; and fourth, such recommendations as they may deem wise in relation to the best method of disposing of the public lands."[15]

The choice for director of the newly created United States Geological Survey resolved itself into a contest between King and Hayden. Wheeler was essentially eliminated, as was the Army presence in the civilian agency. Powell had indicated that he was leaving the field of geology, and threw his support behind King. Hayden was energetic in garnering support, and recommendations on his behalf poured into the White House, urging his appointment by President Rutherford Hayes. During the course of Hayden's surveys he had been especially astute in promoting his accomplishments to politicians, learned societies, and the popular press. It was said that fully two-thirds of the members of Congress had sent recommendations to the President on behalf of Hayden.

James Gardner, by now chief of the topographical survey of New York, endorsed King in a letter to the President. Powell wrote of Hayden's deficiencies in letters to his congressmen friends. He suggested that Hayden would prevent any reform of the system of land surveys, that he had played no part in some of his published works, and that other publications were only for show and were irrelevant.[16] Powell maintained that King, on the other hand, had set the standard for the whole system of mapping in the arid West and, because of his wise and orderly nature, was ideally suited for the directorship.

Recommendations for King were received from Yale, Columbia, Johns Hopkins, New York University, the New York State Museum at Albany, and the American Mu-

seum of Natural History, and from every member of the National Academy of Sciences Committee, except James Dana. Othniel Marsh and William Brewer went to Washington to press the case with President Hayes, as did Professor Newberry, who had been State Geologist of Ohio when Hayes was governor. The historian Mary Rabbitt has written that "President Hayes consulted Charles William Eliot, the President of Harvard, for a confidential opinion and was told that Dr. Hayden did not command the confidence of American men of science, and his appointment would seem to them 'discreditable, discouraging, and unpromising.'"[17]

The President named Clarence King Director of the United States Geological Survey on March 20, 1879, and the Senate confirmed the nomination on April 3. King, however, with the prize in hand, had other duties to attend to. He headed west and spent more than a month accompanying a cattle drive east along the Oregon trail.

He then returned to Washington and took the oath of office May 24. For a still-young man of 37, he had achieved an extraordinary reputation in science and literature, was the youngest member of the National Academy of Sciences, and had a wide circle of influential friends in science, politics, and the arts. King wrote to Powell, "I am sure you will never regret your decision [presumably the decision to eliminate himself as a candidate and support King] and for my part it will be one of my greatest pleasures to forward your scientific work and to advance your personal interest."[18]

When Clarence King took the oath of office, the survey was charged with classifying the public lands and examining the geological structure and mineral resources and products of the national domain. But the meanings of "public lands" and "national domain" were puzzling. Did these constructs include the lands for which the government held title (primarily in the West), or the entire country, including the eastern states? King favored the latter choice, but with the limited first-year budget of $100,000 he first concentrated on the West, where there was the greatest need for systematic geological investigations. The Secretary of the Interior, Carl Schurz, assumed that King's mandate required providing information on the nation's mineral industry for the upcoming tenth national census. Topographical mapping had not been specifically included in the Survey's ruling, but it was now generally assumed that "examining the geologic structure and mineral resources" could not be done without suitable topographic maps.

King chose most of his senior staff from the leaders of the four national surveys that preceded establishment of the U.S. Geological Survey. He appointed as geologists, at $4,000 per year, Samuel Emmons, Arnold Hague, Grove Karl Gilbert, Raphael

FIGURE 12.2 (*opposite*). Profile photograph of Clarence King in formal dress. (U.S. Geological Survey)

Pumpelly, and, graciously, Ferdinand Hayden. Two younger geologists were also hired: George Becker, professor of mining at the University of California, and Charles Walcott, a fossil expert who would become a world leader in Paleozoic paleontology and third director of the U.S. Geological Survey. King appointed as topographers Allen Wilson ($3,000), Frederick Clark ($2,500), and four others at lower salaries. Andrew Blair was appointed chemist at $3,000 per year. Of these, Emmons and Hague had been members of the King survey, Wilson and Clark of both the King and the Hayden surveys, and Gilbert of the Wheeler and Powell surveys. Ferdinand Hayden was grateful for King's generosity in appointing him to the survey, but bitter that he was denied the directorship.

King was always thoughtful about the new scientists he hired, aware that these men represented the future of the organization. Although American colleges were moving forward rapidly in science, he felt that the best earth science education was probably still to be had in Europe. Arnold Hague and Samuel Emmons had both studied in Europe. Of the new men he took on, Raphael Pumpelly had attended the Royal Academy of Mines at Freiburg, and George Becker, also a graduate of that Academy, had received a Ph.D. from Heidelberg in Germany. Charles Walcott, however, who would forge a career of great distinction, had no formal college training.

King organized his bureau into two divisions: Mining Geology and General Geology. He also decentralized the organization so as to reduce travel time for the field parties that would otherwise be shuttling to and from Washington. Samuel Emmons, with an office in Denver, headed up the Rocky Mountain Division, and Karl Gilbert, with headquarters in Salt Lake City, led the Great Basin Division. C. E. Dutton commanded the Colorado Division, and Arnold Hague, the Pacific Division. Allen D. Wilson was appointed first Chief Topographical Engineer. King began his tenure as Director with great enthusiasm, but chafed and became disillusioned with the

FIGURE 12.3 (*opposite*). Official oil portrait of Clarence King that hangs now at the national headquarters of the U.S. Geological Survey, in Reston, Virginia. The painting supposedly was commissioned in 1902 after King's death by the Geological Survey for $1,200 from the artist George Howland, King's half brother. When the fee was not forthcoming, Howland wrote King's old friend John Hay, who suggested that the Century Club should have it. The painting hung in the Club gallery for a time but was ultimately deemed unfitting, either because of a perception of artistic inadequacy or because King's clandestine marriage rendered him unsuitable. Hay, Henry Adams, and other friends raised $500 to compensate Howland, and the painting was donated to the U.S. Geological Survey. (O'Toole, 1990; U.S. Geological Survey) responsibilities of managing a government agency with its seemingly endless bueau-cratic encumbrances.

Because of his patrician tastes, he became tempted by the thought that he could become wealthy in the private sector by discovering and developing promising mining properties. He resigned March 11, 1881, after having remained in office two months short of two years. But during this short time King created the most important government science agency in the country. He brought to the new bureau much of the insight he had developed during his years heading the Fortieth Parallel Survey. The bureau still displays the stamp of King's philosophy, organization, and sense of future growth.

He realized that the key to good science is to acquire the best minds to be had—those with the best training, most imagination, and ability to publish results. He knew that fieldwork was essential in the Earth sciences, and required a special lifestyle dependent on physical and intellectual vigor ruled by personal discipline. He made a strong effort to keep up with new innovative equipment and techniques, such as photography, geophysics, chemical and microscopic analyses, and astronomical and chronological equipment for mapping. He also discovered that to maintain the highest scientific standards, it was important to move senior scientists into management positions so that the philosophy and direction of the organization would not be diverted by the ambitions of petty bureaucrats.

The U.S. Geological Survey still shows the stamp of King's genius. The organization has changed with the ebb and flow of economic and political conditions by shifting its emphasis between pure and applied science, always maintaining its stature as an incorruptible government agency with the highest scientific standards. It remains the most influential, most productive, and most emulated Earth science organization in the world.

CHAPTER THIRTEEN

EPILOGUE

Bring me men to match my mountains.
—Sam Walter Foss (1858-1911)

One of the first matters of business that Clarence King attended to in his new post as director of the U.S. Geological Survey was a four-month tour of the western states by the Public Lands Commission to inspect and assess the potential of the public lands. The Commission had been created by the same act that created the USGS, with King an ex officio member, and four other persons, included John Powell, recommended by King. King assumed his duties as director of the USGS May 24, met with the Commission July 8, and left shortly thereafter for its inspection of the West. Traveling by train first to Cheyenne, Wyoming, to tend to his cattle business, he was late joining the tour. The commissioners systematically visited every state west of Nebraska, investigated local land matters, and held public hearings. King was able to slip away now and then to check in with his field parties in the Rocky Mountains. In the booming Leadville Mining District, Colorado, the topographer Allen Wilson was actively mapping. At Salt Lake City, he found that Karl Gilbert, whose fieldwork would begin in October, had not yet arrived. While the Commission went on to Butte, Montana, King inspected the work underway in the Eureka Mining District, Nevada, where Franklin Clark had begun topographic mapping; George Becker would use the resulting maps as a basis for his geologic studies of the District.

On a tour of the Mother Lode in California, the Public Lands Commission saw the appalling damage wrought by large-scale hydraulic mining for placer gold. The sediment-laden streams from those operations had fouled waters downstream, causing serious sedimentation even in San Francisco Bay, many miles away.

Back in Washington, months later, the Commission assembled the report on its findings for the Department of the Interior. The report reinforced Powell's assessment that much of the West—40 percent of the area of the United States—was incapable of the sort of agriculture practiced in the eastern states. Those lands, to be worked at all, would require extensive irrigation.

Early in 1880 King concentrated on an assessment of the mining industry for the U.S. census. Raphael Pumpelly was well underway on compilation of data dealing with the production of iron ore. This work was concerned not only with the western states but also with the country as a whole, and therefore first established the new survey in work also in the old eastern states. George Becker and Samuel Emmons collaborated with King in an analysis of gold and silver production by compiling available mining documents, and preparing questionnaires sent to mine owners. But the response was dismal. They therefore hired about 50 agents and dispersed them across the country to obtain information and hard data from every significant mine. The avalanche of data obtained by these efforts led to the most complete estimate of gold and silver production yet obtained in the country.

King, however, continued to suffer from bouts of ill health. Early in 1880 he experienced recurring attacks of malaria and rheumatic pain. He also suffered from the never-ending office duties and chafed at the heavy responsibilities of his position. He felt unable to cut away from his mining interests, and in June he headed west on a trip largely concerned with private business, but justified by visits to Emmons at Leadville, Gilbert and Dutton in Salt Lake City, and Becker in San Francisco. In August and September he squeezed in visits to mining properties in Mexico and Arizona, with an eye to private development.

Upon his return to Washington, King found himself marked as the most eligible bachelor in town, and was overwhelmed by dinner engagements and invitations to social functions. He had dinners where he was expected to entertain the wives and daughters of senators, at the Shurz's where the Secretary of the Interior entertained with his piano playing, and at the White House, where the President would host senators and ambassadors in the East Room. He joined with four old friends—Harvard historian Henry Adams and his wife Clover, and Assistant Secretary of State John Hay and his wife Clara—in an informal dinner group called the Five of Hearts. King was the unmatched raconteur of this group, ranging with authority and verve over the realms of art, literature, politics, western adventuring, and science. He was also an unabashed punster. When one of Clover's terriers appeared with an ailing eye, he diagnosed it as a "tom-cataract." When told a story about an oil tycoon who gave a magnificent house to a favorite relative, he joked, "Oil's well that ends swell."[1]

Much of his work time in Washington was devoted to writing the first annual report of the U.S. Geological Survey, but he did manage to head west once again to deal with mining-property affairs in Mexico. And upon returning to Washington in February 1881, he assured himself that the funding for the Survey for the next fiscal year was suitable. But on March 11, 1881, King sent the following letter:

To the President of the United States.
Executive Mansion, Washington, D.C.

Sir: Finding that the administration of my office leaves me no time for personal geological labors, and believing that I can render more important service to science as an investigator than as the head of an executive bureau, I have the honor herewith to offer my resignation as Director of the Geological Survey.

Very respectfully, your obedient servant,
Clarence King[2]

The resignation was accepted on March 12. Clarence King had served as director of the U.S. Geological Survey just 22 months. During that time he had spent more than six months in the West, much of it on private business.

When King resigned, he was succeeded by John Wesley Powell, the man he had recommended as his successor. Quickly freed from matters dealing with federal science, King turned to business and sought his fortune in investment in dozens of promising mines. He visited mining properties across the western part of the country, Canada, Alaska, and Mexico. In the end, notwithstanding his prodigious energies and expertise, financial success would elude him. Business was evidently not one of his strengths.

King had long hoped to visit Europe, and he finally made his first trip in May 1882. He stayed for 27 months, until September 1884, considerably longer than he had served with the USGS. In England he promoted investments in various North American mining properties, but one of his chief interests was in visiting art collections and in acquiring pieces of art. After visiting the Prado Museum in Madrid, he visited Spanish mines, including the famous copper mines of Rio Tinto and the world's then largest quicksilver mine at Almaden. Fulfilling an old dream, he went to La Mancha in Spain, the legendary home turf of Don Quixote, where the knight of the baleful countenance pursued his famous misadventures. As his focus for this excursion, he determined to find a gift for an old friend, Horace Cutter, a retired businessman and habitué of the clubs that King frequented in San Francisco. "Don Horacio," as King called him, was an ardent admirer of the works of Cervantes, and loved to quote from the adventures of Don Quixote.

It was at La Mancha that Don Quixote, arrayed in armor and assisted by his faithful squire Sancho Panza, futilely attacked the windmills, mistaking them for wicked knights. Catching his breath after this debacle, Don Quixote encountered a barber traveling from one village to another. To keep dry in a light rain, the barber had put his brass shaving basin on his head while riding his dappled donkey. The deluded Don Quixote spotted this headgear and declared it was the legendary golden helmet of the knight Mambrino astride his war horse. In the name of chivalry he charged the barber with lowered pike. The frightened barber jumped from his donkey and ran away, leaving the basin on the ground. Don Quixote quickly seized it as his rightful spoils and proudly wore it as a helmet. (Sancho Panza, for his part, exchanged the more opulent trappings on the barber's mount for his own.) This "helmet of Mambrino" thereafter became the prominent headgear for the knight errant.

King, aglow with his visit to the legendary place where these adventures had been reported, decided to search out a primitive La Mancha shaving basin as a gift for his friend in San Francisco, as "Mambrino's helmet." King and a Spanish companion stopped at a humble inn on the outskirts of a decaying village. Behind the inn was the skeletal ruin of a windmill, perhaps not unlike the one that Don Quixote had attacked. The innkeeper, a cheerful chain-smoking lady, listened when he told of his quest, and for whom it was intended. She directed him to an inn beyond the village church, a modest affair operated by an old widow and her son, where she had once seen an old brass basin on the patio.

King noted that "I saw a large, square, walled enclosure bounded on the right by a one-story house, with a waving, sagging, collapsing roof of red tiles. The left or eastern wall which rose to a height of twenty feet or so was pierced by two doorways and several second-story window-openings. Through these we looked out upon the open plain, for the apartments, into which the doorways had once led were ruined and gone. Over the eastern door was traced the half-faded word *Comedor,* and over the other *Barberia.* Still above this latter sign there projected from the solid masonry an ornamental arm of wrought iron, from which hung a barber's basin of battered and time-stained brass, the morning light just touching its disc of green."[3] The widow at this inn found it curious that King wanted this battered old basin, but when King de-

FIGURE 13.1 (*opposite*).   Clarence King in the green velvet suit he reportedly wore on his trip to Europe and while searching for Mambrino's helmet at La Mancha, Spain. (Hague, 1904)

scribed how lovingly his old friend pursued the stories of Don Quixote, she told him
to take the relic. Her son, however, complained, insisting that it was his. Finally, a bar-
gain was struck, the son receiving two silver coins, and King departing with the ancient shaving basin.

King, however, realized that another item would be needed—a certificate signed
by a local official affirming that this barber's basin came from a village in La Mancha.
The magistrate of the village was at first reluctant to prepare such a document, finding it quite irregular, especially since the basin had been purchased from a boy. But after a low whisper from King's Spanish companion, and an almost inaudible clinking
of metal, the paper was duly signed and sealed, and the package was complete. When
the pair left the village and were riding down a nearby gorge, the city official's servant
rapidly approached them on horseback. When he had caught his breath, he took from
under his jacket a glistening brass barber's basin and said that this new basin, provided by the magistrate, was the very one that Cervantes had used while a prisoner at
nearby Argamosillo. The memento was available for the low price of 10 duros. King
thanked the emissary but declined the purchase. He was immediately offered a price
of two and one-half duros, which was also declined, and the travelers left the region
of La Mancha, happy with their original prize.

The helmet had been carefully wrapped in a piece of silk, also from the region of
La Mancha, and was eventually sent to San Francisco to the grateful Don Horacio,
along with the magistrate's certification and a long letter detailing how the basin-hel-
met had been obtained. The letter and the basin remained among Cutter's most
prized possessions. He would wear the helmet on special occasions, to demonstrate
how it must have appeared to Sancho Panza when Don Quixote prepared for battle.

As King matured he became more disenchanted with the Victorian ladies of his own
class, finding them artificial, formal, and unnatural. Rather, his attraction to dark-
skinned women increased, especially those he thought to be primitive, natural, ar-
chaic, and not academic. In 1885, while staying at a hacienda in southern California,
he met Luciana, an Indian woman whose name would appear in many subsequent
letters. He wrote his friend John Hay that she was "as near as Eve can be" to the ideal
woman, and that "I escaped from her by a miracle of self control." He said further that
"I rode with [her] alone in the mountains among the straying cattle. The world was
all flowers, and Luciana's face was the most tender and grave image of Indian wom-
anhood within human conception. . . . I came as near it as I ever shall."[4]

Not long after the Luciana affair, at the age of 45, King met a fetching African-
American woman of 26, a nursemaid in the Manhattan home of a friend. After a

whirlwind courtship, he and Ada Copeland were secretly married in 1888, without benefit of a marriage license. They wed at her aunt's home on 24th street in lower Manhattan, and King lived a double life for the rest of his days. Not only did he keep knowledge of his marriage from his family and friends, but he married Ada under the name *James Todd*, without revealing his true name to her. To cover his frequent traveling, he told her he was a railroad porter from Baltimore. King occupied rooms on 5th Avenue and 26th Street in Manhattan and settled Ada in a house across the river in Brooklyn—a convenient arrangement, allowing him to visit her at night when he was in New York. She soon bore him a son, whom he called Leroy, French for 'the king'—he had thus named the child for himself. Ada eventually bore him four more children.

King wrote Ada often, but few of the letters have been preserved. The marriage was no doubt a source of stress and anxiety to him, owing to the constant fear that their secret would be exposed. After one of his trips to the city he wrote her that "I know just how you love me and how you miss me and how you long for the days and nights to come again when we can lie together and let our love flow out to each other and full hearts have their way. Your letter gave me true joy. I read it over and over and felt like a new man. The reason that I did not come to the house was that I thought there were more boarders and, darling, it will not do to have too many people see me. The most important thing to us of all others is that the property which will one day come to me shall not be torn away from us by some foolish, idle person talking about us and some word getting to my old aunt. For the sake of your darling babies we must keep this secret of our love and our lives from the world."[5]

King's fortunes had not improved by 1893, as one after another of his mining ventures failed to yield a profit. The country, too, was undergoing a financial crisis; when a bank that he had founded in El Paso, Texas, failed, he borrowed $100,000 from his friend John Hay. He also had a chronic back problem, and through it all he felt the keen responsibility of supporting two families, his mother's in Newport, Rhode Island, and Ada's in Brooklyn. In October, while at the lion house at the Central Park Zoo in New York City, he became deranged and inexplicably violent, when apparently jostled by a passerby. He was arrested on a charge of disorderly conduct and booked into the nearest police station. His physician diagnosed his condition as inflammation of the spine that had led to acute depression. Perhaps because he feared that an extended police investigation would unearth his secret family, he allowed himself to be committed to Bloomingdale Asylum, a mental institution in Manhattan.

King remained at Bloomingdale for three months. His old friend and survey associate, James Hague, and his artist friend John LaFarge dropped by frequently, but his most constant visitor was his lifelong friend James Gardner. King, it seems, had taken a dislike for Gardner's second wife, Eliza, the daughter of an Episcopalian bishop, who was in his eyes the epitome of the cold, unnatural, Victorian woman. As Patricia O'Toole has written, "During one dinner at the Gardiner house, King had horrified his hostess by telling stories about Civil War rations covered with mold and fly eggs, and about Cuban cigars being rolled to exquisite smoothness on the bare thighs of beautiful young women."[6] As King expected, Mrs. Gardner was offended and forthwith banned him from her house. Nor did she accompany her husband on his visits to the asylum.

When released from Bloomingdale, King took an extended vacation at his doctor's recommendation. With his old friend Henry Adams, he embarked for the Caribbean in early February 1894 and spent nearly three months in Cuba and several other islands. Back in Washington, King stayed with Adams for a time until he felt quite well again.

In 1900, Horace Cutter (Don Horacio), King's friend in San Francisco, became ill and was taken by friends to the hospital. Sadly, he was unable to be with his books and other treasures again before he died. After King's death, 18 months later, James Hague endeavored to locate among Don Horacio's possessions King's original handwritten copy of the letter about the discovery of the artifact called the "Helmet of Mambrino." The manuscript was indeed found, and Hague—as editor of the *Clarence King Memoirs* published by the Century Club after King's death—included "The Helmet of Mambrino" in the *Memoirs* (King, 1904). Many have acclaimed it King's finest piece of writing.

Despite diligent search and questioning of all those who had access to Cutter's rooms and property, the "helmet" itself could not be found. Thereupon, Hague hired a detective to look into the matter, but again with no results. He placed an ad in a daily newspaper offering a suitable reward for " . . . an old Spanish-made barbers' brass basin, an heirloom, only valuable to advertiser."[7] Still no result. Sometime after Hague returned to New York he received a telegram from Don Horacio's estate executor reporting that the helmet had been found and would be sent soon. The basin arrived, with a note stating that the helmet had been found in a local pawnbroker shop, but was delayed until friends could identify it as the original helmet sent by King to Don Horacio. Hague's examination, however, found it to be made of copper, not brass. Further inquiry found that such basins were a common object in antique shops, and that the pawnbroker who sold it had recently acquired it from another dealer who had received it from Smyrna, Turkey, a principal source for such antiques. Hague gave up his quest, deciding that this basin would do, and hung it on the wall of the meeting room at the Century Club in New York. This copper basin would have to serve as proxy for the brass basin that King had found in La Mancha, that resembled the basin that Don Quixote had believed to be the golden helmet of the knight Mambrino.[8]

King's last years were spent in almost constant travel, examining mining properties and testifying as an expert witness in cases dealing with mining disputes. In February 1900 he arrived at Butte, Montana, and after extensive study of one such embattled mine—commonly in the company of his valet, Alexander—he testified representing the Anaconda Company during a suit involving the Copper Kings. During the trial, in which his testimony was crucial, he acquired a stubborn lingering hoarseness. While recuperating at Butte he wrote Ada, "Ah, my darling, I lie in the lonely hours of the night and long to feel your warm and loving arms about me and your breath on my face and the dear pressure of your lips against mine. My dearest, I love you with all the depth and warmth of my whole heart and will till I die."[9]

Later that year, King traveled to the gold fields of Alaska, and early in 1901 he made an appraisal of lead deposits at Flat River, Missouri. Then on to Chicago, and to Florida and the West Indies for a brief rest, after learning that he had tuberculosis. In April he made a trip to Washington, D.C., to attend a meeting of the National Academy of Sciences, where another old associate, George Becker, was voted into membership and Alexander Agassiz was installed as president. From Washington, he went to Newport, Rhode Island, to visit his mother, and to New York, where he said goodbye to Ada and his family for the last time. Then it was west again, first to Prescott, Arizona, then to a clinic in Pasadena, California, but his sickness was too far advanced to respond to treatment. The dry climate of Phoenix, Arizona, saw him through his last days.

Fearing that letters might not be delivered to him under the name James Todd, he wrote Ada, confessing to her his true name for the first time. He told her to change her name to King, and to record in her Bible the name Clarence King. He wrote her in October that she should "have the children's name changed in the New York State Court at Albany. . . . I have studied it all out and consulted a good lawyer about it, and my only wish before God and for you is to do the very best thing for us all, and I am perfectly sure that what I have advised you is the best."[10]

King maintained his sense of humor to the end. He was given an opiate by his physician to ease his discomfort, but became delirious soon after. In trying to calm him, the doctor said that the heroin must have gone to his head. "At the mention of the word *heroin*, the light of reason returned to King's eyes. He looked at the doctor, cleared his throat, chuckled slightly, and said, 'Well, doctor, I won't be the first man who had a heroine go to his head.'"[11] Clarence King died in Phoenix December 24, 1901, a few weeks before his 60th birthday.

The funeral, held on New Year's Day in New York, was attended by many friends and a 50-man delegation from the Century Club. The pall bearers included his dearest friends Henry Adams (Harvard professor and editor of *North American Review*), Albert Bierstadt (landscape painter), Edward Cary (literary critic), James Gardner (topographer), Samuel Emmons (geologist), Arnold Hague (geologist), and James Hague (geologist).

The bill that established the U.S. Geological Survey also provided for the completion and publication of the study of American ethnology that had been carried on previously by the Geographical and Geological Survey of the Rocky Mountains under John Wesley Powell (1834–1902). Powell was named Director of the Bureau of American Ethnology in the spring of 1879, and allotted $20,000 to conduct this work under the direction of the Smithsonian Institution. For the next two years he managed this bureau, oversaw the fieldwork of Clarence Dutton and William Holmes on the high plateaus of Utah, and pushed his agenda for rethinking the settlement of the arid lands west of the 100th meridian.

President Garfield appointed Powell second Director of the U.S. Geological Survey, and Powell took the oath of office March 19, just seven days after King's resignation on March 12, 1881. Now Powell had two bureaus to manage. He was well-connected in Washington and began immediately to make changes. The appropriation for the USGS had been $106,000 for the first year of King's tenure and $156,000 for the second. Powell managed to increase funding "up above a quarter of a million, and the next year to a third of a million. In 1884–85 he reached $489,000, and in 1885–86 he topped a half million dollars, fabulous for the time and for a mere bureau."[12]

Powell discontinued the regional divisions of the Survey and reorganized on topical grounds—geology, paleontology, chemical and physical sciences, and topography. But more important, he was able to insert into the funding bill for the USGS the concept that the Survey should continue the preparation of a geologic map of the United States. He then took the broad view in interpreting these words, considering them authorization to work over the entire country, not just the government-held territory in the West, and to conduct systematic topographic mapping everywhere, inasmuch as that would be necessary to create a meaningful geologic map.

Powell then turned to the problem of irrigable lands. He was convinced that due to the general aridity of the western lands, a system of mutual development was essential for the welfare of the people. Otherwise, powerful individuals and companies would soon control all the water. In October 1888, Congress approved funding for an Irrigation Survey, administered by Powell, that had as its mission the conduct of surveys of drainage basins in the West, to determine their suitability for irrigation. This ruling took the form of a joint resolution—of March 1888—that withdrew all irrigable lands from development until they could be classified by proper surveys. As Wallace Stegner wrote, "Major John Wesley Powell would not certify any lands until his survey had worked them over." The ruling had made Powell "so far as the development of the West went, the most powerful man in the United States."[13]

Many groups found this legislation intolerable, and they attacked Powell and his agency in every way they could. There were those who questioned whether the government should be funding pure science and mapping at all. Could not the universities and large companies support research, and could not the states map their own territory? This dissent led to a cut in funding for the Geological Survey that in turn forced a reduction in staff. Powell now knew he was defeated, and he resigned in May 1894 after serving 15 years as director.

Powell was justly proud of the organization he had led. The accomplishments and esprit de corps of the bureau, a heritage of King's initial leadership, were bright and had inspired a like psychology in newer government agencies, such as the Forest Service, National Park Service, and Soil Conservation Service. Powell said of the Survey personnel, "I cannot refrain from an expression of profound gratitude for the loyal and loving aid which they have given me, ever working together with zeal and wisdom to add to the sum of human knowledge. The roster of those honored men is found in ten-score volumes of contributions to knowledge and fifty-score maps familiar to the scholars of the world."[14] He nominated Charles Walcott, a paleontologist, as his successor, a man who would steer the course of the Survey back toward an emphasis on geology and its relation to the development of mineral resources.

Powell retreated to his Bureau of American Ethnology in the Smithsonian Institution, and continued his research on the American Indians. He also began an extensive project evaluating the scope of human knowledge, extending from the level of primitive humans, through classical times, to the modern age of scientific enlightenment. One volume of this grand philosophical work, *Truth and Error*, was completed before he died in 1902 at 68.

Ferdinand Hayden (1829–1887), leader of the United States Geological Survey of the

Territories in prior years, was subdued after his defeat in the contentious struggle for the directorship of the combined Geological Survey. King, in a generous gesture, had hired him on as a USGS geologist at an annual salary of $4,000, but Hayden left Washington for Philadelphia to escape the limelight. The move was especially difficult for his wife Emma, who had a wide circle of friends in Washington. A letter to the Director of the Smithsonian, regarding a planned trip to Washington, suggests his feelings at this time, "I am so located here and so utterly removed from all my old troubles that I have put off the time [of my visit]. I do not wish to be in W. much during Congress, so I will start today. . . . I wish to do up my business as quickly as possible and return. Please make no mention of my coming. I wish to attract as little attention as possible."[15]

He then edited, upgraded, and wrote sections of two books. *The Great West* (1880) was a popularized review that trumpeted the glorious scenery and opportunities in the territories, particularly those regions where he had worked. It was clearly intended to be purchased by travelers and settlers moving west. He edited the North America volume of *Stanford's Compendium of Geography and Travel* (1883), which again was essentially a travel book, for which another author added a section on Canada.

Hayden's health declined. He slept poorly, and began showing signs of paralysis. In 1882, he wrote his friend Archibald Geikie at Edinburgh, "In March last I was taken very sick with an acute condition of a chronic nervous disease, which rapidly carried me down to an almost helpless condition. My case was pronounced hopeless, incurable and I prepared for the worst. . . . Within a month or two I have been convalescing so that I can write a few letters, though I do little or no work. The disease has been coming on me for about three years."[16] His condition was caused by syphilis. He had apparently had the disease for some time, and it may have been responsible for the intermittent paranoia that precipitated Gardner's resignation in 1875.

The disease went into remission in 1883, and Hayden—feeling more able—prevailed on Powell to allow him to go into the field. He worked with his longtime associate Albert Peale along the railroad between Bismarck, North Dakota, and Helena, Montana. Their fossil collections established for the first time that the strata in this region were not all of Carboniferous age, but were underlain by Devonian strata.[17] That year he also completed a small-scale geologic map (40 miles to the inch) that included a large part of the western plains and eastern Rockies, virtually all the territory covered by his surveys over the years.[18]

Hayden continued limited fieldwork in 1884 and 1886, but his health resumed its decline, and Emma spent most of her time caring for him. He resigned from the Geological Survey in 1886 and died in December 1887.

George Wheeler (1842–1905) was promoted to Captain after his own survey was abolished in 1879, and continued to work on reports, but increasingly took leave from work. While on sick leave from 1880 to 1884, he attended the Third Geographical Congress and Exhibition in Venice as a delegate for the War Department, and there he persisted in the notion that topographic mapping should be performed by the military. In 1885 and 1886 he returned to active duty, completed unfinished reports, and then took disability retirement in 1888. Poverty-stricken and threatened with court action and eviction in his final years,[19] he died in New York City in 1905, four years after Clarence King's death.

Henry Gannett (1846–1914), a Harvard-trained civil engineer, received his first training in topographic mapping from Charles Hoffmann, in 1869, while attending a Harvard field class in the Rocky Mountains organized by Professor Josiah Whitney. He then joined Hayden's survey to work in Yellowstone for several seasons and accepted a position with the U.S. Census Office at the time of the unification of the western surveys. In 1882 he was named Chief Geographer of the U.S. Geological Survey in charge of topographic mapping. He was a charter member of the U.S. Board on Geographic Names and served as its chair from 1894 until his death in 1914.

The artist-geologist William Henry Holmes (1846–1933) was jobless after the disbandment of the Hayden survey in 1879, but the following year, after a trip to Europe, he was hired by King for the U.S. Geological Survey. With Clarence Dutton, he provided the illustrative support for Powell in his ongoing program in the plateau country.[20] His masterful sketches of the Grand Canyon, as well as those for Hayden's Colorado Atlas, have led many to declare him the greatest American landscape sketcher. He was a founding member of the Cosmos Club in Washington, D.C., and made it an important exhibition venue for fine paintings. Later, he became chief curator of the Field Museum in Chicago, chief of the American Bureau of Ethnology (1902–1920), and the first director of the National Gallery of Art, now the National Museum of American Art. He died in 1933.

The good-natured William Henry Brewer (1828–1910) had been King's staunch friend, mentor, and supporter from the time they met on a Sacramento River steamer in 1863. It was Brewer who first backed King's candidacy for appointment as the leader of the Fortieth Parallel Survey. Brewer also met with President Rutherford Hayes in March 1879, to endorse King for the directorship of the U.S. Geological Survey. He described how King had elevated the standards of all western survey work, and how his method of coupling topographic and geologic mapping had become the model for the other surveys.

Brewer held the chair of Agriculture at the Sheffield Scientific School at Yale until 1903. He brought his California botanical material to Yale, consulted with Harvard Professor Asa Gray, and published a volume on California botany in 1876. But his interests went beyond research and teaching. As Francis Farquhar wrote, "He promoted the establishment of agricultural experiment stations; he helped to organize the Connecticut State Board of Health and served on it for thirty-one years; he also served for a long time on the Board of Health of the city of New Haven."[21]

Sereno Watson (1826–1892) had written the botany volume (1871) for King's Survey, even though he had had no previous training in botany. He was a shy person, well suited to this kind of solitary work, where careful attention to detail was so important. His field notes on habitat greatly enriched the botany volume, which ranked highly among the Survey reports. Professor Asa Gray was impressed with Watson's work, and in 1873 appointed him assistant in the Harvard Herbarium, where he later became curator, a position that lasted until his death in 1892. William Brewer sought Watson's aid in working up his voluminous California collections, and Watson teamed with Brewer and Gray to complete volume 1 of *Botany of California* and worked up volume 2 on his own. He was instructor in phytogeography from 1881 to 1884, and completed the *Manual of the Mosses of North America*, begun by Thomas James and Leo Lesquerieux, which appeared in 1884. At the time of his death, Watson was working on an exhaustive compilation of the flora of North America.

After Richard Cotter (1842–1905) completed the mapping in Yosemite with King and Gardner in late 1864, he returned to San Francisco, and it was there that he signed up to work on the Western Union Telegraph Company expedition to British Columbia and Alaska, with the goal of providing a telegraph link from Asia through Alaska by way of Bering Strait. The project was abandoned in July 1866, when completion of the submarine Atlantic cable established a link from the United States to Europe. But the public interest stimulated by the Alaskan project is credited with influencing the purchase of Alaska from the Russian Empire on March 30, 1867, for $7.2 million.

When abandoned, in the middle of winter, by Eskimo co-workers, Cotter barely escaped with his life and suffered enduring health problems. When he joined the Fortieth Parallel Survey in 1867, Gardner wrote that "His mind is much dimmed, but his glorious heart is as warm as ever. I have hope that affection and sympathetic treatment may restore him."[22] He resigned after two years with the survey and settled in

Montana, where he worked in construction, mining, and ranching. He wrote Professor Brewer occasionally from 1878 to 1898. In one letter he remarked that "I have been a J. P., Post Master, & the last office I was honored with was Sabbath School Supt. I imagine I can see you laughing as I have often seen in Camp. Of course I had other work to do or I should have starved to death long ago."[23]

Charles Hoffmann (1838–1890) arrived in the United States from Frankfurt-am-Main, Germany, at the age of 19. He had an innate skill as a landscape sketcher and became proficient in mapping while working with Frederick West Lander in surveying a wagon road from Fort Kearny, Nebraska, through South Pass, Wyoming, to Honey Lake, California. He joined the California Geological Survey four years later, in 1861. During Josiah Whitney's leave from California to Harvard in 1869, both Hoffmann and Brewer accompanied him to Colorado to teach on a geologic field excursion. One of Hoffmann's students on this trip was Henry Gannett, who later became chief geographer of the U.S. Geological Survey. Another was William Morris Davis, who became a Harvard professor, an authority on the origin of landscape features, and an expert in the tradition of topographic sketching that would serve the western surveys so well in the years to come.

Brewer wrote to Hoffmann much later to say, "All these years I have taken pains, whenever opportunity occurred, to keep in mind that you introduced into America this system of field topographical survey, which now improved greatly, but fundamentally the same, and tho' modified and much more widely extended, is the method employed by the general government. . . . For this, Whitney and you should have credit, and the fact should have a more prominent record than the mere recollections of men."[24] King appointed Hoffmann superintendent of the Sombrerete mine in Mexico in 1881, but by 1885, when King returned from Europe, he was no longer at the mine. No accounts recording the circumstances of his last days have been found.

Robert Ridgeway (1850–1929), the zoologist for the Fortieth Parallel Survey, later became associated with the Smithsonian Institution, first as ornithologist and later as curator of birds. He became a leading American ornithologist and founded the American Ornithologists' Union in 1883. He became an authority on bird color and color description in general, and codified color standards and nomenclature in a work that proved useful in many scientific and practical applications. Ridgeway also published an exhaustive eight-volume work on *The Birds of North and Middle America.*

Timothy O'Sullivan (1840–1882) worked three seasons as photographer with King

(1867, 1868, and 1872), and three with Wheeler (1871, 1873, and 1874). He also spent a year on a Navy expedition to Panama (1870). His outstanding photographs provide perhaps the best visual record of these early explorations and surveys. After trying unsuccessfully to establish himself in the photography business, he was appointed chief photographer of the Department of the Treasury in 1880, but was able to work just five months before tuberculosis forced his retirement. He died on Staten Island, New York, in 1882 at the age of 42.

James Hague (1836–1908) left the Fortieth Parallel Survey after his landmark volume *Mineral Industry* was published in 1871, and quickly turned to mine promotion and development. He became quite successful and found time to team up with King to develop the Murphy Mine in the Toiyabe Range of central Nevada in 1873, the Grizzly Flat Mine in the Mother Lode in 1880, and a silver mine in Idaho in 1890. King visited him often in his New York house and lent him part of his growing collection of paintings and travel memorabilia for safekeeping, where the household could enjoy them. Hague's children delighted in playing games with King and listening to his spellbinding tales.[25] James Hague was a frequent visitor during King's recovery in the Bloomington Asylum, and after King's death he was the editor of the *Clarence King Memoirs* published by the Century Club in 1904.

Arnold Hague (1840–1917), brother of James, took as his first assignment with the U.S. Geological Survey a study of the Eureka Mining District in Nevada. In 1883 he was assigned as geologist-in-charge of Yellowstone National Park, and he spent much of his career concerned with Yellowstone, making detailed investigations of the volcanic rocks, geysers, and thermal waters. In an obituary, Joseph Diller wrote that, "Mr. Hague was not a ready writer nor voluminous, but exact."[26] He worked toward limiting development within the park that would interfere with its unique natural features. He strongly opposed the construction of a railroad into Yellowstone, and played an active role in the forest conservation movement. Hague died in 1917 of a cerebral hemorrhage, undoubtedly hastened by a fall while attending a field meeting of the Geological Society of America in Albany.

Samuel F. Emmons (1841–1911) was initially appointed by King to represent the U.S. Geological Survey in Denver as geologist-in-charge of the Rocky Mountain Division. He mapped and compiled data on the Leadville Mining District, and the main report, with atlas, was published as U.S. Geological Survey Monograph 12 in 1886. He also investigated dozens of other mining districts in the Rocky Mountains, and the information gained allowed him to compare numerous ore deposits with one another. From this insight he generated general concepts on the genesis of metallic ore bodies. He wrote significant papers on the nature of ore-bearing fluids and on the structural relations of ore bodies. These studies were influential in the development of mining geology, and "clearly established Emmons as one of the top-ranking economic geologists in the Nation."[27] He was elected to the National Academy of Sciences in 1892. In 1900, Emmons helped plan Powell's reorganization of the U.S. Geological Survey, and he was placed in charge of its Metalliferous Ores Section.

Allen Wilson (1844–1920), after his appointment with the U.S. Geological Survey, worked on mapping the topography of the Leadville Mining District while Samuel Emmons—his friend and fellow mountaineer on the Mount Rainier climb—studied the district's geology. Wilson left the USGS in 1881 to join the Northern Transcontinental Survey organized by Rafael Pumpelly. This survey, funded by several railroad companies, directed its work toward mapping and evaluating the territory flanking the rail lines. After this enterprise concluded, Wilson was commissioned by the General Land Office in 1885 to investigate the mapping of the western boundary of Colorado. The border had been mandated to follow the 109th meridian, but the original mapping of the line had been challenged. It seems that eleven nights of stormy weather during that survey had rendered astronomical measurements impossible. As a result the surveyed line drifted several miles west off the meridian (the true north-south course) into what should have been Utah Territory. Wilson's later survey confirmed the error and accurately placed the meridian in its true position on the ground. But because the original determination had attained official status, the boundary had to remain as it was. Official boundaries, once fixed by certified survey, cannot be changed without major political intervention.

Wilson next accepted an assignment with the Western Pacific Railroad in laying out a rail line over the Sierra Nevada, via Beckwith Pass some 30 miles north of Donner Pass. Later, he took on business ventures and helped to establish a bank in Oakland, California, which was eventually bought out by the Bank of America. He died a wealthy man in 1920.

Grove Karl Gilbert (1843–1918), having shown exceptional scientific insight and ability on both the Wheeler and Powell surveys, was appointed a geologist with the U.S. Geological Survey from its inception. His first assignment was completion of the study of the ancient Lake Bonneville, the giant lake that covered a vast area of present-day Utah. In Gilbert's first administrative report to Director King on October 1,

1880, he demonstrated his keen insight and clarity of expression in describing the deposits of the former lake: "There is a topography of the land and a topography of the water. The forms of the land are sculptured by the beating of the rain and by the flow of rills, and creeks, and rivers, and they have peculiar characters accordant with their origin. The forms of the beds of lakes and oceans, and especially the forms of shores, are sculptured by the sway of waves and currents, and are distinguished by characters equally peculiar. All the hills and mountains above the shore line of Lake Bonneville bear witness of the play of subaerial agents, while below that line the slopes betray their subaqueous shaping. There is a trenchant line between them, and their peculiarities are beautifully contrasted. A careful inspection, however, shows that subaqueous characters are superimposed on subaerial characters. The forms belonging to the dry land are continued down past the shore line, and the sculpture of the lake has been superficially impressed on them without entirely obliterating them. It is thus made evident that before the epoch of the lake, the land it covered was dry, just as it is now. The lake had a beginning as well as an end. It came, it lingered long enough to make an unmistakable record, and then it departed as it came."[28]

Gilbert took on various managerial tasks and served as Chief Geologist of the U.S. Geological Survey from 1889 to 1892. The Bonneville study, delayed by these duties, was not published until 1890. This study was linked to two other lifelong interests in which he published extensively: the principles of land sculpture by geological processes, and the importance of high-angle faulting in generating Basin and Range structure. Gilbert also made important contributions to many other geologic problems. He studied the origin and history of the Great Lakes, and was asked to investigate the problems caused by the enormous quantities of debris washed into the streams by the hydraulic mining in the California gold region. In 1906, while in Berkeley, California, he experienced the Great San Francisco Earthquake, and published the definitive report on the subject in 1907.

Gilbert was admired for his perceptive methods of scientific investigation, for the completeness and accuracy of his observations, for the skill of his interpretations, and for the clarity of his presentation. He inspired his colleagues and was known for his gentleness of manner. He is considered by many to be the greatest American geologist.

James Gardner (1842–1912) was appointed director of the Topographical Survey of New York State in June 1876, three years before the formation of the U.S. Geological Survey. During periods of fieldwork, he commonly stayed locally, in farmhouses. While working in the region of Rockwood, New York, he answered a letter from his daughter Florence, then nearly seven: "There was a nice little girl about your age

named Alice in the house and she would have let you feed her very little Bantam roos-
ter and hen. They were as white as snow and so tame that they used to come up to Alice and eat out of her hand. Alice was a pretty little girl with very gentle and pleasing
manners but I am sorry to say that when she opened her mouth she talked through
her *nose*. None of these country people with whom I have been this summer had very
large noses but they all make the most of them for conversational purposes. They evidently think their mouths are to eat with, and their noses to talk through."[29]

When working near Cherry Valley, 50 miles west of Albany, he described his lodging as "a little two roomed farm house where kitchen, bedroom, nursery and dining
room are combined in one apartment, and the fare served three times a day consists
of the unvaried items, fat pork, potatoes, buckwheat cakes, squash, apple sauce, coffee and pie. Think of buckwheat cakes three times each day. A great stack of them is
cooked before the meal and placed upon the table and eaten with the food as we use
bread. I could not stand this sort of living even for a few days if the young farmer's
wife was not such a beauty and the entertainment of seeing her performances with
the baby were not so great. This robust infant of thirteen months beside being nursed
from the maternal fount, is fed pickles, coffee, squash, pie, pork, cake, and anything
else that happens to be around. The mystery of its continued existence is too profound for me to penetrate."[30]

The following season, in order to break the monotony of triangulation in the remote farm country, Gardner wrote that "I started for Newport last week where Clare
[i.e., King] has given me day after day of amusement while his mother has supported
my hungry body with food that seems Olympian after the pork and potatoes of the
summer . . . the girls in their picturesque Gainsboroughs, all form a wonderful contrast to the surroundings of the Howlett Hill observatory where I spent my last
month in a pen inhabited by eighteen hogs. In order to get the needed view, I had to
build an observatory right in Mr. Filer's pig pen, and for six or eight hours each day
the grunting of these animals was the only sound that broke the music of the
spheres."[31]

Gardner visited King again early in 1879 and described to his mother a pact that
he had made with his friend, such that "Under the attraction of too rapidly accumu-
lating wealth, controlled by people who spend it largely for ephemeral pleasure, the
country drifts toward sensuous life. Clare and I have had to face this matter in a practical form, passing as we have done from the humble pecuniary inheritance of science
to cattle kingdoms in the West, and at our last meeting in New York we pledged to
each other the promise that however rich we may become we will by simple living
and use of our money for others do our part to stem the tide of selfish extravagance."

He went on to describe the nature of King's new position: "He is Director of the United States Geological Survey. Besides making a geological survey he has power to make such maps as are necessary for geological purposes. He is also ex-officio a member of the commission for the classification of the public lands and recommending to Congress such legislation as may be necessary for their survey and sale. His geological jurisdiction is not confined to the far west. No geological work will be done by the Federal government except under his direction. At present he is the only officer empowered to direct geographical work in the west. All other surveys are suspended. His duties begin July 1st."[32]

Gardner teamed with Frederick Law Olmsted to work on the Niagara Falls Reservation for the New York State Survey in 1879. It was Olmsted who had designed New York's Central Park in 1857, and as commissioner of the newly acquired Yosemite Park, had arranged for Gardner and King to map it and its boundaries. At Niagara, Olmsted used his special genius in designing the trails and accessory structures so as to expose the visitor to the most exhilarating and inspiring views of the falls while maintaining the natural character of the region. Gardner prepared a detailed map of the Niagara Reservation, and together they submitted a special report defining both public areas, and critical areas to be preserved by the state.

In 1880 Gardner became commissioner of the New York State Board of Health, Topographical Section, and in this year he changed the spelling of his name to Gardiner.[33] In April the following year he married Eliza Doane, daughter of the Episcopal Bishop of Albany, New York. In addition to his daughter Florence, he then fathered five more children by 1890, four daughters and one son. The couple moved from New York to Albany in 1883 and built a summer home at Northeast Harbor, Maine.

In 1895 Gardner moved back to New York City, became vice president of Erie Railroad Coal Company, later president of the Mexican Coal and Coke Company and the Pennsylvania Coal and Coke Company. He maintained an office as a consulting coal-mining engineer, and was an active member of the Century Club.

After King's death, Gardner assumed the task of taking care of his friend's affairs, of the storage rooms filled with his art objects and paintings, and of his library and other assets.[34] In March 1903, a part of Kings's paintings—21 oil and 71 watercolor—(primarily landscapes and pastoral, marine, and river scenes, but also portraits and still lifes) were put up for auction at the American Art Galleries in New York.[35] King also had a large collection of art objects and bric-a-brac, including Aztec vases, Indian

FIGURE 13.2 (*opposite*).   James Terry Gardner at about the age of 50. (From William Pier Collection)

blankets, fans of painted silk, samurai swords, and sculptured objects. Other sales disposed of such remaining items as had not been loaned out, or had not disappeared. Some $120,000 was generated by selling King's art collection, and most of this money went to John Hay to satisfy his numerous outstanding loans to King.

King's wife Ada received $65 per month from Gardner's office, and a house was purchased for her, but the deed remained with Gardner. When Ada asked about recovering some of the funds that had apparently been left for her, she was told that any legal action on her part would cause a stop in the monthly checks. When the question came up about the legality of her marriage to King, she said she had a bundle of letters from him that would prove his loving, longstanding relationship with her. She brought them to Gardner's office, but unfortunately they disappeared and were never seen again. Gardner died September 10, 1912 at the age of 70, a month after the death of his wife.

Beginning in 1931, 30 years after King's death, Ada Todd King began legal proceedings against the heirs of James Gardner to seek $80,000, which she believed had been held for her by Gardner, King's trustee. As the case unfolded it was disclosed that John Hay had established a trust fund, of about that amount, with the money owed him by King, and recovered from the sale of King's art objects. Through the years, the monthly support to Ada had come from that fund.

Finally, in 1933, the New York State Supreme Court ruled "that no trust fund had ever been established in favor of Ada or her children. They had merely been the objects of charity."[36] Ada, however, did receive title to the house, and apparently she lived there until she died some four decades after Clarence King, her common law husband.

APPENDIXES

The source abbreviations herein are elaborated in the List of Abbreviations on page xxi.

Appendix A

Engineer Department
Washington, March 21, 1867

Mr. Clarence King
Washington

Sir:

In accordance with directions of the Secretary of War of this date, you are appointed to take charge of the explorations provided for in Sec. 3 of the Act of Congress approved March 2, 1867, authorizing the Secretary of War to direct a geological and topographical exploration of the territory between the Rocky Mountains and the Sierra Nevada mountains, including the route or routes of the Pacific railroad.

The object of the exploration is to examine and describe the geological structure, geographical condition and natural resources of a belt of country extending from the 120th meridian eastward to the 105th meridian, along the 40th parallel of latitude with sufficient expansion north and south to include the lines of the Central and Union Pacific railroads, and as much more as may be consistent with accuracy and a proper progress, which should be not less than five degrees of longitude yearly. The exploration will be commenced at the 120th meridian where it will connect with the geological survey of California, and should, if practicable, be completed in two years.

You will also collect material for detailed maps of the chief mining districts, coal fields, salt basins, &c-as well as material for a topographical map of the region traversed, and conduct a systematic series of barometric and thermometric observations with constant study of the atmospheric conditions bearing upon the subject of refraction and evaporation.

You will also make collections in botany and zoology with the view to memoir on these subjects, illustrating the occurrence and distribution of plants and animals.

You are authorized to employ the following assistants at the monthly rates of compensation set opposite to each respectively, namely:

One assistant geologist	$200.00
One assistant ”	150.00
One topographical assistant	200.00
One ” ”	150.00
One botanical collector	50.00
One zoological ”	50.00
One photographer	100.00
Six laborers at rates of locality	

Your own compensation as geologist in charge of the explorations will be at the rate monthly of $250.00

You are authorized to subsist the employees including yourself while on duty in the field, as is usual in like surveys, and you are authorized by the War Department to purchase subsistence stores from the subsistence department of the Army when practicable. You are also authorized by the War Department to call upon the commanding General of the Divisions of the Pacific to furnish an escort of twenty mounted men (California cavalry if possible) with the proper number of non-commissioned officers and the necessary camp equipage, subsistence and transportation therefor.

You are authorized to make the outfit for your employees embracing camp equipage, subsistence and transportation, to be paid for from the funds applicable to the exploration.

You will make requisition upon the Engineer Department for funds as they may be needed for outfit and for the current expenditures for the month succeeding, all funds expended by you must be in accordance with the rules and regulations prescribed for the disbursement of public funds, with which you will acquaint yourself before proceeding upon your exploration.

You will make reports monthly or more frequently if occasion requires it, the progress of the exploration, stating in general terms the duties upon which the employees have been engaged and the results obtained. If not within reach of the line of mail communication at the time of making up your monthly reports, you will transmit them as soon thereafter as the means at your disposal will admit, either through a messenger or other safe conveyance to the nearest mail station.

You will be required to enter into bonds for the faithful expenditure of such funds in the amount of twenty thousand dollars, with two sureties, according to the form herewith.

Very respectfully,
Your obedt. Servt.
A. A. Humphreys
Brig. Gen. & Chief of Engineers

Source: NA.

Appendix B

Newport, R. I., March 28, 1867
Maj. Gen. A. A. Humphreys
Chief of Engineers

General,

I have the honor to acknowledge your letter of the 21st inst. conveying instructions for a Geological Survey on the Fortieth Parallel, and appointing me Geologist in charge of the same.

I accept with pleasure the position you have given me; and will proceed immediately with the organization of the party and preparation for taking the field at the earliest possible day. The bond called for in the letter of instructions will be forwarded in a few days.

I am very respectfully
Your obedient servant,
Clarence King

Source: NA

Appendix C

Office of Geological Exploration of the 40th Parallel,
New York, April 3, 1867
Maj. Genl. A. A. Humphreys, Chief of Engineers.

General,

Your favor of March 22nd is just received. I shall use the utmost promptness in carrying out the instructions it contains, and hope to leave for San Francisco by the first of May. I enclose duplicate bonds for twenty thousand dollars, as directed by your letter of March 21st. Mr. A. H. Cozzins is a merchant of this city, and Mr. John E. Williams is president of the Metropolitan National Bank: both are well known to the U. S. District Albany, who certifies to their ability to act as bondsman.

I have written to all the Assistants whom I propose to employ but have as yet only heard from Mr. James T. Gardner—the 1st Topographical Assistant. He decided to accompany me and will join me late this week to arrange the list of instruments. Until I hear definitely from the other assistants, I cannot estimate for the funds which will be needed on the Atlantic side before starting.

General Warren has kindly informed me as to the method of disbursements of public funds and I believe I am ready to proceed with the work given into my charge.

Very respectfully,
Your obedient servant,
Clarence King

Know All Men by these Presents

That we, Clarence King of New York as principal and Abraham M. Cozzins of New York City and John E. Williams of Irvington, Westchester County, State of New York as sureties, are held and firmly bound to the United States of America in the sum of Twenty Thousand Dollars, lawful money of the United States to be paid to any officer of the United States duly authorized and empowered to receive the same, to which payment will and truly to be made we jointly and severally bind ourselves our heirs, executors and administrators firmly by these presents, sealed with our seals, and dated this third day of April, One Thousand Eight Hundred and Sixty-Seven.

The condition of this Obligation is such, That, whereas the above named Clarence King has been employed by the Chief of Engineers of the Army of the United States to take charge of and direct a geological and topographical exploration of the territory between the Rocky Mountains and the Sierra Nevada Mountains including the route or routes of the Pacific Railroad, having for its object an examination and description of the geological structure, geographical condition and natural resources of a belt of country extending from the 120th Meridian eastward to the 105th Meridian along the 40th Parallel of Latitude, with sufficient expansion north and south to include the lines of the "Central" and "Union Pacific" railroads, and as much more as may be consistent with accuracy and a proper progress, and to keep and render to the Engineer Department true and accurate accounts for all public money & property that may from time to time be entrusted to him the said Clarence King, in relation thereto, according to the system of accountability prescribed or that may hereafter be prescribed by law or by the Army regulations, and as he may from time to time be instructed by the Chief of Engineers aforesaid.

Now, therefore, if the said Clarence King shall well and truly perform all and singular the duties confided to him by the appointment aforesaid, then this obligation shall be null and void, otherwise to remain in full force and virtue.

(sd.) Clarence King
(sd.) Abraham M. Cozzins
(sd.) John E. Williams

Signed, sealed and delivered in presence of us.

(sd.) Geo. J. Suney
(sd.) B. L. Mitchell

This is to Certify that I am personally acquainted with the above named parties Abraham M. Cozzins and John E. Williams and know them to be perfectly good for the amount named in this bond.

Dated New York, April 3 1867
(sd.) Samuel G. Courtney
U. S. Atty.
Southern Dist.
N.Y.

Source: NA.

Appendix D

Headquarters Corps of Engineers
Washington, D.C., August 31st, 1868

Mr. Clarence King
U. S. Civil Engineer
Virginia City, Nevada. Via Panama

Sir,

Your Accounts for disbursements for Surveys for military Defences for First and Second quarters of 1868 are found to require amendment as follows. Viz:—

For First quarter 1868 *Currency Account.*

Vou 2 The check by which the 37¢ was paid, dates between which the water was delivered and cattle foraged and place from and to which the "hauling" and "carting" was done should be stated.

" 7 Transportation only is allowed and the word transportation should be substituted for "Mileage." SubVouchers should be appended or a Certificate signed by Mr. Gardner that it was impracticable to obtain them. The dates between which the journey was performed should be stated. A certified copy of the "order" authorizing the journey to be made should be appended, and the purpose for which the journey was made stated under head of application.

" 10 The locality of the house and number of rooms should be stated and a certified copy of the order authorizing the expenditure. See Circular No. 47.

" 12 The date in which liability accrued should be stated.

" 14 See note on Voucher No. 10.

" 18 See note on Voucher No. 7.

" 21 See notes on Vouchers 7 & 10.

" 22 A certified copy of the letter referred to herein should be appended—or referred to. See Cir. No. 47.

" 23 The place to and from where the "Moving" was done should be stated.

" 24 See note on Voucher No. 7–Baggage. All the circumstances necessary to a clear understanding of this expenditure should be given in detail as from___ to___ and the articles specified.

" 26 See note on Voucher No. 10.

" 27 See note on Voucher No. 10.

" 28 See note on Voucher No. 2 relative to "Water."

" 32 See Parag. 1002 Reg. 1863.

" 33 the term "Servant" is indefinite and liable to misconstruction. The kind of service should be stated so as to show its proper connection with a *public* duty.

" 34 No. 15. Alteration in amounts receipted for are not admissible without an acknowledgement from the person paid or a witness that the amount receipted for was altered previous to signing, and that the amount paid was $70.00. No. 16. See note on Voucher 33 relative to Servant.

" 35 No. 18. See note on Voucher 34 relative to alterations in amounts and Voucher 33 relative to Servants. Not certified. The month and year in which services were rendered should be stated at the head of Pay roll.

" 36 See note on Voucher No. 7.

For First Quarter Gold Account.

" 8 See note on Voucher No. 10 Currency Acct relative to location of house, no. of rooms and authority. See note on Voucher 34 Currency Acct relative to alterations.

" 9 See note on Voucher no. 34 Currency Acct relative to Erasures.

" 10 See note on Voucher no. 34 Currency Acct relative to Erasures.

" 12 The dates between which the Mules were fed should be stated.

" 13 The dates between which the "Feeding" and "Pasturing" was done should be stated.

" 14 Items 2 & 6, See Voucher no. 12 Coin Acct. Item 15 the place to and from where the "Moving" was done should be stated. SubVouchers should be attached or a Certificate signed by Mr. T. W. O'Sullivan that it was impracticable to obtain them and that the amounts charged are the same as paid by him. Under column of dates the date of liability should be stated.

" 16 See note on Voucher 10 Currency Acct 1st quarter.

" 19 See note on Voucher 10 Currency Acct 1st quarter.

For Second Quarter Currency Account.

" 1 Items 1 & 2 The nature and details of the repairs should be stated.

" 4 See note on Vou 7 Currency Acct 1st quarter.

" 6 The months in which pasturing was done should be stated.

" 9 See note on Vou 7 Currency Acct 1st quarter.

" 10 See note on Vou 7 Currency Acct 1st quarter.

" 14 The items of expenditure should be more clearly stated. They are illegible.

" 21 See note on Vou 10 Currency Acct 1st quarter.

" 23 Full explanations of the nature, value and extent of the notes and plates procured. The object and necessity of procuring. The basis of payment, or the manner of computing their money value of $560.

" 24 The location of Pasture and the rate per day or month should be stated.

" 29 Item 21. See note on Vou 14 2nd quarter.

" 37 See note on Vou 10 Currency Acct 1st quarter.

" 39 Item 10. See note on Vou 14 2nd quarter.

" 43 The receipt is for 30¢ more than the amount shown to be due.

" 44 The dates in which services were rendered should be specified.

" 48 Items 2 & 3. See Vou 34 Currency Acct 1st quarter relative to erasures. The date, number, amount of check and Depository on whom drawn should be stated.

" 49 Item 5. See note on Vou 34 Currency Acct 1st quarter relative to erasures. See note on Vou 48 as to check.

" 50 See note on Vou 48 2nd quarter relative to check.

The duplicates of the above enumerated vouchers should be amended in the particulars above specified and transmitted to this office to be substituted for those now here and on their receipt the defective ones will be returned to you.

Very respectfully,
Your obedt. Servt.
[Signed: name and rank illegible]
By command of Brig. Genl. Humphreys

Source: NA.

Appendix E

HQ Corps of Engineers.
Washington, D.C. December 8, 1868
Clarence King Esq.
In charge Geological Exploration &c.
Washington D.C.

Sir:

Your Letter of the 1st instant is received. You are authorized to rent a building for your office at a monthly rent not to exceed the sum of seventy-five dollars ($75), and to purchase the following articles of furniture for the same office:

(6) Six coal stoves, with the necessary hods, shelves etc.

(1) One coal grate

(18) Eighteen chairs

(7) Seven pine inking tables

(4) Four drawing boards 3' x 5'

(10) Ten tons of coal

(1) One broom

Two baskets, and such drawing paper and as may be required for the proper performance of your duties.

The office hours are from 9 A.M. to 3 P.M. until otherwise ordered.

Very respectfully,
Your obnt. Servant.
By command of Geo. G. Parke
Brig. Gen. Humphreys Major of Engineers

Source: NA.

Appendix F

HQ Corps of Engin.
Washington, D.C. Decr. 9th, 1868
Clarence King Engr.
In charge Geological Exploration &c.
29th Street, Washington, D.C.

Sir,

Your letter of the 8th inst is received. You are authorized to purchase for your office the following instruments ie.vz:

3 three-foot straight edges

1 Five-foot straight edge

3 Triangular Boxwood scales

1 Steel Triangle, 18 inches, long side

3 Steel triangles, 10 or 12 inch, long side

1 small box drawing instruments

1 Table logarithms

The above will be taken up on your return of the instruments in the usual way. One copy of Lee's Tables will be sent to you from this office.

Very Respectfully,
Your Obt. Servt.

Source: NA.

Appendix G

Geological Exploration 40th Parallel
Chico, Cal. Oct. 10, 1870
Maj. Genl. A. A. Humphreys
Commanding Corps of Engineers

General

I have the honor to report that since the date of my last communication I reached Mt. Shasta and spent the entire month surveying and studying the complicated geology of the Butte itself and the country lying between it and our former work. The labor has been extremely severe: our camps were frequently up to 11,000 ft. above sea level, and on one occasion, over 14,000 ft. We completely upset the ideas of Humboldt and of Fremont concerning the mountain itself, and have made the somewhat startling discovery of immense existing glaciers. This is the more surprising when we consider that Whitney, Brewer, Dana, and Fremont all visited the peak without observing them, and that Whitney, Dana, and Agassiz have all published the statement that no true glaciers exist in the United States.

May I ask that this be kept private until my return.

My party under Arnold Hague and S. F. Emmons in Eastern Oregon, were at last report in successful operations; it is, however, three weeks since word has reached me from them.

I reached here from Shasta yesterday, and leave tomorrow for Lassen Peak and the Madeline Plains and the border of Nevada, where, about Nov. 1st I will be joined by the Oregon party, and where I expect to devote six weeks to the volcanic geology bordering my work of 1867.

My plans are all working well and the party continues in good health notwithstanding the terrible physical strain I have called on them to endure.

Very respectfully, Your obedient servant
Clarence King
Geologist in Charge

Source: NA.

Appendix H

OFFICE OF THE GEOLOGICAL EXPLORATION, FORTIETH PARALLEL

San Francisco, November 11, 1872

GENTLEMEN: I have hastened to San Francisco to lay before you the startling fact that the new diamond fields, upon which are based such large investment and such brilliant hope, are utterly valueless, and yourselves and your engineer, Mr. Henry Janin, the victims of an unparalleled fraud.

Having convinced you, verbally, that my investigations have been made upon no other than your own ground, I beg herewith to give a brief statement of my mode of study and its unanswerable results.

Feeling that so marvelous a deposit as the Diamond Fields must not exist within the official limits of the geological exploration of the fortieth parallel unknown and unstudied by me, I availed myself of the intimate knowledge possessed by the gentlemen of my corps, not only of Colorado and Wyoming, but of the trail of every party traveling there, and was enabled to find the spot without difficulty reaching there on November 2.

After examining the camp-ground, water-notices, and general features of the diamond "Mesa," I next traced the boundaries of your claims, and then began in earnest to study the distribution and mode of occurrence of the precious stones.

Our first day was devoted to the sand-stone "Table Rock," at the head of Ruby Gulch, where about all the stones collected by your parties have been gathered; and had our critical work ended with the close of this one day we should have left the ground confident believers in the genuineness and value of the fields.

My suspicions were however aroused early in the second day's work, of which the following are the results:

1st. A nearly uniform numerical ratio exists between the rubies and diamonds.

2d. The gems, in nine cases out of ten, lie directly upon the hard surface of rock or of an indurated crust of soil. In the exceptional cases, where I found them in crevices, there was always ample evidence that the sand or soil had been disturbed and broken up within a year.

3d. With the diamonds and rubies occur quartz-pebbles of varied sizes, and concretions of iron oxide, (containing crystalline particles of quartz) which are found freely mingled with the soil from surface to bedrock; hence, if the gems were a natural deposit, being of a specific gravity intermediate between the quartz and iron concretions, they must have also settled through the earth to bed-rock. I therefore selected ground on and about Table Rock, where the top was more or less strewn with the so-called rubies, carefully shoveled off the surface-inch of ground and gravel, and examined by means of sieves and pan-washing all the material down to bed-rock. About thirty of these tests were made encircling Table Rock, and in no instance was a ruby or diamond found.

4th. Ruby Gulch, leading directly from Table Rock to Arnold Creek, and by necessity receiving the wash of the gem-bearing surface of sand-stone, was found to be extremely rich in rubies at its head, but this richness instead of continuing down the bed, as if genuine it inevitably must have, proved to exist only in the ground directly at the foot of Table Rock, where the soil was clearly disturbed, mixed, and smoothed over. I sank a series of four pits to bed-rock, down the gulch at intervals, excavating probably a couple of tons of material, and although, as in every other instance, quartz and iron concretions were distributed throughout all the gulch-soil, not a ruby or diamond was found.

5th In the top of Table Rock, and in the midst of thickly-sown rubies, are certain crevices not opened by your parties. They are filled with soil and pebbles, and more or less overgrown with grass, sagebrush, and small cactus-plants. We carefully removed the top inch, dug out the whole crack, finding no trace of diamonds, or even rubies. In other crevices, which bore unmistakable evidence of having been tampered with, we never failed to find rubies and often small diamonds.

6th. Upon raised dome-like portions of Table Rock, rubies and diamonds lay upon the summits and inclined sides, in positions where the storms must inevitably have dislodged them, and where, moreover, they were unaccompanied by quartz or iron concretions.

7th. An exhaustive examination of the rock itself, with a field microscope, revealed no grain, however minute, of either gem.

8th. In the ravines and upon the "Mesa," near by, are numerous ant-hills, built of small pebbles, mined by the ants, and which we found to bear rubies in their surfaces. A still closer examination showed artificial holes, broken horizontally, with some stick or small implement through the natural crust of the mound—holes easily distinguished from the natural avenue made by the insects themselves. When traced to its end, each artificial hole held one or two rubies. Moreover, about these "salted" ant-hills, were the old storm-worn foot-prints of a man. Many outside ant-hills were studied, but there were neither artificial holes piercing them, rubies within nor without, nor human tracks.

9th. I discovered on the table three small emeralds. Summing up the minerals, this rock has produced four distinct types of diamonds, oriental rubies, garnets, spinels, sapphires, emeralds, and amethysts—an association of minerals I believe of impossible occurrence in nature.

10th. When altogether satisfied that the gems had been "salted" on and about the table, our party set out upon an outside series of prospects, which were carried on all over the "Mesa" and its flanking canyons, until the absolute valuelessness of the property was finally ascertained.

The results of these ten links of proof are:

That the gems exist in positions where nature alone could never have placed them.

That they do not exist where, had the occurrence been genuine, the inevitable laws of nature must have carried them.

Finally, that some designing hand has "salted" them with deliberate, fraudulent intent.

Furthermore, this is the work of no common swindler, but of one who has known enough to select a spot where detection must be slow, and where every geological parallelism added a fresh probability of honesty. The selection of geological locality is so astonishingly considered, the "salting" itself so cunning and artful, the choice of all conditions so fatally well made, I can feel no surprise that even so trustworthy an engineer as Mr. Janin should have brought home the belief he did, since, as his report states, he was not allowed to prospect exhaustively; nor do I wonder that your second party of ten men brought back a confirmation of Mr. Janin's opinion, since they too were hurried from the ground without actually testing it.

I should add, that on the evening of Wednesday, November 6, when leaving the ground for the last time I met J. F. Berry, of Salt Lake, who had arrived with a prospecting party. I honestly expressed my conviction to him, detailed minutely my mode of investigation, and ended by urging him to remain and satisfy himself by personal examination, since he seemed to accept my result without question.

A sense of my duty as a public officer has impelled me to come directly and frankly to you, gentlemen.

In answer to your request that I accompany General Colten to the ground, while he and his party shall investigate for themselves, I place myself, my camp-men, and field-outfit at his disposal for two weeks, believing that in so doing I shall act as my chief, Maj. Gen. A. A. Humphreys, would order were it possible, in this sudden emergency, to communicate with him.

I am with respect, gentlemen, your obedient servant,
Clarence King,
Geologist in charge
THE BOARD OF DIRECTORS
Of the San Francisco and New York Mining and Commercial Company

Source: From Appendix DD2, King, 1873

Appendix I

Telegram
San Francisco, Cal., Nov 26, 1872
Maj. Gen. A. A. Humphreys,
Chief of Engineers, U. S. Army

In California newspapers of today is published a letter from me to Directors of San Francisco and New York Mining and Commercial Co., signed officially discovering their new diamond fields to be infamous fraud and giving absolute proof. Particulars by letter. Am confident you will approve my conduct.

Clarence King
Geologist in Charge

Source: NA.

Appendix J

Cambridge, Mass., May 18, 1874
J. T. Gardner, Esq.

My dear Sir:

Some ten years ago I made with the assistance of Messrs. Hoffmann and D'Heureuse a thorough examination of all the published work of the U. S. Engineers Corps., in the way of topographical surveys of the country west of the 104th Meridian. My object was to construct a map of the Cordilleras and for this purpose I worked over all the accessible material and carefully compared all the various published maps. I found the work of the Engineer Corps entirely valueless when anything like detail was required, because the topography had always been worked up on erroneous principles. I caused copies of all the Engineer work in Nevada to be made on a uniform scale, and then endeavored to make them harmonize with each other. It could *not* be done. Nothing whatever could be obtained on the State of Nevada which could be used even for a general map of the region on so small a scale as twelve or even twenty four miles to the inch, the different mountain ranges could not be recognized or identified because there was no detail given of any of them, while the uncertainties of the longitude were greater than the width of the valleys between the ranges. I never could use a single line of the Engineer work in California for our geological survey purposes, while the Land Survey in the valleys were an important, and indeed an absolutely essential assistance to us. In my opinion all of the Engineer work in the Cordilleras is worthless as a finality and only valuable as a preliminary reconnaissance to answer until something better can be had. The recently published maps made under the direction of Lieut. Wheeler seems to me very bad, and entirely behind the present requirements of geographical science in this country. You are at liberty to use this letter in any way you may see fit.

Very truly yours,
(signed) J. D. Whitney
Professor of Geology, Harvard University

Source: NYSL.

Appendix K

List of property belonging to the U. S. Geological and Geographical Survey of the Territories abandoned about noon August 16, 1875

Equipment	Cost*
2 Dead mules [and]	
1 Very badly wounded mule [and]	
1 Strayed mule. 2 at $100 and 2 at $75	$350
5 Aparejos [pack saddle]	
1 Pack saddle	15
40 Pr. saddle blankets	180
4 Pr. Hobbles at $1.00 per pair	4
16 Sling ropes	8
16 Lash ropes and cinches	80
5 Prs. Cantinas [saddlebags]	62.50
3 Prs. Panniers [pack basket]	
16 Mantas [pack covers]	76
1 Shoeing outfit	
4 Wagon sheets	24
8 Lunal [?] tents	
1 "A" tent	
2 Hatchets	2.50
3 Axes	6.75
2 Spades	5
2 Dutch Ovens	5
2 Shaving kits	19.50
2 Pr. Mess Chests with cooking and table outfit	90.
3 Halters	7
1 Large eight inch theodolite	
1 Gradiometer	
1 Cassella theodolite	

Equipment	Cost*

5 Small surveying compasses

3 Hand levels

2 Aneroid barometers

1 Thermometer

1 Cistern barometer

2 Medicine cases

1 Camera

50 Prepared dry plates and a box of plates

2 Steel tapes

1 Sextant and artificial horizon

Provisions for seven men for 20 days

* Steven Hovey, Asst. Quartermaster U.S.G&GS will make affidavit to having bought the above articles at the cost.

Source: Draft in Gardner letter to mother of Sept 17, 1875; WPC.

Appendix L

Rocky Mountain News September 17, 1875

We, the undersigned members of the United States Geological and Geographical Survey of the Territories, wishing to express our warm appreciation of the able and successful way in which our chief, James T. Gardner, led us through our recent dangers, do unanimously resolve:

RESOLVED, That our heartfelt thanks are extended to him for the brave and skillful manner of conducting the fight on the 15th and 16th days of August, 1875, with the Sierra La Sal Indians, and for the masterly manner in which he used his topographical skill in leading us over an unknown desert of two hundred miles, in four days, to a place of safety.

RESOLVED, That in our judgment everything was done that wisdom, prudence and courage could dictate to save the property of the survey and party, until it could no longer be preserved without the sacrifice of life.

RESOLVED, That we will never forget his uniform kindness and consideration for our welfare and comfort, on our entire trip.

(Signed)   Cuthbert Mills   Clarence Kelsey
                Shep. Madera   Robert Adams, Jr.,
                Jacque Charpiot   C. C. McCreary

Source: WPC.

Appendix M

Washington, Oct. 28, 1875

My dear Mother:-

I have been considerably perplexed since coming here to know what course to take respecting Dr. Hayden. Some articles that appeared in the North American Review this summer in which all the credit of the geographical work of the Survey, and in fact its present improved condition, was given to me, and other things that have been said and written have fanned again into flame those old fires of jealousy and suspicion which ever smolder in him and have as you know had one outburst after another—the only cessation being when he was in trouble and wanted my help. For the sake of the great work in which we are engaged, I have endeavored to heal these troubles and with patience have borne his abusive tirades. When these inflamed passions have possession of him, all my actions appear in a distorted light. Slight mistakes are magnified into crimes; my services to the Survey seem as nothing in comparison; errors in judgment on questions of policy are ascribed to the basest moral motives, and all explanations are useless. Apparently convinced of the truth of what he sees, and unconscious of the distorting medium, he entertains all the members of the Survey and a great number of uninterested outsiders with accounts of his grievances and my faults. So long as these criticisms were confined, as in times past, within certain bounds, I forebore action and waited till the storm had spent itself, hoping eventually to convince him that I was not seeking to displace him from his position as Chief of the Survey—an idea which seemed ever uppermost in his mind. Soon in the turmoil of events times came when he wanted my help and then all would become serene, and he apologizing for what had passed would express the utmost confidence.

Now however the case is of a more serious nature. Galled by these articles in the leading review and my appearance in the newspapers and the remarks thereon, and taking as a basis my report in respect to the Southern Coal Fields of Colorado which benefited a number of commercial enterprises in the Territory, and more immediately the D. & R.G.R.R.Co. [Denver and Rio Grande Railroad Company], but for which I never received nor expect to receive any compensation, Hayden charges me with having sold the Survey out to a private corporation: and these gross reflections on my honor he began to make long before seeing me or giving any indication that he was displeased with the action or any opportunity to explain the circumstances which made it proper in my opinion. So publicly were these charges made that I first heard of it through some U. S. Engineer Officers before reaching Washington. I immediately went to see Hayden and asked for an opportunity to clear myself by evidence of such witnesses as were competent to testify. This he refused, saying that he would not believe differently from what he did if God Almighty should tell him it was untrue. Hoping that such a storm of increasing passion would pass soon, I waited before taking any steps, until I learned that he was growing more violent in his abuse, giving use to a very strong current of feeling against me in the Survey: he having informed them that I had sold the whole Survey out and disgraced it. It then seemed to me both undignified to myself and undesirable for the Survey that I should remain longer where I was the object of so much unpleasant feeling. Certainly I could not expect to be useful in such a position. Therefore I handed Dr. Hayden my letter of resignation yesterday, expressing the wish that if it was agreeable to him, I should like to finish the primary triangulation and put the record in an intelligible form, so that the proof of the accuracy of the maps might not be lost. This afternoon I received an answer accepting the resignation but not wishing the triangulation finished. Such part however as is completed he would like to have prepared for publication. If he agrees to the terms which I shall propose, I will undertake this work which will require from four to six months; most of which would have to be spent here. This matter will be settled in a day or two and then I can make definite plans for the future.

You must not be anxious, dear mother, for I am in splendid health, and with the help of many good friends am perfectly able to make my way in the world. If there are not open doors we will try to open some. At any rate, I pray hard for wisdom and guidance and fall back on David's life and experience to strengthen my faith. He had a rough time with his faults and his enemies but came out all right. The same loving Power lives and saves today and I can trust in it in trouble.

You must not think of me as alone. I have plenty of good advisors without whose opinion I make no important move. Be very careful what you say about Hayden.

Miss Rines[?] sends much love and many friends ask after your return. With much love to aunty and a kiss to my dear little girl.

Your affectionate
Jamie

Source: NYSL.

Appendix N

Albany, July 13th 1876
To the
Hon. John V. L. Pruyn
President of the Board of Commissioners of the State Survey

Sir.

I have had the honor to receive this day an official copy of the resolutions of the board of Commissioners of the State Survey, appointing me Director of the Survey with a Salary of $4,000 per annum including personal expenses, the State to pay also for all transportation when on duty. Having made no application for the position I feel deeply the honor done me by this action of the Board and accept with thanks the office so generously tendered, trusting that I may discharge its responsibilities so as to maintain and strengthen the confidence most kindly expressed by the distinguished Commissioners.

Very respectfully
Your obedient servant
James T. Gardner

Source: NYSL.

Appendix O

United States Geological Exploration of the 40th Parallel
Manitou Springs, Colorado, Sept. 1, 1877
Brig. Genl. A. A. Humphreys,
Chief of Engineers, U. S. Army

General,

Under my physician's directions I am desirous to spend six or eight weeks at the
Arkansas Hot Springs, but he forbids me to go there until after the frosts early in October. I,
therefore have the honor to ask for an extension of my leave of absence, without pay, until
the middle of November.

Very respectfully,
Your obedient servant,
Clarence King
Geologist in Charge

Source: NA.

Appendix P

Office of the Public Printer
June 1, 1878

Friend King:

If you want your work hurried up, please see to it that your manuscript copy is nearer
what you want it when sent to this office. The part just returned this morning is perfectly
terrible. The additions and erasures you have made cause more than *double* work. In fact
when the book is completed it will be found to have cost nearly or quite twice as much at it
ought. Isn't there *some* way to prevent this extravagance?

Very truly yours,
A. N. Davis

Source: NA.

Appendix Q

Washington, D. C. Jan. 18, 1879
Brig. Genl. A. A. Humphreys.
Chief of Engineers, U. S. Army.

General,

   With the closing of my money accounts of which the last papers were this day transmitted, my duty as Geologist in Charge of the Geological Exploration of the 40th Parallel ceases to exist.
   I have the honor to ask that I may be formally retired.
   Looking back over the twelve years which have elapsed since I first assumed this charge, I can but bear hearty tribute to the unvarying kindness and consideration I have received from your hands.
   Permit me to say that a prominent element in my reflections at the end of this long task is the hope that my scientific results may be found to reach the high level of the Engineer Service.

Very respectfully,
Your obedient Servant
Clarence King
Geologist in Charge.

Source: NA.

Appendix R

The Stone Giant's Bowl

Far in the heart of the desert, over a desolate lowland,
Looms, in the purple of evening, the glorious crest of a mountain;
Snowy the locks of the monarch, and over his broad rocky shoulders
The green perpetual forest hangs close, like an emerald vesture.
The white-haired motionless statue, sitting with gaze never turning,
Holds in his rock-arms a basin, cut from the silvery granite,
Chiseled by ice and by tempest, trimmed with the fir and the pine tree.
Carefully, year after year, this giant pours from the basin
A streamlet as clear as a crystal, which, hour by hour descending,
Reaches at last to the lowland, there by the feet of the statue,
Quenching the thirst of the desert, making for ever a garden.
Thus from his castle of granite, the old stone king of the mountain
Silent and motionless sits, and from eyes never closing
Looks downward and east on the desert, and over the bright blooming garden
Where close to the skirts of his garments and over his sandals of granite,

Blossoms and soft waving grasses, and silvery whispering willows,
Hide in their shadowed recesses the mother-bird patiently sitting,
And waft to the rose of the morning the welcome of caroling thrushes.
The white-haired motionless statue sits with lips ever speechless,
And watches from morning till evening, and on from evening to morning,
The outstretched plain of the desert, where patient and wearily marching
The trains of emigrant people, seeking for ever the sunset,
Urge onward the slow-plodding oxen and long for the cool of the evening
When the sun, low descending, gilds crown-like the brow of the mountain,
And twilight on mountain-side gathers, and far falls the lengthening shadow.
There then burns brightly the camp-fire; there too, the weary and foot-sore
Rest from their toil of the desert—forgetting the sun and the whirlwind;
Over them sail the slow stars, through peaceful, sheltering heavens,
And the kindly Stone Giant pours from his bowl, never failing,
The silvery, musical brooklet, singing the weary to slumber.

Source: King 1870.

Appendix S

The Ice Dragon's Nest

High in the sapphire heaven, where the heart of America rises,
Up o'er a green waved ocean of limitless plain and prairie,
Bright with the snows of the ages, as the crest of a tumbling breaker,
Tower the luminous summits of grand and rocky Uinta.
Why do they watch the red sun from the far off Atlantic arising
Up from the golden aurora, on over desolate deserts
And far white lines of Sierras, till into the starlit Pacific
He sinks, and the twilight behind him glows pale in the purple horizon?
Why thus love they the sunlight—fearful of cold and of darkness?
This is the answering story told by the high Rocky Mountains.
Ages long gone and forgotten, when young were the lofty Uinta,
Born of the snow-cloud and tempest, a white-ice terrible dragon
Rested his hard frozen body, and grew on the flank of the mountain;
Cased in an armor of granite, strong armed—ice-hearted and cruel—
He grew while the sky, ever clouded, buried the peaks in a snow-drift;
Then, dragging his long icy body with slow irresistible movement,
Crawled through the crags and the gorges, till from his den in the mountain,
Reaching the verdurous valley, froze with his breathing the pine tree.
Wild burst the snow-cloud above him, white were the rocky Uinta.
Then from the far azure heaven, high above mountain and snow-cloud,
Shone the red sun in his brightness, warming the icy Uinta,
Melting the snow from their shoulders, dispelling the storm-bearing vapors;
Thick, and like spears swiftly flying, fell the red arrows of sunlight,

Smiting the ice and the armor—slaying the glacier dragon.
Vanished the snow, and to-day—where the terrible monster
Crawled, and with armor of granite, blasted and smote on the snow-cliff,
Wearing huge tracks in the mountain, chilling the air with his breathing—
Green grow the pines, and the flowers breathe their perpetual fragrance
Up to the sun as he sails through the cloudless and sapphire heaven,
And forever the rocky Uinta glow red in the evening and morning.

Source: King 1870.

NOTES

Introduction

1. Adams, 1918.
2. Hay, 1904.

Chapter 1. A Youthful Alliance

1. Park, 1841.
2. Essay by Ann Gardiner Pier, WPC.
3. Wilkins, 1988.
4. Gardner, as quoted in Raymond, 1904.
5. King to Gardner, Jan. 4, 1860, from New York (NYSL).
6. King to Gardner, undated Saturday, 1860? from New York (NYSL).
7. Dascome Greene letter, July 12, 1861, from Troy N.Y. (NYSL).
8. Gardner to his mother, Mar. 1862, from Troy N.Y. (NYSL).
9. King to Gardner, Mar. 18, 1862, from Yale? (NYSL).
10. King to Gardner, Mar. 18, 1862, from Yale? (NYSL).
11. Gardner to his mother, Mar. 1862, from Troy N.Y. (NYSL).
12. Gardner to his mother, May 7, 1862, from Troy, N.Y. (NYSL).
13. King to Gardner, Mar. 18, 1862, from Yale? (NYSL).

14. King to Gardner, undated, 1862, from Yale (NYSL).

15. King to Gardner, Oct. 10, 1861, from Yale (NYSL).

16. Gardner to his mother, June 14, 1862, from New Haven (NYSL).

17. Gardner to his mother, June 24, 1862, from New Haven (NYSL).

18. Gardner to his mother, June 28, 1862, from New Haven (NYSL).

19. Gardner to his mother, Aug. 14, 1862, from Camp Stew (NYSL).

20. Wilkins, 1988.

21. Brewer, 1966.

22. Brewer letter, quoted in Raymond, 1904.

23. Brewer letter, quoted in Raymond, 1904.

24. Gardner to his mother, Jan. 31, 1863, from New York (NYSL).

25. Gardner to his mother, Feb. 13, 1863, from New York (NYSL).

26. Gardner to his mother, March 14, 1863 (NYSL).

27. Gardner to his mother, March 21, 1863, from New York (NYSL).

Chapter 2. Ablebodied Men

1. Redman, 1924.

2. Redman, 1924.

3. Gardner essay in Ann Gardiner Pier collection.

4. Redman, 1924.

5. Redman, 1924.

6. Redman, 1924.

7. Gardner to his mother, Sept. 11, 1863, from San Francisco (WPC).

8. Smith, 1966.

9. Dickason, 1943.

10. Gardner to his mother, March 10, 1864, from San Francisco (WPC).

11. Gardner to his mother, March 10, 1864, from San Francisco (WPC).

Chapter 3. Gold and Guns

1. Raymond, 1904.

2. Brewer, 1966.

3. King, 1871.

4. Brewer, 1966.

5. Brewer, as quoted in Raymond, 1904.

6. Brewer, 1966.

7. Brewer, as quoted in Raymond, 1904.

8. Brewer, 1966.

9. Brewer, 1966.

10. Brewer, 1966.

11. King, 1871.

12. Gardner to his mother, Jan. 6, 1864, from San Francisco (WPC).

13. Gardner to his mother, Jan. 12, 1864, from San Francisco (WPC).

14. Gardner to his mother, Feb. 22, 1864, from San Francisco (WPC).

15. Gardner to his mother, Mar. 26, 1864, from San Francisco (WPC).

16. Muir, 1911.

17. Knight, 1867.

18. Gardner to his mother, Apr. 7, 1864, from San Francisco (WPC).

19. Whitney, 1865.

20. Gardner to his mother, Apr. 7, 1864, from San Francisco (WPC).

21. Gardner to his mother, Apr. 23, 1864 from San Francisco (WPC).

Chapter 4. Almost Inaccessible to Man

1. O'Toole, 1990.

2. King, 1871.

3. King, 1871.

4. Brewer, 1966.

5. King, 1871.

6. King, 1871.

7. King, 1871.

8. King, 1871.

9. King, 1871.

10. King, 1871.

11. King, 1871.

12. King, 1871.

13. King, 1871.

14. King, 1871.

15. King, 1871.

16. Brewer, 1966.

17. Whitney, 1865.

18. King, 1871.

19. King, 1871.

20. King, 1871.

21. King, 1871.

22. Brewer, 1966.

23. Whitney, 1865.

24. Colby, 1918.

25. Brewer, 1966.

26. Wilkins, 1988.

27. Whitney, 1865.

28. Moore, 2000.

Chapter 5. Grand Cold Fury of the Sierra

1. King, 1871.
2. King, 1871.
3. King, 1871.
4. King, 1871.
5. King, 1871.
6. Wilkins, 1988.
7. King, 1871.
8. King, 1871.
9. King, 1871.
10. King, 1871.
11. Wilkins, 1988.
12. King, 1871.

Chapter 6. Mirage and Blizzard

1. Whitney, 1865.
2. Whitney, 1865.
3. Whitney, 1868.
4. Essay by Gardner (WPC).
5. King, 1875.
6. King, 1871.
7. King, 1871.
8. King, 1871.
9. King, 1871.
10. King, 1871.
11. King, 1871.
12. King, 1871.
13. Whitney, 1870.
14. King, 1871.
15. Gardner, as quoted by Raymond, 1904.

Chapter 7. Fever in the Desert

1. Gardner to his mother, March 2, 1867 (WPC).
2. Rabbitt, 1979.
3. Josiah Whitney to Spencer Baird, Nov. 10, 1866 (from S. F. Baird papers, as quoted by Block, 1982).
4. Gardner to his mother, March 6, 1867 (WPC).
5. Gen. Humphreys to King, March 21, 1867, from Washington (Appendix A; NA).
6. O'Toole, 1990.
7. King to Gen. Humphreys, April 3, 1867, from Newport, Rhode Island (Appendices B, C; NA).
8. Gardner to his mother, May 5, 1867, from the steamer *Ocean Queen* (WPC).
9. Bailey to his brother, letter of May 20, 1867, from the Gulf of Panama (HL).
10. Emmons, 1904.
11. Bailey to his brother, letter of May 20, 1867, from the Gulf of Panama (HL).

12. Bailey to his brother, letter of May 20, 1867, from the Gulf of Panama (HL).

13. Bailey essay in Huntington Library, quoted in Wilkins, 1988.

14. Bailey to his brother, June 3, 1867 from San Francisco (HL).

15. Wilkins, 1988.

16. W.D. Whitney to J.D. Whitney, April 9, 1867, Whitney Papers, as quoted by Block, 1982.

17. Bailey to his brother, June 30, 1867, from camp near Sacramento (HL).

18. Bailey to his brother, June 30, 1867, from camp near Sacramento (HL).

19. Gardner to his mother, July 7, 1867, from Camp 5, 4,000 ft. west slope of Sierra (WPC).

20. Gardner to his mother, July 12, 1867, from Camp 9, east side of Sierra (WPC).

21. Gardner to his mother, July 15, 1867, from Hunters Station, western Nevada (WPC).

22. Gardner to his mother, July 18, 1867, from Camp 10, Glendale, Nevada (WPC).

23. Brewer as quoted by Raymond, 1904.

24. King, 1868, p. 504. Baron Louis de La Hontan, a French nobleman who commanded Fort Detroit in the 1680s, had published vivid descriptions of life in the New World that had impressed King.

25. Gilbert, in Wheeler, 1875.

26. Bailey to his brother, Aug. 14, 1867, from Big Bend Truckee River, Nevada (HL).

27. Bailey to his brother, Aug. 14, 1867, from Big Bend Truckee River, Nevada (HL).

28. Bailey to his brother, Sept. 6, 1867, from West Humboldt Mountains, 15 miles from Unionville, Nevada (HL).

29. Bailey to his brother, Sept. 6, 1867, from West Humboldt Mountains, 15 miles from Unionville, Nevada (HL).

30. Gardner to his mother, Sept. 16, 1867, from Unionville, Nevada (WPC).

31. King to Humphreys, December 18, 1867 (NA).

32. Bailey to his brother, Sept. 20, 1867, from Unionville, Humboldt City (HL).

33. King to Humphreys, December 18, 1867 (NA).

34. Wilkins, 1988.

35. Marsh, 1874.

36. Gardner to his mother, Nov. 7, 1867 (WPC).

37. Bailey to his brother, Oct. 16, 1867, from Unionville, Nevada (HL).

38. Bailey to his brother, Nov. 8, 1867, from Glendale, or Stone and Gates Crossing of the Truckee, Nevada (HL).

39. Bailey to his brother, Nov. 8, 1867, from Glendale, or Stone and Gates Crossing of the Truckee, Nevada (HL).

40. Bailey to his brother, Dec. 7, 1867, from Carson City (HL).

41. Gardner to his mother, Dec. 26, 1867, from Virginia City (WPC).

42. Gardner to his mother, Dec. 26, 1867, from Virginia City (WPC).

43. Gardner to his mother, Dec. 26, 1867 from Virginia City (WPC).

44. King to Humphreys, Dec. 18, 1867, Humphreys letters (NA).

45. Bailey to his brother (HL).

46. Bailey to his uncle, Jan. 4, 1868, from Carson City (HL).

47. Smith, 1966.

48. Wilkins, 1988.

49. King to Humphreys, Dec. 18, 1867 (NA).

50. Corps of Engineers to King, Feb. 10, 1868, from Washington, D.C. (NA).

51. Gardner to his mother, Jan. 14, 1868, from Virginia City (WPC).

52. Bailey to his uncle, May 3, 1868, from Carson City (HL).

53. Gardner to his mother, Jan. 20, 1868, from Virginia City (WPC).

54. King's notes for Hague's biographical notice of him, quoted in Wilkins, 1988.

55. King, 1870, and Appendix R.

56. Corps of Engineers to King, Aug. 31, 1868, from Washington (Appendix D; NA).

57. King, 1871.

58. King, 1871.

59. King to Brush, Nov. 2, 1868, as quoted in Wilkins, 1988.

60. King to Humphreys, Nov. 14, 1868 (Appendix D; NA).

61. Corps of Engineers to King, Aug. 31, 1868, from Washington (Appendix D, item 33; NA).

Chapter 8. True Ice and False Summit

1. Humphreys to King, Dec. 8, 1869, from Washington (Appendix E; NA).

2. Humphreys to King, Dec. 9, 1869 from Washington. (Appendix F; NA).

3. King to Humphreys, Aug. 26, 1869, from New Haven (NA).

4. Wilkins, 1988.

5. Raymond, 1904.

6. Gilbert, 1890.

7. Hague, 1904.

8. King, 1870, Appendix S.

9. Gardner to his mother, July 16, 1869, from Parley's Park, Utah (NYPL).

10. Quoted in Hague, 1904.

11. Gardner to his mother, Aug. 19, 1869, from Willow Springs, Utah (NYPL).

12. Gardner to his wife Josephine, July 13, 1869 from Parley's Park, Utah (NYPL).

13. Gardner to his wife Josephine, Aug. 19, 1869 from Willow Springs, Utah (NYPL).

14. Gardner to his wife Josephine, Aug. 28, 1869, from Salt Lake City (NYPL).

15. Gardner to his wife Josephine, Sept. 6, 1869, from Salt Lake City (NYPL).

16. Gardner to his wife Josephine, Aug. 24, 1869, from Willow Springs, Utah (NYPL).

17. Gardner to his wife Josephine, Sept. 2, 1869, from Salt Lake City (NYPL).

18. Gardner to his wife Josephine, Sept. 2, 1869, from Salt Lake City (NYPL).

19. King to Humphreys, Nov. 12, 1870 (NA).

20. Hague, 1870.

21. Hague, 1904.

22. King to Humphreys, Sept. 2, 1870 (NA).

23. King, 1871.

24. King, 1871.

25. Emmons to his brother, Nov. 4, 1870, from Jacksonville, Oregon (LC).

26. Emmons to his brother, Nov. 4, 1870, from Jacksonville, Oregon (LC).

27. Emmons to his brother, Nov. 4, 1870, from Jacksonville, Oregon (LC).

28. King, 1871.

29. Emmons to his brother, Nov. 4, 1870, from Jacksonville, Oregon (LC).

30. King, 1871.

31. King, 1871.

32. King to Humphreys, Oct. 10, 1870 (Appendix G; NA).

33. Emmons to his brother, Nov. 4, 1870, from Jacksonville, Oregon (LC).

34. Emmons to his brother, Nov. 4, 1870, from Jacksonville, Oregon (LC).

35. Emmons to his brother, Nov. 4, 1870, from Jacksonville, Oregon (LC).

36. Emmons to his brother, Nov. 4, 1870, from Jacksonville, Oregon (LC).

37. Emmons to his brother, Nov. 4, 1870, from Jacksonville, Oregon (LC).

38. King, 1871.

39. Humphreys to King, Mar. 21, 1867 (NA).

40. Humphreys to King, Mar. 28, 1871 (NA).

41. King, 1871.

42. King, 1871.

43. King, 1871.

44. King, 1871.

45. Hague, 1870.

46. King, in Hague, 1870.

47. Adams, 1918.

48. Emmons, as quoted in Raymond, 1904.

Chapter 9. An Unparalleled Fraud

1. Gardner to his mother, from Fort Steele, Wyoming, June 18, 1872 (NYSL).

2. King to Humphreys, Apr. 3, 1872 (NA).

3. Stoddard, 1904.

4. La Farge, 1912.

5. Adams, as quoted in Hague, 1904.

6. Wilkins, 1988.

7. Emmons, 1902.

8. King, 1873.

9. Asbury Harpending, as quoted by Rickard, 1925.

10. Wilson, 1904.

11. Emmons papers, quoted by Wilkins, 1988.

12. Wilson, 1904.

13. King to San Francisco and New York Mining and Commercial Company, Nov. 11, 1872, from San Francisco; see Appendix H (King, 1873).

14. Rickard, 1925.

15. King to Humphreys, Nov. 26, 1872, from San Francisco (Appendix I; NA).

16. Humphreys to King, from Washington, Jan. 10, 1873 (NA).

17. Goetzmann, 1966.

18. Goetzmann, 1966.

19. F. H. Bradley, 1873.

20. Goetzmann, 1966.

21. Goetzmann, 1966.

22. Hayden, 1873.

23. Stegner, 1953.

24. Stegner, 1953.

25. Goetzmann, 1966.

26. Goetzmann, 1966.

27. Goetzmann, 1966.

28. Powell, 1875.

29. Stegner, 1953.

30. Dawdy, 1993.

31. Wheeler, Geographical Reports, as quoted in Bartlett, 1962.

32. Goetzmann, 1966.

Chapter 10. Pushed with the Utmost Vigor

1. King to Samuel Emmons, Jan. 30., 1873 from San Francisco (APS).

2. King to Samuel Emmons, April 1, 1873 from San Francisco (APS).

3. Wilkins, 1988.

4. Gardner's appendix in King, 1876.

5. King to General Humphreys in Washington, D.C., Aug. 22, 1875, from New York (NA).

6. Hayden to C. Delano, as quoted in Foster, 1994.

7. King to Gardner, Feb. 15, 1873 (NYPL).

8. Goodyear, 1873.

9. Farquhar, 1965.

10. King to General Humphreys, Dec. 17, 1873, from New York (NA).

11. King, 1871.

12. King, 1871.

13. Moore, 2000.

14. King, 1871.

15. Nelson and Rabbitt, 1982.

16. King, 1876.

17. Gardner's appendix in King, 1876.

18. A. N. Davis to King, June 1, 1878, from Washington, D.C. (see Appendix P).

19. King, 1878.

20. Klein, 2003.

21. William Glen, pers. comm., Sept. 2003.

22. King, 1878.

23. Aalto, 2004.

24. Cary, 1904.

25. Gardner to Henry L. Higginson, Apr. 29, 1879, as quoted in Wilkins, 1988.

26. King, 1877.

27. King, 1877.

28. Glen, 1994.

29. King, in Hague, 1870.

30. Gilbert, in Wheeler, 1875.

31. Nelson and Rabbitt, 1982.

32. King, 1878.

33. King, 1878.

34. King, 1878.

35. Wernicke, 1992.

Chapter 11. Rocky Triangulation

1. Foster, 1994.

2. Gardner, 1874.

3. Gardner, 1874.

4. Goetzman, 1966.

5. Gardner to his mother, June 1, 1873, from Denver (WPC).

6. Gardner to his mother, July 27, 1873, from camp in the Sierra Madre, 10 miles west of Twin Lakes, Colorado (WPC).

7. Gardner to his mother, Aug. 25, 1873, from camp on Eagle River (WPC).

8. Gardner, 1873.

9. Gardner to his mother, Sept. 3, 1873, from Middle Park (WPC).

10. Gardner to his mother, Sept. 11, 1873, from Middle Boulder (WPC).

11. Dickinson, 1879.

12. Gardner to his mother, Sept. 20, 1873, from Denver (WPC).

13. Gardner to his mother, Sept. 20, 1873, from Denver (WPC).

14. Gardner to Whitney, May 13, 1874 (Yale Historical Collection).

15. J. Whitney to Gardner, May 18, 1874, from Cambridge, Mass. (Appendix J; NYSL).

16. Gardner to his mother, June 3, 1874, from Washington (WPC).

17. Gardner to his mother, Aug. 24, 1874, from Kerber Creek, San Luis Valley, Colorado (WPC).

18. Undated Gardner essay. (WPC).

19. Gardner to his mother, Sept. 17, 1874, from Saguache (WPC).

20. Gardner to his mother, Oct. 29, 1874, from Denver (WPC).

21. Gardner to his mother, August 6, 1875, from Camp on the Rio Dolores (NYSL).

22. *Philadelphia Inquirer*, Sept., 1875, as quoted (WPC).

23. *Philadelphia Inquirer*, Sept., 1875, as quoted (WPC).

24. See Appendix K.

25. *Philadelphia Inquirer*, Sept., 1875, as quoted (WPC).

26. Appendix L.

27. Foster, 1994.

28. Gardner to his mother, Oct. 28, 1875, from Washington (Appendix M; NYSL).

29. Gardner to John Pruyn, July 13, 1876, from Albany (Appendix N; NYSL).

Chapter 12. A Grand Fusion

1. Whitney, 1875.

2. Whitney, 1875.

3. Hayden, 1877.

4. Powell, 1878.

5. Stegner, 1953.

6. Congressional Record, as quoted in Rabbitt, 1979.

7. Congressional Record, as quoted in Rabbitt, 1979.

8. House Miscellaneous Document, as quoted in Rabbitt, 1979.

9. Report of the National Academy of Sciences, as quoted in Rabbitt, 1979.

10. Letter from King to Samuel Emmons from 23 Fifth Avenue, New York, Dec. 30, 1878 (APS).

11. King to Othniel Marsh, Jan. 2, 1879, as quoted by Goetzman, 1966.

12. King to Andrew Humphreys, Jan. 18, 1879, from Washington (see Appendix Q).

13. Hayden to James Geikie, Jan. 24, 1879, as quoted by Rabbitt, 1979.

14. Congressional record, as quoted by Rabbitt, 1979.

15. Rabbitt, 1979.

16. Rabbitt, 1979.

17. Rabbitt, 1979.

18. Powell Survey letters, as quoted by Stegner, 1953.

Chapter 13. Epilogue

1. As quoted by Wilkins, 1988.

2. As quoted in Rabbitt, 1980.

3. King, 1904.

4. Wilkins, 1988.

5. King to Ada Todd (undated), from *The New York Daily Mirror*, as quoted by Wilkins, 1988.

6. O'Toole, 1990.

7. Hague, 1904.

8. Hague, 1904.

9. From *The New York Daily Mirror*, Nov. 22, 1933, as quoted by Wilkins, 1988.

10. King to Ada Todd, Oct. 1901, as quoted in Wilkins, 1988.

11. Crosby, 1953.

12. Stegner, 1953.

13. Stegner, 1953.

14. U.S. Geological Survey, 15th Annual Report, 1893–94.

15. Hayden to Spencer Baird, Nov. 19, 1879, as quoted in Foster, 1994.

16. Hayden to Geikie, Dec. 9, 1882, as quoted by Foster, 1994.

17. Nelson et al., 1981.

18. Hayden, 1883.

19. Dawdy, 1993.

20. Stegner, 1953.

21. From Farquhar's Introduction to Brewer, 1966.

22. Gardner to his mother, June 7, 1867.

23. Cotter to Brewer, Sept. 18, 1898, from York, Montana; Francis P. Farquhar, editor's footnote in Brewer, 1966.

24. Brewer to Hoffman, 1900, as quoted in Farquhar's introduction to Brewer, 1966.

25. Wilkins, 1988.

26. Diller, 1917.

27. Rabbitt, 1980.

28. As quoted by Davis, 1926.

29. Gardner to his daughter Florence, Oct. 15, 1877, from Rockwood (NYSL).

30. Gardner to his mother, Oct. 21, 1877, from East Hill, Cherry Valley (WPC).

31. Gardner to his mother, Sept. 11, 1878, from Newport (WPC).

32. Gardner to his mother, Apr. 12, 1879, from Albany (NYSL).

33. Nelson and Rabbitt, 1982.

34. O'Toole, 1990.

35. Kirby, T. E., 1903, Catalogue of valuable paintings and water colors to be sold at unrestricted public sale by order of the executors and trustee of the estates of the late Clarence King and others: American Art Association, New York.

36. Wilkins, 1988.

REFERENCES CITED

Aalto, K. R., 2004, *Clarence King Geology*: Earth Sciences History, v. 23, pp. 9–31.

Abbot, H. L., 1857, Explorations for a railroad route from the Sacramento Valley to the Columbia River under the command of Lieut. R. S. Williamson, v. 6: 33rd Congress, Washington, D.C., 134 pp.

Adams, Henry, 1918, *The education of Henry Adams*: Massachusetts Historical Society, Boston, Mass., 517 pp.

Baker, G. H., 1856, *Map of the mining region of California*: E. L. Barber, Sacramento, Calif.

Bartlett, R. A., 1962, *Great Surveys of the American West*: University of Oklahoma Press, Norman, 408 pp.

Beach, A. E., 1873, *Science record for 1873*: Munn and Company, New York, 590 pp.

Blake, W. P., 1858, *Report of a Geological Reconnaissance in California, Made in Connection with the Expedition to Survey Routes in California, to Connect with the Surveys of Routes for a Railroad from the Mississippi River to the Pacific Ocean under the Command of Lieut. R. S. Williamson, Corps Top. Eng'rs, in 1853*: H. Bailliere, New York, 336 pp.

Block, R. H., 1982, The Whitney survey of California, 1860–74: A study of environmental science and exploration: unpublished Ph.D. thesis, University of California, Los Angeles, 480 pp.

Bradley, F. H., 1873, Explorations of 1872: U.S. Geological Survey of the Territories under Dr. F. V. Hayden, Snake River Division: *American Journal of Science and Arts*, v. 6, pp. 194–207.

Brewer, W. H., 1966, *Up and Down California in 1860–1864*: A new edition edited by, and including a 15–page introduction by F. P. Farquhar: University of California Press, Berkeley, 583 pp.

Brewster, E. T., 1909, *Life and Letters of Josiah Whitney*: Houghton Mifflin Co., Boston and New York, 411 pp.

Cary, E., 1904, *Century necrological note, Clarence King Memoirs*: Century Association by G. P. Putnam's Sons, New York, pp. 227–51.

Colby, W. E., 1918, *Notes and correspondence*: *Sierra Club Bulletin*, v. 10, n. 3.

Crosby, H. H., 1953, So deep a trail, a biography of Clarence King: Ph.D. dissertation, Stanford University, Stanford, 434 pp.

Dana, J. D., 1849, *Notes on Upper California, from observations made during the cruise of the United States Exploring Expedition*: *American Journal of Science*, v. 7, pp. 247–64.

———, 1887, *History of the changes in the Mt. Loa craters*, on Hawaii: *American Journal of Science*, v. 34, pp. 433–51.

———, 1890, *Characteristics of Volcanoes*: Sampson, Low, Marston, Searle, and Rivington, London, 399 pp.

———, 1895, *Manual of Geology, Fourth Edition*: American Book Co., New York, 1087 pp.

Davis, W. M., 1926, *Biographical Memoir of Grove Karl Gilbert*: Memoirs of the National Academy of Sciences, Washington, D.C., v. 11, 303 pp.

Dawdy, D. O., 1993, *George Montague Wheeler—The Man and the Myth*: Swallow Press/Ohio University Press, Athens, 122 pp.

Dickason, D. H., 1943, Clarence King's first western journey: *The Huntington Library Quarterly*, v. 7, pp. 71–87.

———, 1944, Henry Adams and Clarence King—The record of a friendship: *New England Quarterly*, v. 17, pp. 229–54.

Dickinson, A. R., 1879, *A Ragged Register*: Harper & Brothers, New York, pp. 268–71.

Diller, J. S., 1917, Arnold Hague: American Journal of Science, series 4, v. 44, pp. 73–75.

Emmons, S. F., 1897, The geology of government explorations: *Science New Series*, v. 5, pp. 1–15, 42–51.

———, 1902, Clarence King: *American Journal of Science*, series 4, v. 13, pp. 224–37.

———, 1904, Clarence King—Geologist, in J.D. Hague, ed., *Clarence King Memoirs*: Century Association by G. P. Putnam's Sons, New York, pp. 253–94.

Farquhar, F. P., 1947, The story of Mount Whitney IV: *Sierra Club Bulletin*, v. 32, pp. 75–88.

————, 1965, *History of the Sierra Nevada*: University of California Press, Berkeley, 262 ppp.

Foster, M., 1988, Mapping mountains: A. D. Wilson, nineteenth-century Colorado cartographer: *Colorado Heritage*, no. 4, pp. 22–33.

————, 1994, *Strange Genius, the Life of Ferdinand Vandiveer Hayden*: Roberts Rinehart Publishers, New York, 443 pp.

Gardner, J. T., 1873, Hayden and Gardner's survey of the territories, under the direction of the Department of the Interior: *American Journal of Science*, series 3, v. 6, pp. 297–300.

————, 1874, The elevations of certain datum-points on the Great Lakes and rivers and in the Rocky Mountains: Department of the Interior, United States Geological and Geographical Survey of the Territories for the year 1873, F. V. Hayden, U.S. Geologist-in-Charge, Washington, D.C., pp. 627–59.

————, 1878, Geodetical and topographical methods used on the geological exploration of the fortieth parallel, *in* King, 1878, *Systematic Geology: U.S. Geological Exploration of the Fortieth Parallel*, v. 1: Washington, D.C., Government Printing Office, pp. 763–69.

Gilbert, G. K., 1890, *Lake Bonneville*: U.S. Geological Survey monograph, Washington, D.C., 438 pp.

Glen, W., ed., 1994, *The Mass-Extinction Debates: How Science Works in a Crisis*: Stanford University Press, Stanford, 370 pp.

Goetzmann, W. H., 1966, *Exploration and Empire*: History Book Club, New York, 656 pp.

————, 1991, *Army Exploration in the American West, 1803–1863*: Texas State Historical Society, Austin. [Contains Fremont map in pocket.]

Goodyear, W. A., 1873, On the situation and altitude of Mount Whitney: *Proceedings of the California Academy of Sciences*, v. 5, pp. 139–44.

————, 1888, Inyo County, *in* W. Irelan, Jr., *Eighth Annual Report of the State Mineralogist*: California State Mining Bureau, Sacramento, pp. 224–309.

Hague, A., and S. F. Emmons, 1877, Descriptive geology: *Report of the U.S. Geological Exploration of the Fortieth Parallel*, v. 2: Government Printing Office, Washington, D.C., 890 pp.

Hague, J. D., 1870, *Mining Industry: Report of the U.S. Geological Exploration of the Fortieth Parallel*, v. 3: Government Printing Office, Washington, D.C., 647 pp.

———, ed., 1904, *Clarence King Memoirs*, Century Association by G. P. Putnam's Sons, New York and London.

Haines, A. L., 1962, *Mountain Fever, Historic Conquests of Rainier*: Oregon Historical Society, Portland, 255 pp.

Hall, J., and R. P. Whitfield, 1877, *Paleontology*: *Report of the U.S. Geological Exploration of the Fortieth Parallel*, v. 4, pt. 2: Government Printing Office, Washington, D.C., pp. 199–299.

Hart, H. M., 1965, *Old Forts of the Far West*: Bonanza Books, New York, 192 pp.

Hay, J., 1904, Clarence King, *in* J.D. Hague, ed., *Clarence King Memoirs*: Century Association by G. P. Putnam's Sons, New York and London, pp. 117–32.

Hayden, F. V., 1873, *Sixth Annual Report of the United States Geological Survey of the Territories; Progress of the Exploration for the year 1872*: Government Printing Office, Washington, D.C., pp. 120–21.

———, 1874, *[Seventh] Annual report of the United States Geological and Geographical Survey of the Territories, Embracing Colorado, Being a Report of Progress of the Exploration for the Year 1873*: Government Printing Office, Washington D.C., 718 pp.

Hayden, F. V. [and J. T. Gardner and W. H. Holmes], 1877, *Geological and Geographical Atlas of Colorado and Portions of Adjacent Territory*: Julius Bien, New York and Washington, D.C. [6 topographic maps and 6 colored geologic maps, scale 1:253,440, contour interval 200 feet; 4 other maps]

Hayden, F. V. et al., 1880, *The Great West, Its Attractions and Resources*: Charles R. Brodix, Bloomington, 528 pp.

Hayden, F. V., with A. R. C. Selvyn, 1883, *Stanford's Compendium of Geography and Travel: North America*: Edward Stanford, London.

Hoffmann, C., 1873, Topographical map of central California together with a part of Nevada: J. D. Whitney, State Geologist, Geological Survey of California. [Four sheets, scale 1:375,000]

Howard, T. F., 1998, *Sierra Crossing: First Roads to California*: University of California Press, Berkeley, 218 pp.

King, C., 1870, The three lakes: Marion, Lall, and Jan, and how they were named: Three copies privately printed, reprinted by F. P. Farquhar, *Sierra Club Bulletin*, v. 24, 1939, pp. 109–20.

———, 1871, *Mountaineering in the Sierra Nevada*: Edited 1935 with a preface and notes by F. P. Farquhar, and an 1873 addition describing the ascent of the true Mount Whitney: W.W. Norton & Co., New York, 320 pp.

———, 1871, On the discovery of actual glaciers in the mountains of the Pacific Slope: *American Journal of Science*, series 3, v. 1, pp. 157–67.

————, 1873, Annual report of the Geological Exploration of the Fortieth Parallel, in *Report of the Chief of Engineers for 1873* (covers the 1872 season), Appendix DD: Government Printing Office, Washington, D.C., pp. 1203–10.

————, 1875, Bancroft's native races of the Pacific States (a review): *The Atlantic Monthly*, v. 35, n. 208, pp. 163–73.

————, 1876, *Geological and topographical atlas accompanying the report of the Geological Exploration of the Fortieth Parallel*: Chief Engineer, War Department, Washington, D.C. [Contains ten topographic maps and ten colored geologic maps; scale 4 miles:1 inch; grade-curves, 300–ft vertical interval]; Julius Bien, Lithographer, New York and Washington D.C.

————, 1877, Catastrophism and evolution: *American Naturalist*, v. 11, n. 3, pp. 448–53.

————, 1878, *Systematic Geology: Report of the U.S. Geological Exploration of the Fortieth Parallel*, v. 1: Government Printing Office, Washington, D.C., 803 pp.

————, 1904, The helmet of Mambrino, in J. D. Hague, ed., *Clarence King Memoirs*: Century Association by G. P. Putnam's Sons, New York and London, pp. 5–36.

Klein, U., 2003, *Experiments, Models, Papertools: Cultures of Organic Chemistry in the Nineteenth Century*: Stanford University Press, Stanford, 305 pp.

Knight, W. H., 1867, Bancroft's map of the Pacific states: H. H. Bancroft and Co., San Francisco; reproduced in P. E. Cohen, 2002, *Mapping the West*: Rizzoli, New York, 208 pp.

La Farge, J., 1912, *Reminiscences of the South Seas*: Doubleday, New York, 480 pp.

Marsh, O. C., 1874, Notice of new equine mammals from the Tertiary formation: *American Journal of Science*, series 3, v. 7, pp. 247–58.

————, 1880, *Odontornithes: Extinct Toothed Birds of North America: Report of the U.S. Geological Exploration of the Fortieth Parallel*, v. 7: Government Printing Office, Washington, D.C., 201 pp.

Matthes, F. R., 1930, *Geologic History of the Yosemite Valley*: U.S. Geological Survey Professional Paper 160, 137 pp.

Meek, F. B., 1877, *Paleontology: Report of the U.S. Geological Exploration of the Fortieth Parallel*, v. 4, pt. 1: Government Printing Office, Washington, D.C., pp. 1–197.

Mendenhall, T. C., 1993, *The Harvard-Yale Boat Race, 1852–1924, and the Coming of Sport to the American College*: Mystic Seaport Museum, Mystic, Conn., 371 pp.

Middleton, W. E. K., 1969, *Catalog of Meteorological Instruments in the Museum of History and Technology*: Smithsonian Institution Press, Washington, D.C., 128 pp.

Moore, J. G., 1969, *Geology and mineral deposits of Lyon, Douglas, and Ormsby Counties, Nevada, with a section on industrial mineral deposits by N. L. Archbold*: Nevada Bureau of Mines and Geology Bulletin, 75, 45 pp.

————, 1981, Geologic map of the Mount Whitney quadrangle, Inyo and Tulare
    Counties, California: U.S. Geological Survey Geologic Quadrangle Map GQ 1545.

————, 2000, *Exploring the Highest Sierra*: Stanford University Press, Stanford, 427 pp.

Muir, J., 1874, Mountain sculpture, origin of Yosemite valleys: *Overland Monthly*, v.
    12, pp. 393–403.

————, 1887, *Picturesque California: The Rocky Mtns. and the Pacific Slope*: J. Dew-
    ing Publishing Co., New York and San Francisco, 508 pp.

————, 1891, A rival of the Yosemite: The cañon of the South Fork of Kings River,
    California: *Century Magazine*, v. 43, pp. 77–91.

————, 1911, *My First Summer in the Sierra*: Houghton Mifflin, Boston, 104 pp.

National Archives and Records Service, General Service Administration, 1965.
    Records of Geological Exploration of the Fortieth Parallel (King Survey), 1867–81.
    Communications received by and sent from the Office of the Chief of Engineers
    and the Treasury Dept., March 21, 1867, to April 11, 1870.

Nelson, C. M., and M. C. Rabbitt, 1982, The role of Clarence King in the advance-
    ment of geology in the public service, 1867–1881, *in Frontiers of Geological Explo-
    ration of Western North America*: American Association for the Advancement of
    Science, San Francisco, pp. 19–36.

Nelson, C. M., M. C. Rabbitt, and F. M. Fryxell, 1981, Ferdinand Vandiveer Hayden:
    The U.S. Geological Survey years, 1879–1886: *American Philosophical Society*, v.
    125, n. 3. pp. 238–43.

O'Toole, P., 1990, *The Five of Hearts*: Ballantine Books, New York, 459 pp.

Park, R., 1841, *Pantology, or a Systematic Survey of Human Knowledge*: Hogan and
    Thompson, Philadelphia, 587 pp.

Powell, J. W., 1875, *Exploration of the Colorado River of the West and its Tributaries*:
    Government Printing Office, Washington, D.C., 291 pp.

————, 1878, *Report on the Lands of the Arid Region of the United States, with a More
    Detailed Account of the Lands of Utah*: Government Printing Office, 45th Con-
    gress 2nd Session H. R. Exec. Doc. 73,1878, Washington D.C.

Rabbitt, M. C., 1979, *Minerals, Lands, and Geology for the Common Defence and Gen-
    eral Welfare, 1, Before 1879*: Government Printing Office, Washington, D.C., 331 pp.

————, 1980, *Minerals, Lands, and Geology for the Common Defence and General
    Welfare, 2, 1879-1904*: Government Printing Office, Washington, D.C., 407 pp.

Raymond, R. W., 1904, Biographical notice *in Clarence King Memoirs*: Century Asso-
    ciation by G. P. Putnam's Sons, New York, pp. 303–71.

Redman, J. T., 1924, Reminiscences and experiences of my trip across the plains to
    California sixty-one years ago when I drove four mules to a covered wagon: Mar-
    shall, Mo., 6 pp., HM 20462. [Unpublished manuscript in Huntington Library.]

Rickard, T. A., 1925, The great diamond hoax: *Engineering and Mining Journal-Press*, v. 119, pp. 884–88.

Ridgeway, R., 1877, *Ornithology: Report of the U.S. Geological Exploration of the Fortieth Parallel*, v. 4, part 3: Government Printing Office, Washington, D.C., pp. 303–667.

Ringgold, C., 1852, A series of charts with sailing directions for the state of California, 4th ed.: Washington, D.C., 48 pp.

Russell, I. C., 1898, *Glaciers of Mount Rainier: Eighteenth Annual Report of the U.S. Geological Survey*, pp. 355–415.

Scott, Col. R. N., ed., 1880, *The Official Records of the War of the Rebellion of the Union and Confederate Armies*: Published pursuant to act of Congress, Government Printing Office, Washington, D.C.

Shebl, J. M., 1974, *King, of the Mountains*: Pacific Center for Western Historical Studies, University of the Pacific, Stockton, 71 pp.

Smith, G. H., 1966, *The History of the Comstock Lode*: Nevada State Bureau of Mines, University of Nevada Bulletin, v. 37, 305 pp.

Stansbury, H., 1852, *Exploration and Survey of the Valley of the Great Salt Lake of Utah*: U.S. Senate Document, special session March, 1851: Lippincott, Grambo & Co., Philadelphia, 487 pp.

Stegner, W., 1953, *Beyond the Hundredth Meridian, John Wesley Powell and the Second Opening of the West*: Penguin Books, New York, 438 pp.

Stoddard, C. W., 1904, *The Island of Tranquil Delights, A South Sea Idyl and Others*: Herbert B. Turner and Company, Boston, 318 pp.

Thompson and West, 1881, *History of Nevada*: Thompson & West, Oakland, Calif., 678 pp.

U.S. Geological Survey, 1894, *15th Annual Report, 1893-94*: J. W. Powell, Director, Government Printing Office, Washington D.C., 755 pp.

Watson, Sereno, 1871, *Botany: Report of the U.S. Geological Exploration of the Fortieth Parallel*, v. 5: Government Printing Office, Washington, D.C., 297 pp.

Wentworth, G. A., 1903, *Plane and Spherical Trigonometry, Surveying, and Tables*, 2nd ed.: Ginn and Company, New York, 255 pp.

Wernicke, Brian, 1992, Cenozoic extensional tectonics of the U.S. Cordillera, *in The Geology of North America*, v. G-3: Geological Society of America, pp. 553–81.

Wheeler, G. M., 1872, *Preliminary report concerning explorations and surveys principally in Nevada and Arizona during 1871*: Government Printing Office, Washington, D.C., 96 pp. [includes map: scale 24 miles to the inch].

———, 1875, *Geographical and Geological Explorations and Surveys West of the One*

Hundredth Meridian, v. 3, *Geology:* Government Printing Office, Washington, D.C., 681 pp.

————, 1889, *Report upon United States Geographical Surveys West of the 100th Meridian*, v. 1, *Geographical Report:* Chief of Engineers, U.S. Army, Government Printing Office, Washington, D.C., 780 pp.

Whitney, J. D., 1865, *Geology, Report of Progress and Synopsis of the Field-work, from 1860–1864*, v. 1: Geological Survey of California, Sacramento, 498 pp.

————, 1868, *The Yosemite Book: A Description of the Yosemite Valley and the Adjacent Region of the Sierra Nevada, and the Big Trees of California:* Geological Survey of California, Julius Bien, New York, 116 pp.

————, 1870, *The Yosemite Guide-book: A Description of the Yosemite Valley and the Adjacent Region of the Sierra Nevada, and the Big Trees of California:* Geological Survey of California, Sacramento, University Press, Cambridge, 155 pp.

————, 1875, Geographical and geological surveys: *North American Review*, v. 121, pp. 37–85, 270–314.

Wilkins, T., 1988, *Clarence King, a Biography:* University of New Mexico Press, Albuquerque, 524 pp.

Williamson, R. S., 1856, *Explorations in California for Railroad Routes: Explorations and Surveys for a Railroad Route from the Mississippi River to the Pacific Ocean:* War Department, Government Printing Office, Washington, D.C., v. 5, 370 pp.

Wilson, A. D., 1904, The great California diamond mines: *Overland Monthly*, v. 43, pp. 291–96.

Zirkel, Ferdinand, 1876, *Microscopical Petrography: Report of the U.S. Geological Exploration of the Fortieth Parallel*, v. 6: Government Printing Office, Washington, D.C., 525 pp.

INDEX